Criminal Convictions in U.S. Tribal Law

This book is the first comparative law study of collateral consequences of criminal conviction in all federally recognized Indian tribes in the lower 48 U.S. states, and the mechanisms for restoring civil rights in tribal law.

Surveying the constitutions, codes, and ordinances of tribal jurisdictions reveals a broad range of consequences – the impact of which has not been comprehensively and critically examined. Like state and federal jurisdictions, tribal law attaches thousands of legal disabilities to tribal offices, business licenses and permits, social services, and civil rights for persons with criminal convictions. This is especially true in economically important industries such as gaming and resource extraction; additionally, rapidly changing areas such as marijuana regulation and sex offender registries expand the scope still further. This book catalogues restoration of rights procedures in tribal law, to include pardons, expungements, and record sealing. Collateral consequences have proliferated in tribal law because of the limitations of tribal criminal jurisdiction, including over non-tribal members. However, tribal collateral consequences risk contributing to overcriminalization and social exclusion for persons with previous criminal convictions, especially as Native Americans are already disproportionately impacted by the U.S. criminal justice system.

This book will appeal to legal academics, scholars, and practitioners working in tribal criminal law, as well as to others with interests in Indigenous legal issues.

Andrew Novak is Instructional Associate Professor of Criminology, Law, and Society at George Mason University, Virginia, USA.

Part of the
INDIGENOUS PEOPLES AND THE LAW
series

for information about the series and details of previous and forthcoming titles, see https://www.routledge.com/law/series/INDPPL

A GlassHouse book

Criminal Convictions in U.S. Tribal Law

Collateral Consequences, Pardons, and Expungements in Indian Country

Andrew Novak

Routledge
Taylor & Francis Group
a GlassHouse Book

First published 2025
by Routledge
4 Park Square, Milton Park, Abingdon, Oxon OX14 4RN

and by Routledge
605 Third Avenue, New York, NY 10158

A GlassHouse book

Routledge is an imprint of the Taylor & Francis Group, an informa business

British Library Cataloguing-in-Publication Data
A catalogue record for this book is available from the British Library

ISBN: 9781032558462 (hbk)
ISBN: 9781032558479 (pbk)
ISBN: 9781003432548 (ebk)

DOI: 10.4324/9781003432548

Typeset in Sabon
by Deanta Global Publishing Services, Chennai, India

Dedicated to Heather and Matthew Novak

Contents

Preface

This book brings together two distinct literatures that are often not in conversation. The first is the criminological and legal literature on collateral consequences of conviction and restoration of rights, including pardons, expungements, and record clearing procedures. The second is federal Indian law and comparative tribal law, to include the constitutions, codes, and ordinances of separate tribal sovereigns and the decisions of tribal justice systems. Because the interaction between these two literatures is novel, this book tends not to make grandiose conceptual claims. Rather, the main emphasis is on clear presentation of the data that was collected. Because this is a comparative law study of all 347 federally recognized Indian tribes in the lower 48 states, gaps or omissions are expected and unavoidable. Nonetheless, the book will hopefully be of use to persons with criminal convictions who seek to know their rights under tribal law, and the attorneys or lay representatives who are assisting them. The laws presented here reflect only a snapshot in time; the duty is still on the legal practitioner or tribal court official to find and apply the latest laws. The book also makes suggestions and recommendations for improving tribal laws and draws attention to legal innovations that best protect the rights of tribal members and reduce the risk of overcriminalization.

I have presented some of the data in this book at various conferences. I presented the topic of tribal pardons at the Law and Society Association online conference in 2021 and on collateral consequences in tribal law at the Law and Society Association conference in Lisbon in 2022. More recently, I presented on restrictions on running for tribal office at the Academy of Criminal Justice Sciences in National Harbor in 2023 and restrictions in the tribal gaming industry at the American Society of Criminology in Philadelphia in 2023. Thank you to the hardworking panelists, moderators, and discussants at those presentations. Several of the comments proved extremely useful. Also helpful was a call I had with the American Bar Association's Native American Concerns Committee, who alerted me to several conceptual and overarching issues that I had not previously considered. I appreciate the conversations I had with Daniel Pascoe, Sarah Lucy Cooper, Margaret Colgate

Love, Leonard Powell, and others about the material in this book. I am indebted to the work of the Bureau of Justice Statistics and Office of Tribal Justice in the U.S. Department of Justice and the National Indian Gaming Commission for data, as well as the comments of my anonymous reviewers who helped me sharpen the scope and rationale for this book. Finally, thanks to my colleagues at George Mason University, my family, and my friends for providing moral guidance and support.

Andrew Novak
Washington, DC
April 2024

Chapter 1

Introduction to Collateral Consequences in Indian Country

Criminal punishments like imprisonment and fines are best thought of as direct consequences of conviction. *Collateral* consequences of conviction, on the other hand, are hidden, persistent, and ubiquitous. They attach automatically, without legal procedures or an appeal, and defendants are not warned of them before pleading guilty.[1] Collateral consequences can render a person ineligible for public benefits, bar them from certain careers or occupations, or even force them to surrender parental visitation or custody rights. And that is just the tip of the iceberg.[2] Cumulatively, collateral consequences can reduce the voting strength of entire communities through disenfranchisement or ineligibility to run for office; in some jurisdictions, voting rights are suspended for any felony conviction for life.[3] A dizzying array of jurisdictions attach collateral consequences to criminal convictions. Many federal, state, and local government entities have formal policies excluding persons with criminal convictions from certain benefits and roles, but unwritten or informal exclusions also pervade both the public and private spheres.[4] Informal policies, such as exclusions from rental housing, create even more "collateral damage" as it were, as spouses and children may face eviction, denial

1 Keramet A. Reiter, *Mass Incarceration* 58–59 (Oxford University Press, 2018).
2 Michael Pinard, "Collateral Consequences of Criminal Convictions: Confronting Issues of Race and Dignity," 85 *New York University Law Review* 457, 467–69 (2010); John Hagan & Ronit Dinovitzer, "Collateral Consequences of Employment for Children, Communities, and Prisoners," 26 *Crime & Justice* 121, 122 (1999).
3 See, e.g., Christopher Uggen & Jeff Manza, "Democratic Contraction? Political Consequences of Felon Disenfranchisement in the United States," 67(6) *American Sociological Review* 777 (2002); Melanie Bowers & Robert R. Preuhs, "Collateral Consequences of a Collateral Penalty: The Negative Effect of Felon Disenfranchisement Laws on the Political Participation of Nonfelons," 90(3) *Social Science Quarterly* 722 (2009).
4 Gabriel J. Chin, "Collateral Consequences of Criminal Conviction," 18(3) *Criminology, Criminal Justice, Law & Society*, 1, 2 (2017).

DOI: 10.4324/9781003432548-1

of public benefits, or revocation of a driver's license because of restrictions placed on a parent or head of a household.[5]

That federally recognized Indian tribes also attach collateral consequences of conviction in their own tribal laws adds another layer of criminalization that has gone almost entirely unexplored. Tribal law is missing from the National Inventory of Collateral Consequences of Conviction run by Council of State Governments and similar databases of criminal justice reform organizations.[6] Notably, as discussed in Chapter 8, some research has focused on the introduction of sex offender registries to Indian Country through the Sex Offender Registration and Notification Act (SORNA) of 2006, which creates a measure of reciprocity between tribal sex offender restrictions on the one hand and state and federal ones on the other.[7] Beyond this, scholars have said little. Yet, collateral consequences of criminal conviction in tribal law are additive of collateral consequences in state and federal law, creating additional barriers for members of federally recognized Indian tribes that most criminal offenders do not face. Criminological research has shown that Native Americans may be more likely to be criminal justice involved and more harshly punished than other minority groups in the United States, due in part to stereotypes of drunkenness and dependence and to cultural and linguistic barriers.[8] The situation is therefore an urgent one: collateral consequences are more likely to apply to Native American defendants compared to other populations *and* tribal members face more collateral consequences than members of other groups.[9]

The result is both ironic and perverse: tribal governments risk contributing to overcriminalization even though tribal criminal jurisdiction over both

5 Wayne A. Logan, "Informal Collateral Consequences," 88(3) *Washington Law Review* 1103, 1108–09 (2013).

6 National Inventory of Collateral Consequences of Conviction, https://niccc.nationalreentry resourcecenter.org; see also, Collateral Consequences Resource Center, https://ccresource-center.org.

7 See, e.g., Kimberly R. Kras, Morgan McGuirk, Breanne Pleggenkuhle, & Beth M. Huebner, "Compounded Stigmatization: Collateral Consequences of a Sex Offense Conviction," in *Handbook on the Consequences of Sentencing and Punishment Decisions* 188–203, 196 (Beth M. Huebner, Natasha A. Frost, eds., Routledge, 2018); Virginia Davis & Kevin Washburn, "Sex Offender Registration in Indian Country," 6(1) *Ohio State Journal of Criminal Law* 3 (2008).

8 Travis W. Franklin, "Sentencing Native Americans in US Federal Courts: An Examination of Disparity," 30(2) *Justice Quarterly* 310, 314–15 (2013).

9 I note here a continuing disclaimer: many Native Americans are not members of federally recognized Indian tribes, and not all tribes are federally recognized. This book uses the term "Indian tribe" because that is the term used in the U.S. constitution and federal law. Tribal membership is a political category, not an ethnological one, and tribal jurisdictions have their own membership policies. For a discussion of this complexity, see Dwanna L. Robertson, "A Necessary Evil: Framing an American Indian Legal Identity," 37(4) *American Indian Culture and Research Journal* 115 (2013).

Indians and non-Indians is highly restricted. Collateral consequences of criminal conviction may be attractive to tribal governments because their criminal jurisdiction is curtailed within the confines of certain federal statutes such as the Major Crimes Act and U.S. Supreme Court precedent.[10] The tribe may not be able to lock up a convicted person because of jurisdictional limitations, but it can take away the car keys.[11] Attaching collateral consequences to tribal office or economic activity can also be a strategy for the tribe to assert its jurisdiction over non-tribal members. Tribes, for instance, have designated some regulatory codes as civil rather than criminal in nature to ensure that they can enforce the rules against non-tribal members and have established civil forfeiture laws as a means of preventing crime by non-tribal members.[12] Furthermore, collateral consequences may attach even in tribal jurisdictions that do not prosecute criminal offenses at all; in these jurisdictions, state and federal convictions are sufficient to exclude a tribal member from running for tribal office or receiving a license or a permit. One of the most far-reaching observations in this book is how federal statutes and officials in federal agencies encourage tribes to create new collateral consequences of conviction in tribal law. For instance, federal officials must approve tribal sex offender registries, gaming and casino ordinances, ordinances providing for sale of alcohol on reservations, and even tribal constitutions under the Indian Reorganization Act of 1934.[13] Besides direct regulatory authority, federal officials (and sometimes state officials) have soft power, such as drafting model ordinances for sex offender registries and lawful gambling that tribal leadership can follow.[14] As tribal self-government expands, federal and state pressure to increase collateral consequences provides a powerful growth factor for overcriminalization.

10 Angelique Wambdi EagleWoman & Stacy L. Leeds, *Mastering American Indian Law* 56–63 (2d ed., Carolina Academic Press, 2019).

11 For this observation, I am indebted to a conversation with the American Bar Association's Native American Concerns Committee on one of their monthly conference calls (May 2023). Thank you to the Committee and the ABA staff members for their invitation.

12 Joseph Thomas Flies-Away, Carrie Garrow, & Miriam Jorgensen, "Native Nation Courts: Key Players in Nation Rebuilding," in *Rebuilding Native Nations: Strategies for Governance and Development* 115, 135 (Miriam Jorgensen, ed., University of Arizona Press, 2007).

13 For sex offender registries, this is done by the Office of Sex Offender Sentencing, Monitoring, Apprehending, Registering, and Tracking (SMART), Office of Justice Programs, U.S. Department of Justice. For alcohol sales and tribal constitutions, it is the U.S. Secretary of the Interior. For gaming ordinances, it is the National Indian Gaming Commission.

14 Office of Sex Offender Sentencing, Monitoring, Apprehending, Registering, and Tracking, Office of Justice Programs, U.S. Department of Justice, "Model Tribal Sex Offender Registration Code" (2017), available at: https://smart.ojp.gov/model-tribal-code (last accessed November 1, 2023); National Indian Gaming Commission, Revised Model Gaming Ordinance, Bulletin No. 2018-1 (January 10, 2018), available at: https://www.nigc.gov/images/uploads/bulletins/Bulletin_2018-1_Revised_Model_Ordinance.pdf.

An Overview of Collateral Consequences of Criminal Conviction

A full search of the National Inventory of Collateral Consequences of Conviction, to include federal law and the law of all 50 states plus Washington, DC, Puerto Rico, and the U.S. Virgin Islands, reveals a total of 42,756 collateral consequences as of the end of 2023.[15] This number, however, does not include collateral consequences imposed under tribal law, the subject of this study. It also does not include collateral consequences that apply simply to arrests without conviction; an arrest alone can lead to suspension of a professional license, eviction from public housing, or onerous fees.[16] In jury selection, the reach is even further: association with a person who has a criminal conviction, one's status as a crime victim, or membership in any relevant personal network may be enough to prevent service on a jury.[17] Federal employment discrimination law does not specifically protect persons with arrest records who have not been convicted, though federal courts have ruled and guidance from the Equal Employment Opportunity Commission now holds that blanket policies against hiring applicants with any arrest record might have a disparate impact on racial minorities.[18]

This survey generally focuses on explicit collateral consequences of criminal conviction: that is, exclusions that are written directly into tribal law. However, the landscape is more complicated because collateral consequences may be indirect, hidden, or discretionary. This is to say that collateral consequences may be incorporated into an ordinance by reference to a different law or inferior regulation (*indirect*), subsumed into another element of eligibility (such as a revocation or removal provision) or operated according to an informal or unwritten policy (*hidden*), or left to a secondary actor to decide, such as a gaming commission determining an applicant's eligibility for a gaming license (*discretionary*). The explicit collateral consequences explored here therefore represent an undercount of potential restrictions on persons with previous convictions. Automatic collateral consequences are by definition overbroad, but at least are uniformly applied and potentially provide public notice of their existence. Discretionary or informal collateral

15 National Inventory of Collateral Consequences of Conviction, "Collateral Consequences Inventory," https://niccc.nationalreentryresourcecenter.org/consequences (last accessed December 12, 2023) (check "federal" box and select all jurisdictions).

16 Eisha Jain, "Prosecuting Collateral Consequences," 104(5) *Georgetown Law Journal* 1197, 1207 (2016).

17 Matthew Clair & Alix S. Winter, "The Collateral Consequences of Criminal Legal Association During Jury Selection," 56 *Law & Society Review* 532 (2022).

18 Benjamin D. Geffen, "The Collateral Consequences of Acquittal: Employment Discrimination on the Basis of Arrests without Convictions," 20(2) *University of Pennsylvania Journal of Law and Social Change* 81, 89–90 (2017).

consequences, by contrast, can be more parsimoniously distributed but also create the risk of unequal or arbitrary application.[19]

Discretionary collateral consequences may also manifest as character review standards. By the turn of the twentieth century, established professions such as architects, engineers, accountants, nurses, and lawyers came under stricter regulation. As vocational standards proliferated to other professions, blanket exclusions for felony convictions regardless of their relevance to the position became more common, seemingly "more vindictively punitive than … selectively preventive."[20] Even when a person with a criminal record receives a license to practice in a learned profession, she or he may still face adverse action since licensing boards have discretion to suspend, revoke, or refuse to renew licenses or allow disciplinary complaints from other members of the profession on the basis of prior convictions.[21] While only at the margins of the technical definition of collateral consequences, criminal convictions also come with indirect financial costs, beyond fines and fees imposed as part of a sentence or mandatory post-conviction program costs. Unpaid child support, for instance, can compound during involvement in the criminal justice system and lead to new charges. Financial legal obligations lead to reduced credit scores, which in turn affect housing applications or tuition subsidies or loans.[22] The effects of collateral consequences may produce unintended results. Failure to find employment may increase the likelihood of a parole violation if a condition of parole is to secure a job. Similarly, prison vocational programs in fields such as hairstyling or firefighting can transmit useful skills to prisoners who are then excluded from these careers after release.[23]

Collateral consequences may reproduce and exacerbate other disparities in the criminal justice system and broader society. "Like the carceral state generally, collateral consequences enact racial hierarchy, disadvantaging people of color" and threatening many advancements of the civil rights movement, "as measured by employment, education, and other socioeconomic

19 Christopher Gowen & Erin Magary, "Collateral Consequences: How Reliable Data and Resources Can Change the Way Law Is Practiced," 39(1) *Fordham Urban Law Journal* 65, 67 (2011).

20 Deborah L. Rhode, "Virtue and the Law: The Good Moral Character Requirement in Occupational Licensing, Bar Regulation, and Immigration Proceedings," 43(3) *Law & Social Inquiry* 1027, 1031 (2018), quoting Walter Gellhorn, *Individual Freedom and Government Restraints* 138 (LSU Press, 1956).

21 Marlaina Freisthler & Mark A. Godsey, "Going Home to Stay: A Review of Collateral Consequences of Conviction, Post-Incarceration Employment, and Recidivism in Ohio," 36(3) *University of Toledo Law Review* 525, 540 (2005).

22 Breanne Pleggenkuhle, "The Financial Costs of a Criminal Conviction: Context and Consequences," 45(1) *Criminal Justice and Behavior* 121 (2018).

23 Zachary Hoskins, *Beyond Punishment? A Normative Account of the Collateral Legal Consequences of Conviction* 15 (Oxford University Press, 2019).

markers."[24] They perpetuate a Jim Crow stereotype of a criminal as irredeemable. Women may be especially vulnerable to collateral consequences: they have greater caregiving responsibilities than men but also higher unemployment rates after incarceration and less access to rehabilitative and vocational programs while incarcerated.[25] In 1996, Congress prohibited persons with drug-related felony convictions from food stamps or other welfare benefits, a provision that received only two minutes of legislative debate and proved so onerous that most U.S. states have modified the rule or opted out altogether.[26] Possibly, exclusion from social welfare or public benefits programs on the basis of prior convictions affects public health, either directly as a loss of access to food programs or indirectly as a loss of access to employment training or job placement services.[27] Persons with drug convictions have also been excluded from access to federal student loans and grants since the Higher Education Act of 1992, adding additional barriers to reintegration and employment.[28]

Collateral consequences do not only manifest as felony bars; they attach to minor crimes too. Even low-stakes misdemeanors can rope in serious civil sanctions. The category does not simply include formal legal or regulatory exclusions. Rather, exclusions extend to the private sector, as for instance in rental housing or employment, and may be hidden or discretionary.[29] Similarly, collateral consequences do not only attach at the state and federal level. Municipal governments across the United States control vital access to public housing and entrepreneurial opportunities, such as licenses for street vendors or taxicabs. Onerous collateral consequences in these jurisdictions can effectively work as a form of banishment, preventing certain persons with criminal records from living or working in the municipality at all.[30] The analogy to municipal governments also applies to tribal governments, which add another layer of bureaucratic sanctions that are for all intents and

24 Abigail E. Horn, "Wrongful Collateral Consequences," 87(2) *George Washington Law Review* 315, 319 (2019).

25 Joni Hersch & Erin E. Meyers, "The Gendered Burdens of Conviction and Collateral Consequences on Employment," 45(8) *Journal of Legislation* 171 (2018).

26 Hoskins, supra note 23 at 18.

27 Amanda Sheely & Shawn M. Kniepp, "The Effects of Collateral Consequences of Criminal Involvement on Employment, Use of Temporary Assistance for Needy Families, and Health," 55(5) *Women & Health* 548, 560–61 (2015).

28 Rouzhna Nayeri, "The Forever Scarlet Letter: The Need to Reform the Collateral Consequences of Criminal Convictions," 5(2) *Widener Journal of Law, Economics & Race* 109, 118 (2014).

29 Alessandro Corda, "Collateral Consequences and Criminal Justice Reform: Successes and Challenges," 52 *Crime and Justice* 447, 449 (2023).

30 Amy P. Meek, "Street Vendors, Taxicabs, and Exclusion Zones: The Impact of Collateral Consequences of Criminal Convictions at the Local Level," 75(1) *Ohio State Law Journal* 1, 4–5 (2014).

purposes invisible and cumulative. In addition, tribal governments are separate sovereigns and therefore tribal collateral consequences are more durable: that is, they are less likely than municipal collateral consequences to be preempted by state law.

The many unsuccessful legal challenges to collateral consequences of conviction have tended to focus on two arguments. The first is that specific collateral consequences, such as sex offender registration, termination of parental rights, civil commitment, or disenfranchisement, are excessively punitive, retroactive, or double jeopardy. The second is that due process requires that defendants be warned of the deleterious effects of collateral sanctions before pleading guilty. Courts have reasoned that collateral consequences are civil rather than criminal penalties and therefore outside the due process jurisprudence.[31] Even this rule works injustices so harsh that federal courts have carved out exceptions. Despite their supposed legality, these restrictions are also unpopular. Research on public opinion and collateral consequences finds that respondents of all political persuasions oppose restrictions on formerly incarcerated people's ability to participate in job placement programs and were at worst ambivalent about exclusions from public housing or food assistance.[32] In 2004, the American Bar Association issued guidelines for reform of collateral consequences, advocating that criminal defendants be fully informed of their impact before arraignment and trial and proposing that judges consider the impact of collateral and other non-punitive sanctions in their sentencing decisions.[33]

The relatively modern invention of most collateral consequences of conviction does not negate the ancient origins of the concept. "Civil death" existed in ancient Greece and Rome and many medieval societies on the theory that those who commit crimes should not participate in public affairs.[34] If collateral consequences are a form of punishment, then they must be justified based on normative theories of punishment; otherwise they immorally subject citizens to coercive pain without justification. Even if collateral consequences are construed strictly as civil (non-criminal) disqualifications, the

31 Michael Pinard, "An Integrated Perspective on the Collateral Consequences of Criminal Convictions and Reentry Issues Faced by Formerly Incarcerated Individuals," 86(3) *Boston University Law Review* 623, 639–45 (2006).

32 Travis Johnston & Kevin H. Wozniak, "Public Opinion and the Politics of Collateral Consequence Policies," 23(2) *Punishment & Society* 190, 208–09 (2020).

33 Alec C. Ewald & Marnie Smith, "Collateral Consequences of Criminal Convictions in American Courts: The View from the State Bench," 29(2) *Justice System Journal* 145, 148 (2008).

34 Danielle R. Jones, "When the Fallout of a Criminal Conviction Goes Too Far: Challenging Collateral Consequences," 11(2) *Stanford Journal of Civil Rights and Civil Liberties* 237, 244–45 (2015).

social costs may clearly outweigh any benefit to be gained.[35] Another normative argument is that collateral consequences undermine a previously convicted person's opportunity to reform, which shows unjustifiable contempt to that person and fails to treat her or him with moral dignity and respect.[36]

An estimate of potential risk may be key in justifying a collateral consequence. Avoiding potentially unsuitable employees can justify an exclusion, depending on how narrowly the risk is construed: a candidate with a history of gun possession convictions may not be a suitable schoolteacher. In other contexts, the scope of acceptable risk may be broader. For offices of public trust or authority, such as a judge, prior criminal convictions may be inconsistent with the moral qualities demanded of these professions.[37] Most collateral consequences are intended not to punish people for prior offenses, but rather to control and restrain them for what they might do in the future. They are consistent with other mechanisms of predictive surveillance and control that exist throughout the justice system.[38] This kind of risk prediction, besides being notoriously unreliable, also exacerbates disparities in the criminal justice process. Collateral consequences, many of which came into existence with the War on Drugs and the so-called "punitive turn" during the 1980s and 1990s, are extensions of longstanding criminal justice policy decisions that disproportionately impact racial minorities.[39] The immigration consequences of a criminal conviction, up to and including automatic deportation for so-called "aggravated felonies," to be defined as any offense resulting in incarceration or confinement, were so severe that even the U.S. Supreme Court in *Padilla v. Kentucky* ruled that defense counsel have an obligation to warn their clients before pleading guilty.[40]

One of the significant themes of this book is the degree to which state and federal law promote collateral consequences in tribal law. The federal government has a long history of attaching collateral consequences to federal benefits, even when the underlying conviction is not a federal one. Under federal law, persons with drug convictions are excluded from all federal benefits. This does not include retirement or health benefits, but it sweeps in a huge

35 Jeffrey M. Brown, "Collateral Legal Consequences of Criminal Convictions in a Society of Equals," 15 *Criminal Law and Philosophy* 181 (2021).

36 Hoskins, supra note 23 at 30.

37 Milena Tripkovic, "Collateral Consequences of Conviction: Limits and Justifications," 18(3) *Criminology, Criminal Justice, Law & Society* 18, 19 (2017).

38 Sandra G. Mayson, "Collateral Consequences and the Preventative State," 91(1) *Notre Dame Law Review* 301, 303 (2015).

39 Pinard, supra note 2 at 465.

40 Anita Ortiz Maddali, "*Padilla v. Kentucky*: A New Chapter in Supreme Court Jurisprudence on Whether Deportation Constitutes Punishment for Lawful Permanent Residents," 61(1) *American University Law Review* 1, 18, 22 (2011), citing *Padilla v. Kentucky*, 130 S. Ct. 1473 (2010).

range of grants, contracts, loans, professional licenses, or employment in federally regulated industries such as airlines. It also impacts federal housing benefits, food stamps, federally funded health care programs, and educational loans and scholarships.[41] In this study, federal law requires or encourages collateral consequences in specific areas of tribal law either directly (as with sex offender employment or cannabis licensing) or indirectly (as with gaming and casino ordinances). While more subtle, states also have a role to play in the proliferation of tribal collateral consequences; for instance, states may exclude persons with criminal convictions from alcohol sales licenses or may require such exclusions in the Tribal-State Gaming Compacts required by the Indian Gaming Regulatory Act, which regulates casinos in Indian Country.

Although federal law may impose or encourage collateral consequences in tribal law, federal and state courts have come to differing conclusions as to whether a tribal court conviction constitutes a "conviction" for purposes of enhanced sentencing or "career offender" status. As a threshold matter, enhanced sentencing for subsequent crimes can be considered a collateral consequence of conviction.[42] This is a matter of some importance, because the Indian Civil Rights Act only requires tribes to provide indigent defendants with a lawyer when imposing a prison sentence longer than one year. Whether tribal court convictions without the benefit of legal representation can constitute prior convictions under federal law has caused a split among the U.S. Courts of Appeal.[43] For federal courts, U.S. Federal Sentencing Guidelines permit, but do not require, consideration of prior tribal court convictions in the sentencing process, leaving significant discretion to judges who may not be familiar with tribal court operations or jurisdiction.[44] The result is a contradiction in federal Indian law that increasingly respects tribal court authority and yet provides that tribal court convictions may be disregarded when calculating an offender's criminal history.[45]

41 Gabriel J. Chin, "Race, the War on Drugs, and the Collateral Consequences of Criminal Conviction," 6(2) *Journal of Gender, Race and Justice* 253, 259–60 (2002).

42 Id. at 261.

43 Nicholas LeTang, "*United States v. Bryant* and the Subsequent Use of Uncounseled Tribal Court Convictions in State or Federal Prosecution," 77(1) *Montana Law Review* 211, 211–12 (2016).

44 Matthew L.M. Fletcher, "Sovereign Comity: Factors Recognizing Tribal Court Criminal Convictions in State and Federal Courts," 45 *Court Review* 12, 16 (2009).

45 William C. Canby, "Commentary: Treatment of Tribal Court Convictions," 17(3) *Federal Sentencing Reporter* 220, 220 (2005).

Organization of the Book and Typology of Collateral Consequences

This book establishes a typology of collateral consequences of conviction in tribal law. The chapters of this book are organized accordingly. In general, the book categorizes collateral consequences into four categories: (1) restrictions on tribal office, (2) restrictions on occupational licenses or business permits, (3) limitations on tribal civil rights, and (4) exclusions from tribal social services. The final typology is broken down further than this because of the complexity of restrictions on tribal office and because of the cross-cutting nature of the gaming industry, which is a dense source of collateral consequences spanning both employment and licensing. On the other hand, limitations on tribal civil rights and social services are combined into a single chapter because they are comparatively less common than the other categories. For simplicity, this book does not include whether prior convictions count toward sentencing enhancements or may be used to impeach a witness's testimony.

Chapter 2 of this book looks at the status of federal Indian law, including criminal jurisdiction in and organization of tribal justice systems. The proliferation of collateral consequences in tribal law may be a byproduct of constrained criminal jurisdiction, the result of Congressional statutes and Supreme Court precedent that create a delicate tripartition among federal, state, and tribal courts based on the identities of the offender and victim. Because collateral consequences are construed as civil sanctions rather than criminal ones, tribal law is not always limited by these same jurisdictional boundaries. Over the past 50 years, the growth and increasing complexity of tribal administration and regulation have increased the opportunities for attaching collateral consequences to tribal office, employment, or regulatory permissions. This chapter also addresses the methodology and limitations of this study, including the challenges of finding and summarizing the laws of 347 separate tribal jurisdictions, each of which has its own legal sources and organization. I am confident, however, that the perfect is the enemy of the pragmatic; these unavoidable gaps in legal sources do not prevent observations and conclusions about the general state of tribal law.

The most common collateral consequences in this book, measured by number of jurisdictions, are restrictions on running for elected tribal council or executive leadership, the subject of Chapter 3. Restrictions on running for tribal office are common because they are contained primarily in tribal constitutions rather than codes or election ordinances and are replicated in influential constitutional templates. Restrictions on running for office are frequently tempered by sunset dates or restoration of rights mechanisms, such as a tribal council waiver to restore the right to run for tribal office. Far more varied are restrictions that attach to *appointed* tribal office, including tribal judges, boards, committees, or administrator positions, covered in

Chapter 4. These provisions are idiosyncratic, including restrictions on tribal law enforcement positions, natural resource managers, election administrators, tribal authorities governing public utilities or education, or employees of tribal-owned corporations or businesses.

The second-most common area of tribal collateral consequences pertains to occupational licenses and business permits, in Chapter 5. These can affect controlled economic activity, such as alcohol sales, or attach to specific roles or professions, such as lawyers or security guards. Also explored in this chapter are the complex regulations governing natural resource permits, such as hunting or shellfish licenses or specific permissions for grazing or fishing. Restrictions on natural resource extraction are generally most common among tribes in the Upper Midwest or Pacific Northwest. Collateral consequences may also attach to licensing for lawyers or lay advocates in tribal court and to other licensed professions, such as pawnbrokers, veterinarians, sports betters, private security guards, or day care center operators.

The longest chapter of this book and the densest area of tribal collateral consequences relate to the gaming and casino industry, the topic of Chapter 6. Here, collateral consequences generally take two forms: first, restrictions on serving in gaming regulatory or management offices, such as tribal gaming commissions; and second, restrictions on receiving a gaming license, which is required under federal law for persons serving in management positions. Many tribes, however, extend background checks and exclusions for prior convictions to non-gaming employees in casinos or other gaming operations. A wide range of restoration of rights mechanisms exist. Many tribes provide for a gaming waiver to restore eligibility for a gaming license, especially for tribal members. With some important exceptions, the most common versions of these collateral consequences tend to be narrowly tailored specifically to crimes of dishonesty, theft, or moral turpitude. Since gaming ordinances must be approved by the National Indian Gaming Commission and only after tribes negotiate Tribal-State Compacts with their state governments, this area of collateral consequences is especially prone to legal sharing among jurisdictions and influence from federal and state authorities.

Chapter 7 is on collateral consequences that pertain to civil rights and social services, the most problematic realm but also the least common, itself an important normative conclusion of this study. Among civil rights exclusions, the right to serve on a tribal court jury is the most frequent; more serious civil rights burdens, such as banishment from the reservation or denial of the right to vote in tribal elections, are far less common. For tribal social services, the most common exclusions are for tribal housing or homesteading benefits or employment with the tribe. This may manifest as an exclusion from a tribal hiring preference on the grounds of a prior criminal conviction. Federal law applies to certain types of tribal employment involving children, such as employment with early childhood education centers. In addition to background checks and disclosure policies, some tribes have also created per se exclusions from these roles for certain prior convictions.

Although the harms of tribal collateral consequences stem, in part, from state and federal law, the solution may well come from within tribal law. As explored in Chapter 8, tribal constitutions, codes, and ordinances lay out hundreds of possibilities for pardons, expungements, automatic record clearing, waivers for specific rights, or juvenile record sealing. Included in this chapter is an analysis of tribal sex offender registries, including whether sex offender registration periods can be reduced through a discretionary petition process. Marijuana expungements are another active area of tribal lawmaking. Tribal law has become a laboratory for innovation: restoration of rights procedures run the full spectrum from traditional executive pardon processes to court-driven or automatic expungements to traditional forgiveness rituals involving a panel of elders. Unlike some states, federal law does not currently permit "deferred adjudication," that is, requiring a defendant to fulfill certain conditions such as community service *before* charges are brought, thereby avoiding a criminal record altogether.[46] Like post-conviction relief such as pardons and expungements, deferred adjudication allows offenders to demonstrate respect for the law without the stigma of a conviction. Positively, some tribal courts have adopted deferred adjudication policies, such as the Tulalip Tribes in Washington State.[47] Restoring rights to persons with a criminal record or avoiding a conviction altogether are important steps toward reducing collateral harm of criminal convictions.

Concluding Recommendations on Tribal Collateral Consequences

When drawn too broadly, collateral consequences of conviction have diminishing returns in protecting community members from future harm; they also undermine important rehabilitative and reintegrative goals of the justice system. Tribal governments may see collateral consequences as functions of political sovereignty, part and parcel of their criminal legal jurisdiction. Strengthening elements of tribal criminal law in the model of state and federal law may contribute to tribal legal autonomy, but it may also lead to increased social control. Adding an additional layer of criminalization to a criminal justice system that already has its fair share of layers has a "net-widening" consequence and simply ropes in more people for longer into a labyrinth of punishment, surveillance, and control.[48] As noted above, Indian

46 Margaret Colgate Love, "Alternatives to Conviction: Deferred Adjudication as a Way of Avoiding Collateral Consequences," 22(1) *Federal Sentencing Reporter* 6, 8 (2009).

47 Tulalip Tribes (WA) Law and Order Code, Ordinance 49, § 5.11.2.

48 See Scott H. Decker, "A Systematic Analysis of Diversion: Net Widening and Beyond," 13 *Journal of Criminal Justice* 207 (1985).

tribes face unique vulnerabilities in the U.S. criminal justice system: Native Americans are more likely to be victims and offenders; jurisdictional gaps hamper straightforward investigation and prosecution; and the procedures used to adjudicate criminal cases are culturally and sometimes linguistically distant. For this reason, some of the strongest critiques against overcriminalization in Indian Country come from the movement for prison minimalism and abolition. Tribal jurisdictions "are uniquely positioned to reconsider systems of punishment," both because of legal limitations on sovereignty and a rich tradition of restorative and reparative practices.[49]

It may be premature to complain about overcriminalization in Indian Country when tribal criminal jurisdiction is so curtailed. This is especially true given the limitations of tribal civil and criminal jurisdiction over non-Indians who live and work on Indian reservations; collateral consequences may be a way to assert tribal authority over non-Indians. One must also acknowledge that per se exclusions for prior criminal convictions can help reduce the cost of burdensome background checks, especially in the gaming industry where strict and expensive background checks are required by federal law. However, the thousands of collateral consequences of conviction across hundreds of tribal legal systems, as documented in this book, are testament to the fact that overcriminalization might already exist in tribal law even without the expansive formal jurisdiction of criminal courts. Because of the peculiarities of the U.S. federal system, tribal governments have authority to create additional layers of surveillance and social control that are cumulative of already existing federal, state, and municipal burdens. For instance, tribe-specific sex offender registries may be symbolically important areas of autonomy for tribes, independent of state criminal databases, but to persons forced to register as sex offenders this adds another layer of byzantine rules and procedures that they must comply with or else face further harm. One may also critique the degree to which collateral consequences really are less burdensome than background checks or discretionary hiring policies: criminal records databases are notoriously unreliable; interpretation of collateral consequences often requires analysis of complex legal terms such as "moral turpitude" or "crimes of dishonesty"; and placing the burden on the applicant to "prove" that he or she is eligible may wrongfully exclude applicants who are eligible for the position or the license.[50]

I propose a few observations to assist tribal lawmakers and legislative drafters. First, the narrower a collateral consequence and the more well-tailored it is to the job in question, the more defensible it is. Collateral consequences that are too broad have deleterious social consequences, including

49 Grace L. Carson, "Tribal Sovereignty, Decolonization, and Abolition: Why Tribes Should Reconsider Punishment," 69(4) *UCLA Law Review* 1076, 1121 (2022).

50 Horn, supra note 24 at 323–24.

possible discrimination and undermining the goal of indigenizing tribal employment. Second, collateral consequences that have a sunset date or that automatically restore eligibility after a period of years are preferable to collateral consequences that are perpetual or lifelong. While perhaps justifiable in narrow circumstances, lifelong exclusions from tribal employment or licensing because of a single conviction risk creating a second class of citizenship. Third, requiring disclosure of prior criminal convictions in a background check is a morally and practically defensible policy, but creating a system of purely discretionary decision making may produce arbitrary results. Better would be a system of more transparent criteria for employment or licensing in which applicants could provide statements or evidence, while hiring or licensing commissions could provide reasons or conditions for approval or denial. Fourth, provisions that extend collateral consequences to juvenile convictions, arrests without conviction, civil judgments for damages or bankruptcy proceedings, or association with a person with a criminal conviction, such as a spousal exclusion, are highly disfavored since they expand collateral harm to groups that are unlikely to be high risk. Finally, the problem of wrongful convictions deserves special attention. Per se exclusions for persons with criminal convictions may always sweep in persons who are factually and legally innocent. Legislative drafters should be cognizant of this risk, especially when creating burdensome petition processes or lengthy waiting periods for pardons, expungements, or record sealing.

Waivers or restoration of rights mechanisms, especially for tribal members seeking employment or occupational licenses, are favored. However, procedures that create a waiver or restoration of rights for a single collateral consequence (such as a special waiver for a gaming license or tribal elected position) may needlessly create more bureaucracy and be confusing to applicants. An open, general restoration of rights procedure such as a pardon, expungement, certificate of rehabilitation, or record sealing process that is available to all persons with a previous criminal conviction (including non-tribal members seeking tribal office or licenses) would be the most equitable and administratively efficient way to reduce the harms of collateral consequences of conviction. Exclusions from waiver or pardon processes, such as gratuitous exceptions for sex, drug, or alcohol offenses, are rarely based on criminological risk data and are often unjustified expressions of penal populism. A jurisdiction may have good reasons to exclude, but it also has many good reasons to forgive.

Chapter 2

Tribal Justice Systems in Comparative Perspective

This book is about comparative tribal law: it takes tribal constitutions and codes on their own terms. It is not about the well-trodden realm of federal Indian law or the boundaries of concurrent criminal jurisdiction among the federal government, states, and the tribes. It is also not a book about the historical development of tribal law or about the clash between traditional custom and Anglo-American influence. But some discussion of these areas cannot be avoided: "the experience of native peoples in the United States is entwined with law to an unusual degree."[1] Treaties with the U.S. federal government, Supreme Court precedent, and Congressional action have to a degree defined tribal membership, and tribal membership in turn has helped define Native American identity. This chapter proceeds in four parts. First, the chapter will summarize the origins of federal Indian law with an emphasis on criminal jurisdiction in Indian Country. Second, the chapter will describe the basic legal architecture and contemporary practice of drafting a tribal constitution and codifying tribal law. Third, the reader will be introduced to tribal justice systems, including tribal courts, which now comprise the dominant paradigm of dispute resolution in Indian Country. Finally, the last section will elaborate on the methodology of this book, including the limitations caused by the unavailability of tribal legal sources, the great diversity of tribal political and legal structure, and the resulting peculiarities of citation format.

Introduction to Federal Indian Law

The bedrock of the federal–tribal legal relationship is Chief Justice John Marshall's characterization in *Cherokee Nation v. Georgia* (1831) that tribes are not foreign sovereigns but rather "domestic dependent nations" over which the U.S. federal government has a fiduciary duty to protect tribal lands,

1 Carole Goldberg-Ambrose, "Of Native Americans and Tribal Members: The Impact of Law on Indian Group Life," 28(5) *Law and Society Review* 1123, 1124 (1994).

DOI: 10.4324/9781003432548-2

people, and resources.[2] This followed an earlier case, *Johnson v. McIntosh* (1823), in which the Marshall Court found that the doctrine of discovery gave the U.S. government superior and exclusive title to land as the successor of the British Crown. Tribes might have had right to occupancy of that same land, but they did not have fee title.[3] In *Worcester v. Georgia* (1832), another dispute involving Georgia's attempted interventions in the Cherokee Nation, the Court restricted states' abilities to regulate tribes, providing that Congress alone had plenary power over Native nations.[4] These three cases, the so-called Marshall Trilogy, still primarily define the boundaries of federal Indian law. We can characterize the basic rule emerging from these cases as follows: (1) the federal government, not the states, has plenary authority over Indian Country; (2) state law has no force unless Congress has specifically authorized it; (3) Indian tribes are sovereign nations but domestic in the sense that Congress, and only Congress, has authority to regulate their affairs; and (4) the U.S. federal government has accepted a fiduciary duty to govern Indian Country for the benefit of individual Indians and tribes.[5] In these interlocking decisions, Chief Justice Marshall "attempted to mediate the tension between colonialism and constitutionalism."[6]

In the realm of criminal law, the division of jurisdiction between federal, state, and tribal governments dates to the early republic. Since 1790, the federal government has had jurisdiction over non-Indians who commit crimes against Indians on tribal lands; similarly, early Indian treaties allowed state and territorial governments to prosecute Indians who commit crimes against non-Indians. Until 1871 with the end of the treaty period with tribal nations, federal courts enforced the rule that states had no jurisdiction over crimes occurring in Indian Country.[7] In *United States v. McBratney* (1881), the U.S. Supreme Court ruled that state governments had exclusive jurisdiction over non-Indians who commit crimes against other non-Indians on tribal lands.[8] However, this tripartite division between federal, state, and tribal governments broke down over the gaps that were created when the competing

2 Samuel E. Ennis & Caroline P. Mayhew, "Federal Indian Law and Tribal Criminal Justice in the Self-Determination Era," 38(2) *American Indian Law Review* 421, 425 (2013); see also, Cherokee Nation v. Georgia, 30 U.S. (5 Pet.) 1, 17 (1831).

3 Johnson v. McIntosh, 21 U.S. (8 Wheat.) 543 (1823).

4 Worcester v. Georgia, 31 U.S. (6 Pet.) 515 (1832); Harvard Project on American Indian Economic Development, *The State of the Native Nations: Conditions under U.S. Policies of Self-Determination* 38 (Oxford University Press, 2008).

5 Matthew L.M. Fletcher, "Federal Indian Law as Method" (2023), Social Science Research Network, available at: https://papers.ssrn.com/sol3/papers.cfm?abstract_id=4505559.

6 Philip P. Frickey, "Marshalling Past and Present: Colonialism, Constitutionalism, and Interpretation in Federal Indian Law," 107(2) *Harvard Law Review* 381, 385 (1993).

7 M. Brent Leonhard, "Criminal Jurisdiction in Indian Country," 69(2) *Department of Justice Journal of Federal Law and Practice* 45, 47–48 (2021).

8 United States v. McBratney, 104 U.S. 621, 624 (1881).

sovereigns had different conceptions of criminal behavior and how to punish it. In *Ex Parte Crow Dog* (1883), the U.S. Supreme Court held that the U.S. federal government did not have criminal jurisdiction over a tribal member for crimes committed on tribal territory.[9] In that case, the defendant, who murdered another tribal leader, had already been punished by the tribe and subsequently prosecuted and sentenced to death under federal law. The fallout over this punishment was the Major Crimes Act of 1885, in which Congress granted federal courts concurrent jurisdiction to prosecute an enumerated list of felony-level crimes that are committed by tribal members on tribal lands.[10] For other crimes not covered by the Major Crimes Act that are committed on reservations and involve a non-tribal member as either perpetrator or victim, the federal government has criminal jurisdiction under the Indian Country Crimes Act.[11] Additionally, the Assimilative Crimes Act allows the federal government to prosecute based on a state criminal offense if the activity is not a crime under federal law. This was applied to Indian Country in *Williams v. United States* (1946). As a result, federal courts have jurisdiction over Indian perpetrators who commit acts against non-Indians on tribal lands based on state criminal law.[12]

In the realm of criminal law, it is now axiomatic after *Oliphant v. Suquamish Indian Tribe* (1978) that tribal courts do not have criminal jurisdiction over non-tribal members, unless Congress has specifically created this jurisdiction. For instance, Congress did so under the Violence Against Women Act owing to Indian Country's enforcement gap in domestic violence cases.[13] Arguably, *Oliphant* departs from the spirit of the Cherokee cases and federal statutes because it essentially flips the presumption of tribal sovereignty: tribal legal jurisdiction is now the exception rather than the rule.[14] Excluding non-tribal members is a large omission from tribal criminal jurisdiction because of the 4.6 million people who live on Indian reservations, only 1.1 million are tribal members, though this gap is not uniform across Indian Country. The large number of non-Indians on Indian reservations is partly the legacy of allotment in which tribes were encouraged to sell off land as parcels, partly due to the success of economic development operations on Indian reservations

9 Ex Parte Crow Dog, 109 U.S. 556 (1883).

10 Angelique Wambdi EagleWoman & Stacy L. Leeds, *Mastering American Indian Law* 56 (2d ed., Carolina Academic Press, 2019); see also, 18 U.S.C. § 1153.

11 EagleWoman & Leeds, supra note 10 at 58; see also, 18 U.S.C. § 1152.

12 EagleWoman & Leeds, supra note 10 at 58; see also Williams v. United States, 327 U.S. 711 (1946); 18 U.S.C. § 13.

13 Alex Tallchief Skibine, "Constitutionalism, Federal Common Law, and the Inherent Powers of Indian Tribes," 39(1) *American Indian Law Review* 77, 78 (2014); see also Oliphant v. Suquamish Indian Tribe, 435 U.S. 191 (1978).

14 Frank Pommerscheim, *Broken Landscape: Indians, Indian Tribes, and the Constitution* 212 (Oxford University Press, 2009).

such as casinos, and partly the result of marriages between tribal members and non-members.[15] Tribes do have criminal jurisdiction over Indians who are members of other tribes ("nonmember Indians"). After the U.S. Supreme Court ruled in *Duro v. Reina* that members of different tribes could not be prosecuted because they were not tribal members, Congress passed legislation (the so-called "*Duro* fix") specifically giving tribal courts jurisdiction to prosecute non-member Indians who violate tribal law.[16] Where a crime occurs on an Indian reservation and *neither* the perpetrator nor the victim are tribal members, then neither tribal nor federal law applies: rather, state prosecutors may prosecute under state law in state court.[17]

In 1953, perceiving a lapse in law enforcement in Indian Country, Congress passed Public Law 280, which "fundamentally disrupted the traditional allocation" of legal jurisdiction among federal, state, and tribal governments.[18] This law delegated federal civil and criminal authority under the Major Crimes Act and Indian Country Crimes Act to state governments. Six U.S. states, the so-called "mandatory" PL-280 states, have accepted the full delegation of federal criminal jurisdiction. These are, respectively, Alaska (except the Metlakatla Indian Community of the Annette Islands), California, Minnesota (except the Red Lake Reservation), Nebraska, Oregon (except the Warm Springs Reservation), and Wisconsin, which combined cover about two-thirds of federally recognized Indian tribes, though not generally the most populous ones.[19] In these six states, the state government has taken the place of the federal government for purposes of concurrent jurisdiction in criminal matters and (excluding the Red Lake Reservation and Warm Springs Reservation only, but including the Metlakatla Indian Community) for civil matters as well. In addition to these six "mandatory" states under PL-280, other states may optionally accept delegation of federal criminal jurisdiction over specific categories of crimes or cases; Idaho, for instance, accepted jurisdiction over juvenile delinquency cases. After passage of the Indian Civil Rights Act (ICRA) of 1968, however, tribal consent is necessary for the federal government to transfer criminal jurisdiction to state courts and with the Tribal Law and Order Act (TLOA) of 2010, tribes can request return of federal criminal jurisdiction where it has been delegated to the state.[20]

15 Julia M. Bedell, "The Fairness of Tribal Court Juries and Non-Indian Defendants," 41(2) *American Indian Law Review* 253, 256–57 (2017).

16 Stephen L. Pevar, *The Rights of Indians and Tribes* 100 (4th ed., Oxford University Press, 2012); see also, Duro v. Reina, 495 U.S. 676 (1990); United States v. Lara, 541 U.S. 193 (2004) (upholding "*Duro* fix").

17 EagleWoman & Leeds, supra note 10 at 59; see also *U.S. v. McBratney*, 104 U.S. 621 (1882).

18 Vanessa J. Jimenez & Soo C. Song, "Concurrent Tribal and State Jurisdiction under Public Law 280," 47(6) *American University Law Review* 1627, 1632 (1998).

19 Id. at 1632–33, including n. 21.

20 EagleWoman & Leeds, supra note 10 at 60–61.

Background on Tribal Constitutions and Codes

Tribal constitutions have a long history, dating to the Cherokee adoption in 1827, a move partly designed to fend off Georgia's encroachment on Cherokee land. More than 60 tribal nations had written constitutions on file with the U.S. Department of the Interior before the passage of the Indian Reorganization Act of 1934 (IRA).[21] The IRA, also known as the Wheeler-Howard Act, was a major plank in the "Indian New Deal," which refers to the policy turn during the Franklin Roosevelt administration toward tribal autonomy and away from 50 years of assimilation and allotment of tribal lands.[22] The IRA created a template for tribal polities to organize their internal governments, but only provided them 2 years to make an irreversible selection; subsequently, the legislation was amended to include tribes in Oklahoma and Alaska without the deadline. Roughly 60% of tribes accepted the IRA in those 2 years and thereby began the process of creating a tribal constitution, heavily influenced by Anglo-American legal principles including through the model constitutions famously drafted by Felix Cohen, an attorney in the Office of the Solicitor in the U.S. Department of the Interior.[23]

Tribal constitutions are more than simply boilerplate constructions imposed on tribes by the Bureau of Indian Affairs. Native communities frequently had "a fair amount of self-determination to decide what kinds of provisions they wanted to have in their organic charters."[24] IRA-style constitutions may have a parliamentary-style structure in which upper-level officials are selected by the tribal council from among its members or they may provide for the direct election of the tribal council chair and usually vice chair. In some cases, the constitution provides for a single general council as its legislature, and in others the constitution creates a smaller business committee to run the daily operations of the tribe with the general council's powers restricted to major constitutional issues.[25] These constitutions often reflect underlying cultural norms. For instance, the Lakota people, who have a long history of representative councils, have selected a parliamentary-style political structure that better reflects that tradition.[26] In addition, some social science evidence suggests that tribal constitutions "have a positive and significant correlation on

21 Robert J. Miller, "American Indian Constitutions and Their Influence on the United States Constitution," 159(1) *Proceedings of the American Philosophical Society* 32, 44 (2015).

22 Philip Weeks, *The American Indian Experience: 1524 to the Present* 252–57 (Forum Press, 1988).

23 Miller, supra note 21 at 44–46.

24 David E. Wilkins & Sheryl Lightfoot, "Oaths of Office in Tribal Constitutions: Swearing Allegiance, but to Whom?" 32(4) *American Indian Quarterly* 389, 391 (2008).

25 Joseph P. Kalt, "The Role of Constitutions in Native Nation Building: Laying a Firm Foundation," in *Rebuilding Native Nations: Strategies for Governance and Development* 78, 86–88 (Miriam Jorgensen, ed., University of Arizona Press, 2007).

26 Id. at 88–89.

the economic well-being of tribes," especially among constitutions drafted later.[27] This may be because constitutions provide tribal jurisdictions with a blueprint for political stability, though tribes with the most economic growth potential may also be more likely to adopt constitutions.[28]

In the decades after tribal IRA constitutions went into force, direct federal interference in tribal legal and judicial systems waned, which reduced oversight over some internal tribal operations. Federal courts also began to consider whether the U.S. constitution applied to tribal courts through the IRA. As political entities, Indian tribes predate the U.S. constitution, which in turn recognizes tribes as having inherent sovereignty. As a result, the U.S. constitution does not directly apply to intra-tribal governmental operations, though it does apply to U.S. government agencies like the Bureau of Indian Affairs that oversee the trust relationship with tribes.[29] The position of tribes in the U.S. political system faces a fundamental contradiction. Fully accepting tribes into the U.S. political and legal landscape would ensure that their laws are coequal with other political divisions and that tribal court decisions are entitled to "full faith and credit." On the other hand, placing tribes directly into this system would no doubt have an assimilating effect, especially if U.S. federal courts were able to directly review tribal court decisions.[30] At different times and in different contexts, the U.S. Supreme Court has validated both approaches.

Shortly after building the architecture of modern federal civil rights law, Congress passed the ICRA in 1968 with mixed reactions from tribal leaders to include a direct protest of the Senate Judiciary Committee.[31] The new law gave tribal members the ability to go to U.S. federal court to challenge tribal justice procedures on due process grounds, though the U.S. Supreme Court blunted the assimilationist threat by effectively limiting this aspect of the ICRA to criminal cases in *Santa Clara v. Martinez* in 1978.[32] While ICRA extends many traditional civil and political rights (speech, self-incrimination, double jeopardy, equal protection, etc.) to tribal governments, it does not do so completely. Absent are provisions on establishment of religion, right of an indigent accused to counsel, or indictment by a grand jury.[33] Restricting

27 R. Warren Anderson, "Native American Reservation Constitutions," 27 *Constitutional Political Economy* 377, 392 (2016).

28 Id. at 395.

29 Bedell, supra note 15 at 258.

30 Alex Tallchief Skibine, "Troublesome Aspects of Western Influences on Tribal Justice Systems and Laws," 1 *Tribal Law Journal* 1, 4 (2000).

31 Vine Deloria & Clifford M. Lytle, *American Indians, American Justice* 127–28 (University of Texas Press, 1983).

32 Carey N. Vicenti, "The Reemergence of Tribal Society and Traditional Justice Systems," 79(3) *Judicature* 134, 136 (1995); see also Santa Clara v. Martinez, 436 U.S. 49 (1978).

33 Deloria & Lytle, supra note 31 at 130–31.

the ICRA to criminal rather than civil cases also protects the broad inherent jurisdiction of tribal courts over civil cases. This is powerful for tribes because they can characterize civil wrongs broadly, protect tribal tax and enforcement mechanisms, and even assert civil jurisdiction over non-tribal members, limited only at the margins by the Secretary of the Interior's duty to protect the federal government's trust responsibility.[34]

Since the 1960s, tribal governments have adopted increasingly complex and organized tribal codes. Tribal codes may not always be public or readily available, but at least some are compiled into collections or regularly published with revisions.[35] A major influence on drafting tribal codes is the tribal attorney or in-house counsel, who may look to the laws of other tribal jurisdictions or consult with outside legal experts before the matter is put to the tribal council for a vote.[36] Drafters of codes routinely look to the codes of other jurisdictions, including from other tribes, state law, or model provisions, and the final wording is refined by legislative committees or the tribal council. In tribal jurisdictions where final legislation must be approved by all adult citizens in a referendum, another layer of refinement may take place. Code drafters may not be members of the tribe but rather hired counsel, immersed in Western rather than tribal law, who struggle in tailoring the language to local conditions or reflecting all viewpoints.[37]

Following the disastrous Termination Era of the 1950s and 1960s, when many tribes partitioned tribal lands and dissolved, the U.S. federal government has since tended to pursue a policy of tribal self-determination, envisioning federal backing for tribal programs to replace directly administered federal services.[38] The Indian Self-Determination and Education Assistance Act of 1975 authorizes tribes to submit "self-determination" contracts to federal government agencies that, if approved, require the agency to transfer all allocated funding to the tribe to administer the relevant program. These may involve operating schools, water treatment facilities, health clinics, or law enforcement programs.[39] As tribal jurisdictions fully realize their inherent sovereignty by developing modern legal and regulatory architecture, they become increasingly secure against state encroachment. This is because if tribes have already regulated on a subject, they can argue that

34 Robert D. Cooter & Wolfgang Fikentscher, "Indian Common Law: The Role of Custom in American Indian Tribal Courts," 46(2) *American Journal of Comparative Law* 287, 305–06 (1998).

35 Robert D. Cooter & Wolfgang Fikentscher, "American Indian Law Codes: Pragmatic Law and Tribal Identity," 56(1) *American Journal of Comparative Law* 29, 32–35 (2008).

36 Id. at 35–37.

37 Bruce G. Miller, "The Individual, the Collective, and Tribal Code," 21(1) *American Indian Culture and Research Journal* 107, 110 (1997).

38 Ennis & Mayhew, supra note 2 at 426–27.

39 Pevar, supra note 16 at 63–64.

state interference is preempted by federal law and that the tribe has sovereign immunity from state lawsuits; they are not at the mercy of an exemption from the state.[40]

Tribal Justice Systems and Courts

Tribal justice systems were also beneficiaries of this trend toward tribal self-determination beginning in the 1970s. Many tribal constitutions did not originally provide for tribal courts and judiciaries. In traditional tribal systems of justice, mediating chiefs or elders sought satisfactory compromises with the parties to the dispute, which often involved compensation or restitution, sometimes from the chief himself.[41] Today, tribes are complex political and administrative organs with formalized relationships with states and the federal government. An independent judiciary, separate from the tribal council and executive, has tended to improve management of social services and economic development. The Confederated Tribes of the Colville Reservation amended its tribal constitution in 1990 to create a tribal court and court of appeals, specifically laying out the conditions of judicial service and removal from office.[42] Effective tribal courts no doubt help define and reinforce the boundaries of the tribe's legal jurisdiction. Consistent with notions of legal pluralism, tribal court authority can be empowered in many ways: through restorative justice practices, developing tribal common law through jurisprudence, professionalizing tribal judiciaries, and consolidating small tribal courts into inter-tribal appellate systems.[43] The U.S. Supreme Court has ruled that tribes have exclusive jurisdiction to interpret tribal law unless Congress has explicitly limited this authority.[44] Tribal courts therefore have a potentially broad, if not fully realized, role to play in asserting tribal sovereignty.

According to a census of tribal justice systems performed by the U.S. Bureau of Justice Statistics in 2002, about 60% (188) of all federally recognized Indian tribes had some form of tribal justice system. Thirty-nine of these jurisdictions (21%) had an indigenous forum such as a peacemaking process, sentencing circle, or council of elders. About 25% of them (46) had a Court of Indian Offenses for less serious criminal offenses and disputes

40 Lance Morgan, "The Rise of Tribes and the Fall of Federal Indian Law," 49 *Arizona State Law Journal* 115, 121–22 (2017).

41 Deloria & Lytle, supra note 31 at 112–13.

42 Kalt, supra note 25 at 92–93.

43 Joseph Thomas Flies-Away, Carrie Garrow, & Miriam Jorgensen, "Native Nation Courts: Key Players in Nation Rebuilding," in *Rebuilding Native Nations: Strategies for Governance and Development* 115, 117, 123–34 (Miriam Jorgensen, ed., University of Arizona Press, 2007).

44 Douglas B.L. Endreson, "The Challenges Facing Tribal Courts Today," 79(3) *Judicature* 142, 146 (1995); see also, Williams v. Lee, 359 U.S. 217, 220 (1959).

between tribal members. These courts were initially set up by the Bureau of Indian Affairs in 1883. Today, they number five in total and serve multiple tribes.[45] Usually called CFR Courts (so termed because they are governed by the U.S. Code of Federal Regulations), they are staffed by magistrate judges who are employees of the U.S. Department of the Interior. About 175 (or 56%) of all tribes had a tribal court on their reservations, of which 103 also had a tribal appellate court. The IRA encouraged tribes to create their own tribal courts rather than the BIA-created Courts of Indian Offenses. Finally, about 15 of the 188 tribes (8%) had an intertribal court system in which they shared a consolidated court with other small jurisdictions, allowing them to pool prosecutors, judges, and other resources. About 84% of all tribes with a justice system handled criminal misdemeanor cases.[46]

Western legal influences on tribal notions of justice are apparent from the workings of tribal courts, paramount among them the language used in a proceeding and the emphasis on written decisions. For instance, the Navajo Supreme Court takes care not to translate critical Navajo words and instead defines them, reflecting the idea that some indigenous concepts of justice can only be expressed in their original context.[47] The indigenous justice paradigm is non-adversarial, based on a holistic philosophy that is guided by unwritten customary traditions that are passed orally by elders or other specialists. Legal disputes are not isolated from their social contexts and individual litigants are not separate from their communities, while resolution of these disputes tends to focus on restorative and reparative solutions.[48]

At the same time, conceiving of a pure dichotomy between indigenous justice and Anglo-American adversarial values risks being overgeneralized and ahistorical. The "return" to an authentic, pre-contact custom presupposes that customs can be ascertained in the first instance and applied in a manner that modern society would find fair and equitable. Given the great variation tribal governments have had in the duration and intensity of European contact, this is easier in some cases than others.[49] The relationship between Anglo-American courts and tribal courts is also not necessarily unidirectional, with legal ideas and influences flowing only one way. Reflecting on the intrinsic role of tribal courts in the U.S. legal system, U.S. Supreme Court Justice Sandra Day O'Connor pointed to peacemaking courts as a potentially

45 U.S. Department of the Interior, Indian Affairs, "Court of Indian Offenses," available at: https://www.bia.gov/CFRCourts (last accessed December 23, 2023).

46 Bureau of Justice Statistics, *Census of Tribal Justice Agencies in Indian Country, 2002*, https://www.bjs.gov/content/pub/pdf/ctjaic02.pdf.

47 Skibine, supra note 30 at 2.

48 Ada Pecos Melton, "Indigenous Justice Systems and Tribal Society," 79(3) *Judicature* 126, 126 (1995).

49 Elizabeth E. Joh, "Custom, Tribal Court Practice, and Popular Justice," 25(1) *American Indian Law Review* 117, 118–20 (2000).

long sought after alternative to adversarial approaches, especially in cases involving child custody or juvenile delinquency.[50] Peacemaking courts and circle sentencing have commonalities both to victim-offender mediation, used across the Western world (including in U.S. federal court), and to the family group conference model used in New Zealand courts with influences from the Māori indigenous model of justice.[51]

Tribal court proceedings have several unique characteristics, blending traditional customs with modern notions of jurisprudence. Attorneys often do not lead the proceedings; rather, a non-attorney advocate, usually a tribal member with command of the language and familiarity with customs, presents evidence and testimony. Many tribal judges do not have law degrees. Courtroom proceedings tend toward the informal and in some systems the judge may play a more active role.[52] In criminal proceedings specifically, tribal courts have out of necessity adopted some Anglo-American innovations. Tribal courts employ prosecutors and increasingly public defenders. Under TLOA, tribal courts meeting additional due process safeguards are granted the ability to sentence a tribal member up to 3 years of incarceration (instead of the ordinary 1 year) or up to a $15,000 fine (instead of $5,000). These additional safeguards include providing counsel for indigent defendants, ensuring judges have legal training, making publicly available criminal laws and procedures, and maintaining records of the proceedings.[53]

Methodology and Limitations of This Study

This is a comparative analysis of collateral consequences of criminal convictions and restoration of rights mechanisms in the laws of all federally recognized Indian tribes in the lower 48 U.S. states, which number 347 separate jurisdictions as of 2024. The method used in this book, therefore, is focused on black letter law and the rule as written, the most traditional, structural, and positivistic version of comparative law. This means, naturally, that researchers concerned with the application of law in practice will find this study limiting.[54] However, this analysis is only a first step. Future researchers will find many avenues of inquiry to explore how tribal authorities use their discretion and how different jurisdictions interpret the same rule more

50 Sandra Day O'Connor, "Lessons From the Third Sovereign: Indian Tribal Courts," 33(1) *Tulsa Law Journal* 1, 6 (1997).

51 Gordon Bazemore & Mark Umbreit, "A Comparison of Four Restorative Conferencing Models," Office of Juvenile Justice and Delinquency Prevention Juvenile Justice Bulletin (February 2001), available at: https://www.ojp.gov/pdffiles1/ojjdp/184738.pdf.

52 Deloria & Lytle, supra note 31 at 149–51.

53 48 EagleWoman & Leeds, supra note 10 at 48-50.

54 Esin Örücü, "Methodological Aspects of Comparative Law," 8(1) *European Journal of Law Reform* 29, 31 (2006).

stringently or leniently. In the meantime, this study of black letter law will hopefully assist defense counsel, tribal court personnel, legislative drafters, and policy researchers in the fields of both criminal justice reform and tribal self-determination.

By sheer number of jurisdictions, tribal law surveys may be the largest comparative law studies of all time. Collateral consequences and restoration of rights may exist in tribal constitutions, codes, ordinances, or soft policy documents. First, a general disclaimer. Tribal political entities encompass an astonishing variation of size, structure, complexity, and legal development. The smallest tribes number fewer than a dozen members and the very largest number in the hundreds of thousands. More than several have no internal legal organization or any published laws or constitutions, while large jurisdictions such as the Cherokee and Navajo Nations have a sophisticated legal framework on par with a small U.S. state. The federal government holds 326 reservations in trust for these tribes, which can range anywhere from little more than an acre (Pit River Tribe cemetery) to 16 million acres (Navajo Nation).[55] Some tribes are consolidated into single political units, such as the Fort Peck Indian Reservation in Montana, which is home to Assiniboine, Lakota, and Dakota communities; by contrast, others like the Minnesota Chippewa Tribe are split up into bands, sharing a constitution but with separate tribal codes. These variations too have deep cultural and historical roots. The Confederated Salish and Kootenai Tribes of the Flathead Reservation in Montana, for instance, has opted for a decentralized parliamentary system to ensure effective representation for both Salish and Kootenai communities. The Minnesota Chippewa Tribe has historically operated as a confederation; today it has a national tribal executive committee representing the highest officials of the six business committees of each autonomous band.[56]

Complicating these political realities are the significant gaps in published tribal law codes. Tribes may opt not to make their codes public or may not release ordinances online in a timely manner. No single database or publication consolidates all tribal codes or even simply constitutions that have been approved by the Bureau of Indian Affairs. Though uncommon, several tribes, such as the Havasupai Tribe in Arizona and the Cheyenne and Arapaho Tribes in Oklahoma, have requirements in their tribal constitutions to make tribal legal materials publicly available.[57] Formal codifications of tribal law may quickly become out of date if they do not include subsequent ordinances. For instance, the Oglala Sioux Tribe in South Dakota enacted

55 U.S. Department of the Interior, Indian Affairs, "What Is a Federal Indian Reservation?," available at: https://www.bia.gov/faqs/what-federal-indian-reservation.

56 Kalt, supra note 25 at 89–90.

57 Bonnie Shucha, "Whatever Tribal Precedent There May Be: The (Un)Availability of Tribal Law," 106(2) *Law Library Journal* 199, 201 (2014).

hundreds of resolutions and ordinances since its 1996 codification of tribal law, but the online database that stored these laws was only accessible to tribal members and contained scanned documents that could not be word searched.[58] This poses a challenge not just for advocates, but for tribal leaders as well, who may not be able to determine what an existing rule is and may therefore pass a supplementary rule without resolving the original law's status. While the failure to publish tribal codes may simply be the result of resource constraints, at least some tribes have an affirmative policy of keeping their tribal codes private. This may be to protect the sacred nature of tribal law or to discourage criticism or legal action.[59] This book unavoidably has serious omissions that must be supplemented in future years, perhaps by a survey of tribal court administrators. Defense lawyers, lay advocates, and their clients are encouraged not to consider this book a finished product but rather as inspiration to check relevant tribal laws in their respective jurisdictions.

Nonetheless, some areas of tribal law were easier to find than others. Constitutions were more likely to be available than other tribal law materials. Liquor regulations must be approved by the Secretary of the U.S. Department of the Interior and published in the Federal Register; a somewhat similar approval process applies for the industrial hemp and medical marijuana industries. Gaming and casino ordinances must be approved by the National Indian Gaming Commission and are published on that agency's website. The existence of lawful gambling on an Indian reservation presupposes a certain amount of tribal legal infrastructure since it often demands the tribal code cover issues such as insurance, collective bargaining, or land use, for instance. Tribal sex offender registry laws are approved by the Office of Sex Offender Sentencing, Monitoring, Apprehending, Registering, and Tracking (SMART) in the Office of Justice Programs in the U.S. Department of Justice. In these areas of law, this study worked with a more or less complete set of tribal laws. Certain federal laws, such as TLOA and the Violence Against Women Reauthorization Act of 2013, also require participating tribal nations to make their laws and codes publicly available, especially since in the case of the Violence Against Women Act participating tribes are given criminal jurisdiction over non-tribal members.[60]

For pragmatic purposes, this study does not include the laws of the 231 Alaskan Native tribal entities, which are considered Indian tribes for purposes of federal law. The difficulty in finding and researching these codes and

58 Jacob Franchek, "Digitizing Tribal Law: How Codification Projects Such as Tribal Law Online Could Give New Rise to American Indian Sovereignty," 94(5) *Washington University Law Review* 1025, 1026–27 (2017).

59 Shucha, supra note 57 at 202.

60 Id. at 200.

ordinances is greater than for tribes in the lower 48 states. However, the chapter on the gaming and casino industry does include the four Alaskan Native villages with lawful gambling since gaming ordinances must be approved by the National Indian Gaming Commission and therefore are publicly available. In this instance, it was easier to deal with the complete set of gaming ordinances rather than exclude Alaska. In 1936, Congress extended the Indian Reorganization Act to Alaska, which authorized creation of reservations for Alaskan Natives and gave these communities opportunity to create constitutional systems. In 1971, this legal framework became more complex when Congress abolished Alaskan Native reservations (except the Annette Islands Reserve of the Metlakatla Indian Community) and instead reorganized Alaskan Native communities into village corporations, which are not strictly speaking subordinate political units like tribes are.[61] Though Alaskan state courts have tended not to protect Native Village sovereignty on par with Indian reservations, federal courts continue to place Native Villages in the same "ward-guardian relationship" with the federal government as other Indian tribes.[62] Periodically, research for this study did come across collateral consequences of conviction in Alaskan Native tribal law. For instance, the constitution of the Chilkat Indian Village in Klukwan excludes persons convicted of major felonies from serving in elected tribal office for a period of two years, a provision that is unpardonable and irreducible.[63] Likely, many more examples can be found. We offer an open invitation to researchers on Alaskan Native law to close this gap.

Finally, one must address the issue of citation format, which has no uniform rules across Indian Country. This study makes no normative claims about any particular naming convention and recognizes that tribal entities do change their names to better reflect their identities. For the avoidance of doubt, this study will consistently use the formal name of a tribal jurisdiction in the parlance of the U.S. Bureau of Indian Affairs as of 2024, regardless of tribal naming conventions. For instance, the BIA uses the cumbersome "Muscogee (Creek) Nation" and this study will as well. The citations herein will also provide the state in which the tribe is headquartered, even if the tribe crosses state boundaries. Having the state listed is to help the reader locate the correct jurisdiction: the Ponca Tribe of Oklahoma, for instance, rather than the Ponca Tribe of Nebraska (though the reader should still take care: the Delaware Tribe and the Delaware Nation are both in Oklahoma). Where a single tribal code has been consolidated, it is usually, but not always,

61 Patricia Thompson, "Recognizing Sovereignty in Alaska Native Villages after the Passage of ANCSA," 68(2) *Washington Law Review* 373, 378–79 (1993).

62 Id. at 381–82.

63 Chilkat Indian Village (Tlingit Indians), Village of Klukwan, Alaska, Constitution, Art. 7 § 1(a).

divided into titles; these may or may not be consecutively numbered. This study will uniformly refer to these consolidated codes as "tribal codes," to prevent confusion with tribal jurisdictions that have multiple, non-consolidated codes (such as Law and Order Codes) that are not numbered by title.[64] The tribal code citations used in this study therefore will tend to be more rather than less comprehensive, even if they provide redundant information. Since tribal constitutions, bylaws, articles of incorporation, tribal-state compacts, or codifications are rarely changed, as superior law, the reader should assume that the citation is to the most recent version as of 2024 unless otherwise noted in the footnotes. For ordinances, resolutions, or other legal materials such as codes of conduct, the date is also provided along with as much identifying information as possible. This is especially important in Chapter 6 because gaming ordinances change routinely. The reader should assume that the legal citation is good through the year listed in the citation, considering any amendments or subsequent changes. Despite this study's best efforts at consistency, some legal materials simply have anomalies: inconsistent numbering, missing pages, duplicate provisions, illegible text, or non-final wording. Where relevant, these are simply noted in the footnote.

64 In particular, the Navajo Nation Code has a non-uniform numbering system. This code is partially consolidated with partially consecutive numbering, but the reader is advised that the numbers may start over not only with each title, but with some chapters, subchapters, or parts. When citing the Navajo Nation Code, this book has tried to provide as much information as possible, but the reader is advised to double check the number of each provision, including the chapter, subchapter, or part. In addition, the Navajo Nation Code has not been codified since 2009, so amendments since then are not codified. See Diné Nihi Kéyah Project, "Navajo Nation Code (2009) & Uncodified Amendments," available at: https://dinelanduse.org/nnc (last accessed January 17, 2024).

Chapter 3

Restrictions on Running for Tribal Executive or Legislature

This chapter focuses on restrictions pertaining to running for tribal council or tribal executive. Typically, the legislative branch of a tribal government is composed of a tribal council, the members of which are often elected but in some traditional systems may be selected by clans or, in the case of some Pueblos, by a special body of elders. Some tribal councils are elected by district and others at-large. In many constitutions based on the Indian Reorganization Act of 1934 (IRA), the legislative and executive branches are not separate: the tribal executive may be elected from among the members of the tribal council, though in larger jurisdictions the tribal executive is often elected separately.[1] Other constitutions create a general council composed of all adult citizens of the tribe, though if this consensus-based structure is not supplemented by a smaller legislative body it can produce instability.[2] "[W]hich structure will work best for a tribe depends critically on its own Indigenous cultural norms regarding governmental systems, because these norms define legitimate and illegitimate forms of political authority and power."[3] To that end, tribal nations with a history of hierarchical leadership may find a directly elected chief executive is the best fit. Nonetheless, while IRA-era constitutions generally reflect Anglo-American values and influence, tribes exercise agency in choosing whether to adopt an IRA-style constitution in the first instance and whether to install traditional decision-making structures and authorities.[4]

1 Vine Deloria & Clifford M. Lytle, *American Indians, American Justice* 108–09 (University of Texas Press, 1983); Logan Trombley, "The Constitutional Tribe: Rethinking Governance in the Developing World," B.A. Thesis, University of Michigan (2014).

2 Joseph P. Kalt, "The Role of Constitutions in Native Nation Building: Laying a Firm Foundation," in *Rebuilding Native Nations: Strategies for Governance and Development* 78, 87–88 (Miriam Jorgensen, ed., University of Arizona Press, 2007).

3 Id. at 88.

4 Keith Richotte, "Legal Pluralism and Tribal Constitutions," 36(2) *William Mitchell Law Review* 447, 448 (2010).

DOI: 10.4324/9781003432548-3

Restrictions on serving in or running for tribal office are among the most common types of collateral consequences found in this project. This is partly because under the IRA, tribal constitutions must be approved by the Bureau of Indian Affairs before they enter into force and must satisfy specific criteria. As a result, many IRA-style tribal constitutions follow a template or model; therefore, collateral consequences, as restrictions on tribal office or candidacy for persons with prior criminal convictions, are widely copied or replicated across jurisdictions. In addition, because they are approved by the Bureau of Indian Affairs, constitutions are often easier to find for many tribes than bylaws, tribal codes, or ordinances. As a result, this chapter has a selection bias with the types of legal documents that are most readily available.

Based on this survey, at least 51 tribal jurisdictions had no provisions in their tribal constitutions, bylaws, codes, or election ordinances excluding persons with criminal convictions from running for or serving in tribal office. However, even though these legal documents were negative for collateral consequences, removal from office or ineligibility for running for office may still occur for criminal convictions. For instance, some tribal constitutions authorize removal from office for misconduct, without specifying a criminal conviction, so these jurisdictions may be false negatives since criminal convictions may be determined to be misconduct.[5] In another variation, the Pit River Tribe authorizes automatic removal from tribal office for violations of its Government Code of Conduct, which prohibits conflicts of interest, violations of confidentiality, receiving unauthorized gifts, or nepotism in government contracts.[6] However, this law does not require a criminal conviction and therefore it is not a true collateral consequence of conviction. On the other hand, the Navajo Nation has an Ethics in Government Law that states that persons who are convicted of misdemeanors under this law for crimes such as nepotism, use of public office for private gain, or receiving unauthorized gifts are guilty of misdemeanors and barred from running for elective public office or serving in appointive office for a period of 5 years.[7] This law requires a criminal conviction and therefore is a true collateral consequence of conviction.

5 For instance, "improper conduct or gross neglect of duty" are the terms used in the Confederated Tribes of the Grand Ronde Community (OR) Tribal Council Ordinance, Chapter 106; Constitution of Tule River Indian Tribe (CA), art. 5, § 2 (1936); and the Constitution of Yerington Paiute Tribe (NV), art. 5, § 2 (1937).

6 Pit River Tribe (CA), Tribal Government Code of Conduct, Ordinance No. 09-03-03, § 802(E).

7 Navajo Nation (AZ) Tribal Code, Title 1, Chapter 6, § 3782.

Removal from Tribal Office for Criminal Convictions

At least 41 tribal nations provide for automatic ouster of tribal council members or other executive officials upon conviction of a felony.[8] At least 55 tribes provide for automatic removal for felonies and some misdemeanors. Most commonly, the misdemeanors must involve dishonesty (35 jurisdictions) to be eligible for automatic removal from office, though moral turpitude (6 jurisdictions), moral integrity (3 jurisdictions), or some combination (4 jurisdictions) also exist.[9] A handful of tribes delineate specific

8 Constitution of the Apache Tribe (OK), art. 8; Constitution of the Assiniboine and Sioux Tribes of the Fort Peck Indian Reservation (MT), art. 5, § 5 (1960); Constitution of the Bridgeport Indian Colony (CA), art. 10, § 1(c) (1994); Constitution of the Cold Springs Rancheria of Mono Indians (CA), art. 6, §§1, 3 (1980); Constitution of the Cortina Indian Rancheria (Kletsel Dehe Band of Wintun Indians) (CA), art. 6, § 1 (1973); Constitution of the Crow Tribe of Montana (MT), art. 7, § 1 (executive), § 2 (legislative); Constitution of the Death Valley Timbi-Sha Shoshone Tribe (CA), art. 10, § 1(c) (2014); Delaware Nation (OK) Election Ordinance, § 301(D) (2018); Constitution of the Dry Creek Rancheria (CA), art. 7 (1972); Constitution of the Eastern Shawnee Tribe (OK), art. 13, § 2 (as amended to 2018); Constitution of the Elem Indian Colony of Pomo Indians (CA), art. 6, § 1 (1972); Articles of Association of the Fort Independence Indian Community (CA), art. 4, § 1 (1999); Constitution of the Guidiville Rancheria (CA), art. 7, § 3(b) (2006); Constitution of the Iowa Tribe of Kansas and Nebraska (KS), art. 6, § 1 (1937, as amended to 2013); Constitution of the Kaibab Band of Paiute Indians (AZ), art. 11, § 4 (1951, as amended to 1987); Constitution of the Kickapoo Tribe of Indians (KS), art. 4, § 4 (1936); Constitution of the Mashpee Wampanoag Tribe (MA), art. 8, § 3(a) (2004); Constitution of the Mesa Grande Band of Diegueno Mission Indians (CA), art. 6, § 1 (1971); Constitution of the Miami Tribe (OK), art. 10 (1996); Constitution of the Minnesota Chippewa Tribe (MN), art. 10, § 2(d) (1964); Constitution of the Mooretown Rancheria of Maidu Indians (CA), art. 5; Constitution of the Northern Cheyenne Tribe (MT), art. 7, § 1(a) (1935, amended through 2006); Oneida Tribe of Indians (WI) Tribal Code, Title 1, § 104.4; Constitution of the Otoe-Missouria Tribe of Indians (OK), art. 9, § 3 (1984); Constitution of the Paiute Indian Tribe (UT), art. 7, § 3 (1991); Constitution of the Passamaquoddy Tribe (ME), art. 6, § 4 (1993); Constitution of Picayune Rancheria of Chukchansi Indians (CA), art. 10, § 3 (1988); Constitution of the Poarch Band of Creeks (AL), art. 4, § 4(Q) (1985); Constitution of the Pueblo of Isleta (NM), art. 7, § 1 (2016); Articles of Association of the Rincon Band of Luiseno Mission Indians (CA), § 6(c); Constitution of the Santa Rosa Indian Community (CA), art. 5, § 1 (1962); Constitution of the Shawnee Tribe (OK), art. 8, § B; Constitution of the Sherwood Valley Rancheria of Pomo Indians (CA), art. 5, § 1 (1974); Constitution of the Standing Rock Sioux Tribe (SD), art. 3, § 8; Constitution of the Susanville Indian Rancheria (CA), art. 4, § 3; Constitution of the Table Mountain Rancheria (CA), art. 6, § 1 (1980); Constitution of the Tonkawa Tribe of Indians (OK), art. 2 (1938, as amended to 2020); Constitution of the Tunica-Biloxi Indian Tribe (LA), art. 15, § 2(A) (1999); Constitution of the Turtle Mountain Band of Chippewa Indians (ND), art. 8, § 2; Constitution of the Wilton Rancheria (CA), art. 9, § 5 (2011); Constitution of the Yocha Dehe Wintun Nation (CA), art. 7, § 1 (1976).

9 Constitution of the Ak-Chin Indian Community (AZ), art. 7, § 1 (1961); Constitution of the Bad River Band of the Lake Superior Tribe of Chippewa Indians (WI), art. 5, § 4; Constitution of the Bay Mills Indian Community (MI), art. 5, § 1 (1970); Constitution of the Chippewa Cree Indians of the Rocky Boy's Reservation (MT), art. 5, § 1 (1935); Constitution of the Colorado River Indian Tribes (AZ), art. 9, § 1 (1974); Constitution of the Confederated

misdemeanors which, in addition to felonies, would result in automatic removal of a tribal executive or legislator. These include crimes of theft or fraud (Chitimacha Tribe of Louisiana), any two misdemeanors (Round Valley Indian Tribes), any three misdemeanors (Hualapai Indian Tribe, Crow Creek Sioux Tribe), accepting a bribe (Ponca Tribe of Oklahoma, Quechan Tribe of the Fort Yuma Indian Reservation), or serious or "Class A" misdemeanors (Northwestern Band of Shoshone Nation).[10] Two tribes have automatic

Tribes of the Chehalis Reservation (WA), art. 6, § 1 (1973); Constitution of the Confederated Tribes of the Colville Reservation (WA), art. 4, § 1 (1938, as amended to 1946); Constitution of the Coquille Indian Tribe (OR), art. 6, § 6(a); Constitution of the Duckwater Shoshone Tribe (NV), art. 5, § 1 (1940); Constitution of the Ely Shoshone Tribe (NV), art. 5, § 1 (1990); Constitution of the Fort Belknap Indian Community (MT), art. 8, § 1 (2001); Constitution of the Fort McDowell Yavapai Nation (AZ), art. 9, § 1(A)(1) (1999); Constitution of the Fort Mojave Indian Tribe (AZ), art. 9, § 1 (1957); Constitution of the Gila River Indian Community (AZ), art. 12, § 1 (1960); Constitution of the Hoh Indian Tribe (WA), art. 6 (1969); Constitution of the Hoopa Valley Tribe (CA), art. 7, § 1; Constitution of the Hopi Tribe (AZ), art. 5, § 1 (1936); Constitution of the Hopland Band of Pomo Indians (CA), art. 5, § 3 (1982, as amended to 2009); Constitution of the Iowa Tribe of Oklahoma (OK), art. 9, § 3(b)–(c) (1937, as amended to 2008); Constitution of Jamul Indian Village (CA), art. 6, § 3 (1981); Constitution of Kalispel Indian Community (WA), art. 5, § 1(b); Constitution of the Kiowa Indian Tribe (OK), art. 12, § 1; Constitution of the Little Shell Band of Chippewa Indians (MT), art. 1, § 5 (1977, as amended to 2015); Constitution of the Lower Elwha Tribal Community (WA), art. 6, § 1 (1968); Constitution of the Lower Sioux Indian Community (MN), art. 7, § 2 (1936, as amended to 2007); Constitution of the Lummi Tribe (WA), art. 5, § 1 (1970, as amended to 2006); Constitution of the Mashantucket Pequot Indian Tribe (CT), art. 7, § 1 (2012); Constitution of the Mechoopda Indian Tribe (CA), art. 6, § 3(c); Constitution of the Muckleshoot Indian Tribe (WA), art. 5, § 1 (1936); Constitution of the Nisqually Indian Tribe (WA), art. 5, § 1 (1946); Constitution of the Ottawa Tribe (OK), art. 9, § 3(c)–(d) (1979); Constitution of the Peoria Tribe of Indians (OK), art. 11, § 3(c)–(d); Constitution of the Prairie Island Indian Community (MN), art. 7, § 2 (1936, as amended to 2017); Constitution of the Puyallup Tribe (WA), art. 5, § 1 (1936); Governing Resolution of the Quapaw Tribe of Indians (OK), § 6(b); Constitution of the Robinson Rancheria (CA), art. 6, § 3(b)–(c) (2013); Constitution of the San Carlos Apache Tribe (AZ), art. 9, § 1 (1954); Constitution of the Shoshone-Bannock Tribes of the Fort Hall Reservation (ID), art. 5, § 1 (1936); Constitution of the Shoshone-Paiute Tribes of the Duck Valley Reservation (NV), art. 5, § 1 (1936); Constitution of the Squaxin Island Tribe (WA), art. 7, § 1; Constitution of the Suquamish Indian Tribe (WA), art. 7, § 1 (1965); Constitution of the Swinomish Indian Tribal Community (WA), art. 5, § 1 (1936); Constitution of the Tulalip Tribes (WA), art. 5, § 1; Constitution of the United Auburn Indian Community (CA), art. 6, § 3 (b)–(c); Draft Constitution of the Upper Mattaponi Tribe (VA), art. 7, § 1 (2019); Constitution of the Ute Indian Tribe of the Uintah & Ouray Reservation (UT), art. 5, § 1 (1937); Constitution of the Wiyot Tribe (CA), art. 10 (1978); Constitution of the Yomba Shoshone Tribe (NV), art. 5, § 1.

10 Constitution of Chitimacha Tribe (LA), Art 5, § 3(B)(1) (1970)(a); Constitution of the Crow Creek Sioux Tribe (SD), art. 5, § 5(C)(1)–(2); Constitution of Round Valley Indian Tribes (CA), art. 4, § 10 (1994); Constitution of the Hualapai Indian Tribe (AZ), art. 4, § 10 (1991); Constitution of Ponca Tribe of Indians of Oklahoma (OK), art. 5, § 1 (1950); Constitution of Quechan Tribe of the Fort Yuma Indian Reservation (AZ), art. 6, § 2 (1936); Constitution of Northwestern Band of Shoshone Nation (UT), art. 11, § 3 (1987).

removal for all misdemeanors resulting in imprisonment, excluding traffic, hunting, or fishing violations. These include the Nez Perce Tribe and the Tejon Indian Tribe.[11] One of the more unusual provisions is the Oglala Sioux Tribe, which provides for automatic forfeiture of tribal office solely for a conviction involving distribution of alcoholic beverages or other controlled substances.[12] The Karuk Tribe authorizes automatic removal from the tribal council for a variety of specifically enumerated felonies: murder, manslaughter, rape, assault with intent to kill, burglary, child or elder abuse, assault resulting in serious bodily injury, theft, fraud or embezzlement, or a crime requiring registration as a sex offender.[13]

Instead of automatic removal provisions, many tribes instead have a discretionary process where the tribal council votes to remove an official who was convicted of certain crimes. Some tribal constitutions require a supermajority or unanimity for these decisions and a handful authorize tribal court review. In all, at least 12 jurisdictions authorize, but do not require, the tribal council to remove a tribal official upon conviction of a felony,[14] and one additional one (Big Lagoon Rancheria) restricts this solely to felonies involving dishonesty.[15]

More common are jurisdictions that authorize the tribal council to remove, at its discretion, tribal officials who are convicted of felonies and some misdemeanors. These number at least 27 in total. These provisions are more varied than the jurisdictions with automatic removal provisions. The most common scenario is to include misdemeanors of moral turpitude (six jurisdictions), dishonesty (nine jurisdictions), or a combination of the two (two jurisdictions).[16] However, some tribes depart from this template to include

11 Constitution of Nez Perce Tribe (ID), art. 7, § 1 (1961); Constitution of Tejon Indian Tribe (CA), art. 7, § 1 (2015).

12 Oglala Sioux Tribe (SD) Law and Order Code, Chapter 27, § 6(G) (applies to both candidates for office and current officeholders).

13 Constitution of the Karuk Tribe (CA), art. 9, § 1 (1985).

14 Articles of Association of the Cabazon Band of Mission Indians (CA), § 5 (1965); Constitution of the Cachil DeHe Band of Wintun Indians (CA), art. 4, § 2 (1941); Constitution of the Chemehuevi Indian Tribe (CA), art. 7, § 1 (1993); Constitution of the Forest County Potawatomi Community (WI), art. 8, § 2(a)(2) (1982); Constitution of the Jamestown S'Klallam Tribe (WA), art. 6, § 1(a)(3); Constitution of the Miccosukee Tribe of Indians (FL), art. 3, § 4; Constitution of the Mississippi Band of Choctaw Indians (MS), art. 6, § 6 (1945); Constitution of the Nooksack Indian Tribe (WA), art. 5, § 2 (1973); Constitution of the Northfork Rancheria of Mono Indians (CA), art. 5, § 2 (1996); Constitution of the Potter Valley Tribe (CA), art. 4, § 6(a) (2004); Samish Indian Nation (WA) Tribal Code, § 2.02.050(4).

15 Constitution of Big Lagoon Rancheria (CA), art. 8, § 3 (1985).

16 Constitution of Blue Lake Rancheria (CA), art. 6, § 3 (1994); Constitution of the Confederated Tribes of the Coos, Lower Umpqua and Siuslaw Indians (OR), art. 10, § 1 (1987); Constitution of the Delaware Tribe of Indians (OK), art. 10, § 1 (1982); Constitution of the Fort Bidwell Indian Community (CA), art. 7, § 2 (1936, as amended

fraud (Cowlitz Indian Tribe), embezzlement (Enterprise Rancheria of Maidu Indians), financial crime (Kashia Band of Pomo Indians), use of a weapon to do bodily harm (Upper Sioux Community), misdemeanor resulting in jail time (Cocopah Tribe), or multiple misdemeanor convictions (Winnebago Tribe of Nebraska).[17] A handful of tribes provide an exhaustive list of offenses that could result in discretionary removal. The Saint Regis Mohawk Tribe allows removal from office for serious misdemeanors, sex-related misdemeanors, or three other misdemeanor convictions.[18] In addition to felony convictions, the Yavapai-Apache Nation allows removal for sex-related crimes, drunk and disorderly conduct, any other three misdemeanors, or contempt of court.[19] The Nottawaseppi Huron Band of the Potawatomi authorizes discretionary removal for felonies, crimes of theft, fraud, violence against persons, sex offenses, or convictions resulting in prison terms longer than 1 year.[20] The broadest category are those jurisdictions that allow discretionary removal for any criminal conviction, regardless of whether it is a felony or misdemeanor. These include the Arapaho Tribe of the Wind River Reservation and the Sault Ste. Marie Tribe of Chippewa Indians.[21] The Pawnee Nation of Oklahoma goes so far as to permit removal from tribal office for any "felony, misdemeanor, or otherwise," even if pardoned or expunged.[22]

Another 13 jurisdictions have automatic removal for felonies but discretionary removal for certain kinds of misdemeanors. Four of these jurisdictions (Ely Shoshone Tribe, Hoh Indian Tribe, Sauk-Suiattle Indian Tribe,

to 1940); Constitution of the Ione Band of Miwok Indians (CA), art. 5, § 5(d) (2002); Constitution of the Lac Courte Oreilles Band of Lake Superior Chippewa Indians (WI), art. 3, § 7(c) (1966); Constitution of the Mohegan Tribe of Indians (CT), art. 8, § 3(b); Constitution of the Paskenta Band of Nomlaki Indians (CA), art. 5, § 1 (1998); Sac & Fox Tribe of the Mississippi (IA) Law and Order Code, Title 8, § 8-4206(c)(2); Constitution of the Scotts Valley Band of Pomo Indians (CA), art. 5, § 1 (excluding driving offenses) (1994); Constitution of the Seminole Tribe of Florida (FL), art. 4, § 5 (1957); Constitution of the Southern Ute Indian Tribe (CO), art. 3, § 7 (1936); Constitution of the Stillaguamish Tribe of Indians (WA), art. 5, § 9, § 1(a)(1) (1986); Constitution of the Tuolumne Band of Me-Wuk Indians (CA), art. 6, § 2 (1936, as amended to 1940); Constitution of the Ute Mountain Ute Tribe (CO), art. 3, § 5 (1940, as amended to 1983).

17 Constitution of Cowlitz Indian Tribe (WA), art. 6, § 1(a); Constitution of the Enterprise Rancheria of Maidu Indians (CA), art. 9, § 3 (1993); Kashia Band of Pomo Indians (CA) Tribe Ethics and Conduct Ordinance, Ord. No. 11 (2009), § 3.2; Constitution of Upper Sioux Community (MN), art. 5 (1995); Constitution of Cocopah Tribe (AZ), art. 9, § 1 (1958); Constitution of Winnebago Tribe of Nebraska (NE), art. 6, § 4(b)(2) (three class 2 convictions in tribal court or equivalent).

18 Constitution of Saint Regis Mohawk Tribe (NY), art. 7, § 1(a)–(d) (1995).

19 Constitution of Yavapai-Apache Nation (AZ), art. 4, § 6(a)(2) (1992).

20 Constitution of Nottawaseppi Huron Band of the Potawatomi (MI), art. 4, § 8(a)(2).

21 Constitution of Arapaho Tribe of the Wind River Reservation (WY), § 1(C) (1938); Sault Ste. Marie Tribe of Chippewa Indians (MI) Tribal Code, § 16.105(3).

22 Constitution of Pawnee Nation (OK), art. 7, § 4(iii) (1938, as revised through 2008).

and Tohono O'odham Nation of Arizona) have automatic removal for felonies and misdemeanors involving dishonesty, and discretionary removal for other misdemeanors (only misdemeanors of moral turpitude for the Tohono O'odham Nation).[23] Another six jurisdictions have automatic removal for felonies, plus discretionary removal for crimes of moral turpitude or dishonesty.[24] Jurisdictions departing from these templates include the Jicarilla Apache Nation, which provides for automatic removal for felonies and discretionary removal for misdemeanors involving misconduct, and the San Juan Southern Paiute, which authorizes automatic removal for felonies and discretionary removal after three misdemeanors.[25] Most complex of all is the Koi Nation of Northern California, which has a mandatory removal provision for murder, sexual offenses, larceny, embezzlement, burglary, mayhem, or arson, but a discretionary removal provision for crimes involving dishonesty or other felonies.[26]

Restrictions on Running for Tribal Office

Restrictions on running for tribal office because of past criminal convictions are numerous and varied. This section is organized according to increasing severity: first are requirements simply to disclose criminal convictions; second are discretionary provisions; third are exclusions for a term of years, that is, with a sunset date; and the final category are lifelong exclusions. The following section describes tribal jurisdictions that permit restoration of rights to run for tribal office, either through a pardon or expungement from an appropriate authority or through a process to waive the ineligibility criterion.

Disclosure Provisions

At least two jurisdictions, the Little River Band of Ottawa Indians and the Picayune Rancheria of Chukchansi Indians, do not bar persons with criminal convictions from running for tribal office but do require disclosure of convictions to be eligible to run for office. For the Little River Band of Ottawa

23 Constitution of the Ely Shoshone Tribe (NV), art. 5, §§ 1–2 (1990); Hoh Indian Tribe (WA) Election Ordinance, §§ 2.223–2.224; Sauk-Suiattle Indian Tribe (WA), art. 5, §§ 1–2 (1975); Constitution of the Tohono O'odham Nation (AZ), art. 8, § 1.

24 Constitution of the Mescalero Apache Tribe (NM), art. 10, § 1; Draft Constitution of the Monican Indian Nation (VA), art. 11, § 2 (2019); Constitution of the Prairie Band Potawatomi Nation (KS), art. 10, § 2 (1976); Constitution of the Salt River Pima-Maricopa Indian Community (AZ), art. 9, § 1 (1990); Constitution of the San Pasqual Band of Diegueno Mission Indians (CA), art. 7, §§ 1–2 (1970); Constitution of the Zuni Tribe (NM), art. 17, § 1.

25 Constitution of Jicarilla Apache Nation (NM), art. 8, § 1 (1937, as revised to 1969); Constitution of San Juan Southern Paiute Tribe (AZ), art. 9, §§ 1(a)(1), (3) (1996).

26 Constitution of Koi Nation of Northern California (CA), art. 13, §§ 1–2 (2012).

Indians, candidates must disclose convictions for fraud or misrepresentation, convictions within the past 10 years for crimes under the Major Crimes Act, convictions within the past 10 years in which the tribe was a victim, and all convictions for sexual crimes committed as an adult.[27] The Picayune Rancheria requires disclosure of all convictions within the past 10 years of felonies or misdemeanors involving moral turpitude or dishonesty.[28] Likely, there are more jurisdictions in this category because these eligibility rules tend to be contained in election ordinances rather than in tribal constitutions, which are often harder to find.

Discretionary Provisions

A discretionary and indeterminate restriction was found in the law of the Mesa Grande Band of Diegueno Mission Indians. In that jurisdiction, persons with felony convictions resulting in serious bodily injury or death, any convictions for sexual assault, conversion, theft, fraud, or embezzlement, or convictions resulting in sex offender registration are ineligible to run for tribal office for life. However, for other types of convictions, the General Council will review candidates' prior convictions and determine eligibility on a case-by-case basis.[29] This is the only instance in this chapter where a tribal council was found to have discretion to determine which criminal convictions could bar a candidate from running for tribal office.

Restrictions for Terms of Years

At least 50 tribal jurisdictions were found to have ineligibility restrictions on running for tribal office for a term of years, such that the right to run for office will be automatically restored after the sunset date. Another seven jurisdictions, described in the section below on waivers or restoration of rights, also have ineligibility restrictions for a term of years but have a pardon or waiver process to restore eligibility for persons with certain criminal convictions.

One tribe has an ineligibility restriction of 1 year after a felony conviction (Redwood Valley Rancheria).[30] Three others exclude persons with criminal convictions from running for tribal office for 1 year for felonies or misdemeanors of moral turpitude (Gila River Indian Community) or dishonesty

27 Constitution of Little River Band of Ottawa Indians (MI), art. 4, § 3 (1998).

28 Picayune Rancheria of Chukchansi Indians (CA) Amended Election Ordinance (2021), art. 6, § 5(B).

29 Mesa Grande Band of Diegueno Mission Indians (CA) Election Ordinance, No. 3 of 2018, § 2(A)–(B).

30 Constitution of Redwood Valley Rancheria (CA), art. 5, § 2 (1987).

(Kalispel Indian Community and Stillaguamish Tribe of Indians).[31] Two tribes provide for a 2-year period of ineligibility on running for office: Caddo Nation of Oklahoma (felony conviction only) and Wiyot Tribe (conviction for felony or crime of moral turpitude).[32] Eight tribes have a 3-year bar on running for tribal office. These include five for felony convictions alone: Miccosukee Tribe, Mooretown Rancheria of Maidu Indians, Northern Cheyenne Tribe, Potter Valley Tribe (excluding juvenile offenses), and Zuni Tribe.[33] The latter tribe, the Zuni Tribe of the Zuni Reservation in New Mexico, calculates the 3-year exclusion from the date of release from custody rather than the date of conviction.[34] Three other tribes have a 3-year bar following felony convictions and some misdemeanors: Mechoopda Indian Tribe of Chico Rancheria (includes misdemeanors involving moral turpitude or dishonesty), Tejon Indian Tribe (all convictions resulting in imprisonment, excluding minor traffic, hunting, or fishing violations), and United Auburn Indian Community (crimes of dishonesty, regardless whether they are felonies or misdemeanors).[35]

Twelve tribes have a 5-year bar on running for office after a felony conviction, although three of these (Iowa Tribe of Oklahoma, Sac & Fox Nation of Missouri, and Scotts Valley Band of Pomo Indians) count the 5 years from the date of completion of sentence rather than the date of conviction.[36] Three others have a specific exclusion rendering certain types of felonies ineligible for life, meaning that after 5 years eligibility to run for tribal office is not restored. These are the Iowa Tribe of Kansas and Nebraska (5-year bar on felonies, unless tribe is a victim, then ineligible for life), Jamestown S'Klallam Tribe (5-year bar on felonies, unless crime is domestic, elder, or child abuse, a drug felony, or child molestation), and Kashia Band of Pomo Indians (5-year bar unless crime involves violence, financial crime, or dishonesty,

31 Constitution of Gila River Indian Community (AZ), art. 6, § 2 (1960); Constitution of Kalispel Indian Community (WA), art. 4, § 9 (1969); Constitution of Stillaguamish Tribe of Indians (WA), art. 5, § 7 (1986).

32 Constitution of Caddo Nation (OK), art. 4, § 4 (1976); Constitution of Wiyot Tribe (CA), art. 5, § 4(d).

33 Constitution of Miccosukee Tribe of Indians (FL), art. 3, § 5; Constitution of Mooretown Rancheria of Maidu Indians (CA), art. 4, § 2; Constitution of Northern Cheyenne Tribe (MT), art. 7, § 1(a); Constitution of Potter Valley Tribe (CA), art. 4, § 5 (2004); Constitution of Zuni Tribe (NM), art. 5, § 5(4).

34 Constitution of Zuni Tribe (NM), art. 5, § 5(4) (1970).

35 Constitution of Mechoopda Indian Tribe of Chico Rancheria (CA), art. 5, § 2(b) (1998); Constitution of Tejon Indian Tribe (CA), art. 7, § 3(b) (2015); Constitution of United Auburn Indian Community (CA), art. 5, § 2 (2014).

36 See Constitution of Iowa Tribe of Oklahoma, art. 12(d) (1937, amended to 2008); Constitution of Sac & Fox Nation of Missouri in Kansas and Nebraska (KS), art. 4, § 4 (1990); Constitution of Scotts Valley Band of Pomo Indians (CA), art. 4, § 2 (1994).

then ineligible for life).[37] The remaining six tribes with a 5-year exclusion are the Absentee-Shawnee Tribe of Indians, Fort Sill Apache Tribe, Mashpee Wampanoag Tribe, Ottawa Tribe of Oklahoma, Bishop Paiute Tribe, and Prairie Band Potawatomi Nation.[38] Besides the 12 tribes with a 5-year bar for felony convictions, another five tribes have a 5-year bar for certain types of misdemeanor convictions. The Chippewa Cree Indians of the Rocky Boy's Reservation has a 5-year bar for federal or state court convictions involving dishonesty and a 5-year bar on misdemeanor convictions involving dishonesty or bribery in tribal court, calculated from the date of sentence completion.[39] The Elk Valley Rancheria has a 5-year ineligibility period following criminal convictions involving moral turpitude or completion of a sentence for a crime of moral turpitude.[40] The Spokane Tribe has a 5-year bar for felonies or misdemeanors involving dishonesty, calculated either from the date of conviction or release from custody, whichever is later.[41] Prairie Island Indian Community has a 5-year bar for either felony or misdemeanor convictions that involve fraud, embezzlement, deceit, theft, cheating, or perjury.[42] Finally, with a narrower restriction, the San Juan Southern Paiute Tribe has a 5-year bar on running for office by any former tribal council member who was removed from office for a felony or three misdemeanors.[43] As noted in the introduction, the Navajo Nation's Ethics in Government Law operates as a collateral consequence of conviction, as persons convicted under that law for ethical violations are guilty of misdemeanors and barred from running for elective public office or serving in appointive office for a period of 5 years.[44]

Two tribal jurisdictions have a 7-year bar on running for office after a felony conviction (Little Traverse Bay Band of Odawa Indians and Pueblo of Pojoaque).[45] One has an 8-year bar after a felony conviction (Round Valley

37 Constitution of Iowa Tribe of Kansas and Nebraska (KS), art. 9, § 4 (1937, amended to 2013); Constitution of Jamestown S'Klallam Tribe (WA), art. 5, § 2(a) (1980, amended to 2014); Kashia Band of Pomo Indians (CA) Election Ordinance (2011), § 3(A)(4)–(7).

38 Constitution of the Absentee-Shawnee Tribe of Indians (OK), art. 14, § 1(e); Constitution of the Fort Sill Apache Tribe (OK), art. 5, § 4 (1976, as amended to 2003); Constitution of the Mashpee Wampanoag Tribe (MA), art. 6, § 1(b) (2004); Constitution of the Ottawa Tribe of Oklahoma (OK), art. 8, § 4 (1979); Bishop Paiute Tribe (CA) Election Ordinance, § 7.1(c) (1998); Constitution of the Prairie Band Potawatomi Nation (KS), art. 6, § 4(d).

39 Chippewa Cree Indians of the Rocky Boy's Reservation (MT) Election Board Ordinance, No. 1-89, art. 2, § 1(d).

40 Elk Valley Rancheria (CA) Election Ordinance, No. 2002-02, § 20.06.01(c)–(d).

41 Constitution of the Spokane Tribe of the Spokane Reservation (WA), art. 5, § 3 (1951, amended to 2021).

42 Prairie Island Indian Community (MN) Election Ordinance, Res. 21-9-8-142, art. 11, § 3(A).

43 Constitution of San Juan Southern Paiute Tribe (AZ), art. 9, § 1(c) (1996).

44 Navajo Nation (AZ) Tribal Code, Title 1, Chapter 6, § 3782.

45 Constitution of Little Traverse Bay Band of Odawa Indians (MI), art. 7, § H(3) (Tribal Council), art. 8, § E(1) (Chairperson and Vice-Chairperson); Pueblo of Pojoaque (NM) Law and Order Code, Subpart U, § 3(b)(6) (2023 edition).

Indian Tribes) and another has an 8-year bar after a felony conviction or a conviction for theft, fraud, violence against persons, sex offense, or any other crime resulting in a prison term longer than 1 year (Nottawaseppi Huron Band of the Potawatomi).[46]

Six tribes render a candidate ineligible for tribal office for 10 years following a felony conviction. These include the following: Grand Traverse Band of Ottawa and Chippewa Indians, Penobscot Nation, Pokagon Band of Potawatomi Indians (except crimes related to assertion of treaty rights), Snoqualmie Indian Tribe, and United Keetoowah Band of Chippewa Indians.[47] In addition, the Death Valley Timbi-Sha Shoshone Tribe calculates the 10-year bar from the date of sentence completion rather than the date of conviction.[48] Two other tribes, the Karuk Tribe and the Yurok Tribe, add special exclusions for sex offenders. The Karuk Tribe has a 10-year bar for candidates who have been convicted of murder, manslaughter, rape, assault with intent to kill, burglary, child or elder abuse, assault resulting in serious bodily injury, theft, fraud, or embezzlement, calculated from the date of completion of sentence.[49] However, for the Karuk Tribe, convictions resulting in sex offender registration result in a lifelong bar.[50] The Yurok Tribe has a similar 10-year exclusion for felonies and crimes of moral turpitude, but a lifelong exclusion for convictions resulting in sex offender registration.[51]

Additionally, six more tribes have a 10-year ineligibility period following a felony conviction or certain misdemeanor convictions. Three of these, Chitimacha Tribe of Louisiana, Hoh Indian Tribe, and Swinomish Indian Tribal Community, calculate the date from conviction.[52] The other three (Cedarville Rancheria, Greenville Rancheria, and Hoopa Valley Tribe) calculate the date from sentence completion rather than conviction.[53] The misdemeanor exclusions among these six tribes vary: misdemeanors involving moral turpitude (Cedarville Rancheria, Greenville Rancheria, and Hoopa

46 Round Valley Indian Tribes (CA) Election Ordinance (2013), art. 6, § 6.01(A)(3); Nottawaseppi Huron Band of the Potawatomi (MI) Tribal Code, Title 3, § 3.1–6(A)(4)–(5).

47 Constitution of Grand Traverse Band of Ottawa and Chippewa Indians (MI), art. 7, § 4 (1988); Final Draft Constitution of Penobscot Nation (ME), art. 7, § B(2)(b) (Tribal Council), § B(3)(a) (Chief), § B(4)(a) (Vice-Chief); Constitution of Pokagon Band of Potawatomi Indians (MI), art. 10, § 2 (2005); Snoqualmie Indian Tribe (WA) Tribal Council Act 2.2, § 7.0(e); United Keetoowah Band of Chippewa Indians (OK) Election Ordinance (2022), Chapter 5, § 501(B)(1).

48 Death Valley Timbi-Sha Shoshone Tribe (CA) Election Ordinance, No. 2006-01, § 4.2.

49 Constitution of Karuk Tribe (CA), art. 7, § 4 (1985).

50 Id.

51 Constitution of Yurok Tribe (CA), art. 3, § 5(a) (1993).

52 Constitution of Chitimacha Tribe (LA), art. 5, § 2(E); Hoh Indian Tribe (WA) Tribal Code, Title 2.200, § 2.205(a); Swinomish Indian Tribal Community (WA) Tribal Code, Title 2, Chapter 1, § 2-01.120(C)(2).

53 Cedarville Rancheria (CA) Election Ordinance (2003), § 6(1)(c); Constitution of Greenville Rancheria (CA), art. 9, § 2 (1995); Constitution of Hoopa Valley Tribe (CA), art. 6, § 6(c).

Valley Tribe), crimes of theft or fraud (Chitimacha Tribe of Louisiana), all drug crimes or crimes against a person (Hoh Indian Tribe), and misdemeanors involving dishonesty (Swinomish Tribal Community). Finally, two tribes have an even longer sunset provision for eligibility to run for tribal office, of 15 years. The Lac Courte Oreilles Band of Lake Superior Chippewa Indians have a 15-year bar for felonies or other serious offense charges, calculated from the date of sentence completion.[54] The Omaha Tribe of Nebraska has a 15-year bar for felony convictions resulting in a loss to the tribe or a felony resulting in imprisonment, calculated from conviction or the date of release from prison, whichever is later.[55]

At least four tribes have a hybrid restriction. Among the Nez Perce Tribe, felony convictions are subject to a 10-year bar on the ability to run for tribal office following the release from confinement. For all other convictions, except minor traffic, hunting, or fishing violations, the bar is 3 years running from the date of conviction.[56] The Yavapai-Apache Nation has a 15-year bar on eligibility for persons with felony convictions and a 5-year bar for misdemeanor convictions.[57] The Habematolel Pomo of Upper Lake render ineligible persons with felony convictions for a period of 5 years or persons who are incarcerated for a period of 3 years after release.[58] In another complex variation, the Paskenta Band of Nomlaki Indians renders ineligible for life persons with criminal convictions for both felonies and misdemeanors involving dishonesty, fraud, theft, or moral turpitude, with a 10-year bar for persons convicted of all other felonies, calculated from completion of the sentence. However, in that jurisdiction, candidates for tribal chairperson, vice-chairperson, and treasurer cannot have any previous felony convictions.[59]

Lifelong Restrictions

Lifelong restrictions on running for tribal office are more common than ineligibility restrictions that sunset after a term of years. In total, at least 36 tribes have lifelong exclusions for felony (or major crime) convictions that do not make provision for restoration of rights.[60] Besides these 36, several

54 Lac Courte Oreilles Band of Lake Superior Chippewa Indians (WI) Tribal Code, Title 5, Chapter 1, § 1.503(1)(c).

55 Constitution of Omaha Tribe of Nebraska (NE), art. 5, § 4 (1936, provision added by amendment in 1981).

56 Constitution of Nez Perce Tribe (ID), art. 8, § 4(a)–(b) (1961).

57 Constitution of Yavapai-Apache Nation of the Camp Verde Indian Reservation (AZ), art. 8, § 3 (1992).

58 Constitution of Habematolel Pomo of Upper Lake (CA), art. 4, § 2(6)–(7) (2019).

59 Constitution of Paskenta Band of Nomlaki Indians (CA), art. 4, § 2 (1998).

60 Constitution of the Apache Tribe of Oklahoma (OK), art. 8; Bylaws of the Cheyenne River Sioux Tribe (SD), art. 2(b) (1935); Constitution of the Chickasaw Nation (OK), art. 6, § 6 (legislature), art. 10, § 6 (executive) (1983); Constitution of the Choctaw Nation (OK), art.

tribal constitutions have interesting variations on a simple lifelong exclusion for felony convictions for tribal council members. The Muscogee (Creek) Nation has a lifelong felony exclusion for Principal Chief and Second Chief and for appointive offices, to include members of the National Council.[61] The newly recognized Virginia tribe, the Monacan Indian Nation, has a lifelong felony exclusion only for *mala-in-se* (inherently wrong) felony crimes and not *mala prohibitum* (prohibited only by statute) felony crimes, which narrows the exclusion.[62] For the San Juan Southern Paiute Tribe, the exclusion from candidacy for a tribal council seat is not for a felony conviction, but rather for serving 12 or more months in jail or prison.[63] More troublingly, the Standing Rock Sioux Tribe, which has an elaborate pardon mechanism under tribal law, makes clear that a pardon under tribal law does not restore the eligibility to run for tribal office.[64] In another interesting variation, the

---

6, § 5 (1983); Bylaws of the Confederated Tribes of the Warm Springs Reservation (OR), art. 2 (1938); Constitution of the Crow Tribe (MT), art. 4, § 4; Constitution of the Delaware Nation (OK), art. 7, § 5 (1976); Charter and Governing Document of the Eastern Band of Cherokee Indians (NC), § 17 (1986); Bylaws of the Fort Belknap Indian Community (MT), art. 2 (2001); Bylaws of the Fort McDermitt Paiute and Shoshone Tribes (NV), art. 2 (1936); Constitution of the Kickapoo Tribe of Indians (KS), art. 3, § 5(f) (1936); Constitution of the Kiowa Indian Tribe (OK), art. 6, § 4 (legislators), art. 7, § 3(b) (chairman or vice-chairman); Constitution of the Menominee Indian Tribe (WI), art. 4, § 4; Constitution of the Modoc Tribe (OK), art. 4, § 3 (2007); Constitution of the Northfork Rancheria of Mono Indians (CA), art. 4, § 2 (1996); Constitution of Ohkay Owingeh (NM), art. 11, § 1 (1996); Constitution of the Osage Nation (OK), art. 6, § 4 (members of Osage Nation Congress), art. 7, § 3 (principal chief) (2006); Constitution of Otoe-Missouria Tribe of Indians (OK), art. 7, § 5(e) (1984); Constitution of the Paiute Indian Tribe of Utah (UT), art. 14, § 6; Constitution of the Pawnee Nation (OK), art. 4, § 4; Constitution of the Peoria Tribe of Indians (OK), art. 9, § 5 (1997); Constitution of the Poarch Band of Creeks (AL), art. 6, § 3 (1985); Constitution of the Ponca Tribe of Indians (OK), art. 9 (1950); Constitution of the Pueblo of Isleta (NM), art. 4, § 3(c) (2016); Constitution of the Red Lake Band of Chippewa Indians (MN), art. 5(b) (1958, as amended to 1982); Constitution of the Saginaw Chippewa Indian Tribe (MI), art. 6, § 12 (1986); Constitution of the Seneca Nation of Indians (NY), § 10 (1993); Constitution of the Southern Ute Indian Tribe (CO), art. 3, § 4 (1936); Constitution of the Susanville Indian Rancheria (CA), art. 3, § 2(b) (2005); Te-Moak Tribe of Western Shoshone Indians (NV) Tribal Code, §§ 13-5-1(a)(5), 13-5-2(c); Three Affiliated Tribes of the Fort Berthold Reservation (ND) Election Ordinance, Chapter 2, § 2(A)(4); Constitution of the Tonkawa Tribe of Indians (OK), art. 2 (1938, as amended to 2020); Constitution of the Torres Martinez Desert Cahuilla Indians (CA), art. 9, § 2 (1997); Draft Constitution of the Upper Mattaponi Tribe (VA), art. 11, § 1 (2019); Constitution of the Ute Mountain Ute Tribe (CO), art. 3, § 4 (1940, as amended to 1983); Constitution of the Wilton Rancheria (CA), art. 9, § 5 (2011).

61 Constitution of Muscogee (Creek) Nation (OK), art. 5, § 1(f) (1979). Note that the exclusion on felony convictions was broadened to include "or has been convicted of a felony crime against the Muscogee (Creek) Nation" in a 2015 constitutional amendment.

62 Draft Constitution of the Monacan Indian Nation (VA), art. 9, § 4 (2019).

63 San Juan Southern Paiute Tribe (AZ) Election Code, art. 4, § 401(D).

64 Standing Rock Sioux Tribe (SD) Tribal Code, Title 4, Chapter 4, § 4-405(b).

St. Croix Chippewa Indians have a lifelong bar for persons with violent felony convictions or any civil or criminal judgment against him or her related to misappropriation, embezzlement, theft, conversion, or misappropriation of any funds or other property.[65] This is the only instance found in this survey where a civil judgment for monetary damages could render a prospective candidate ineligible for tribal office.

Nine tribal jurisdictions provide for lifelong ineligibility on running for tribal office for persons with felony convictions but provide for a sunset period for at least some misdemeanor convictions. The most common formulation of these provisions is that a person with a felony conviction is ineligible from running for office for life, but a person with a misdemeanor conviction is only ineligible for 1 year. These include Hualapai Indian Tribe (three misdemeanors only), Jamul Indian Village (misdemeanors involving dishonesty), Robinson Rancheria (misdemeanors involving dishonesty), San Carlos Apache Tribe (misdemeanors involving moral integrity), and Shoalwater Bay Indian Tribe (all misdemeanors).[66] Three tribes, notably all based in Arizona, have nearly identical provisions that provide an exhaustive list of covered misdemeanors. The Tonto Apache Tribe has a lifelong bar for felony convictions and a 1-year bar for misdemeanors involving moral integrity, defined as adultery, bribery, embezzlement, extortion, fraud, forgery, misbranding, perjury, and theft.[67] The Yavapai-Prescott Indian Tribe has an identical list.[68] The White Mountain Apache Tribe has the same list but adds convictions for public intoxication.[69] Using a different structure altogether, the Ione Band of Miwok Indians prohibits from election or appointment to the tribal council any person convicted of a violent felony or any crime involving violence, dishonesty, or moral turpitude.[70] In this jurisdiction, then, at least some felonies do not render a candidate ineligible while some misdemeanors can.

This leaves a total of 21 jurisdictions that have a lifelong ban on running for office by persons with felony convictions *and* a lifelong ban for persons with at least some misdemeanor convictions, which is the broadest formulation possible in this typology. The misdemeanors that are included in these exclusions vary dramatically among these 21 jurisdictions. Other than felonies, the following misdemeanor convictions result in a lifelong bar from running for tribal office:

65 St. Croix Chippewa Indians (WI) Tribal Code, Title 2, Chapter 1, § 01.05(2).
66 Constitution of Hualapai Indian Tribe (AZ), art. 8, § 5 (1991); Constitution of Jamul Indian Village (CA), art. 5, § 4 (1981); Constitution of Robinson Rancheria (CA), art. 5, § 2 (2013); San Carlos Apache Tribe (AZ) Bylaws, art. 2 (1954); Constitution of Shoalwater Bay Indian Tribe (WA), art. 5, § 1(b)(2) (1982).
67 Constitution of Tonto Apache Tribe (AZ), art. 5, § 1(d) (1980).
68 Constitution of Yavapai-Prescott Indian Tribe (AZ), art. 11 (1960).
69 Constitution of White Mountain Apache Tribe (AZ), art. 12, § 1 (1993).
70 Constitution of Ione Band of Miwok Indians (CA), art. 5, § 5(a) (2002).

- Dishonesty (Coquille Indian Tribe)[71]
- Moral turpitude (Flandreau Santee Sioux Tribe, Fort McDermitt Paiute and Shoshone Tribes, Koi Nation, Pueblo of Laguna, Tolowa Dee-ni' Nation)[72]
- Moral integrity (Fort Mojave Indian Tribe)[73]
- Dishonesty or moral turpitude (Federated Indians of Graton Rancheria)[74]
- Dishonesty, bribery, or embezzlement (Comanche Nation)[75]
- Fraud or moral turpitude (Cowlitz Indian Tribe)[76]
- Embezzlement (Enterprise Rancheria of Maidu Indians)[77]
- Theft or embezzlement (Guidiville Rancheria)[78]
- Theft, misappropriation, or embezzlement from the tribe (Minnesota Chippewa Tribe)[79]
- Theft, embezzlement, forgery, or theft of money from the tribe (Turtle Mountain Band of Chippewa Indians)[80]
- Serious (or Class A) misdemeanors (Northwestern Band of Shoshone Nation)[81]
- Dishonest act or distribution of alcoholic beverages or controlled substances (Oglala Sioux Tribe)[82]
- Misconduct in tribal affairs, perjury, forgery, bribery, dishonesty, abuse of public office (Rosebud Sioux Tribe)[83]

71 This is not made explicitly but is implicit in reading together the constitutional provision on automatic forfeiture of office and the qualifications for electoral candidates that import the same language. Coquille Indian Tribe (OR) Tribal Code, Chapter 194, § 194.310(1)(C). See also Constitution of Coquille Indian Tribe, art. 6, § 5.

72 Flandreau Santee Sioux Tribe (SD) Tribal Code, Title 20, Chapter 4, § 2(3); Fort McDermott Paiute and Shoshone Tribes (NV) Bylaws, art. 2(a) (1936); Constitution of Koi Nation (CA), art. 11, § 2(b)–(c) (2012); Constitution of Pueblo of Laguna (NM), art. 7, § 3 (2012); Constitution of Tolowa Dee-Ni' Nation (CA), art. 9, § 3 (1987).

73 Bylaws of the Fort Mojave Indian Tribe (AZ), art. 2 (1957).

74 Constitution of the Federated Indians of Graton Rancheria (CA), art. 4, § 1(B)(1)–(2) (2012).

75 Constitution of Comanche Nation (OK), art. 9, § 2 (1966, amended to 2019).

76 Constitution of Cowlitz Indian Tribe (WA), art. 5, § 5. Note that the felony bar applies to all candidates, but the misdemeanors involving fraud or moral turpitude only appear to apply to former tribal officers who were removed as the result of a criminal conviction for these crimes.

77 Constitution of Enterprise Rancheria of Maidu Indians (CA), art. 9, § 3 (1993).

78 Constitution of Guidiville Rancheria (CA), art. 6, § 2 (2006).

79 Constitution of Minnesota Chippewa Tribe (MN), art. 4, § 4 (1964, added by amendment in 2006).

80 Constitution of Turtle Mountain Band of Chippewa Indians (ND), art. 5, § 4(4) (amended to 2005).

81 Constitution of Northwestern Band of Shoshone Nation (UT), art. 12, § 3(3) (1987).

82 Oglala Sioux Tribe (SD) Law and Order Code, Chapter 27, § 6(G).

83 Constitution of Rosebud Sioux Tribe (SD), art. 3, § 6-*bis* (1935, added by amendment in 2006). Note that the 2006 amendments added two different art. 3, § 6 provisions. I have renumbered the second one § 6-*bis* for clarity.

- Election fraud or misdemeanors involving gambling, theft, dishonesty, or fraud (Sault Ste. Marie Tribe of Chippewa Indians)[84]
- Misdemeanors resulting in imprisonment (Upper Sioux Community)[85]
- Intentional harm to another tribal member with a dangerous weapon (Kickapoo Traditional Tribe of Texas)[86]

Finally, in the broadest formulation of any tribe found in this survey, the Tunica-Biloxi Indian Tribe has a lifelong ban for all persons on running for office who have any felony conviction or a misdemeanor conviction involving financial crime, sex crime, fraud, violent crime, or crimes of moral turpitude, even if these crimes are later pardoned or expunged, even if the laws are later repealed, even if the crimes were committed as a juvenile, and even if the felony crime is reduced to a misdemeanor conviction after the fact.[87]

Restoration of the Right to Run for Tribal Office

As noted above, the Standing Rock Sioux Tribe does not allow a tribal pardon to restore the right to run for tribal office.[88] Perhaps a more famous example comes from the Muscogee Supreme Court in 1890. In that decision, the Chief Justice wrote that the Muscogee organic law prohibited a person who was convicted of a felony to be eligible for any office of profit, honor, or trust, despite provision for executive clemency. The Chief Justice wrote that executive clemency "does not restore to the felon any political rights forfeited by him by reason of his felony, but only saves his back from the lash and restores him to personal liberty."[89]

By contrast, at least 23 tribal jurisdictions allow a pardon from the appropriate convicting jurisdiction to restore the right to tribal office even where a person with a criminal conviction is otherwise ineligible. Of these, seven tribal jurisdictions have an ineligibility exclusion of a term of years, which can be shortened by a pardon. For the Assiniboine and Sioux Tribes of the Fort Peck Indian Reservation and Seminole Nation of Oklahoma, the felony exclusion for running for tribal office is 5 years, but this may be shortened with a pardon.[90] For the Lac Vieux Desert Band of Lake Superior Chippewa Indians and Lower Brule Sioux Tribe, the felony exclusion is 10 years, but

84 Sault Ste. Marie Tribe of Chippewa Indians (MI) Tribal Code, Chapter 10, § 10.110(1)(i).
85 Constitution of Upper Sioux Community (MN), art. 5(K) (1995).
86 Constitution of Kickapoo Traditional Tribe (TX), art. 5, § 5(c) (1989).
87 Tunica-Biloxi Indian Tribe (LA) Election Ordinance (2020), No. TBN-O-2020-004.
88 Standing Rock Sioux Tribe (SD) Tribal Code, Title 4, Chapter 4, § 4-405(b).
89 Matthew L.M. Fletcher, *American Indian Tribal Law* n.p. (Aspen Publishing, 2020), citing 7 Mvskoke Law Reporter 389 (Mvskoke Supreme Court, Oct. 10, 1890).
90 Constitution of the Assiniboine and Sioux Tribes (MT), art. 5, § 5(b) (1960); Constitution of the Seminole Nation (OK), art. 3, § 2 (chief and assistant chief), art. 4, § 3 (general council).

pardonable.[91] Another jurisdiction, the Cheyenne and Arapaho Tribes, has a combination of both: a 5-year pardonable felony exclusion for district legislators and a 10-year exclusion for governor and lieutenant governor.[92] The Citizen Potawatomi Nation also applies a pardonable 10-year exclusion for district legislators, governor, and lieutenant governor, but extends the proscription to a conviction of "a felony or other serious crime involving incarceration for moral turpitude," or a crime resulting in incarceration of at least 6 months.[93]

Another nine tribal jurisdictions have lifelong exclusions for felony convictions alone but allow a pardon to restore eligibility.[94] An additional jurisdiction, the Ponca Tribe of Nebraska, allows a pardon to restore eligibility to run for tribal office except when the tribe was the victim of theft, in which case a pardon cannot restore eligibility.[95] Five more jurisdictions also have lifelong exclusions for felonies, pardonable, but also include some misdemeanors. Four of these jurisdictions, all in Oklahoma, have lifelong ineligibility for at least some misdemeanors but allow for a pardon to restore eligibility. These are the Eastern Shawnee Tribe of Oklahoma (serious misdemeanors), Wyandotte Nation (serious misdemeanors), Kaw Nation (misdemeanors of moral turpitude), and Miami Tribe (misdemeanors of moral turpitude).[96] In the Wyandotte Nation, a tribal officer who was removed from tribal office for cause is "forever barred" from holding any other office or position, so the pardon provision does not apply.[97] Similarly, in a fifth jurisdiction, the Pascua Yaqui Tribe, no person who has been convicted of a felony or any

91 Constitution of the Lac Vieux Desert Band of Lake Superior Chippewa Indians (MI), art. 7, § 4(b) (note also in the next section that a judge may restore this right through a certificate of rehabilitation); Constitution of the Lower Brule Sioux Tribe (SD), art. 4, § 8 (1942).

92 Constitution of the Cheyenne and Arapaho Tribes (OK), art. 4, § 4(b) (district legislators), art. 7, § 3(b) (governor and lieutenant governor).

93 Constitution of the Citizen Potawatomi Nation (OK), art. 12, § 1 (1938, as amended to 2007).

94 Constitution of the Blackfeet Tribe (MT), art. 5, § 3 (1998); Constitution of the Cherokee Nation (OK), art. 9, § 2 (1975); Constitution of the Ho-Chunk Nation (WI), art. 5, § 7 (legislators), art. 6, § 3 (president); Constitution of the Hopland Band of Pomo Indians (CA), art. 5, § 2; Constitution of the Jicarilla Apache Nation (NM), art. 6, § 4 (1937, as revised to 1969); Constitution of the Mississippi Band of Choctaw Indians (MS), art. 4, § 5(b) (1945); Constitution of the Passamaquoddy Tribe (ME), art. 7, § 1(c) (1993) (note that the Sipayik Pleasant Point reservation has its own subordinate constitution, but with an identical provision, see Sipayik Pleasant Point Constitution, art. 5, § 1 (2003)); Constitution of the Reno-Sparks Indian Colony (NV), art. 3, § 2(c) (1936); Shawnee Tribe (OK) Tribal Code, § 6.16.020(D) (for chief only).

95 Ponca Tribe of Nebraska (NE) Law and Order Code, Title 9, Chapter 2, § 9-6-2(4)-(5).

96 Eastern Shawnee Tribe (OK) Election Ordinance (2021), art. 6, § 7; Wyandotte Nation (OK) Election Ordinance (1999), art. 6, § 1; Constitution of Kaw Nation (OK), art. 9, § 3(B); Constitution of Miami Tribe (OK), art. 18, § 2 (1996).

97 Wyandotte Nation (OK) Election Ordinance (1999), art. 6, § 1.

crime involving deceit, fraud, or misappropriation of funds is eligible to run for tribal council or serve as tribal officer, "unless, in the event of a felony conviction, his or her voting rights have been legally restored, or unless the criminal conviction has been expunged."[98] A pardon or expungement would not restore the right to run or serve in tribal office for deceit, fraud, or misappropriation of funds.

Several jurisdictions have specially created processes to allow otherwise ineligible persons with criminal convictions to run for tribal office. Three jurisdictions (Big Lagoon Rancheria, Jicarilla Apache Nation, and Mescalero Apache Tribe) allow the tribal executive to restore the right to run for tribal office for a candidate who is ineligible because of a criminal conviction.[99] Presumably this process may also restore eligibility to run for office for a candidate who was removed from office for a conviction. The Mescalero Apache Tribe requires the candidate to attach a copy of the pardon to the statement of intent to run for office. Notably, the tribe's pardon statute prohibits self-pardons, so the Tribal President cannot restore his or her own eligibility to run for tribal office.[100]

Two jurisdictions allow tribal courts or tribal judges to grant a certificate of rehabilitation or otherwise waive the ineligibility exclusion. For the Eastern Band of Cherokee Indians, an ineligible prospective candidate for office may file a petition with the tribal court supported by three affidavits requesting civil rights to be restored.[101] For the Lac Vieux Desert Band of Lake Superior Chippewa Indians, a tribal judge is authorized to certify that a candidate has been rehabilitated and thereby negate the 10-year bar on running for office with a felony conviction.[102] In one jurisdiction (Lac Courte Oreilles Band of Lake Superior Chippewa Indians), the election board itself is permitted to grant a waiver for a candidate who is otherwise ineligible to run for office.[103] In this process, the prospective candidate must establish that 15 years or more has passed since the completion of the punishment of the felony or other serious offense. For the Mohegan Tribe of Indians of Connecticut, a person seeking election to the Tribal Council must not have been convicted of a felony or a misdemeanor involving moral turpitude, such as forgery or bribery. However, this exclusion may be waived by a majority

98 Constitution of the Pascua Yaqui Tribe (AZ), art. 5, § 5 (legislature), art. 6, § 6 (executive).

99 Constitution of Big Lagoon Rancheria (CA), art. 8, § 3 (1985); Constitution of Jicarilla Apache Nation (NM), art. 6, § 4 (1937, amended to 1969); Constitution of Mescalero Apache Tribe (NM), art. 4, § 1.

100 Mescalero Apache Tribe (NM) Tribal Code, Chapter 1, §§ 1-3-7, 9-4-1.

101 Eastern Band of Cherokee Indians (NC) Tribal Code, § 14-1.4(c).

102 Constitution of Lac Vieux Desert Band of Lake Superior Chippewa Indians (MI), art. 7, § 4 (1997).

103 Lac Courte Oreilles Band of Lake Superior Chippewa Indians (WI) Tribal Code, Title 5, Chapter 1, § 1.503(1)(c)(i).

vote of the Council of Elders. Candidates for the Council of Elders itself are subject to the same bar, but the Council of Elders may also waive by majority vote ineligibility for candidacy on that body as well.[104] The Hopland Band of Pomo Indians has a specific process for proving a pardon that restores eligibility to run for tribal office. In this jurisdiction, the prospective candidate must submit to the Chief of Police supporting documentation showing that she or he has been pardoned. The Chief of Police must consult with the Tribal Attorney to determine whether the pardon has restored the right to run for office, and then provide a joint recommendation to the Election Board as to whether the candidate is eligible.[105]

While not a restoration of rights mechanism, at least one jurisdiction specifically allows a prospective tribal council member who was deemed ineligible because of a previous conviction to run as a write-in candidate. The Quileute Tribe prohibits a person from running for tribal council who was convicted of crimes of dishonesty or of felonies, other than convictions for asserting tribal treaty rights, but she or he may still be voted on as a write-in candidate.[106]

104 Constitution of the Mohegan Tribe of Indians (CT), art. 6, § 1(c)–(d), § 2(c)–(d) (as amended in 2014).
105 Hopland Band of Pomo Indians (CA) Tribal Code, Title 1, Chapter 3–4, § 3–4.20(b).
106 Quileute Tribe (WA) Election Ordinance, § 22 (2021).

Chapter 4

Restrictions on Serving in Tribal Office or Administration

For many jurisdictions, tribal government has become sophisticated: elected councils perform legislative functions; professional bureaucrats manage administration; tribal courts handle adjudication of disputes; and economic development authorities take care of resource extraction and revenue generation.[1] Undoubtedly, this shift is the result of Anglo-American influence on organizational management and reform, which may conflict with traditional Indian values concerning, for instance, consensus-based decision-making or a non-hierarchical distribution of political power.[2] The increased growth of tribal administrative apparatuses in the last several decades reflects a turn toward self-government and enhanced institutional knowledge building. "Predictably, this transfer of authority [from federal to tribal control] has been accompanied by rapid growth in tribal bureaucracies: more offices, more programs, more people, and more activity."[3] As one example, the federal government gradually transferred administrative control to the Eastern Band of Cherokee Indians during the second half of the twentieth century, to include deputizing Cherokee police officers, establishing tribal sanitation and fire departments, and building a new tribal high school to replace busing to county public schools.[4] In Montana, the Confederated Salish and Kootenai Tribes of the Flathead Nation went through a major administrative reorganization in the 1980s after an inefficient tribal council and committee structure needed professional upgrades. The reorganization consolidated departments with a new chain of command headed by an executive secretary

1 Vine Deloria & Clifford M. Lytle, *American Indians, American Justice* 104 (University of Texas Press, 1983).

2 Id. at 109.

3 Stephen Cornell & Miriam Jorgensen, "Getting Things Done for the Nation: The Challenge of Tribal Administration," in *Rebuilding Native Nations: Strategies for Governance and Development* 146, 151 (Miriam Jorgensen, ed., University of Arizona Press, 2007).

4 John R. Finger, *Cherokee Americans: The Eastern Band of Cherokees in the Twentieth Century* 150–53 (University of Nebraska Press, 1992).

DOI: 10.4324/9781003432548-4

with professional rather than political experience, the centerpiece of which is a highly specialized and acclaimed tribal department of natural resources.[5]

The growth and increased sophistication of tribal administrative agencies have attached collateral consequences to many more tribal offices. This chapter explores each of four broad areas of tribal administration in which collateral consequences most commonly attach to appointed office: tribal court judges and personnel, election management positions, law enforcement roles, and natural resource authorities. Then, the chapter turns to less common positions, many of which reflect a tribe's unique administrative structure. These can concern, for instance, positions in tribal public utilities, housing authorities, public businesses or economic development agencies, educational authorities or tribal schools or colleges, or tax and financial agencies. Of these, the strictest and most common restrictions tend to be on appointments of tribal judges or other personnel in the tribal legal or court sector, which is not a surprise given the special expertise, training, and public trust that these positions require.

Tribal Court Personnel

Collateral consequences frequently attach to tribal court judge positions and to other positions in tribal legal systems. Depending on the structure of the specific tribal judiciary, these exclusions may attach to tribal prosecutors, public defenders, peacemakers, clerks or deputy clerks, administrative law judges, tribal attorneys general, magistrates, court administrators, or members of judicial commissions or other governing bodies of tribal judiciaries. Finally, this section summarizes restoration of rights mechanisms that may restore an applicant's right to be appointed to a position as a tribal judge or court administrative staff.

Tribal Court Judges

Restricting the appointment of persons with criminal convictions to tribal judge positions is common: this study found at least 93 tribal jurisdictions that did so. Persons convicted of a felony cannot serve as a tribal judge for the Assiniboine and Sioux Tribes of the Fort Peck Indian Reservation, Coushatta Tribe of Louisiana, Habematolel Pomo of Upper Lake, Kickapoo Tribe of Oklahoma, Kickapoo Traditional Tribe of Texas, Kiowa Indian Tribe, Las Vegas Tribe of Paiute Indians, Mississippi Band of Choctaw Indians, Moduc Tribe, Muscogee (Creek) Nation, Nez Perce Tribe, Pueblo of Acoma, Pueblo of Isleta, Pueblo of Laguna, Pueblo of San Ildefonso, Scotts Valley Band of

5 James J. Lopach, *Tribal Government Today: Politics on Montana Indian Reservations* 165–69 (Routledge, 1990).

Pomo Indians, Stockbridge Munsee Community, and Tunica-Biloxi Indian Tribe.[6] Using slightly different wording, the Penobscot Nation in Maine bars reappointment to another 3-year term if a judge is convicted of a felony; the ordinance also provides for automatic removal upon conviction for a felony or crime of violence of fraud.[7] The Delaware Tribe of Indians only excludes persons convicted of felonies within the previous 7 years.[8] Another version of this provision is found among the Menominee Tribe of Wisconsin, which states that persons with convictions for "major crimes" (defined in the Major Indian Crimes Act, 18 U.S.C. § 1153) for which jurisdiction lies in U.S. federal court are excluded from serving as tribal judges or legislators.[9] The Little Traverse Bay Bands of Odawa Indians prohibit a person from serving as a tribal court judge or tribal appellate judge who has been convicted of a felony unless 10 years have passed since he or she completed his or her sentence or probation.[10]

An interesting variation on the felony exclusion are the tribes that do not consider political offenses on behalf of Native American sovereignty to be a bar to tribal court employment. The Lac Vieux Desert Band of Lake Superior Chippewa Indians extends its felony exclusion for tribal court judges to 10 years, "unless such offense is demonstrated to the satisfaction of the Tribal Council to be related to an assertion of a treaty protected right," which is an exception for political offenses.[11] The Pokagon Band of Potawatomi Indians has the same 10-year felony exclusion, "excepting those crimes determined by the Election Board to relate to the furtherance of the Band's tribal sovereignty rights."[12]

6 Assiniboine and Sioux Tribes of the Fort Peck Indian Reservation (MT) Comprehensive Code of Justice, § 301; Coushatta Tribe of Louisiana (LA) Judicial Codes, § 1.4.03; Habematolel Pomo of Upper Lake (CA) Judicial Code, Chapter 3, § 3(c); Kickapoo Tribe of Oklahoma (OK) Judicial System Ordinance, Chapter 1, § 6(A)(6)(b); Kickapoo Traditional Tribe of Texas (TX), Tribal Code, Chapter 1, § 1.6(M); Constitution of the Kiowa Indian Tribe (OK), art. 8 § 4(d); Las Vegas Tribe of Paiute Indians (NV) Tribal Code, § 1-40-020(b); Mississippi Band of Choctaw Indians (MS) Tribal Code, § 1-3-3(1); Constitution of the Moduc Tribe (OK), art. 7 § 5; Constitution of the Muscogee Nation (OK), art. 7 § 2; Nez Perce Tribe (ID) Tribal Code, § 1-1-16(d) ("no person having been convicted of a crime"); Pueblo of Acoma (NM) Tribal Code, § 1-5-6(D); Constitution of the Pueblo of Isleta (NM), art. 9 § 3; Pueblo of Laguna (NM) Tribal Code, § 5-1-1(2); Pueblo of San Ildefonso (NM) Tribal Code, Part 4.1.2.10(d); Constitution of the Scotts Valley Band of Pomo Indians (CA), art. 9 § 3(2); Stockbridge Munsee Community (WI) Tribal Court Code, § TCT.01.06(c)(1)(G); Tunica-Biloxi Indian Tribe (MS) Judicial Code, § 15.2(a).

7 Final Draft Constitution of the Penobscot Nation (ME), art. 8(C)(b), art. 8(H)(6).

8 Constitution of the Delaware Tribe of Indians (OK), art. 12 § 3.

9 Constitution of the Menominee Tribe of Wisconsin (WI), art. 4 § 4, art. 5 § 4.

10 Constitution of the Little Traverse Bay Bands of Odawa Indians (MI), art. 9(E)(1)–(2).

11 Constitution of the Lac Vieux Band of Lake Superior Chippewa Indians (WI), art. 5 § 5(b).

12 Constitution of the Pokagon Band of Potawatomi Indians (MI), art. 12 § 7(d).

Some tribes extend the felony exclusion to some misdemeanors. The Standing Rock Sioux Tribe excludes as tribal court judges and justices anyone convicted of a crime other than traffic offenses for which imprisonment was imposed.[13] The Upper Sioux Community of Minnesota states that judges may not have felony convictions or misdemeanor convictions that would disqualify an attorney from legal practice.[14]

The most common construction across Indian Country is to exclude, along with felonies, misdemeanors within the previous 1 year. This is the case for the Blackfeet Tribe, Chickasaw Nation, Confederated Tribes of the Warm Springs Reservation, Hopland Band of Pomo Indians, Kaibab Band of Paiute Indians, Klamath Tribes, Lac du Flambeau Band of Lake Superior Chippewa Indians, Lower Sioux Indian Community in Minnesota, Mescalero Apache Tribe, Grand Portage Band of the Minnesota Chippewa Tribe, Prairie Island Indian Community, Reno-Sparks Indian Colony, St. Croix Chippewa Indians, Sokaogon Chippewa Community, Suquamish Indian Tribe of the Port Madison Reservation, Swinomish Indian Tribal Community, Washoe Tribe of Nevada and California, and Yomba Shoshone Tribe.[15] Two others, Hoh Indian Tribe and Mille Lacs Band of the Minnesota Chippewa Tribe, have the same provision but restricted to "gross misdemeanors" only.[16] In addition to excluding persons with felony convictions as potential tribal court judges, the Confederated Salish and Kootenai Tribes exclude persons with misdemeanor convictions within 1 year but make an exception for

13 Standing Rock Sioux Tribe (SD) Tribal Code, Title 1, Chapter 3, § 1-301(3).

14 Upper Sioux Community (MN) Judicial Code, Chapter 3, § 4.

15 Blackfeet Tribe (MT) Law and Order Code, Chapter 1, § 2(2); Constitution of the Chickasaw Nation (OK), art. 12; Confederated Tribes of the Warm Springs Reservation (OR) Tribal Code, § 200.255(2); Constitution of the Hopland Band of Pomo Indians (CA), art. 8 § 4l; Constitution of the Kaibab Band of Paiute Indians (AZ), art. 13 § 5; Klamath Tribes (OR) Tribal Codes, Title 2, Chapter 11, § 11.18(a); Lac du Flambeau Band of Lake Superior Chippewa Indians (WI) Tribal Code, § 80.103(2); Little Sioux Indian Community (MN) Judicial Code, Resolution 10-53 (enacted March 10, 2010), § 1.12; Mescalero Apache Tribe (NM) Tribal Code, § 2-1-4(A); Minnesota Chippewa Tribe (MN), Grand Portage Band Judicial Code, Title 1, Chapter 3, § 4(b); Prairie Island Indian Community (MN) Judicial Code, Title 1, Chapter 3, § 4(b); Reno-Sparks Indian Colony (NV) Tribal Code, § 1-40-020; St. Croix Chippewa Indians (WI) Tribal Court Code, § 103(B)(2)(c)–(d); Sokaogon Chippewa Community (WI) Community Codes, § 1.1.3(B)(c)–(d); Suquamish Indian Tribe of the Port Madison Reservation (WA) Tribal Code, § 3.3.1; Swinomish Indian Tribal Community (WA) Tribal Code, § 3-01.100(B); Washoe Tribe of Nevada and California (NV) Tribal Code, §§ 1-40-020 (chief judge), 1-40-030 (associate judges and court masters); Yomba Shoshone Tribe of the Yomba Reservation (NV) Law and Order Code, Title 1(C), §§ 7–8.

16 Hoh Indian Tribe (WA) Tribal Code, Title 1, § 1.3.1; Minnesota Chippewa Tribe (MN), Mille Lacs Band Tribal Code, Title 5, §§ 9(b), 10(a).

minor traffic violations.[17] Other tribes in accord include the Confederated Tribes of the Coos, Lower Umpqua, and Siuslaw Indians, Keweenaw Bay Indian Community (for chief or associate judges), Paiute-Shoshone Tribe of the Fallon Reservation and Colony (if not alcohol-related), and Saginaw Chippewa Indian Tribe.[18]

Other tribes extend the time bar beyond 1 year. The Confederated Tribes of the Chehalis Reservation in Washington extend the misdemeanor exclusion to 2 years but allow the General Council to waive the requirement for minor traffic offenses.[19] The Winnebago Tribe of Nebraska excludes as tribal judges persons convicted of a felony or, within the past 2 years, a misdemeanor excluding traffic offenses.[20] The Blue Lake Rancheria of the Wiyot, Yurok, and Hupa Indians in California and the Quechan Tribe of the Fort Yuma Indian Reservation extend the misdemeanor exclusion to 3 years.[21] The Crow Tribe of Montana, Dry Creek Rancheria Band of Pomo Indians, and Salt River Pima-Maricopa Indian Community extend it to 5 years.[22] Hannahville Indian Community in Michigan makes the restriction stronger: felonies and misdemeanors within 10 years, excluding minor traffic violations.[23] The Picayune Rancheria of Chukchansi Indians has a lifelong bar for felony convictions and a 10-year bar for misdemeanors, excluding non-alcohol related traffic offenses.[24]

In another variation, the Iowa Tribe of Oklahoma excludes as judges of the district court persons convicted of felonies or any offense punishable by banishment, even if banishment did not occur, as well as "any offense, except traffic offenses" for 2 years prior to the appointment. The clock begins to run not at conviction, but on the date that the person was unconditionally released from supervision.[25] For justices of the Iowa Tribe Supreme Court,

17 Confederated Salish and Kootenai Tribes of the Flathead Reservation (MT) Tribal Code, Title 1, § 1-2-202(5).

18 Confederated Tribes of the Coos, Lower Umpqua, and Siuslaw Indians (OR) Tribal Code, § 1-1-32(c); Keweenaw Bay Indian Community (MI) Tribal Code, § 1.110; Paiute-Shoshone Tribe of the Fallon Reservation and Colony (NV) Law and Order Code, § 1-40-020; Saginaw Chippewa Indian Tribe (MI) Tribal Code, Title 1, § 1.509(b)–(c).

19 Confederated Tribes of the Chehalis Reservation (WA) Tribal Code, § 3.10.030(F)–(G).

20 Winnebago Tribe (NE) Tribal Code, § 1-204(b).

21 Blue Lake Rancheria (CA) Tribal Code, § 11.1.1.040(A); Quechan Tribe of the Fort Yuma Indian Reservation (AZ) Tribal Code, § 2.2.2(C) (excepting traffic offenses).

22 Crow Tribe of Montana (MT) Tribal Code, §§ 3-3-303(1), 3-3-304; Dry Creek Rancheria Band of Pomo Indians (CA) Judicial Code, Chapter 2, § 7(B)(3); Salt River Pima-Maricopa Indian Community (AZ) Community Code of Ordinances, §§ 432(b)(4), 432(c)(6) (excluding civil traffic violations).

23 Hannahville Indian Community (MI) Legal Code, Chapter 1.5, § 1.509(2)–(3).

24 Picayune Rancheria of Chukchansi Indians (CA) Tribal Court Ordinance, § 5.2(d)–(e).

25 Iowa Tribe (OK) Tribal Code, Title 26, § 102(C).

the period for non-felony offenses is extended to 5 years.[26] The Tulalip Tribes of Washington also have a 5-year bar for misdemeanor convictions.[27] The Kaw Nation, Pawnee Nation, and Kickapoo Tribe of Kansas have identical provisions—so similar, in fact, that the section numbers of the tribal code are the same. In these jurisdictions, district court judges must not have been convicted of a felony, crime punishable by banishment, or crime of moral turpitude, for 2 years for district court judges and 5 years for supreme court justices.[28] The Wyandotte Nation has an identical provision, except that the exclusion is only 2 years for both district court judges and supreme court justices.[29] The Seminole Nation of Oklahoma's criminal conviction exclusion for tribal court judges follows this same model, but the time bar is for 10 years instead of 5 for both the district court and the supreme court.[30] The Yavapai-Apache Nation of the Camp Verde Indian Reservation also has a 5-year misdemeanor bar, excluding minor traffic offenses but running the clock at release from supervision rather than conviction.[31]

Other tribes exclude judges who have been convicted of felonies or specifically enumerated misdemeanors. The simplest expression of this model is along the lines of the Mashpee Wampanoag Tribe, which excludes persons with felonies or crimes (misdemeanors) of moral turpitude from serving as tribal court judges.[32] For tribal court judges, including traffic court judges, the Saint Regis Mohawk Tribe has a similar prohibition on felony convictions and convictions for crimes of moral turpitude, but also exempts "act[s] of civil disobedience" to encompass political crimes.[33] The Confederated Tribes of the Grand Ronde Community and the Coquille Indian Tribe, both in Oregon, exclude felonies or crimes involving dishonesty, as does the Fort McDermott Paiute and Shoshone Tribes in Nevada.[34] The Morongo Band of Mission Indians excludes felonies and crimes involving moral turpitude

26 Id. at § 203(C).

27 Tulalip Tribes of Washington (WA) Tribal Code, § 2.05.040.

28 Kaw Nation (OK) Tribal Code, Title 11, art. 1, §§ 102(c), 203(c); Kickapoo Tribe of Indians (KS) Tribal Code, Title 9, Chapter 1, §§ 102(c), 203(c); Pawnee Tribe (OK) Tribal Code, Title 1, §§ 102(c), 203(c).

29 Wyandotte Nation (OK) Tribal Code, Title 4, §§ 102(c), 203(c).

30 Seminole Nation of Oklahoma (OK) Tribal Code, Title 5, §§ 102(a)(3), 203(a)(4).

31 Yavapai-Apache Nation of the Camp Verde Indian Reservation (AZ) Tribal Code, Title 3, § 111(c).

32 Constitution of the Mashpee Wampanoag Tribe (MA), art. 10 § 4(b).

33 Saint Regis Mohawk Tribe (NY) Tribal Court and Judiciary Code, § 3 (defines "serious crime" as felonies and crimes of moral turpitude and defines "crimes of moral turpitude" as "contrary to community standards of justice, honesty and good morals"), § 8.

34 Confederated Tribes of the Grand Ronde Community (OR) Tribal Court Ordinance, Chapter 302(e)(C); Coquille Indian Tribe (OR) Tribal Court Ordinance, § 610.300(2); Fort McDermott Paiute and Shoshone Tribes (NV) Tribal Code, Chapter 2, § 2.

or dishonesty.[35] For tribal judges, the Nottawaseppi Huron Band of the Potawatomi has a bar on felonies, violent crimes, or crimes of fraud.[36] The Pascua Yaqui Tribe excludes all felonies, as well as crimes of deceit, fraud, or misappropriation of funds.[37] The Spirit Lake Tribe excludes persons convicted of all felonies or persons convicted of crimes for which the punishment was more than 60 days' imprisonment, which would include more serious misdemeanors.[38]

Some jurisdictions also add a time bar to the list of specifically enumerated misdemeanors. The Kalispel Indian Community (Washington), Confederated Tribes of the Umatilla Indian Reservation (Oregon), and Te-Moak Tribe of Western Shoshone Indians (Nevada) exclude as judges of the tribal court anyone with a felony conviction or, within 1 year, a conviction for a misdemeanor involving moral turpitude.[39] In other jurisdictions the time bar is longer. The San Manuel Band of Mission Indians has a lifelong felony exclusion for tribal court judges and a 5-year bar for persons with convictions for crimes of moral turpitude.[40] For the Northern Cheyenne Tribe, the bar is lifelong on felonies and within 10 years for misdemeanors of moral turpitude.[41] The Hoopa Valley Tribe and the Jamestown S'Klallam Tribe have a 10-year bar for potential judges for felonies or misdemeanors involving moral turpitude, corruption, or dishonesty.[42] The Little River Band of Ottawa Indians is substantially the same, a 10-year bar for felonies or misdemeanors involving moral turpitude or dishonesty.[43] For its tribal court judges, the Stillaguamish Tribe of Indians has a 5-year bar for both felonies and misdemeanors involving moral turpitude or dishonesty.[44] The Miami Tribe of Oklahoma has a more elaborate list of excluded misdemeanors. In that jurisdiction, persons are excluded from serving as a tribal court judge persons who were convicted of felonies or, within the previous 1 year, bribery, embezzlement, extortion, fraud, perjury, theft, or drunk and disorderly conduct.[45]

35 Morongo Band of Mission Indians (CA) Tribal Court Ordinance, #28, Title 1, § 1.2.05(3).
36 Constitution of the Nottawaseppi Huron Band of the Potawatomi (MI), art. 11 § 5(a)(4).
37 Constitution of the Pascua Yaqui Tribe (AZ), art. 8 § 6.
38 Spirit Lake Tribe (ND) Tribal Code, § 2-6-104(2)–(3).
39 Kalispel Indian Community (WA) Law and Order Code, § 1-4.03(3); Confederated Tribes of the Umatilla Indian Reservation (OR) Tribal Court Code, § 2.02(C); Te-Moak Tribe of Western Shoshone Indians (NV) Tribal Code, § 1-3-12(B).
40 San Manuel Band of Mission Indians (CA) Tribal Code, § 22.2.1(b).
41 Northern Cheyenne Tribe (WY) Tribal Code, Title 1A, §§ 1A-8-5, 1A-8-6.
42 Hoopa Valley Tribe (CA) Tribal Code, Title 1, § 1.2.07(2); Jamestown S'Klallam Tribe (WA) Tribal Code, Title 13, § 13.05.02. Note that the Jamestown S'Klallam Tribe has "judicial officers" rather than judges.
43 Little River Band of Ottawa Indians (MI) Tribal Court Ordinance, #12-300-01, art. 15(a)–(b).
44 Stillaguamish Tribe of Indians (WA) Law and Order Code, § 2.05.030(2).
45 Miami Tribe of Oklahoma (OK) Judicial Code, § 2.8(B)(2).

Another model is for a tribe to have staggered collateral consequences, depending on the level of the court. The Sac and Fox Tribe of Mississippi disqualify from serving as a district court judge any person with a felony conviction or, within the past 2 years since release from custody, a misdemeanor conviction excluding traffic offenses. For justices of the Sac and Fox Supreme Court, however, justices are subject to a lifelong ban not only on felonies, but also on crimes of moral turpitude; the exclusion for other misdemeanors is 5 years instead of 2 years.[46] Other jurisdictions also have staggered collateral consequences. For judges of the Hopi Tribe's appellate court, only felony convictions are excluded. For chief judge or associate judges of the trial court, the exclusion is for felonies or misdemeanors involving fraud or dishonesty.[47] For the Spokane Tribe, the Chief Judge of the tribal court must not have been convicted of felonies or, within the past year, misdemeanors concerning dishonesty. However, the justices of the appellate court must never have been convicted of felonies or misdemeanors concerning dishonesty—the prohibition is lifelong.[48]

Finally, some tribes are hard to classify. The Sauk-Suiattle Indian Tribe excludes as tribal judges anyone with a conviction for "an offense involving dishonesty or impugning his moral character" within the previous 5 years.[49] Such a provision appears to apply to both felonies and misdemeanors but has the disadvantage of leaving to discretion what offenses are excluded. In another variation, the Tule River Indian Tribe excludes from serving as a tribal court judge persons who were convicted of "act involving moral turpitude, dishonesty, corruption, or a violent felony," which apparently excludes some (non-violent) felonies but includes some misdemeanors.[50]

Other Court Personnel

Other appointed court personnel may also have collateral consequences attach to their positions. The Standing Rock Sioux have a lifetime felony bar for tribal prosecutors and public defenders and a 10-year felony bar for tribal court administrators and court clerks.[51] The Alabama-Coushatta Tribe of Texas prohibits from serving as tribal court administrators those who

46 Sac and Fox Nation (OK) Tribal Code, Title 9, §§ 102(c), 203(c).

47 Hopi Tribe (AZ) Tribal Code, Title 1, §§ 1.2.2, 1.3.3, 1.3.4.

48 Spokane Tribe of the Spokane Reservation (WA) Law and Order Code, §§ 1-3.02(a), 1-7.04(a).

49 Sauk-Suiattle Indian Tribe (WA) Law and Order Code, § 2.060.

50 Tule River Indian Tribe (CA) Judicial Ordinance, § 4.02.

51 Standing Rock Sioux Tribe (SD) Tribal Code, Title 1, Chapter 4, Subchapter A, § 1-402(4); Title 1, Chapter 4, Subchapter B, § 1-408(4); Title 1, Chapter 5, Subchapter A, § 1-502(a)(5); Title 1, Chapter 5, Subchapter B, § 1-509(a)(5).

have committed a felony; the same exclusion applies to peacemakers.[52] The Assiniboine and Sioux Tribes of the Fort Peck Indian Reservation has a felony exclusion for court clerks and tribal court administrators.[53] The Choctaw Nation excludes from peacemaker positions those who were convicted of felonies or misdemeanors involving moral turpitude.[54] Klamath Tribes of Oregon also have a felony exclusion for peacemakers.[55] The Hopland Band of Pomo Indians excludes from the position of peacemaker persons who have been convicted of any crime within the previous 5 years.[56] The Spirit Lake Tribe excludes persons with felony convictions or with sex offense convictions from serving as peacemakers for the Wodakota Traditional Court.[57] The Arapaho Tribe of the Wind River Reservation excludes persons convicted of a felony or a misdemeanor of moral turpitude from serving as a magistrate.[58] Hannahville Indian Community excludes from serving as court clerks or magistrates anyone with a felony conviction or, within 1 year, a misdemeanor conviction (excluding traffic violations).[59] The Kalispel Indian Community extends its bar on felonies and misdemeanor convictions involving moral turpitude to administrative law judges.[60] The Muscogee (Creek) Nation has a felony exclusion for attorney general of the tribe.[61] The Comanche Nation provides for automatic removal of tribal prosecutors upon conviction of a crime "other than a misdemeanor traffic offense."[62] For the Grand Traverse Band of Ottawa and Chippewa Indians, the felony exclusion for tribal prosecutor is 10 years.[63] The Little River Band of Ottawa Indians has a more explicit exclusion for tribal prosecutor. There, candidates for tribal prosecutor must not have been convicted within the previous 10 years of a felony, any crime involving theft, fraud, or dishonesty, or any crime of violence, threats of violence, or criminal sexual conduct.[64]

52 Alabama-Coushatta Tribe (TX) Tribal Code, Title 1, § 204(D) (on tribal court administrators); Title 2, § 112(B) (providing automatic removal for peacemakers upon conviction of a felony).
53 Assiniboine and Sioux Tribes of the Fort Peck Indian Reservation (MT) Comprehensive Code of Justice, Title 2, §§ 402(5), 405(4).
54 Choctaw Nation (OK) Peacemaking Act, § 3.
55 Klamath Tribes (OR) Tribal Code, Title 2, § 18.07(e).
56 Hopland Band of Pomo Indians (CA) Tribal Code, § 12-1.100.030.
57 Spirit Lake Tribe (ND) Tribal Code, § 21-1-110(3).
58 Northern Arapaho (WY) Tribal Code, Title 17, § 402(c).
59 Hannahville Indian Community (MI) Legal Code, Chapter 1.5, §§ 1.512(2)–(3), 1.520(2).
60 Kalispel Indian Community (WA) Law and Order Code, § 21-3.03. Misdemeanors are only excluded if they occurred within the previous year.
61 Muscogee (OK) Tribal Code, Title 16, § 3-109(B).
62 Comanche Nation (OK) Tribal Code, Title 1, § 5.01(E).
63 Grand Traverse Band of Ottawa and Chippewa Indians (MI) Tribal Code, Title 3, Chapter 1, § 102(a)(2).
64 Little River Band of Ottawa Indians (MI) Office of the Prosecutor Ordinance, #11-400-09, art. 7, § 7.01(c)–(e).

For court clerks, Pueblo of Acoma, Pueblo of San Ildefonso, and Stockbridge Munsee Community exclude only felony convictions.[65] The Coquille Indian Tribe excludes persons convicted of a felony or misdemeanors involving dishonesty from serving as court clerks.[66] The Nez Perce exclude from serving as court clerks or deputy clerks any person "convicted of a felony or of a misdemeanor within the year prior to appointment."[67] The Suquamish Indian Tribe of the Port Madison Reservation also has a lifelong felony bar and a 1-year misdemeanor bar.[68] The Saginaw Chippewa Tribe excludes persons convicted of felonies or, within the past year, of misdemeanors excluding traffic offenses.[69] The Seminole Nation of Oklahoma has a lifetime bar on felony convictions for potential court clerks and deputy clerks, and a 10-year bar for all other offenses excluding traffic offenses, the date to run from the end of incarceration or supervision rather than the date of conviction.[70]

Tribal Judicial Commissions

Some tribes have a judicial commission to govern the tribal judiciary. Membership on the Hopi Tribe's commission excludes persons convicted of an "offense" (defined in the tribal code as a crime punishable by 1 year in custody), "serious offense" (2 years in custody), or "dangerous offense" (3 years in custody).[71] The Kiowa Tribe of Oklahoma and the Stockbridge Munsee Community exclude from their judicial commission any person convicted of a felony, while the Klamath Tribes of Oregon exclude as judicial commissioners persons convicted either of a felony or of a misdemeanor involving dishonesty or moral turpitude within the past 10 years.[72] Similarly, the Picayune Rancheria of Chukchansi Indians excludes from its judicial council any person with a felony conviction or a misdemeanor conviction involving dishonesty.[73] The Judicial Conduct and Discipline Commission of the Salt

65 Pueblo of Acoma (NM) Law and Order Code, Title 1, § 1-5-10; Pueblo of San Ildefonso (NM) Tribal Code, Part 4.1.6.010(b)(2); Stockbridge Munsee Community (WI) Tribal Court Code, § TCT.01.11(b)(1).

66 Coquille Indian Tribe (OR) Tribal Court Ordinance, § 610.400(2).

67 Because of the placement of the second word "of," the best reading of this provision is that the felony exclusion is lifelong, but the misdemeanor exclusion is only for 1 year. Nez Perce Tribe (ID) Tribal Code, § 1-1-21(b)(2).

68 Suquamish Indian Tribe of the Port Madison Reservation (WA) Tribal Code, § 3.5.2.

69 Saginaw Chippewa Tribe of Indians (MI) Tribal Code, Title 1, § 1.511(b)–(c).

70 Seminole Nation of Oklahoma (OK) Tribal Code, Title 5, §§ 402, 403.

71 Hopi Tribe (AZ) Tribal Code, Title 1, § 1.1.2(a) (for Judicial Commission qualifications); Title 3, § 3.4.1 (for definitions of offenses).

72 Constitution of the Kiowa Tribe (OK), art. 8 § 9(a); Klamath Tribes (OR) Tribal Code, Title 1, § 5.06(a)(3);); Stockbridge Munsee Community (WI) Tribal Court Code, § TCT.01.07(c)(1)(E).

73 Picayune Rancheria of Chukchansi Indians (CA) Tribal Court Ordinance, § 4.2.

River Pima-Maricopa Indian Community in Arizona has an exclusion for felony convictions or "two or more misdemeanors (other than non-criminal traffic tickets)" within the past 7 years.[74]

Restoration of Rights for Tribal Court Personnel Appointments

Several tribes have restorations of rights built into the criminal conviction exclusion for tribal court positions. For the Cayuga Nation in New York, the exclusion is on felonies or any crimes of misrepresentation or fraud, unless the conviction is more than 10 years old and has been pardoned or expunged.[75] The Enterprise Rancheria of Maidu Indians states that no person who has been convicted of a felony can serve as Chief Judge or Associate Judge "unless pardoned."[76] The Ho-Chunk Nation of Wisconsin also has a felony exclusion for Chief Justice and Associate Justices of the Ho-Chunk Supreme Court and Chief Judge and Associate Judges of the trial court "unless pardoned" in the jurisdiction where the conviction took place.[77] In another interesting variation, the Oneida Tribe of Wisconsin prevents persons convicted of felonies or other crimes involving fraud or misrepresentation from serving as a tribal judge, unless 10 years have passed since the conviction was pardoned either according to the tribe's pardon law or a pardon by another competent authority.[78] The Pascua Yaqui Tribe restores the ability of a person with a felony conviction to serve as a tribal court judge if his or her voting rights have been restored or the conviction has been expunged.[79] Other tribes that contemplate a restoration of the right to serve as a tribal judge through a pardon or similar process include the Paiute-Shoshone Tribe of the Fallon Reservation and Colony, Picayune Rancheria of Chukchansi Indians, Reno-Sparks Indian Colony, Washoe Tribe of Nevada and California, and the Yomba Shoshone Tribe in Nevada.[80]

74 Salt River Pima-Maricopa Indian Community (AZ) Community Code of Ordinances, § 4-35(e)(3).

75 Cayuga Nation (NY) Judiciary Law, § 11.1(a)(3).

76 Constitution of the Enterprise Rancheria of Maidu Indians (CA), art. 8 § 8(a)–(b).

77 Constitution of the Ho-Chunk Nation (WI), art. 7 § 8(a)–(c).

78 Oneida Tribe of Indians (WI) Tribal Code, Title 8, § 801.11-1(a).

79 Constitution of the Pascua Yaqui Tribe (AZ), art. 8 § 6.

80 Paiute-Shoshone Tribe of the Fallon Reservation and Colony (NV) Law and Order Code, § 1-40-020; Picayune Rancheria of Chukchansi Indians (CA) Tribal Court Ordinance, § 5.2; Reno-Sparks Indian Colony (NV) Tribal Code, § 1-40-020; Washoe Tribe of Nevada and California (NV) Tribal Code, §§ 1-40-020, 1-40-030; Yomba Shoshone Tribe of the Yomba Reservation (NV) Tribal Code, Title 1(C), §§ 7–8.

Election Administration

Some tribes restrict persons with criminal convictions from serving in positions related to management of elections. The most common provision involves exclusions from the election oversight body. The Te-Moak Tribe of Western Shoshone Indians excludes persons with felony convictions from appointments to the Tribal Election Board and the subordinate Band Election Committees for the tribe's four constituent bands.[81] The Assiniboine and Sioux Tribes of the Fort Peck Indian Reservation exclude persons with felony convictions as Election Supervisor, Election Commissioners, or Election Judges, "unless such person has received a full pardon from an appropriate official authorized to grant such pardon by the government in which they received the felony conviction."[82] The Kiowa Indian Tribe not only has an exclusion for persons with felony convictions from appointment to its election commission, but also automatic removal upon conviction of a felony, a crime of dishonesty, or an election-related crime.[83] The Oglala Sioux Tribe excludes persons convicted of a felony "and/or dishonest act."[84] The Keetoowah Band of Cherokee Indians excludes from its Election Board persons "convicted of a felony, imprisonment [*sic.*], or crime punishable by tribal banishment."[85] Even more vague and encompassing is the exclusion in the tribal law of the Caddo Nation of Oklahoma for any potential member with a felony conviction or a misdemeanor conviction for a crime involving the misuse of money or that "inhibits the promotion and protection of the health, peace, morals, education and general welfare of the tribe."[86] Other tribes that have felony exclusions for election oversight bodies include the Enterprise Rancheria of Maidu Indians, Fort Belknap Indian Community, Northfork Rancheria of Mono Indians, Susanville Indian Rancheria, and Poarch Band of Creeks.[87] The Lower Brule Sioux Tribe's felony exclusion only applies to convictions within the past 10 years.[88] The Ponca Tribe of Indians of Oklahoma and

81 Te-Moak Tribe of Western Shoshone (NV) Tribal Code, Title 13, at §§ 13-14-1(a)(2) and 13-15-1(a)(2).

82 Assiniboine and Sioux Tribes of the Fort Peck Indian Reservation (MT) Comprehensive Code of Justice, Title 5, § 106(d).

83 Constitution of the Kiowa Indian Tribe (OK), art. 9 § 3(d).

84 Oglala Sioux Tribe (SD) Tribal Code, Chapter 27, § 2.

85 Keetoowah Band of Cherokee Indians (OK) Election Ordinance, § 203(B).

86 Caddo Nation (OK) Election Ordinance, § 4(4)(d).

87 Constitution of the Enterprise Rancheria of Maidu Indians (CA), art. 9 § 6; Fort Belknap Indian Community (MT) Election Ordinance 10-28-11, § 5(D)(e); Constitution of the Northfork Rancheria of Mono Indians (CA), art. 4 § 5; Susanville Indian Rancheria (CA), Ordinance 2006-001, § 1(b); Poarch Band of Creeks (AL) Tribal Code, Title 22, § 22-2-1.

88 Constitution of the Lower Brule Sioux Tribe (SD), art. 4 § 3(b).

the Delaware Nation of Oklahoma have automatic removal procedures for Election Board members convicted of a felony.[89]

Less common election management-related restrictions include appointments as poll workers and election appeals bodies. The Te-Moak Tribe of Western Shoshone Indians prohibits persons with felony convictions from serving as polling officials.[90] The Oglala Sioux Tribe excludes individuals with felony convictions or convictions for "dishonest act[s]" from its Court of Election Appeals, which hears challenges to candidacy determinations and conduct of elections.[91] The Standing Rock Sioux Tribe has a felony bar for members of its election commission, election judges, and election clerks.[92] Several tribes have more complex provisions than these. For the Pokagon Band of Potawatomi Indians, members of the Election Board may not be currently incarcerated or have been convicted of a felony within the past 10 years to a crime subject to imprisonment for 1 year or longer, "excepting those crimes determined by the Election Board to relate to the furtherance of the Band's tribal sovereignty rights," which is an exception for political or protest-related crimes.[93] The Quileute Tribe has a non-mandatory removal procedure for Election Board members convicted in the past 7 years of felonies "other than convictions for asserting tribal treaty rights" (a safe harbor for political offenses) or a misdemeanor involving controlled substances or dishonesty.[94]

In other jurisdictions, the exclusion for persons with criminal convictions is discretionary. The tribal code of the Confederated Tribes of the Coos, Lower Umpqua, and Siuslaw Indians in Oregon authorizes, but does not require, the Tribal Council Chairperson to remove Election Board members for conviction of a felony or crime involving dishonesty, with the consent of the Tribal Council.[95] The Paiute Indian Tribe of Utah also has a provision authorizing the tribal council or band chair to remove an Election Board member for conviction of a felony or any crime involving dishonesty or moral turpitude.[96] This removal, though, is discretionary.

89 Constitution of the Ponca Tribe of Indians (OK), art. 5 § 1; Delaware Nation (OK) Election Ordinance (2018), § 301(D).
90 Te-Moak Tribe of Western Shoshone Indians (NV) Tribal Code, Title 13, § 13-16-1(a).
91 Oglala Sioux Tribe (SD) Tribal Code, Chapter 27, § 3.
92 Standing Rock Sioux Tribe (SD) Tribal Code, Title 15, § 15-205.
93 Pokagon Band of Potawatomi Indians (MI) Election Code, § 2(C)(5).
94 Quileute Tribe of the Quileute Reservation (WA) Election Ordinance, § 14(1).
95 Confederated Tribes of the Coos, Lower Umpqua and Siuslaw Indians (OR) Tribal Code, § 7-3-2(n).
96 Paiute Indian Tribe of Utah (UT), Election Ordinance (2020), § 4(1).

Law Enforcement and Corrections Officers

Serving in a tribal law enforcement capacity also comes with collateral consequences of criminal conviction. As with election administration, these come in three general types: first, qualifications for members of police oversight bodies or public safety commissions; second, qualifications for appointed or elected police chiefs or sheriffs; and finally, qualifications for hiring police officers. In at least one jurisdiction, the Seminole Nation of Oklahoma, the collateral consequence is not on hiring police officers, but rather on cross-deputizing tribal police with state and county law enforcement. In that jurisdiction, police officers may not be cross-deputized if they have a felony conviction, domestic violence conviction with an inability to carry a firearm, or a misdemeanor conviction within the previous year, traffic offenses excluded.[97]

Membership of the police commission for the Oneida Tribe excludes anyone with a felony conviction, a felony arrest that results in a misdemeanor conviction as the result of a plea bargain, or a conviction for "any ordinance violation that could bring discredit to the Commission." Notably, these crimes are *unpardonable*—that is, a pardon for these convictions does not restore eligibility to serve on the Oneida Police Commission, one rare such example in tribal law.[98] The Red Cliff Band of Lake Superior Chippewa Indians, also of Wisconsin, has a substantially similar exclusion including the provision finding such convictions unpardonable for purposes of police commissioner eligibility.[99] The Menominee Tribe of Wisconsin bars persons with felony convictions from serving as police chief, including tribal offenses punishable by more than 1 year in prison and any crime that would prohibit a candidate from working with children.[100] The Menominee Tribe's exclusion for its police commission, however, is much broader: no candidates may have a felony conviction, a misdemeanor sexual assault or domestic violence conviction, a drug- or alcohol-related misdemeanor conviction within 5 years, or any other misdemeanor conviction within 1 year.[101] Interestingly, the Saint Regis Mohawk Tribe in New York has a police commission with the same four eligibility exclusions as the Menominee Tribe.[102] In the Lac Courte Oreilles Band of Lake Superior Chippewa Indians, a person convicted of a felony or crime involving fraud or misrepresentation is ineligible to serve

97 Seminole Nation of Oklahoma (OK) Tribal Code, Title 24, § 112(c)(4).
98 Oneida Tribe of Indians (WI) Tribal Code, Title 3, § 301.6-3(c).
99 Red Cliff Band of Lake Superior Chippewa Indians (WI) Tribal Code, § 42.5.3(c).
100 Menominee Tribe (WI) Tribal Code, art. 3, § 132-16(1)–(2).
101 Id. at art. 8, § 132-53.
102 Saint Regis Mohawk Tribe (NY) Police Commission Act, § 7(C)(2).

on the public safety commission.[103] By contrast, the Ho-Chunk Nation has a legislative waiver provision for members of its police commission. In that jurisdiction, a law enforcement commissioner must not have a felony conviction within the preceding 10 years "unless waived by the Legislature when the person has demonstrated and shown that his/her prior activities do not pose a threat to the credibility and integrity of the Commission."[104]

As for reservation police officers, exclusions based on criminal convictions vary in scope. The famous Lighthorse Administration of the Muscogee (Creek) Nation excludes as lighthorsemen any person with a felony conviction or any misdemeanor conviction concerning violence, theft, fraud, embezzlement, gaming-related crimes, or crimes of moral turpitude.[105] The tribal police of the Confederated Tribes of the Coos, Lower Umpqua, and Siuslaw Indians in Oregon exclude persons with felony convictions or Class A misdemeanors (crimes punishable by up to 1 year in prison).[106] The Lac Courte Oreilles Band of Lake Superior Chippewa Indians has the same exclusion.[107] The Assiniboine and Sioux Tribes of the Fort Peck Indian Reservation exclude as reservation police persons with felony convictions, unless pardoned, or with misdemeanor convictions within the previous year.[108] In accord are the Chippewa Cree Indians of the Rocky Boy's Reservation, Confederated Tribes of the Colville Reservation, Lummi Tribe, Pueblo of Pojoaque, Quechan Tribe of the Fort Yuma Indian Reservation, and Swinomish Indian Tribal Community.[109]

The Makah Indian Tribe excludes as potential police officers anyone convicted of a felony or Class A misdemeanor, or within the past year, any other offense.[110] The Omaha Tribe of Nebraska, Tulalip Tribes of Washington State, and Ute Indian Tribe of the Uintah and Ouray Reservation in Utah

103 Lac Courte Oreilles Band of Lake Superior Chippewa Indians (WI) Tribal Code, Title 10, § 1.302(3)(d).
104 Ho-Chunk Nation (WI) Tribal Code, Title 1, § 14(7)(b)(2)(d).
105 Muscogee (Creek) Nation (OK) Tribal Code, Title 16, § 4-102.
106 Confederated Tribes of the Coos, Lower Umpqua, and Siuslaw Indians (OR) Tribal Code, § 1-3-12(c).
107 Lac Courte Oreilles Band of Lake Superior Chippewa Indians (WI) Tribal Code, Title 10, § 1.505(3).
108 Assiniboine and Sioux Tribes of the Fort Peck Indian Reservation (MT) Comprehensive Code of Justice, Title 3, § 205(3).
109 Chippewa Cree Indians of the Rocky Boy's Reservation (MT) Law and Order Code, Title 4, § 1.5(2)(c)–(d); Confederated Tribes of the Colville Reservation (WA) Tribal Code, § 1-3-61(c); Lummi Tribe of the Lummi Reservation (WA) Tribal Code, § 9.04.020(c); Pueblo of Pojoaque (NM) Law and Order Code, § D-6(a)(3); Quechan Tribe of the Fort Yuma Indian Reservation (AZ) Tribal Code, § 9.3.2(C); Swinomish Indian Tribal Community (WA) Tribal Code, § 2-07.090(A).
110 Makah Indian Tribe of the Makah Indian Reservation (WA) Tribal Code, § 8.3.02(c).

have the same exclusion.[111] The Cheyenne-Arapahoe Tribes of Oklahoma has a felony exclusion as well but extends the misdemeanor exclusion to the past 3 years, traffic offenses excepted.[112] The Kickapoo Traditional Tribe of Texas has a felony exclusion and a 3-year misdemeanor exclusion both for its entry-level professional police positions and its volunteer reserve police force.[113] The Port Gamble S'Klallam Tribe excludes as police officers anyone with a felony conviction, anyone with a domestic violence conviction, and any misdemeanor conviction within 3 years of appointment.[114]

The Sac and Fox Tribe of the Mississippi in Iowa has an eligibility exclusion for its probation-parole officers in the event of a previous conviction of a felony or misdemeanor involving perjury or false statement. This exclusion applies even if the applicant received a deferred adjudication or a suspended sentence.[115]

Natural Resource Management

Many tribes have collateral consequences of conviction for commissions or boards that oversee the use of natural resources or that grant permits or licenses for natural resource privileges. The Navajo Nation has an unusually specific restriction on previous criminal convictions for members of its Land Board, Farm Board, and Grazing Committee, which are elected positions. Candidates for these positions must not have been convicted in the previous 5 years of any felony or

> any misdemeanor in any court involving crimes of deceit, untruthfulness and dishonesty, including but not limited to extortion, embezzlement, bribery, perjury, forgery, fraud, misrepresentation, false pretense, theft, conversion, or misuse of Navajo Nation funds and property, and crimes involving the welfare of children, child abuse, child neglect, aggravated assault and aggravated battery.[116]

111 Omaha Tribe (NE) Tribal Code, § 6-1-3(a)(3); Tulalip Tribes of Washington (WA) Tribal Code, §2.45.030(2)(c); Ute Indian Tribe of the Uintah and Ouray Reservation (UT) Tribal Code, § 11-1-3(2)(c).

112 Cheyenne-Arapahoe Tribes (OK) Law and Order Code, Title 2, Subpart F, §§ 103(d)(3), 302(b)(2).

113 The misdemeanor exclusion for reserve police excludes traffic offenses; the exclusion for tribal police does not. Kickapoo Traditional Tribe (TX) Tribal Code, Chapter 3, § 302(b)(2); Tribal Police Ordinance, § 103(d)(3).

114 Port Gamble S'Klallam Tribe (WA) Tribal Code, Title 5, § 5.12.03(c).

115 Sac & Fox Tribe of the Mississippi (IA) Law and Order Code, § 13-6608(b)(5).

116 Navajo Nation (AZ) Tribal Code, Title 11, Chapter 1, § 8(D)(1)–(3).

Notably, restrictions on membership of natural resource commissions or boards are particularly common in tribes of the Pacific Northwest. The Tulalip Tribes have a collateral consequence attached to membership on the tribe's Hunting Commission, which excludes as members anyone with a felony conviction or "Class E" or "Class F" convictions, which encompass serious misdemeanors like property damage, violent crimes, use of controlled substances, or domestic violence.[117] The Puyallup Tribe states that members of the Fisheries Management Commission must not have had a fishing-related conviction in the previous 2 years.[118] For the tribe's Shellfish Commission, a potential member must not have had a tribal fishing or shellfish-related violation in 2 years.[119] The Port Gamble S'Klallam Tribe also excludes for 2 years persons with fishing-related convictions from serving on the tribe's Fisheries Committee. A committee member convicted of a fishing violation may be removed from office at the discretion of the tribal council.[120] A similar provision is found in the law of the Confederated Tribes of the Grand Ronde Community. That tribe's Fish and Wildlife Committee excludes from membership any person found guilty of a hunting, fishing, or gathering violation within the 2 years preceding appointment.[121] The Natural Resources Committee of the Jamestown S'Klallam Tribe has a 2-year bar for committee membership and employment with the fisheries program for persons with violations of the tribe's natural resources ordinances.[122] The Swinomish Indian Tribe also has a 2-year exclusion for members of its Fish and Game Management Commission who are convicted under the tribal code for any natural resources violation or criminal offense, and mandates removal from the commission for 2 years for any current member with such a conviction. The provision also authorizes denial of employment with the tribal fisheries and game programs for a period of 2 years for similar convictions.[123]

Some tribes instead provide for removal from the commission or board upon conviction for certain crimes. At the discretion of the Tribal Council, the Lower Elwha Tribal Community excludes from its Game Committee any person who was convicted of a violation of the Treaty Hunting Ordinance for a period of 2 years.[124] The Sault Ste. Marie Tribe of Chippewa Indians requires members of its Conservation Committee to report violations of any conservation-related laws; violations of the tribe's fishing and hunting

117 Tulalip Tribes of Washington (WA) Tribal Code, § 8.10.050(3)(a)(iii).
118 Puyallup Tribe (WA) Tribal Code, § 12.04.060.
119 Id. at § 12.04.060.
120 Port Gamble S'Klallam Tribe (WA) Tribal Code, § 17.08.02(g)(ii).
121 Confederated Tribes of the Grand Ronde Community (OR) Tribal Code, Chapter 801(c)(1)(C).
122 Jamestown S'Klallam Tribe (WA) Tribal Code, §§ 6.07.03, 6.11.06.
123 Swinomish Indian Tribe (WA) Tribal Code, §§ 18-02.020, 18-02.030.
124 Lower Elwha Tribal Community (WA) Treaty Hunting Ordinance, § 1.1.3.

regulations result in automatic removal.[125] The Suquamish Indian Tribe authorizes removal of members of its Fish and Wildlife Committee and Shellfish Committee for persons with felony or serious misdemeanor convictions and renders ineligible for employment any member found guilty of a violation of the fish and wildlife or shellfish provisions for 1 year.[126] The Spirit Lake Tribe has a broad provision providing that members of the Environmental Quality Commission are automatically disqualified if convicted of any felony or misdemeanor while serving in the position.[127]

Finally, at least one tribe extends collateral consequences to its natural resources law enforcement officers. The Little Traverse Bay Bands of Odawa Indians exclude from serving as a Tribal Conservation Enforcement Officers anyone with a criminal conviction for felonies (including expunged convictions) or misdemeanor domestic violence.[128]

Other Tribal Boards, Commissions, and Committees

This section summarizes conviction-related exclusions for membership on other tribal boards, commissions, and committees. The Jamestown S'Klallam Tribe has a blanket exclusion for persons with criminal convictions from serving on any tribal board or committee.[129] The Kickapoo Traditional Tribe of Texas also has a blanket exclusion for persons convicted of any crime that is punishable by exclusion or banishment from serving in any public office or on any tribal board for at least 5 years, up to the length of the banishment term.[130] Unusually, though, this tribe allows restoration to serve in tribal office or on a tribal board by petitioning the Tribal Council for a pardon at least 7 years after conviction (or upon evidence of innocence) or for a reduction of a sentence of banishment or exclusion 10 years after conviction.[131] Notwithstanding this provision, the Kickapoo Traditional Tribe of Texas also has separate exclusions for specific tribal commissions such as the tribe's Housing Authority, below.

Tax authority: the Standing Rock Sioux Tribe excludes any person with a felony conviction from serving as a tax commissioner.[132] The Standing Rock Sioux Tribe has two five-member tax commissions, one for North Dakota and one for South Dakota, owing to the different arrangements that tribe has with

125 Sault Ste. Marie Tribe of Chippewa Indians (MI) Tribal Code, Chapter 22, § 10(b).
126 Suquamish Indian Tribe (WA) Tribal Code, §§ 14.1.8(e), 14.1.47(a).
127 Spirit Lake Tribe (ND) Tribal Code, § 16-1-104(6).
128 Little Traverse Bay Bands of Odawa Indians (MI) Tribal Code, Title 4, § B(1)(d)–(e).
129 Jamestown S'Klallam Tribe (WA) Tribal Code, Title 30, Article 8, § 1.
130 Kickapoo Traditional Tribe of Texas (TX) Penal Code, § 3.
131 Id.
132 Standing Rock Sioux Tribe (SD) Tribal Code, § 16-203(B).

these respective state governments. The Cherokee Nation, Shawnee Tribe, and the Assiniboine and Sioux Tribes of the Fort Peck Indian Reservation have a broader exclusion on any person with a criminal conviction (excluding traffic offenses) from serving as a tax commissioner.[133] For the Cherokee Nation and the Fort Peck Indian Reservation, the tax commissioner serves as part of a three-member tax commission; for the Shawnee Tribe the tax commissioner is a single tribal office.

Utility authority: the Kickapoo Tribe of Oklahoma authorizes removal of any director of the Tribal Utility Management Board upon conviction of a crime "reflecting upon such Director's honesty" or ability to "fulfill the fiduciary obligations" of the position.[134] The Mohegan Tribe in Connecticut has an identical provision, in an interesting example of cross-country sharing.[135] An alternative formulation may be found in the laws of some Western and Pacific Northwestern tribal jurisdictions. The Nez Perce Tribe has a provision for automatic removal of a member of the tribe's Utility Board upon conviction for "a felony or major crime" in any court.[136] The Pueblo of Pojoaque, Sauk-Suiattle Indian Tribe, Shoalwater Bay Indian Tribe, and Swinomish Indian Tribal Community use the same formulation for their utility commissions.[137] The Navajo Nation has a bar for members of its Tribal Utility Authority for felony convictions alone.[138] The Assiniboine and Sioux Tribes of the Fort Peck Indian Reservation have a collateral consequence of conviction attached to membership on the reservation's Municipal, Rural, and Industrial Water Commission, which oversees the tribe's rural water supply. Members of this five-person commission must never have been convicted of a felony or an offense involving fraud or theft.[139] This tribe additionally has a Water Resources Control Commission, which grants permits for irrigation and other uses. This Commission has a broader restriction for its members, excluding those who have been convicted of any criminal offense except traffic offenses.[140]

133 Assiniboine and Sioux Tribes of the Fort Peck Indian Reservation (MT) Comprehensive Code of Justice, Title 23, § 302(b); Cherokee Nation (OK) Tribal Code, Title 68, Chapter 2, § 12(A); Shawnee Tribe (OK) Tribal Code, § 5.08.020.
134 Kickapoo Tribe of Oklahoma (OK) Tribal Utility Ordinance, § 108(e)(2).
135 Mohegan Tribe of Indians (CT) Utility Code, § 1-318(e)(2).
136 Nez Perce Tribe (ID) Tribal Code, § 8-2-7(b).
137 Pueblo of Pojoaque (NM) Utility Board Ordinance, § T-6(c)(8); Sauk-Suiattle Indian Tribe (WA) Utility and Environmental Services Ordinance, § 3.08; Shoalwater Bay Indian Tribe (WA) Tribal Code, Title 22, § 3.08; Swinomish Indian Tribal Community (WA) Tribal Code, § 11-02.100(B)(2).
138 Navajo Nation (AZ) Tribal Code, Title 21, Chapter 1, Subchapter 2, § 54(A)(3).
139 Assiniboine and Sioux Tribes of the Fort Peck Indian Reservation (MT) Comprehensive Code of Justice, Title 20, § 1301(3)(4).
140 Id. at Title 20, § 303(4).

Enrollment authority: exclusions for persons with criminal convictions from enrollment and membership authorities tend to take the form of removal of the board member upon criminal conviction rather than as an eligibility bar. The Bad River Band of the Lake Superior Tribe of Chippewa Indians has a removal provision for any member of the Membership Enrollment Committee upon conviction of a felony or a misdemeanor involving dishonesty.[141] The Ponca Tribe of Nebraska also authorizes removal from its Enrollment Committee for conviction of any crime "against the tribe."[142] The Yavapai-Apache Nation authorizes the Enrollment Board to recommend to the Tribal Council removal of any board member to be removed upon conviction for a felony or "serious misdemeanor," defined as a crime punishable by more than 3 months in jail or a fine of $1,000.[143]

Tribal-owned corporation or economic development authority: some tribes have collateral consequences for directors and shareholders of tribal-owned business enterprises or economic development authorities. The Kashia Band of Pomo Indians excludes from its Economic Development Committee any person convicted of a felony or who was found to have embezzled or mismanaged money from the tribe.[144] For the Ponca Tribe of Nebraska, members of the boards of directors of any tribally owned corporations must have no felony convictions or other convictions involving tax evasion, tax fraud, embezzlement, or moral turpitude.[145] The Winnebago Tribe excludes from the Board of Trustees of its Economic Development Authority any person convicted of a felony or other crimes involving embezzlement, fraud, or moral turpitude.[146] The Confederated Tribes of the Goshute Reservation has a Goshute Federal Corporation to manage its economic development priorities. To serve on the Board of Directors, one must never have been convicted of a felony involving violence or lack of integrity, to include crimes against children, fraud, embezzlement, theft, conversion, misrepresentation, sexual misconduct, or misuse of a weapon.[147] The Little Traverse Bay Band of Odawa Indians runs the Ziibimijwang Farm, which engages in sustainable agriculture. One may not serve on the Board of Directors of this tribal-owned

141 Big River Band of the Lake Superior Tribe of Chippewa Indians (WI) Tribal Code, § 601.05(f).
142 Ponca Tribe of Nebraska (NE) Tribal Code, § 10-2-6(g).
143 Yavapai-Apache Nation (AZ) Tribal Code, Title 1, § 407(A)(5).
144 Kashia Band of Pomo Indians (CA) Economic Development Committee Operating Procedures, § 3.1.
145 Ponca Tribe of Nebraska (NE) Tribal Code, § 15-9-32(1)(c)–(d).
146 Winnebago Tribe (NE) Tribal Code, § 11A-308(4).
147 Confederated Tribes of the Goshute Reservation (NV), "CTGR Board of Directors Needed for Goshute Federal Corporation" (January 24, 2018), https://ctgr.us/home/2018/01/24/ctgr-board-of-directors-needed-for-goshute-federal-corporation.

corporation "within seven (7) years of completion of a sentence or probation" for a felony conviction, unless the conviction was overturned or vacated.[148] The Menominee Tribal Enterprises, which produces lumber and other sustainable forest products, prohibits any person with a felony conviction in the previous 10 years from serving as a member of the Board of Directors. However, a pardon from the appropriate authority or certificate of rehabilitation from the tribal court would restore this right.[149] The Menominee tribe also has an Economic Development Authority, which excludes from its Board of Directors any person with a conviction in the past 10 years for a felony or a misdemeanor involving theft, fraud, or misrepresentation. This right may also be restored through a pardon.[150]

Construction authority: Yavapai Apache Construction, a public corporation managed by the Yavapai Apache Tribal Council, provides for removal from its board of directors any person convicted of a felony or any of the following offenses: assault on a law enforcement officer or judge; obstruction of justice; tampering with physical evidence; perjury; bribery; fraud; extortion or theft.[151] The Little River Band of Ottawa Indians operates the Muschigon Construction Company, which authorizes removal of any member of the board of directors for conviction of a felony or of a misdemeanor "that infringes on the professional responsibilities and integrity of the member."[152]

Tribal housing authority: for the Standing Rock Sioux Tribe, members of the Board of Commissioners of the Housing Authority must never have been convicted of a felony.[153] The Eastern Band of Cherokee Indians has a broader exclusion for members of the Housing Committee, for persons with convictions for felonies or crimes of moral turpitude, defined as "a criminal offense involving dishonesty, fraud, or deceit."[154] The Yurok Tribe excludes from its Housing Authority Board of Commissioners any person convicted within 10 years of a felony or crime of moral turpitude, and provides for automatic removal from the position upon conviction.[155] The Kickapoo Traditional Tribe of Texas Tribal Code states that no person convicted of a felony or, within the last 5 years, a misdemeanor may serve on that tribe's Housing

148 Little Traverse Bay Band of Odawa Indians (MI) Tribal Code, § 7.1105(B)(2).
149 Menominee Indian Tribe (WI) Tribal Code, § 692-8.
150 Id. at § 652-5(A)(4)(e).
151 Yavapai-Apache Nation (AZ) Tribal Code, Title 31, § 304(6)(b)(i).
152 Little River Band of Ottawa Indians (MI) Muschigon Construction Company Ordinance, # 05-800-04, § 6.10(c)–(d).
153 Standing Rock Sioux Tribe (SD) Tribal Code, § 15-501(d).
154 Eastern Band of Cherokee Indians (NC) Tribal Code, § 117-43.4(b).
155 Yurok Tribe (CA) Tribal Code, § 24.05.080(a)–(b).

Authority Board of Directors.[156] The Little River Band of Ottawa Indians authorizes removal from its Housing Commission any member who has been convicted of a felony.[157] In California, the Pit River Tribe has a felony bar for members of its Housing Committee, while the Round Valley Indian Tribes deems ineligible for its Housing Commission any person with a felony conviction in the previous 8 years.[158] For the Northern Ponca Housing Authority of the Ponca Tribe of Nebraska, a Housing Commissioner must not have been convicted of any sex offense or any criminal or civil offense involving fraud or dishonesty.[159]

Education authority: the Mescalero Apache School Board excludes persons convicted of felonies from serving on the board.[160] The Muscogee (Creek) Nation also has a felony record exclusion for board members of the Eufaula Boarding School.[161] The Standing Rock Sioux Tribe excludes persons with felony convictions from running in school board elections.[162] The Navajo Nation Board of Education excludes persons with felony convictions or convictions for any crime involving child abuse or neglect from serving.[163] In addition, the Navajo Nation also excludes persons with felony convictions in the previous 5 years from serving on the Board of Regents for Diné College.[164] For the Navajo School Board, the criminal conviction exclusion is broader than for the Board of Education and the College Board of Regents, encompassing a lifelong restriction for any felony or any misdemeanor

> involving elements of deceit, untruthfulness and dishonesty, including but not limited to extortion, bribery, forgery, fraud, theft, embezzlement, perjury, misrepresentation, false pretense, conversion, or misuse of public funds or property, any crimes involving the welfare of children, child abuse, or child neglect, aggravated assault or aggravated battery, [or] any crimes involving the use of intoxicating alcohol or illegal substance abuse including unlawful transport, sales or distribution of controlled substances.[165]

156 Kickapoo Traditional Tribe of Texas (TX) Tribal Code, § 23.4(B)(4).
157 Little River Band of Ottawa Indians (MI) Housing Commission Ordinance, 04-700-01, § 4.04(a).
158 Pit River Tribe (CA) Housing Committee Policy and Procedures, Resolution No. 03-10-09, art. 3, § 302(B); Round Valley Indian Tribes (CA) Housing Authority Ordinance, RV-2005-1, art. 3 § 3(f).
159 Ponca Tribe of Nebraska (NE) Tribal Code, § 5-2-4(1)(b).
160 Mescalero Apache Tribe of the Mescalero Reservation (NM) Tribal Code, § 26-1-2(C).
161 Muscogee (Creek) Nation (OK) Tribal Code, Title 18, § 3-203(A)(1)(d).
162 Standing Rock Sioux Tribe (SD) Tribal Code, § 15-401.
163 Navajo Nation (AZ) Tribal Code, Title 10, § 106(D)(4).
164 Id. at Title 10, Chapter 19, § 2003(C)(e).
165 Id. at Title 11, Chapter 1, § 8(D)(4)(g)–(h).

Tribal employment authority: as with its utility authority, the Nez Perce Tribe has a provision for automatic removal for any member of its Tribal Employment Rights Commission who is convicted of a felony or major crime.[166] For the Standing Rock Sioux Tribe, members of its Tribal Employment and Contracting Rights Commission must never have been convicted of a felony.[167] The Assiniboine and Sioux Tribes of the Fort Peck Indian Reservation have a three-person Tribal Employment Rights Review Board that also has a felony exclusion for its members.[168] The Navajo Nation Labor Commission excludes from its membership any person "convicted of any crime reflecting upon such member's honesty or ability to fulfill the fiduciary obligations imposed by law."[169] The Tulalip Tribes exclude from their Tribal Employment Rights Office (TERO) Commission any person convicted of a felony or misdemeanor involving dishonesty or controlled substance use.[170]

Financial services authority or financial institution: the Pueblo of Pojoaque have a Consumer Financial Services Regulatory Authority, which is governed by one or more Regulatory Agents appointed by the Tribal Council. No person may be appointed as Regulatory Agent if he or she has had a criminal conviction in the past 10 years for any felony or misdemeanor involving a breach of trust or dishonesty.[171] The Salt River Pima-Maricopa Indian Community has an automatic removal procedure for any member on the board of Salt River Financial Services Institution upon conviction for a felony or finance-related misdemeanor.[172] The Yavapai Apache Nation excludes from its Board of Directors of the Yavapai Apache Community Development and Financial Institution any member convicted of a felony or other crime involving "extortion, theft, possession of stolen property, fraud, refusing to aid law enforcement officers, false reporting, obstruction of justice, criminal contempt of court, perjury, possession of dangerous drugs, bribery, or tampering with physical evidence."[173]

Ethics authority: the Mohegan Tribe of Indians may remove a member of the tribe's Ethics Commission for any conviction of a misdemeanor or felony.[174]

166 Nez Perce Tribe (ID) Tribal Code, § 9-1-9(b).
167 Standing Rock Sioux Tribe (SD) Tribal Code, § 30-106(A)(1)(c).
168 Assiniboine and Sioux Tribes of the Fort Peck Indian Reservation (MT) Comprehensive Code of Justice, Title 13, § 302.
169 Navajo Nation (AZ) Tribal Code, Title 15, Chapter 4, § 303(E).
170 Tulalip Tribes (WA) Tribal Code, § 9.05.050(1)(c).
171 Pueblo of Pojoaque (NM) Tribal Code, Subpart R, § R-2(d)(D)(b).
172 Salt River Pima-Maricopa Indian Community (NM) Community Code of Ordinances, Division 6, § 1-151(b)(2).
173 Yavapai-Apache Nation (AZ) Tribal Code, Title 34, § 304(B)(6)(b).
174 Mohegan Tribe of Indians (CT) Tribal Code, Article 3, § 1-254(d).

The Poarch Band of Creeks has a felony exclusion for members of its Ethics Board.[175]

Freedom of information authority: the Mohegan Tribe of Indians may remove a member of the tribe's Freedom of Information Commission for any misdemeanor or felony conviction.[176]

Public health or hospital authority: the Eastern Band of Cherokee Indians excludes from the tribe's Hospital Authority Governing Board any person convicted of a felony or crime involving moral turpitude.[177] The tribe has the same exclusion for members of its Advisory Board on Public Health and Human Services.[178] The Navajo Nation has a felony bar for its Nursing Home Administrator.[179]

Tribal-state agreements oversight authority: the Assiniboine and Sioux Tribes of the Fort Peck Indian Reservation has a three-member Tribal-State Agreements Oversight Commission, which excludes from serving persons who have been convicted of a felony "for which he/she has not received a pardon."[180]

Pardon authority: the Lac Courte Oreilles Band of Lake Superior Chippewa Indians has an exclusion for members of its Pardon Screening Committee any person convicted of a felony or any crime involving fraud or misrepresentation, "unless pardoned."[181] The Assiniboine and Sioux Tribes of the Fort Peck Indian Reservation have a Tribal Pardon Commission that allows removal of any person convicted of "an offense involving dishonesty" by a two-thirds vote of the Tribal Executive Board.[182]

Athletics authority: the Confederated Tribes of Siletz Indians authorizes removal of athletic commission members for crimes involving moral turpitude or dishonesty.[183] For the Pascua Yaqui Tribe, athletic commission members

175 Poarch Band of Creeks (AL) Tribal Code, § 28-1-7(b).
176 Mohegan Tribe of Indians (CT) Tribal Code, Article 6, § 1-407(d).
177 Eastern Band of Cherokee Indians (NC) Tribal Code, § 130B-4(b).
178 Id. at § 130A-8(b)(2).
179 Navajo Nation (AZ) Tribal Code, Chapter 17, Subchapter 11, § 2751(D).
180 Assiniboine and Sioux Tribes of the Fort Peck Indian Reservation (MT) Comprehensive Code of Justice, Title 26, § 103(4).
181 Joe Morey, "Final Call for Members to Important Pardon and Forgiveness Committee," Lac Courte Oreilles Tribe News and Information (February 19, 2021), https://www.lcotribe.com/post/final-call-for-important-pardon-and-forgiveness-committee-members.
182 Assiniboine and Sioux Tribes of the Fort Peck Indian Reservation (MT) Comprehensive Code of Justice, Title 6, § 906.
183 Confederated Tribes of Siletz Indians (OR) Tribal Code, § 6.505.

must not have been convicted of a felony "unless … his or her voting rights have been restored, or unless the criminal conviction has been expunged." In addition, a member must not have been convicted of any crime involving deceit, fraud, or misappropriation of funds.[184]

Insurance authority: the Ho-Chunk Nation has a felony exclusion for members of its Insurance Review Commission. Unlike for its Law Enforcement Commission above, this felony bar cannot be waived by the Ho-Chunk legislature for rehabilitation.[185]

Blanket Exclusions

Some tribes have a blanket exclusion on all personnel serving in tribal office. The Yavapai-Apache Nation has a General and Special Events Committee Code that applies to all subordinate standing, ad hoc, and special event committees that the tribal council creates. This Code excludes persons with a felony in the previous 5 years from serving on any committee and precludes a person with a conviction for a crime against a child from serving on any committee that provides activities for children. This provision may be waived, however, if the tribal council finds mitigating factors justify a waiver.[186] The Omaha Tribe of Nebraska states that no tribal member may serve on the tribal council or as a tribal judge, court clerk, or policeman for 15 years after conviction or release from prison for any felony causing loss to the tribe or any felony resulting in imprisonment.[187] In its government ethics law, the Navajo Nation has a blanket misdemeanor exclusion for 5 years following the date of conviction for all candidates for elective office or appointees to any tribal office or tribal entity.[188]

Other Tribal Offices

Collateral consequences also attach to a range of tribal offices not listed above. These include the following:

- **Tribal administrator**: the Comanche Nation has a tribal administrator to manage the budget and operations of the tribe. To be eligible for this position, a candidate must not have had a previous conviction for a felony or misdemeanor involving dishonesty, bribery, or embezzlement, or a failed

184 Pascua Yaqui Tribe (AZ) Tribal Code, 2 P.Y.T.C. § 4-2-10.
185 Ho-Chunk Nation (WI) Tribal Code, 1 H.C.C. § 13(6)(c)(2)(a).
186 Yavapai-Apache Nation (AZ), General and Special Event Committee Code, § C(7)(d).
187 Constitution of the Omaha Tribe (NE), art. 5 § 4.
188 Navajo Nation (AZ) Tribal Code, Title 1, Chapter 6, § 3782.

drug test or court judgment determining that she or he inappropriately disposed of tribal assets.[189]

- **Controller or treasurer**: the Muscogee (Creek) Nation does not permit persons with felony convictions to serve as the tribal controller, in charge of budgetary matters. Conviction of a felony is also grounds for removal from the position.[190] The Osage Nation has a felony bar for its position of treasurer.[191] For the Fort McDowell Yavapai Nation, the treasurer must not have been convicted of a felony or a misdemeanor of moral turpitude.[192]
- **Secretary of the Nation**: the Muscogee (Creek) Nation does not permit persons with felony convictions to serve as Secretary of the Nation.[193] To serve as Secretary of the Nation of the Osage Nation, one must also have no previous felony convictions or "previous misdemeanor convictions where the underlying acts involve moral turpitude."[194] The Fort McDowell Yavapai Nation also excludes as tribal secretary any person with a felony conviction or a misdemeanor conviction involving moral turpitude.[195]
- **Coroner**: the Flandreau Santee Sioux Tribe excludes as tribal coroner any person convicted of a felony or, within the previous 1 year, a misdemeanor; it also provides for removal from the position upon conviction.[196] The Oglala Sioux Tribe has the same exclusion for its tribal coroner.[197]
- **Water administrator**: the Lummi Tribe requires that its Water Resources Manager must never have been convicted of a felony or a misdemeanor involving dishonesty.[198] The Standing Rock Sioux Tribe has a felony bar for any person serving as that tribe's Water Administrator.[199] The Assiniboine and Sioux Tribes of the Fort Peck Indian Reservation also have a Water Administrator, who enforces the tribal water resources law before the tribe's two water commissions, described above. The Fort Peck Water Administrator must never have been convicted of a criminal offense other than a traffic offense, which is a stronger exclusion than for the Lummi Tribe and Standing Rock Sioux.[200]

189 Constitution of the Comanche Nation (OK), art. 5, § 8 (1966, as amended to 2019).
190 Muscogee (Creek) Nation (OK) Tribal Code, Title 37, §§ 2-703, 2-707(B).
191 Osage Nation (OK) Tribal Code, Title 15, § 2-304(A).
192 Fort McDowell Yavapai Nation (AZ) Tribal Code, Chapter 3, § 3.5(A).
193 Muscogee (Creek) Nation (OK) Tribal Code, Title 16, § 8-102.
194 Osage Nation (OK) Tribal Code, Title 15, § 2-103(A)(2)–(3).
195 Fort McDowell Yavapai Nation (AZ) Tribal Code, Chapter 3, § 3.5(A).
196 Flandreau Santee Sioux Tribe (SD) Tribal Code, § 22-1-2(4).
197 Oglala Sioux Tribe (SD) Tribal Code, Chapter 42, § 1(d).
198 Lummi Tribe of the Lummi Reservation (WI) Tribal Code, § 17.02.020(c).
199 Standing Rock Sioux Tribe (SD) Tribal Code, § 34-1002(4).
200 Assiniboine and Sioux Tribes of the Fort Peck Indian Reservation (MT) Comprehensive Code of Justice, Title 20, § 1002(4).

Chapter 5

Restrictions on Tribal Business Licenses and Permits

Other than restrictions on running for or serving in tribal office, the most common area of collateral consequences in tribal law is in the regulation of economic activity or in occupational licensing. That tribal authorities are interested in regulating in this sphere is no surprise. In Indian Country, economic growth is often fragile and linked to federal projects, grants, or exemptions; as a result, the benefits may not distribute equitably and may reduce rather than increase economic independence.[1] By issuing licenses, governments assert control over public employment opportunities and economic benefits. Given the limited criminal jurisdiction that tribes have over non-tribal members, permits and licenses may be useful for another reason as well: applicants, including non-members, may need to consent to tribal court jurisdiction to apply for something like a tribal hunting permit.[2] Licenses and permits may therefore be a significant assertion of tribal sovereignty above and beyond the activities that they regulate.

Licensing laws are generally categorized in two types, though these may overlap in practice: revenue-raising licenses and regulatory licenses. Both may impact a person with a criminal record, intending to exclude her or him from starting a business or entering a profession.[3] This chapter includes both types. Some of these are restrictions on engaging in certain controlled economic activity (such as liquor sales, pawnbrokers, day care centers, or waste disposal) and others operate as restrictions on certain roles or professions (such as lawyers, veterinarians, or private security guards). Restrictions on natural resources licenses can be a mixture, depending on whether the license

1 Harvard Project on American Indian Economic Development, *The State of the Native Nations: Conditions Under U.S. Policies of Self-Determination* 121 (Oxford University Press, 2008).

2 Joseph Thomas Flies-Away, Carrie Garrow, & Miriam Jorgensen, "Native Nation Courts: Key Players in Nation Rebuilding," in *Rebuilding Native Nations: Strategies for Governance and Development* 115, 135 (Miriam Jorgensen, ed., University of Arizona Press, 2007).

3 Bruce E. May, "The Character Component of Occupational Licensing Laws: A Continuing Barrier to the Ex-Felon's Employment Opportunities," 71(1) *North Dakota Law Review* 187, 189 (1995).

DOI: 10.4324/9781003432548-5

is for extraction of a natural resource or for a specific role or position, such as a ceremonial hunter.

This chapter generally covers three well-regulated spheres of economic activity that require licensing, expertise, or privileged access. The first of these spheres are controlled substances like alcohol, tobacco, and cannabis, which take advantage of tribal semi-sovereignty on matters such as taxation.[4] In this, these industries are similar to gaming and casino operations explored in the next chapter. The second sphere involves licenses for natural resource extraction, either as a mode of economic development for the tribe or as a protection of a historically or culturally important activity like subsistence hunting or fishing. The other major area of occupational licensing is the practice of law before tribal courts, either as an attorney or lay advocate. The final sections of this chapter list the wide range of other collateral consequences found in occupational licensing and business permits, on par with that of a municipal or state government in the United States.

Licenses for Sales or Distribution of Controlled Substances

Because of the potential harms arising from alcohol, tobacco, and drug abuse on Indian reservations, tribal governments have established sophisticated regulatory structures for distribution and sales of controlled substances. The complexity of this area of tribal law, like gaming and casino ordinances, provides fertile ground for formal collateral consequences of criminal conviction. The alcohol mortality rate for Native Americans is as high as six times the general U.S. population, in part the legacy of destructive multigenerational alcohol cultures and practices that arose after European contact and white settlement.[5] Similarly, because of its addictive qualities tobacco use is "on a par with alcohol" as a cause of dependency and public health risks for Native American social groups, a residue of changing social and cultural contexts concerning tobacco that date back to the precontact period.[6] This section also considers the changing federal legal context of industrial hemp and medical and recreational uses of marijuana and its implications for tribal regulatory authorities.

4 Raymond I. Orr, et al., "Up in Smoke: A Tradeoff Study between Tobacco as an Economic Development Tool or Public Health Liability in an American Indian Tribe," 39(3) *American Indian Culture and Research Journal* 25, 26 (2015).

5 John W. Frank, Roland S. Moore, & Genevieve M. Ames, "Historical and Cultural Roots of Drinking Problems among American Indians," 90(3) *American Journal of Public Health* 344, 348–49 (2000).

6 Christina M. Pego, et al., "Tobacco, Culture, and Health among American Indians: A Historical Review," 19(2) *American Indian Culture and Research Journal* 143, 144 (1995).

Alcoholic Beverage Control

A search of ordinances permitting alcoholic beverage sales on tribal lands was especially fruitful. This area of tribal law has been highly regulated since the legalization of alcohol sales on reservations in 1953.[7] Federal law requires the U.S. Secretary of the Interior to approve tribal liquor ordinances and publish them in the Federal Register, which makes these ordinances more accessible to researchers than other tribal laws.[8] In 1983, the U.S. Supreme Court ruled that state liquor control authorities can require liquor licenses on tribal lands, reversing a lower court ruling that applying state liquor laws to reservations was preempted by federal law.[9] Requiring a state-approved liquor license to sell alcohol on reservations has become increasingly common since the 1960s.[10] Like tribal gaming ordinances, alcohol sales ordinances are influenced by state law to a greater degree than other areas of tribal law.

According to a 2006 survey of tribal alcohol sales ordinances in the lower 48 states, about 65% of federally recognized Indian tribes legalized alcohol sales to some degree since the end of federal prohibition on tribal alcohol sales in 1953.[11] Over that time, these ordinances also became more complex, to include tribal taxation, licensing standards, special restrictions for resorts and gaming facilities, and public health provisions, reflecting more sophisticated tribal regulatory structures.[12] Whether tribes can tax alcohol sales or have their own licensing standards has caused legal conflicts with state alcohol authorities. In 1999, the Yakama Tribe passed an alcohol sales ordinance that levied a tax and required a tribal distributor's license with a fee for any person introducing alcohol to the reservation. The State of Washington sued the tribe on the grounds that the ordinance burdens non-tribal members who sell alcohol on the reservation. A federal district judge dismissed the suit based on the wording of the ordinance.[13] Alaska provides another example of how state alcohol control laws can influence tribal lawmaking: statehood in 1959 legalized alcohol distribution and ended a previously existing policy that allowed local communities, including Alaskan Native Villages, to prohibit alcohol. However, in 1980, the state legislature reinstated the ability of unincorporated rural communities to ban the importation of alcohol. Unlike

7 Public Law 83-277 (August 15, 1953), codified at 18 U.S.C. § 1161.

8 18 U.S.C. § 1161.

9 Rice v. Rehner, 463 U.S. 713 (1983).

10 Phillip May, "Alcohol Beverage Control: A Survey of Tribal Alcohol Statutes," 5 *American Indian Law Review* 217, 220 (1977).

11 Anne E. Kovas, et al., "Survey of American Indian Alcohol Statutes, 1975–2006: Evolving Needs and Future Opportunities for Tribal Health," 69(2) *Journal of Studies on Alcohol and Drugs* 181, 186 (2008).

12 Id. at 187–88.

13 Mark T. Baker, "The Hollow Promise of Tribal Power to Control the Flow of Alcohol into Indian Country," 88(3) *Virginia Law Review* 685, 699–703 (2002).

federally recognized Indian tribes in the lower 48 states, Alaskan Native Villages may not sell alcohol without a vote of the full community (not just tribal members) but may import and distribute alcohol unless the community affirmatively passes an ordinance prohibiting this.[14]

Many tribal jurisdictions have an alcoholic beverage ordinance that excludes at least some persons with felony convictions from applying for a liquor license. These ordinances nonetheless have considerable variation. The most common exclusion is on felonies alone.[15] The Standing Rock Sioux Tribe extend the felony exclusion to the applicant and his/her spouse.[16] The Chickasaw Nation excludes from alcohol sales licenses persons with criminal convictions under alcohol licensing and gambling laws, but not other crimes.[17] The Muscogee (Creek) Nation has a similar provision.[18] The Nisqually Tribe only excludes persons convicted under laws concerning manufacturing, possession, or sale of alcoholic beverages.[19] The Pueblo of Santa Ana exclude persons convicted only of "any felony in any jurisdiction involving theft, corruption, dishonesty or embezzlement."[20] At the other end of the spectrum are ordinances that have blanket exclusions on all felonies and even some misdemeanors. The Mohegan Tribe in Connecticut excludes not only the applicant for a liquor license, but also his or her spouse, for all felonies and misdemeanors involving moral turpitude.[21] The Ponca Tribe of Nebraska excludes all persons with felony convictions or alcohol-related convictions.[22] Similarly, the Pueblo of Tesuque exclude persons with felony convictions or alcohol-related misdemeanors within the last 5 years, a provision that applies not only to liquor licenses but also to temporary event-specific permits.[23] The St. Croix Chippewa have an elaborate exclusion for felony convictions, but also for misdemeanors within the last 5 years for alcohol-related crimes, financial crimes, obstruction of justice, crimes involving children, gambling, crimes against tribal property, and crimes involving violence, theft, or bribery.[24]

Some ordinances give officials discretion to deny the liquor license for reason of prior criminal conviction. The Bay Mills Indian Community in Michigan has an ordinance stating that the Executive Council will consider

14 Matthew Berman & Teresa Hall, "Alcohol Control by Referendum in Northern Native Communities: The Alaska Local Option Law," 54(1) *Arctic* 77, 80 (2001).

15 See, e.g., Reno-Sparks Indian Colony (NV) Liquor Control Ordinance, Ordinance No. 14-A, § 5(A)(vi); Sac and Fox Tribe of the Mississippi (IA), Tribal Code, Title 21, § 21-3109(a)(4).

16 Standing Rock Sioux (SD) Tribal Code, Title 8, § 8-104(g).

17 Chickasaw Nation (OK) Tribal Code, Title 3, Chapter 2, § 3-201.7(C).

18 Muscogee (Creek) Nation (OK) Tribal Code, Title 36, Chapter 7, § 7-303(B).

19 Nisqually Indian Tribe (WA) Tribal Code, Title 29, § 29.03.04(c)(iv).

20 Pueblo of Santa Ana (NM), Liquor Ordinance (2006), § 153.

21 Mohegan Tribe of Indians (CT), Liquor Control Code, art. 5 § 3-278(a)(6).

22 Ponca Tribe of Nebraska (NE) Tribal Code, Title 16, § 16-3-9(2).

23 Pueblo of Tesuque (NM) Liquor Control Ordinance (2007), §10(C)(6) and § 12.

24 St. Croix Chippewa Indians (WI) Alcoholic Beverage Control Ordinance (2009), § 8(6).

an applicant's prior criminal record in deciding whether to issue the license, and therefore the exclusion is discretionary.[25] The Mashantucket Pequot Tribe in Connecticut also permits the tribe's land use commissioner to deny a liquor permit if the applicant has a felony conviction but does not require this.[26] The Sault Ste. Marie Tribe of Chippewa Indians requires disclosure of felony convictions, but the law does not automatically bar persons with felony convictions from receiving a license.[27]

Another collateral consequence that arises in liquor ordinances is exclusion of persons with criminal convictions from serving as liquor control authorities. In this typology, this is considered a restriction on tribal office rather than a restriction on a business license. In the Jicarilla Apache Nation, the tribe's Alcohol and Gaming Commission is responsible for liquor licenses; the liquor control ordinance excludes from membership on the Commission any person convicted of a liquor-related misdemeanor within the past five years.[28] This ordinance also excludes any person with a felony conviction or a misdemeanor conviction involving alcohol within the past 5 years from owning a 10% or greater stake in a company holding a liquor license.[29] The Ponca Tribe of Nebraska excludes from membership on its Liquor Control Board any person with a conviction in the previous 5 years of any felony or alcohol-related crime, unless he or she received a pardon or restoration of rights.[30]

Tobacco Control

Tribal tobacco control can serve as an economic development strategy for the tribe; however, like alcohol sales, greater access to tobacco is associated with a host of public health and other harms.[31] State excise taxes do not generally apply to Indian reservations and therefore, in high tax states, non-tribal buyers of cigarettes are attracted to the lower prices in reservation smoke shops, many of which now have an Internet presence.[32] The U.S. Supreme Court has ruled that tribes may collect tribal cigarette taxes from non-Indians who purchase cigarettes on the reservation.[33] However, in a separate case arising

25 Bay Mills Indian Community (MI), Ordinance Providing for the Introduction of Intoxicating Liquors (1984), § 666.
26 Mashantucket Pequot Indian Tribe (CT), Tribal Code, Title 17, Chapter 1 § 16(a).
27 Sault Ste. Marie Tribe of Chippewa Indians (MI), Tribal Code, Chapter 41, §41-302(3)(e).
28 Jicarilla Apache Nation (NM) Tribal Code, Title 18, §3(1).
29 Id., § 4(1).
30 Ponca Tribe of Nebraska (NE), Tribal Code, Title 16, Chapter 2, § 16-2-3(3).
31 Orr, et al., supra note 4 at 26–27.
32 Kari A. Samuel, Kurt M. Ribisl, & Rebecca S. Williams, "Internet Cigarette Sales and Native American Sovereignty: Political and Public Health Contexts," 33 *Journal of Public Health Policy* 173 (2012).
33 Washington v. Confederated Tribes of the Colville Reservation, 447 U.S. 134 (1980).

from New York, the Supreme Court ruled that states cannot collect state cigarette taxes on sales to tribal members, but may collect them from non-tribal members who purchase cigarettes from a tribal smoke shop.[34] Most states have not sought to tax these sales, and even in those states like New York and Oklahoma that have, tax evasion and avoidance are extremely common without a tribal-state compact that allows state excise tax on cigarettes in exchange for sharing the revenue with the tribe.[35]

Because tobacco sales are a dense area of tribal regulation, they sometimes contain formal collateral consequences, either on tobacco sales licenses or on tribal regulatory offices. The Muscogee (Creek) Nation will deny a tobacco retail permit to any applicant who was convicted of a felony.[36] The Pueblo of Acoma exclude only persons with criminal convictions related to contraband cigarettes, stolen cigarettes, or counterfeit stamps.[37] On the Salt River Reservation in Arizona, the felony bar for a cigarette license is 5 years.[38] The Flandreau Santee Sioux Tribe prohibits persons with certain criminal convictions from serving as a member of the Board of Directors of the Tobacco Product Control Authority. Those convictions include all felonies or misdemeanors within 5 years related to the manufacture, transportation, sale, and possession of tobacco and tobacco products.[39]

Cannabis Control

Cannabis control laws have been an active area of lawmaking in tribal law over the last decade. At least 25 tribes have ordinances that exclude persons with certain criminal convictions from licenses concerning the medical, recreational, research, or industrial use of hemp, cannabis, or marijuana. The 2014 Farm Bill, passed by Congress, included a pilot program to allow states and Indian tribes to cultivate industrial hemp for research purposes in states where cultivation was lawful.[40] The 2018 Farm Bill removed certain strains of the hemp plant from the federal list of controlled substances, which legalized industrial production of hemp nationwide, including on Indian

34 Department of Taxation and Finance of New York v. Milhelm Attea & Bros., 512 U.S. 61 (1994).

35 Xu Wang, et al., "Tax Avoidance and Evasion: Cigarette Purchases from Indian Reservations among US Adult Smokers, 2010–2011," 132(3) *Public Health Report* 304 (2017).

36 Muscogee (Creek) Nation (OK) Tribal Code, Title 36, § 5–115(B).

37 Pueblo of Acoma (NM) Tribal Code, § 14-7-8(G)(3).

38 Salt River Pima-Maricopa Indian Community of the Salt River Reservation (AZ) Tribal Code, Chapter 15, § 15-116(a).

39 Flandreau Santee Sioux Tribe (SD) Tribal Code, Title 33, § 33-18-8.

40 Marc Adesso, Pirjin Laser & Alex Mills, "*An Overview of Industrial Hemp Law in the United States*," 22 *U.D.C. L.* Rev. 85, 86–87 (2019) (also noting the popularity of state hemp ordinances after 2014 across 39 states).

reservations.[41] Under the 2018 Farm Bill, states or Indian tribes that want to regulate hemp production in their jurisdictions must submit a regulatory plan for approval by the U.S. Department of Agriculture (USDA).[42] USDA's final regulation on industrial hemp cultivation requires ordinances to have licensing programs that exclude individuals with previous drug convictions:

> State and Tribal plans also must prohibit any person convicted of a felony related to a controlled substance under State or Federal law from participating in the State or Tribal plan and from producing hemp for 10-years following the date of conviction. An exception applies to a person who was lawfully growing hemp [for research purposes] under the 2014 Farm Bill before December 20, 2018, and whose conviction also occurred before that date. This exemption language must be included in all State and Tribal hemp plans, whether they administered a 2014 Farm Bill research pilot program or not.[43]

If a conviction is subsequently overturned, expunged, or pardoned, however, USDA's guidance states that the criminal conviction will not bar an applicant from an industrial hemp cultivation license.[44] Because this collateral consequence is required under federal law, the distinction is imported into tribal law. For instance, the Colorado River Indian Tribes exclude from hemp production licenses anyone with felony convictions for controlled substance crimes for a period of 10 years following conviction, unless the conviction occurred before December 20, 2018, and the individual was lawfully growing hemp for research purposes under the 2014 Farm Bill.[45] Other tribal ordinances that relate to industrial hemp production are substantially similar. The Little Traverse Bay Bands of Odawa Indians makes clear that the drug felony exclusion applies to all key participants and those with ownership interests in hemp cultivation firms.[46] Some tribal ordinances have criminal conviction exclusions broader than what federal law requires. The Standing Rock Sioux Tribe has a broader 10-year bar on felonies and drug-related misdemeanor convictions, which is not limited to felonies related to controlled

41 Robert Rowe, "*What Bankers Need to Know about Fast-Moving Hemp Rules*," 112(2) American Bankers Association Banking Journal 20 (2020).
42 Id.; see generally, Sungeun Julie Kim & Jessica Roberts, "*Green Means Go: Tribes Rush to Regulate Cannabis in Indian Country*," *8 Am. Indian L.J. 255 (2019)*
43 86(11) Fed. Reg. 5596, 5606 (Jan. 29, 2021). See also, 7 C.F.R. Part 990.
44 86(11) Fed. Reg. 5596, 5613.
45 Colorado River Indian Tribes of the Colorado River Indian Reservation (AZ & CA), Agriculture Code, art 5 § 1-203(1)(ii)(g), § 1-204(1). The Yurok Tribe of the Yurok Reservation (CA) Tribal Code contains a similar exclusion at Title 22, § 22.05.150(2)–(4).
46 Little Traverse Bay Bands of Odawa Indians (MI) Tribal Code, Chapter 19, §3.

substances as required by federal law.[47] In addition, the Standing Rock Sioux Tribe does not have an exception for pre-2018 criminal convictions under the 2014 Farm Bill.[48]

Another collateral consequence related to cannabis control is the exclusion of persons with criminal convictions from appointment to tribal offices that oversee hemp cultivation. The Miccosukee Tribe in Florida disallows persons with felony or drug-related misdemeanor convictions from becoming a Hemp Control Officer, which is appointed by the Business Council to manage the hemp program.[49] The Seminole Tribe of Oklahoma excludes persons with convictions "involving breach of trust or dishonesty" from appointment to the Seminole Hemp Commission, and, more vaguely, where a person's criminal record and other past associations are a "threat to the public interest" or to "effective regulation."[50] The Winnebago Tribe of Nebraska excludes all persons with felony convictions from appointment to the Hemp Oversight and Licensing Commission.[51]

Unlike hemp, which has low levels of the chemical tetrahydrocannabinol or THC, federal law still prohibits marijuana or cannabis for medical or recreational use, though the U.S. Department of Justice issued prosecutorial guidance in 2014 (the so-called Cole Memorandum and its supplement for Indian tribes, the Wilkinson Memorandum) that deemphasized marijuana prosecutions for persons complying with rigorous state laws.[52] Tribes have taken dramatically different positions on marijuana cultivation and legalization. Some tribes, such as the Flandreau Santee Sioux Tribe in South Dakota, have moved toward legalization in states that do not allow legal marijuana, while the Navajo Nation in Arizona has resisted legalization even though Arizona and neighboring states allow medical marijuana. Other states such as California that have legalized marijuana have attempted to regulate marijuana on tribal lands.[53] The result is a complex and uncertain regulatory framework for tribes to navigate, though this has not stopped some tribes from passing comprehensive marijuana ordinances.

The exclusions for legal marijuana sales encompass appointment to tribal office, licenses for business operations, and employment. For tribal office, the Puyallup Tribe's exclusion is relatively narrow in both covered crimes and duration, excluding from the Tribal Cannabis Committee persons who have

47 Standing Rock Sioux (SD) Tribal Code, Title 43, Chapter 4, § 501(c).
48 Id. ("No application shall be granted if an applicant ... has been convicted of a state, federal, or tribal felony or drug-related misdemeanor within the last 10 years").
49 Miccosukee Tribe of Indians (FL) Hemp Plan, Chapter 4, § 30-4-3(a).
50 Seminole Nation of Oklahoma (OK) Tribal Code, Title 35, § 205.
51 Winnebago Tribe of Nebraska (NE) Tribal Code, Title 8, § 8-305(5).
52 Courtney Lewis, Confronting Cannabis: Legalization on Native Nation Lands and the Impacts of Differential Federal Enforcement, 43 Amer. Indian Q. 408, 415 (2019).
53 Id. at 425; Kim & Roberts, supra note 42 at 268–70, 273.

criminal convictions for any drug or controlled substance violations, excluding cannabis-related convictions, for a period of 7 years.[54] However, an additional exclusion on all personnel working for "cannabis-related businesses" is broader, denying employment to anyone with a "felony criminal record."[55] The Flandreau Santee Sioux Tribe also has a felony conviction bar for employees of marijuana businesses (within 5 years for felony convictions and 10 years for controlled substance convictions).[56] The Tribe has a lifelong felony conviction bar for appointees to the Marijuana Control Commission.[57] By contrast, the Suquamish Evergreen Corporation, the tribal corporation that processes and sells marijuana for the Suquamish Tribe, specifically restricts the conviction bar only to managers who "exercise control" over the corporation and not to all employees.[58] However, the list of excluded offenses is more extensive: within the past 10 years, any felony or any crime involving dishonesty, with the latter category including forgery, counterfeiting, fraud, theft, embezzlement, tax evasion, perjury, bribery, obstruction of justice, mail fraud, and related crimes.[59] The Picayune Rancheria of Chukchansi Indians will deny a cannabis license to anyone convicted of a felony offense or, in the preceding 10 years, of a non-cannabis-related misdemeanor. The tribe also excludes anyone with a conviction for theft or embezzlement, regardless of whether it was a felony or a misdemeanor.[60]

Not all tribes attach collateral consequences to marijuana licenses directly. After Michigan legalized recreational marijuana by referendum in November 2018, the Sault Ste. Marie Tribe of Chippewa Indians passed a commercial marijuana ordinance that requires applicants to have a marijuana license from the state, even though it was not required to do so under the state law.[61] Although the ordinance does not exclude persons with criminal convictions from receiving a tribal license, collateral consequences may attach under state law since a background check from the state licensing authority is required.[62] On the other hand, the Shoalwater Bay Indian Tribe in Washington does not exclude persons with criminal convictions from business licenses to

54 Puyallup Tribe of the Puyallup Reservation (WA) Tribal Code, § 14.08.030.
55 Id. at § 14.08.080.
56 Flandreau Santee Sioux Tribe (SD) Tribal Code, § 29-3-5(c).
57 Id. at § 29-9-1(d).
58 Suquamish Indian Tribe of the Port Madison Reservation (WA) Tribal Code, § 11.10.10(c).
59 Id. at § 11.10.10(c)(1)–(2).
60 Picayune Rancheria of Chukchansi Indians, Commercial Cannabis Ordinance, § 10.4(A).
61 Sierra Clark, "*Tribe Authorizes Marijuana Business*," *Record Eagle* (Aug. 29, 2021); Joey Boomgaard, "*Leveraging Tribal Sovereignty Gives Cannabis Firm Entry to Off-Limits Michigan Markets*," *MiLive.com* (Aug. 2, 2020).
62 Sault Ste. Marie Tribe of Chippewa Indians (MI) Tribal Code, Chapter 47, §§ 47.104(3) (application requirements); 47.108 (revocation).

sell recreational marijuana because it does not require such licenses at all.[63] Another option is to leave the collateral consequence to the discretion of a tribal official. For the Confederated Tribes of the Warm Springs Reservation in Oregon, the Executive Director of the tribe's Cannabis Commission may deny a permit to cultivate marijuana for a previous criminal conviction, "if the conviction is substantially related to the fitness and ability of the applicant to lawfully carry out activities under the permit."[64] However, the Executive Director may only consider convictions within the past 2 years under federal felony statutes, and only of offenders with a previous conviction; she or he may not consider prior possession of marijuana.[65]

In states where medical marijuana is legal, tribes may have restrictions on who is eligible not only for a license to sell medical marijuana, but also a license to buy it. The Pyramid Lake Paiute Tribe in Nevada excludes all persons with convictions for an "excluded felony offense," defined as a felony conviction for "distribution of a controlled substance," from receiving a marijuana registry identification card, operating a medical marijuana establishment, or serving as a medical marijuana business agent.[66] Reno-Sparks Indian Colony, also in Nevada, has a similar medical marijuana ordinance as the Pyramid Lake Paiute, encompassing issuing medical marijuana cards, authorizing business agents, and operating a medical marijuana-related business. However, unlike the Pyramid Lake Paiute, its definition of "excluded felony offense" is not restricted to drug convictions; here, the term is defined as a felony conviction for any offense that would be a Class A felony in the state of Nevada or for two or more felony convictions, excluding criminal offenses for which the individual completed incarceration or supervision more than 10 years prior.[67]

Perhaps the most novel aspect of tribal marijuana laws are expungements for marijuana convictions. The Arapaho Tribe of the Wind River Reservation dropped all pending charges and expunged all previous convictions from the tribal court for personal use of marijuana.[68] Other jurisdictions created a petition process to expunge marijuana possession convictions. The Mashantucket Pequot Tribe states that any person convicted of possession of

63 Shoalwater Bay Indian Tribe (WA) Code of Laws, § 10A.2.07 (explaining no entity or employment license required).
64 Confederated Tribes of the Warm Springs Reservation (OR) Tribal Code, § 703.405(4).
65 Id. at § 703.405(5).
66 Pyramid Lake Paiute Tribe (NV) Tribal Code, Chapter 16, §§ 3.16.104, 3.16.225(1), 3.16.322(3), 3.16.332(4), 3.16, 342(1). The restriction on business agents also excludes persons who completed a term of probation, incarceration, or supervised release within the preceding 5 years. Id. at § 3.16.332(4)(a).
67 Reno-Sparks Indian Colony (NV) Tribal Code, Ordinance 61, §§ 61.1.104, 61.1.225(1), 61.1.322(3), 61.1.332(4), 61.1.342(1), 61.1.843(5).
68 Arapaho Tribe of the Wind River Reservation (WY) Tribal Code, Title 24, § 205(a)–(b).

small amounts of a "cannabis-type substance" may petition the tribal court for erasure of the conviction.[69] The Nez Perce Tribe also has proposed an ordinance to expunge convictions for possessing less than 40 grams of marijuana or marijuana paraphernalia.[70] On the other hand, some tribes have moved in the opposite direction, making collateral consequences irreversible. The Tohono O'odham Nation of Arizona states that the repeat offense of delivering marijuana to a minor is "not … eligible for suspension or commutation of sentence, probation, pardon or parole or release on any other basis."[71]

Natural Resource Permits

Like questions of controlled substances, management of natural resources on Indian reservations involves a complex interaction of federal, state, and tribal law. Generally, tribal governments have the authority to tax tribal members for extraction of natural resources; tribes also may zone their own land for specific purposes, though in portions of reservations that are primarily demographically non-Indian state and county zoning may apply.[72] Whether state governments can regulate non-tribal members on tribal lands depends on whether the federal government has preempted jurisdiction through comprehensive legislative or regulatory policy. For instance, the federal government has regulated timber harvesting and mineral extraction, preempting state taxation and oversight without the approval of the U.S. Secretary of the Interior.[73] The U.S. Supreme Court has also ruled that owing to the historical importance of hunting and fishing, tribal jurisdictions had exclusive authority to regulate hunting and fishing for both tribal and non-tribal members on lands owned by or held in trust for the tribe.[74] For water rights, tribes have authority to regulate uses of water where doing so has no impact off the tribal lands, but states can regulate excess water uses on the reservation by non-Indians.[75] Though the jurisdictional landscape is complex, tribes have significant authority to regulate natural resources on their own lands. These tribal legal and regulatory frameworks are also a dense area of collateral

69 Mashantucket Pequot Indian Tribe (MA) Tribal Code, Title 2, Chapter 2, § 1(d).
70 Nez Perce Tribe (ID) Tribal Code, § 2.10.57 (proposed).
71 Tohono O'odham Nation (AZ) Tribal Code, Title 7, Chapter 13.5(C).
72 Mary Beth West, "Natural Resources Development on Indian Reservations: Overview of Tribal, State, and Federal Jurisdiction," 17(1) *American Indian Law Review* 71, 88–91 (1992); Brendale v. Confederated Tribes & Bands of Yakima Indian Nation, 492 U.S. 408 (1989).
73 West, supra note 72 at 92.
74 Montana v. United States, 450 U.S. 544 (1981).
75 West, supra note 72 at 97–98.

consequences, both for licensing or permits to extract natural resources and in tribal regulatory offices that govern natural resource management.

Many tribes deny fishing, hunting, shellfish, grazing, or other licenses to persons for convictions of certain crimes. The Pueblo of Santa Ana will deny a hunting permit to any tribal member who has been convicted of a felony or battery against a family member. The tribal governor may also revoke a hunting permit for up to 5 years for hunting convictions under federal, state, or tribal law.[76] The Yankton Sioux Tribe authorizes suspension or revocation of hunting or fishing privileges for up to 5 years for violations of its Hunting, Fishing, and Outdoor Recreation Code. Criminal offenses that may result in forfeiting the license include taking game during closed season, exceeding catch quotas, unlawful fishing, unlawful possession of a license, and similar offenses.[77] The Swinomish Indian Tribe may revoke fishing privileges for "good cause," defined as any three fishing-related violations in 3 years, conviction of a felony, conviction for failure to appear in a fish and game citation hearing, conviction for assault of an enforcement officer, conviction for reckless disregard for others while fishing, or conviction of wasteful practices.[78]

In another jurisdiction, the Puyallup Tribe, persons with shellfish-related convictions in other jurisdictions are disallowed from receiving shellfish privileges under tribal law, until the entire sentence has been served including any post-incarceration supervision. The tribe does not provide for review or appeal of this denial, unless the conviction was for a good faith exercise of a protected tribal treaty right.[79] This reference to "protected tribal treaty right" is important, because it relates to the "Fish-In" civil rights protests of the 1960s. In 1964, the National Indian Youth Council launched fish-in protests primarily across the Pacific Northwest to protest arrests of Native fishermen by Washington State game officials. The protestors argued that federal treaties with the tribes guaranteed fishing privileges, even out of season. The episode was one of the first examples of inter-tribal civil disobedience and a precursor to the Red Power Movement of the 1970s.[80]

In a few jurisdictions, collateral bars for hunting and fishing licenses may extend to non-Indian spouses of tribal members. The Nooksack Tribe has restrictions for both shellfish and fishing privileges. A violation of the shellfish ordinance may result in suspension or revocation of shellfish licenses.[81] The tribe has a more complex and harsher restriction on spousal fishing

76 Pueblo of Santa Ana (NM) Hunting, Fishing, and Trapping Regulations, art. 3, §§ 1.0, 7.0(A).
77 Yankton Sioux Tribe (SD) Tribal Code, §§ 11-7-090, 11-11-020(B).
78 Swinomish Indian Tribe (WA) Tribal Code, § 18-03.100(B).
79 Puyallup Tribe (WA) Tribal Code, § 12.12.160.
80 Bradley G. Shreve, "'From Time Immemorial': The Fish-In Movement and the Rise of Intertribal Activism," 78(3) *Pacific Historical Review* 403 (2009).
81 Nooksack Indian Tribe (WA) Shellfish Ordinance, § 11-108.

privileges that even extends to spouses. A non-Indian person may receive a fishing permit after 2 years of marriage to a tribal member who also has a fishing permit. Spousal fishing permits are automatically revoked upon divorce or upon suspension of the tribal member's permit. Any spouse who violates the fishing regulations will have the permit permanently revoked for life: "[t]his penalty is mandatory; the Court does not have the authority to reduce, waive, or suspend the lifetime revocation." In addition, the tribe imposes a legal responsibility on tribal members whose spouses have fishing permits. If a non-member spouse is convicted of a criminal or civil offense under the fishing ordinance, the tribal member loses his or her fishing license for 1 calendar year.[82] The Pokagon Band of Potawatomi Indians also extends collateral consequences to spouses of tribal members but does not automatically revoke a spouse's rights under the ordinance to criminal convictions committed by the other spouse. The Band will revoke the hunting or fishing licenses of a trial member or non-member spouse for 1 year and bar reapplication for licenses for an additional 1 year for illegal killing, possessing, or transporting a wild animal. A subsequent conviction results in a 3-year bar.[83]

In Washington State, subsistence hunting on open and unclaimed lands is a right protected by treaty between the federal government and the tribal nations at the time of statehood.[84] These tribes have "designated hunter" licenses to allow a tribal hunter to harvest an animal for an elder or a family member who cannot themselves hunt. Traditional tribal hunters are filling a public service role not a personal one.[85] At least six Washington State tribes attach collateral consequences of criminal conviction to "designated hunter" status. The Lower Elwha Tribal Community excludes from designated hunter status any person with a tribal or state hunting conviction for a period of 2 years, or any person who is prohibited from carrying a firearm.[86] The Port Gamble S'Klallam Tribe and Suquamish Indian Tribe have an identical exclusion as the Lower Elwha.[87] Using simpler phrasing, the Puyallup Tribe excludes from "designated hunter" status any person with a hunting

82 Id. at §§ 30.02.040, 30.10.040, 30.10.050.

83 Pokagon Band of Potawatomi Indians (MI) Tribal Code, § 10.04(a).

84 Northwest Indian Fisheries Commission, "Treaty Hunting Rights FAQ," https://nwifc.org/about-us/wildlife/treaty-hunting-rights-faq (last accessed June 18, 2022).

85 Id.; Scott M. McCorquodale, "*Cultural Contexts of Recreational Hunting and Native Subsistence and Ceremonial Hunting: Their Significance for Wildlife Management," 25(2) Wildlife Soc. Bull. 568, 570 (1997).*

86 Lower Elwha Tribal Community (WA) Treaty Hunting Ordinance, § 1.1.12(2)(D)–(E); Suquamish Indian Tribe (WA) Tribal Code, § 14.3.6(b).

87 Port Gamble S'Klallam Tribe (WA) Tribal Code, § 18.01.13(4)–(5).

conviction in the previous 2 years.[88] The exclusions for the Skokomish Indian Tribe and Snoqualmie Indian Tribe are the same as that for the Puyallup Tribe.[89]

At least two tribes attach collateral consequences to grazing permits. The Oglala Sioux Tribe will deny a grazing permit to any person who was convicted of a felony or misdemeanor related to land or land use, convictions for theft of livestock, or violations of the grazing ordinance.[90] The Pueblo of Santa Ana will suspend or cancel grazing permits for persons who have three or more violations of the tribe's livestock code, in addition to any penalties from the tribal court.[91]

Practice of Law and Legal Representation

Tribal codes may regulate attorney licensing at tribal trial and appellate courts and the appointment of lay advocates. For attorneys, this is often a matter of reciprocity with lawyers licensed in the state where the tribe is located or sometimes in other states.[92] Collateral consequences may be imposed by the tribe, but often are more likely to be imported from the rules of the state bar. Unlike most state and federal courts, tribal courts rely more heavily on lay advocates to represent clients, especially in rural areas where licensed attorneys are in short supply. Lay advocates, who are often tribal members, may also have greater expertise in languages, traditions, or customs that attorneys may not have.[93] To that end, many tribes apply ethical rules to lay advocates as well, which may contain exclusions for certain criminal convictions.

Lawyer Licensing

For licensed attorneys, collateral consequences of conviction may not be directly stated in tribal law as the tribe may reciprocally license lawyers from other jurisdictions. The Rosebud Sioux Tribe, for instance, historically admitted law-trained attorneys who were licensed to practice law in South Dakota or before the highest court of any other state or the U.S. Supreme Court. However, in 1995, the tribe authorized its first bar examination to specifically test tribal and federal Indian law. The tribe also created the Sicangu

88 Puyallup Tribe (WA) Tribal Code, § 12.08.220(d).
89 Skokomish Indian Tribe (WA) Tribal Code, § 7.03.014(d); Snoqualmie Indian Tribe (WA) Tribal Council Act 6.3, An Act Relating to Hunting and Gathering, § 6.6(c)(iv).
90 Oglala Sioux Tribe (SD) Tribal Code, Chapter 35, § 15.
91 Pueblo of Santa Ana (NM) Tribal Code, § 16-3-6(E).
92 Frank Pommerschein, "Tribal Court Jurisprudence: A View from the Field," 21(1) *Vermont Law Review* 7, 13–14 (1996).
93 Lauren van Schilfgaarde, "Indigenizing Professional Responsibility: The Role of Ethics in Tribal Courts," 59(2) *Judges Journal* 6, 10 (2020).

Oyate Bar Association to regulate continuing legal education, judicial qualifications, and disciplinary standards.[94] Many tribal courts, by contrast, still reciprocally license attorneys who are licensed in other tribal, state, or federal jurisdictions.

Besides importing collateral consequences from other licensing jurisdictions, some tribes are more restrictive and have special rules that exclude persons with certain criminal convictions from representing clients in tribal court. The Mohegan Tribe of Indians and the Upper Sioux Community of Minnesota have a simple felony exclusion for attorneys practicing before the tribal court.[95] The Sisseton-Wahpeton Oyate of the Lake Traverse Reservation also has a felony exclusion for tribal court practice unless the attorney has received a pardon or restoration of rights.[96] The Shoshone Tribe of the Wind River Reservation licenses attorneys to practice law so long as they do not have felony convictions or misdemeanor convictions involving moral turpitude.[97] In a slightly different formulation, the Hoh Indian Tribe allows attorneys to practice by motion before the tribal court, so long as they have not been convicted in the past year of a felony or a misdemeanor.[98] The Mashpee Wampanoag Tribe has a softer exclusion. There, applicants for admission to the tribal bar must certify that they have not been charged with or investigated for a felony or misdemeanor other than minor traffic charges. If the applicant is unable to do so, he or she may request a meeting with the chief judge to determine whether the applicant is of good character and qualified to practice.[99]

A more complex provision is found in the laws of several Great Plains tribes. The Kickapoo Tribe of Indians in Kansas, Pawnee Nation, Seminole Nation of Oklahoma, and Wyandotte Nation automatically suspend from the practice of law any attorney who is convicted of a felony or any crime punishable by banishment or involving moral turpitude. If the attorney is disciplined in another jurisdiction, disqualification is reciprocal unless the attorney can show that the disciplinary procedure in the other jurisdiction was lacking in notice, due process, or evidence.[100] Other tribes frame

94 Pommerschein, supra note 92 at 13–14.

95 Mohegan Tribe of Indians (CT) Tribal Code, Article 1, § 1-37(a); Upper Sioux Community (MN) Judicial Code, Chapter 6, § 4.

96 Sisseton-Wahpeton Oyate of the Lake Traverse Reservation (SD) Tribal Code, Chapter 32, § 1-1(5).

97 Shoshone Tribe of the Wind River Reservation (WY) Tribal Code, § 1-5-1(3).

98 Hoh Indian Tribe (WA) Tribal Code, § 1.8.16(c).

99 Mashpee Wampanoag Tribe (MA) Administrative Order #20, Admission to Tribal Court Bar Amended, § 5(f).

100 Kickapoo Tribe of Indians (KS) Tribal Code, Title 2, Appendix: Rules Relating to Attorneys and Lay Advocates, Rule 106(k); Pawnee Nation of Oklahoma (OK) Tribal Code, Title 1, Attorney and Lay Advocate Rules, Rule 101(k); Seminole Nation of Oklahoma (OK) Attorney and Lay Advocate Rules, Rule 102(c); Wyandotte Nation (OK) Attorneys and Lay Advocates Rules, Rule 101(k).

their collateral consequences for legal representatives not as a qualification to practice but as a removal procedure. The Coushatta Tribe of Louisiana authorizes discipline or disbarment for any licensed attorney who commits a felony or a misdemeanor of moral turpitude.[101] The Nez Perce Tribe authorizes suspension or disbarment for any attorney found guilty of a felony.[102]

Lay Advocates

The role of lay advocates in tribal court is more expansive than in non-tribal jurisdictions. In 2000, a survey by the American Indian Law Center found that 75.6% of tribal courts surveyed employed lay advocates who are trained in law but not licensed as an attorney. Many of these lay advocates are community members with low turnover and deep institutional knowledge of tribal law and custom.[103] As a result of their ubiquity across Indian Country, many tribes have enacted regulations to govern the conduct and ethical obligations of lay advocates. For instance, the Sault Ste. Marie Tribe of Chippewa Indians requires a lay advocate to be 21 years old with a high school diploma, have some legal training or experience and knowledge of tribal customs, and possess good character and fitness.[104] Other tribes may require an examination process or payment of fees. Helping to professionalize this role, certificate programs for lay advocates have appeared at Sitting Bull College, National Tribal Trial College at University of Wisconsin Law School, and Lac Courte Oreilles Ojibwe Community College.[105] Legal aid or law school clinics may also allow law students to represent clients in tribal court under the supervision of a licensed attorney.[106]

101 Coushatta Tribe of Louisiana (LA) Judicial Codes, § 1.7.07.

102 Nez Perce Tribe (ID) Tribal Code, § 1-1-37(a).

103 Lindsay Cutler, "Tribal Sovereignty, Tribal Court Legitimacy and Public Defense," 63(6) *UCLA Law Review* 1752, 1800–01 (2016).

104 Danielle J. Mayberry & Carrie E. Garrow, "A Portrait of Tribal Courts: Tribal Court Tools and Levers to Ensure Procedural Fairness for Self-Represented Litigants," 23(2) *Journal of Appellate Practice and Process* 221, 259 (2023).

105 Joe Morey, "LCO College Offers New Program to Provide Lay Advocates to Tribal Court," *LCO Tribe News and Information* (June 3, 2019), https://www.lcotribe.com/post/lco-college-offers-new-program-to-provide-lay-advocates-to-tribal-court; W.L. Shelley, "Training Tribal Lay Advocates at Sitting Bull College," 27(2) *Tribal College: Journal of American Indian Higher Education* (Nov. 8, 2015), https://tribalcollegejournal.org/training-tribal-lay-advocates-at-sitting-bull-college; University of Wisconsin Law School Division of Extension, National Tribal Trial College, "Certificate in Tribal Court Legal Advocacy," https://nttc.extension.wisc.edu (last accessed Dec. 12, 2023).

106 Aliza G. Organick, "Creating a Tribal Law Practice Clinic in Kansas: Carving the Peg to Fit the Hole," 82(3) *North Dakota Law Review* 849 (2006) (describing tribal law clinics at University of New Mexico, University of Washington, and University of Arizona, among others).

For lay representatives, who are not licensed attorneys, tribal jurisdictions do not "import" credentials the way they might with reciprocal attorney licensing. These decisions must be made on a case-by-case basis by the tribal court itself. The Pokagon Band of Potawatomi Indians, Confederated Salish and Kootenai Tribes, and Coushatta Tribe of Louisiana have a simple exclusion for felony convictions for any lay representative.[107] The Picayune Rancheria of Chukchansi Indians prevents from serving as a lay advocate any person with a felony conviction or, within the last 5 years, a misdemeanor conviction other than a traffic offense.[108] Some tribes have the same exclusions for attorneys and lay representatives, or do not distinguish between them. The Mississippi Band of Choctaw Indians has an identical prohibition for both attorneys and lay advocates on felony convictions or misdemeanor convictions within the previous 1 year.[109] Reno-Sparks Indian Colony does not distinguish between attorneys and lay representatives. In that jurisdiction, any personal representative may appear before tribal court so long as he or she has never been convicted of a crime in the previous year.[110] The Washoe Tribe makes a distinction between lay advocates who are members of federally recognized Indian tribes and those who are not. In that tribe, attorneys who are licensed to practice in another state may practice in the Washoe tribal courts so long as they have never been convicted of a felony or, within the past year, of a gross misdemeanor. Lay advocates who are members of federally recognized Indian tribes may be admitted so long as they have not been convicted of a felony. Lay advocates who are not tribal members may be admitted at the discretion of the Chief Judge so long as they have not been convicted of a felony or, within the past year, of a gross misdemeanor.[111] The Pueblo of Laguna may temporarily authorize to practice before the tribal court a person who is not a licensed attorney but who has 1 year of legal experience or 1 year of legal training, so long as he or she has not been convicted of a felony in the past 3 years.[112] This rule would also allow paralegals or current law students to practice before tribal courts.

107 Pokagon Band of Potawatomi Indians (MI) Tribal Court Code, No. 10-21-2002, § 13(B); Confederated Salish and Kootenai Tribes (MT) Tribal Code, § 1-2-506(2); Coushatta Tribe of Louisiana (LA) Judicial Codes, § 1.7.02(d).
108 Picayune Rancheria of Chukchansi Indians (CA) Tribal Court Ordinance, § 9.3(c)(2).
109 Mississippi Band of Choctaw Indians (MS) Tribal Code, §§ 1-4-2(2), 1-4-3(2).
110 Reno-Sparks Indian Colony (NV) Tribal Code, § 1-80-030(a)(2).
111 Washoe Tribe of Nevada and California (NV) Law and Order Code, Tribal Court Rules, § 2, Rule 1(b).
112 Pueblo of Laguna (NM) Tribal Code, § 5-3-1(B).

Blanket Exclusions on Business Operations

Though uncommon, a tribe may have a blanket exclusion for persons with criminal convictions from doing any business with the tribe whatsoever. The Navajo Nation has an expansive provision that applies to any business organization or individual who seeks to do business with the tribe in any capacity (contractor, grantee, broker, dealer, supplier, and so on) or who seeks a contract, purchase order, direct payment, lease, loan, or permit of any kind. This provision excludes anyone with a criminal conviction within the previous 10 years for "embezzlement, theft, forgery, bribery, falsification or destruction of records, receiving stolen property, or committing a criminal offense relating to obtaining a public/private contract or in the performance of such contract."[113] However, the tribe has a waiver process to restore eligibility for potential business partners and suppliers if the ineligibility is caused by unpaid debt to the tribe.[114] The Code also permits a potential business partner an opportunity for a written appeal against a finding of ineligibility, to be determined by a hearing officer within 30 days.[115]

Other Restrictions on Business Licenses and Permits

Tribal jurisdictions have an array of other exclusions for business licenses or permits to applicants with criminal convictions. In general, these are far less common than the ones mentioned above, but they illustrate the diversity and breadth of collateral consequences of this type:

General business license: some tribes have a blanket exclusion for preventing persons with criminal convictions from operating any business. The Standing Rock Sioux Tribe prevents individuals, directors or officers of a corporation, or majority or controlling shareholders from receiving a business license for certain criminal convictions within the previous 5 years, to include felony convictions involving fraud, misrepresentation, conversion, or dishonesty, and any other convictions for unfair or unscrupulous business practices.[116]

Labor or collective bargaining license: the Muscogee (Creek) Nation requires licenses for labor organizations, defined as committees or unions representing employees in their negotiations with management, to conduct business or perform services.[117] As a condition of obtaining these licenses, neither the principals nor the officers may have a previous felony

113 Navajo Nation (AZ) Tribal Code, Title 12, Chapter 15, § 1505.
114 Id. at § 1506(B).
115 Id. at § 1508(A).
116 Standing Rock Sioux Tribe (SD) Tribal Code, § 16-407.
117 Muscogee (Creek) Nation (OK) Tribal Code, Title 37, Chapter 8.

conviction.[118] The Nisqually Indian Tribe has a felony exclusion for licenses for agents of labor organizations, unless their civil rights have been restored.[119] The Squaxin Island Tribe prohibits licenses for agents of labor organizations who have been convicted of a crime of dishonesty or moral turpitude.[120]

Handgun sales permit: the Eastern Band of Cherokee Indians has a prohibition on sales permits for handguns to persons with previous felony convictions.[121]

Pawnbrokers permit: the Eastern Band of Cherokee Indians also has a prohibition on pawnbrokers permits for persons with previous felony convictions, but unlike the handgun sales permits, this only applies to felonies within the last 10 years.[122] The Navajo Nation also prohibits persons with felony convictions from receiving a pawnbroker permit, but with no sunset date.[123]

Solid waste disposal permit: several tribes restrict the ability of a person with a criminal conviction to receive a permit to dispose of solid waste, such as debris from demolition or construction. The Apache Tribe of Oklahoma prohibits persons with felony convictions from receiving solid waste disposal permits from the Apache Tribe Environmental Program.[124] The Northern Cheyenne Tribe and the Snoqualmie Indian Tribe also have an exclusion on solid waste disposal permits for persons convicted of felonies or with felony charges pending.[125]

Motor vehicle parts recycler license: the Confederated Tribes of the Chehalis Reservation require business licenses for recyclers of motor vehicle parts. This tribe excludes persons with felony convictions from these licenses and allows the planning department discretion to deny an application for a misdemeanor conviction.[126]

Sports license: the Mississippi Band of Choctaw Indians licenses boxing announcers, booking agents, matchmakers, promoters, and referees. These licenses, granted by the tribe's boxing commission, have a vague exclusion for any applicant who has been convicted of "a violation of any applicable state, Tribal, or federal statutes," presumably including crimes

118 Id. at § 8-103(B).
119 Nisqually Indian Tribe (WA) Tribal Code, § 26.05.01(c)(i).
120 Squaxin Island Tribe (WA) Tribal Code, § 12.09.030(C)(2).
121 Eastern Band of Cherokee Indians (NC) Tribal Code, § 144-2.
122 Id. at § 91-2.
123 Navajo Nation (AZ) Tribal Code, Title 5, Chapter 7, Subchapter 5, § 1140(b).
124 Apache Tribe (OK) Solid Waste Code, § 606(b)(G).
125 Northern Cheyenne Tribe of the Northern Cheyenne Indian Reservation (MT) Solid Waste Code, § 6-2(8)(C); Snoqualmie Indian Tribe (WA) Act Relating to Solid Waste Management, Tribal Council Act 6.2, § 17.1(b)(9)(C).
126 Confederated Tribes of the Chehalis Reservation (OR) Tribal Code, § 9.05.110.

like match-fixing.[127] Whether the exclusion reaches beyond these types of offenses is not clear from the wording.

License for door-to-door sales: the Nottawaseppi Huron Band of the Potawatomi Indians requires individuals who sell goods door-to-door or from a temporary location to have a solicitor's license. This license requires disclosure of any convictions in the previous 10 years for any crime, including misdemeanors, gross misdemeanors, or criminal ordinance violations. In addition, the Chief of Police is authorized to deny permits to any person convicted of a sex offense or, within the previous 10 years, any misdemeanor or felony related to the occupation of the vendor, such as those involving moral turpitude, fraud, or misrepresentation.[128] The Tulalip Tribes of Washington also requires a peddler's license for persons engaged in door-to-door sales. This provision is virtually identical to the one by the Nottawaseppi Huron Band, except that sex offenses is changed to "child molestation and/or rape" and the denial by the Tax and License Division is not discretionary.[129]

Amusement license: the Salt River Pima-Maricopa Indian Community of Arizona requires amusement licenses for carnivals and other entertainment-related events. Applicants must not have been convicted of a felony within the previous 5 years.[130] Interestingly, this tribe has a blanket exclusion on all licenses or permits for anyone with a felony conviction within the past 5 years "unless such person has been pardoned by appropriate authority or has had his or her civil rights restored under [the] appropriate statute."[131] However, the amusement license does not contain this provision for pardons or restoration of rights.

Private security guard license: the Sault Ste. Marie Tribe of Chippewa Indians requires private security guards to have licenses. These licenses exclude any person who has a felony conviction or, within the previous 5 years, any misdemeanor conviction concerning dishonesty, fraud, disclosure of private information, impersonation of a law enforcement officer, illegal use or possession of a dangerous weapon, controlled substances, or two or more alcohol-related offenses.[132]

Veterinary license: the Navajo Nation's veterinary board may revoke a veterinary license for conviction of "a felony or other crime involving moral turpitude in the practice of veterinary medicine."[133]

127 Mississippi Band of Choctaw Indians (MS) Tribal Code, § 27-1-7(1)(a)(iii).
128 Nottawaseppi Huron Band of Potawatomi Indians (MI) Tribal Code, §§ 8-13.4(B)(7), 8-13.5(B)(3)–(4).
129 Tulalip Tribes of Washington (WA) Tribal Code, §§ 10.10.070(2)(a)(7), 10.10.070(3)(b).
130 Salt River Pima-Maricopa Indian Community (AZ) Tribal Code, § 15-153.
131 Id. at § 15-33.
132 Sault Ste. Marie Tribe of Chippewa Indians (MI) Tribal Code, § 49.401(1)(c)–(d).
133 Navajo Nation (AZ) Tribal Code, Chapter 7, § 1022.

Bail bond license: the Eastern Band of Cherokee Indians prohibits individuals with felony convictions or convictions for controlled substances from receiving a license to serve as a bail bondsman or a runner working for the bondsman.[134]

Consumer credit license: the Eastern Band of Cherokee Indians will deny a consumer credit license to a check cashing servicer who has been convicted of a felony or any misdemeanor involving fraud, misrepresentation, or deceit.[135]

Fuel distributor's license: the Navajo Nation requires persons importing and selling fuel to pay an excise tax and have a license issued by the Tax Commission, conditional on not having a felony conviction within the previous 10 years.[136]

Manufactured housing license: the Navajo Nation does not permit individuals with convictions for felonies or offenses involving moral turpitude to receive a license or certificate of qualification to build, sell, or repair manufactured housing.[137]

Consumer financial services license: the Pueblo of Pojoaque require licenses to perform consumer financial services, excluding owners, partners, or other management officials of financial services firms who have a felony conviction or a conviction for breach of trust or dishonesty within the previous 10 years.[138]

Day care center license: the Mohegan Tribe of Connecticut has a complex exclusion for childhood day care centers. This provision excludes as licensees any person convicted of a felony involving physical force, cruelty, injuring or impairing the morals of children, abandonment of children, or any felony in which the victim was under 18.[139] The Swinomish Indian Tribal Community also requires a license for day care centers, which is denied or revoked for convictions related to child abuse or physical harm to another person or felony convictions "reasonably related to the competency of the person" to meet the standards of the license.[140]

134 Eastern Band of Cherokee Indians (NC) Tribal Code, § 58-5(c). See also, Cherokee One Feather, "Cherokee Code Discussion: Bondsmen, Bail Bonds, and Forfeiture" (January 13, 2022), https://theonefeather.com/2022/01/13/cherokee-code-discussion-bondsmen-bail-bonds-and-forfeiture.
135 Eastern Band of Cherokee Indians (NC) Tribal Code, § 53-22(a)(6).
136 Navajo Nation (AZ) Tribal Code, Title 21, Chapter 9, § 911(C)(1).
137 Id. at Title 5, Chapter 8, § 1311(I).
138 Pueblo of Pojoaque (NM) Tribal Code, Subpart R, § R-2(e)(3)(A)(ii).
139 Mohegan Tribe of Indians (CT) Tribal Code, Article 8, § 19a-87a(a).
140 Swinomish Indian Tribal Community (WA) Tribal Code, § 15-01.110(B)(1).

Chapter 6

Restrictions in the Tribal Gaming Industry

Though their impact is uneven across Indian Country, gaming enterprises are major sources of economic development for Indian reservations, providing employment for tribal members and revenue for tribal authorities.[1] The industry has grown exponentially. In 1988, total revenue from Indian gaming was $100 million. This increased to $26.5 billion in 2009, though more than a third of Indian casinos earn less than $10 million per year and just 20 facilities account for more than 40% of the total earnings.[2] The Indian gaming industry has existed since the 1960s. However, not until 1987 in *California v. Cabazon Band of Mission Indians* did the U.S. Supreme Court definitively prevent state encroachment into tribal sovereignty to regulate gaming.[3] Under pressure from state governments, Congress passed the Indian Gaming Regulatory Act (IGRA) in 1988, which created the National Indian Gaming Commission (NIGC). Under the IGRA, states must negotiate in good faith with tribes to legalize casinos, bingo halls, lotteries, or other gaming facilities on Indian reservations. Under these Tribal-State Gaming Compacts, tribes may be required to share revenues with the state or provide state gaming officials some oversight over casino operations.[4] If a compromise cannot be reached, the IGRA authorizes mediation between the tribe and the state; if that fails, the U.S. Secretary of the Interior may override state objections and legalize tribal gaming.[5]

Under the IGRA, once tribes have negotiated Tribal-State Compacts with their state governments, they must submit a tribal gaming ordinance to the NIGC. Because gaming and casinos may involve large amounts of unregulated money, especially cash, Congress had an interest in preventing money

1 Harvard Project on American Indian Economic Development, *The State of the Native Nations: Conditions Under U.S. Policies of Self-Determination* 145 (OUP 2008).
2 Stephen L. Pevar, *The Rights of Indians and Tribes* 275 (OUP, 4th ed., 2012).
3 Id. at 276; California v. Cabazon Band of Mission Indians, 480 U.S. 202 (1987).
4 Pevar, supra note 2 at 281.
5 Id. at 278–79.

DOI: 10.4324/9781003432548-6

laundering and organized crime through background checks and other hiring provisions.[6] Collateral consequences in the gaming industry reflect the overall pattern in other areas of tribal law: they are most likely to attach to tribal legal privileges, offices, and benefits, which are clearly under tribal control, rather than to tribal social services or civil rights. In the 313 gaming ordinances reviewed here, collateral consequences generally manifest through restrictions on tribal gaming regulatory offices, gaming licensing, employment in the gaming industry, or third-party contracts. Under the IGRA, the tribe must issue gaming licenses to primary management officials (PMOs) and key officers or employees (KOs), the terms used in the Act, which require background checks.[7] However, neither the IGRA nor Title 25, Part 556 of the Code of Federal Regulations specifically exclude persons with criminal convictions from serving as PMOs and KOs; rather, consideration of previous criminal convictions is part of the background check process and left to the discretion of the tribal gaming authorities in conjunction with state regulators, with results provided to the NIGC.[8] Similarly, neither the IGRA nor the Code of Federal Regulations exclude a person with a criminal conviction from serving on a tribal gaming commission or board. Except for the background check requirement, exclusions on tribal gaming offices, licenses, employment, or most contracts due to previous criminal convictions go "above and beyond" what federal law requires of gaming tribes.

As of July 1, 2023, 301 federally recognized Indian tribes in the lower 48 U.S. states have gaming and casino ordinances approved by the NIGC. To this number, we may add the four Alaskan Native Villages with lawful gaming (Klawock Cooperative Association, Central Council of Tlingit and Haida Indian Tribes of Alaska, Metlakatla Indian Community, and Organized Village of Kake). In addition, we add to the total two tribes, the Minnesota Chippewa Tribe and the Capitan Grande Band of Diegueno Mission Indians of California, which are divided into six bands and two bands, respectively, that have separate NIGC-approved ordinances.[9] In total, then, the NIGC-approved ordinances of 313 tribal jurisdictions were reviewed in this survey. All tribes with NIGC-approved ordinances are included even if they have not yet built gaming or casino facilities as of the time of writing.

6 Kevin K. Washburn, "Recurring Problems in Indian Gaming," 1(1) *Wyoming Law Review* 427–44, 433 (2001).

7 29 U.S.C. § 2710(b)(2)(F).

8 25 C.F.R. §§ 556.4, 556.5, and 556.6 (2023).

9 The Minnesota Chippewa Tribe is a confederation of six bands, each with their own tribal codes although they share a single tribal constitution. These are the Bois Forte Band, Fond du Lac Band, Grand Portage Band, Leech Lake Band, Mille Lacs Band, and White Earth Band. The Capitan Grande Band of Diegueno Mission Indians is divided into two bands that have separately negotiated their gaming ordinances: the Barona Group and the Viejas Group. Where relevant, this paper will refer to the appropriate band.

Though difficult to detect and quantify, indirect, hidden, and discretionary collateral consequences are common in tribal gaming law. A common indirect collateral consequence is the requirement that gaming commissioners also be eligible for gaming licenses in that jurisdiction, importing the eligibility requirements for PMOs and KOs and applying them to tribal gaming regulators. Note that the IGRA distinguishes among Class I gaming, which are traditional games regulated by the tribe alone; Class II gaming, which applies to games of chance such as bingo; and Class III gaming, which refers to Vegas-style casino games that are played against the house.[10] Tribes, therefore, may require different types of licenses. One common discretionary provision is the vaguely worded eligibility requirement for gaming commissioners that their "prior activities, criminal record, if any, reputation, habits and associations" do not threaten tribal interests or gaming authority.[11] This type of provision has an advantage and a disadvantage: it can permit exception in special cases, but it can also work a detriment by giving a secondary actor permission to deny an otherwise meritorious case. Another variation on discretionary collateral consequences is for a tribe to distinguish between "mandatory denial" of a gaming license and "permissive denial." The Sac and Fox Nation of Missouri, for instance, has a mandatory denial provision for upper management for embezzlement or gaming offenses and discretionary denial for other felony convictions, crimes of moral turpitude, and other categories.[12] As explained below, dual or multi-tiered exclusions for prior criminal convictions are not uncommon.

Although the IGRA and associated regulations do not require tribal gaming commissions to have per se license exclusions for persons with criminal convictions, the NIGC influences tribal gaming ordinances in less overt ways. First, Class II and Class III tribal gaming ordinances must be approved by the NIGC, which gives federal officials final say over whether an ordinance is compliant with the IGRA. The NIGC can and does make recommendations to tribes to improve their background check requirements. For instance, in a 2019 opinion letter to the Sauk-Suiattle Indian Tribe, the NIGC recommended further changes to the tribe's amended ordinance that required applicants to disclose all previous felony convictions.[13]

10 W. Dale Mason, *Indian Gaming: Tribal Sovereignty and American Politics* 65–66 (University of Oklahoma Press 2000).

11 See, e.g., Confederated Tribes of the Umatilla Indian Reservation (OR) Gaming Ordinance (1994), § 10(B)(4)(a).

12 Sac and Fox Nation of Missouri (KS) Gaming Ordinance (1998), § 5(G)(1)–(2).

13 Letter from NIGC to Sauk-Suiattle Indian Tribe, 3 September 2019, available at: https://www.nigc.gov/images/uploads/gamingordinances/20190903AmendedGamingOrdinance-SaukSuiattle.pdf. Compare Sauk-Suiattle Indian Tribe (WA) Gaming Ordinance (2000), § 2.4.9 with Sauk-Suiattle Indian Tribe (WA) Gaming Ordinance (2019), § 10.12.1.8.

The second way in which NIGC influences tribal gaming ordinances is by issuing a Model Gaming Ordinance on the NIGC website. Other than providing for background check procedures, this Model Gaming Ordinance introduces collateral consequences of conviction for appointments of tribal gaming commissioners. At Section 8(E) of the Revised Model Gaming Ordinance (2018), non-tribal members are ineligible to serve as gaming commissioners if they have a previous conviction for any felony or certain misdemeanors, to include embezzlement, theft, or any offense related to money or honesty. Tribal members face the same exclusion, but with a waiver: the tribal council could determine that "a significant amount of time has passed and the person is now of trustworthy character."[14] The leniency of this provision for tribal members evidences a more general policy favoring indigenization of gaming management and operations. This is consistent with Congress's intent in the IGRA that the benefits of tribal gaming should accrue to the tribe. The Model Gaming Ordinance is influential. As explained below, at least 32 tribal jurisdictions use a version of Section 8(E) of the Revised Model Gaming Ordinance in their local ordinances, including the waiver provision for tribal members.

Extensive background checks are burdensome to tribes. Some jurisdictions have reduced background check requirements because of the complexity and expense involved or because of the shortage of applicants. In a resolution of the tribal council, the Pueblo of Santa Ana explained that the background check requirement for lower-level employees made hiring difficult for restaurant, maintenance, and other non-gaming employees. Since federal law did not require a background check for these positions, the tribe repealed the background check requirement "so as to make clear that licensing requirements for persons who are not employed in any gaming-related activity should be limited to a minimum reasonable level of inquiry."[15] The new provision states that "only a limited investigation shall be required" though this still includes prior criminal record, if any.[16]

Given the difficulty of extensive background checks, some tribes may use explicit exclusions for persons with criminal records to reduce the costs of the investigation. Several California tribes divide gaming licenses between Class A (for PMOs and KOs) and Class B (for lower-level or non-gaming employees). These tribes provide for an intensive background check process for Class A license applicants, who then must face a discretionary eligibility

14 NIGC, Revised Model Gaming Ordinance, Bulletin No. 2018-1 (January 10, 2018), available at: https://www.nigc.gov/images/uploads/bulletins/Bulletin_2018-1_Revised_Model_Ordinance.pdf.

15 Pueblo of Santa Ana (NM) Resolution No. 99-R-42 (2000), available at: https://www.nigc.gov/images/uploads/gamingordinances/pueblosantaana-santaanaamend042700.pdf.

16 Pueblo of Santa Ana (NM) Gaming Ordinance (2000), § 4(E)(3).

determination. However, Class B licenses simply exclude persons with criminal convictions without conducting such an intensive background check.[17] In this case, the collateral exclusion may spare the tribe the burden of the background check for Class B employees, but the wording may also highlight the possibility of a "hidden" collateral consequence for Class A employees who do not have an automatic bar to eligibility but whose records face greater scrutiny.

Though generalizing about the gaming ordinances of 313 different jurisdictions is hazardous, we may make a few normative claims. First, the public policy rationale for background checks in the gaming and casino industry is perhaps stronger than in other industries because of the threat of organized crime and money laundering. Owing to the expense of background checks for tribal gaming commissions, categorical exclusions for persons with previous convictions could be a cost-effective means of excluding at the initial application persons who would likely be excluded later in the consideration process for gaming licenses. Second, many of the normative claims we have made in other areas of tribal law apply here: the more narrowly tailored criminal conviction exclusions are, the more they may be justified by a "future harm principle."[18] In the tribal gaming industry, categorical exclusions for financial crimes or dishonesty are naturally common. However, an exclusion that runs too broad is less justifiable based on the "future harm principle." To this end, exclusions specifically for drug crimes or sex crimes may be less justifiable than for economic or financial crimes. The Little River Band of Ottawa Indians, for instance, allows a pardon to restore eligibility for employment or gaming license for previous convictions of gaming offenses, fraud, and misrepresentation but not for sex offenses, which may not fully satisfy a "future harm principle" approach.[19]

Along the same lines, provisions that sunset are preferred over provisions that are lifelong, bearing in mind that the public policy rationale for excluding applicants may be stronger with certain crimes than with others. Third, a provision that recognizes pardons from other governmental actors or that has an internal waiver process for exceptional cases is favored over completely discretionary provisions because pardon and waiver processes are more transparent and prevent arbitrary decision making (though they may increase the cost for the tribe). On the other hand, provisions that attach collateral consequences even to convictions that have been pardoned or expunged, that

17 See, e.g., Sherwood Valley Rancheria of Pomo Indians (CA) Gaming Ordinance (1997), § 10(d)(2); Scotts Valley Band of Pomo Indians (CA) Gaming Ordinance (1999), § 10(d)(2); Hopland Band of Pomo Indians (CA) Gaming Ordinance (1996), § 10(d)(2).

18 Zachary Hoskins, "Criminalization and the Collateral Consequences of Conviction," 12 *Criminal Law & Philosophy* 625, 628–30 (2018).

19 Little River Band of Ottawa Indians (MI) Gaming Ordinance (2011), § 10.02(b)(2), (3), (6); § 10.03(b)(3), (4), (7).

extend to defendants in civil suits, or that apply to associations with persons with criminal convictions run too broadly. Though it has a waiver provision, the Burns Paiute Tribe excludes applicants with criminal convictions that have been expunged, potentially roping in wrongfully convicted persons. The tribe also extends its bar on criminal convictions to persons who were the defendants in a civil suit based on facts that constitute a felony.[20] The Klamath Tribes of Oregon authorize denial of a gaming license to defendants in civil lawsuits that constitute the elements of the excluded crimes.[21] The Pueblo of Acoma review a person's business or employment relationships with anyone convicted of any felony "other than a traffic offense," potentially importing convictions to innocent parties.[22] Though we may recognize that employment in the gaming industry is a privilege and not a right, it is not the case from a policy or cost efficiency perspective that a broader exclusion is always preferred over a narrower exclusion.

Gaming and casino ordinances are frequently altered or replaced. However, I did not observe a general trend toward harsher collateral consequences over time. The record has many counterexamples both of jurisdictions that have become stricter over time and those that became more lenient. An example of a tribe that has become more lenient is the Arapaho Tribe of the Wind River Reservation. A 2002 ordinance prohibited employment for all non-gaming employees who had been convicted of a felony; this was replaced with a new ordinance in 2017 that allows the tribe to issue a work permit to a non-gaming employee if she or he passes a suitability determination and would not pose a risk to the tribe.[23] By contrast, we can point to examples of jurisdictions that have become harsher over time. The Sac and Fox Nation of Oklahoma provided for a waiver for tribal members in its 2008 ordinance; in its 2018 ordinance, however, the waiver provision was removed.[24] I tentatively observe that jurisdictions that have broader collateral consequences across more categories of stakeholders tend also to recognize pardons or have internal waiver processes. Even a waiver exclusively for tribal members is beneficial because it may serve the goal of encouraging tribal employment in the gaming industry. This can, for instance, reduce reliance on outside contractors or other third parties and could serve the cause of tribal economic development. The record has numerous examples of jurisdictions that have broad exclusions for certain criminal convictions but that have generous

20 Burns Paiute Tribe (OR) Gaming Ordinance (2004) [section number missing in the ordinance on the NIGC website].
21 Klamath Tribes (OR) Gaming Ordinance (1995), § 45.14(e)(1).
22 Pueblo of Acoma (NM) Gaming Ordinance (2011), § 11-1-18(A)(1)–(2).
23 Arapaho Tribe of the Wind River Reservation (WY) Gaming Ordinance (2002), § 704; Arapaho Tribe of the Wind River Reservation (WY) Gaming Ordinance (2017), § 705(a)–(b).
24 Sac and Fox Nation (OK) Gaming Ordinance (2008), § 1-401(I) (no equivalent in 2018 ordinance).

waiver or pardon provisions. Two examples of jurisdictions that have comprehensive collateral consequences balanced with broad waiver or pardon provisions include the Stockbridge Munsee Community in Wisconsin and the Spirit Lake Tribe in North Dakota.[25]

Restrictions on Tribal Gaming Offices

Tribal gaming ordinances typically create special tribal offices to administer gaming facilities and monitor compliance with the IGRA, the tribal-state compacts, and the tribe's own gaming regulations.[26] Collateral consequences may attach to these tribal offices, excluding persons with criminal convictions from serving. In total, 153 tribal jurisdictions out of the total 313 jurisdictions (48.9%) covered in this chapter attach collateral consequences of criminal conviction to tribal gaming offices. Because each tribal jurisdiction has its own internal gaming structure, it is best to divide these tribal gaming offices by function rather than title. To that end, this survey will separate regulatory offices, managerial offices, and judicial or quasi-judicial offices.

Tribal Gaming Commissions

Gaming regulatory offices, usually referred to as tribal gaming commissions, are typically independent of other tribal offices. Frequently, these commissions are responsible for performing background checks, inspecting gaming facilities, auditing finances, issuing licenses, and promulgating rules.[27] Tribal gaming commissions are regulatory offices, not managerial ones. They have unfettered access to gaming facilities on tribal lands and conduct oversight to ensure compliance with tribal, state, and federal law. Gaming commissions typically have clear authority to take enforcement action, including revocation of gaming licenses or barring certain individuals from gaming facilities.[28] In total, at least 141 tribal jurisdictions attach collateral consequences of conviction to tribal gaming commissioner positions.

For appointment of gaming commissioners, the most common exclusion is for persons convicted of felonies plus misdemeanors of embezzlement and theft or other money- or honesty-related offenses. A total of 34 tribal

25 Stockbridge Munsee Community (WI) Gaming Ordinance (2021), § GMG.01.15(j)(2)–(3), (8); § GMG.01.09(l)(37); Spirit Lake Tribe (ND) Gaming Ordinance (1994), § 8-14-101(b).

26 Kathryn R.L. Rand & Stephen Andrew Light, *Indian Gaming Law & Policy* 121 (2nd ed., Carolina Academic Press, 2014).

27 Rand & Light, supra note 26 at 121.

28 Tracy Burris, "How Tribal Gaming Commissions Are Evolving," 8(4) *Gaming Law Review* 243–46 (2004).

jurisdictions have this exclusion, including 10 in Oklahoma.[29] This is evidence of the influence of the NIGC Model Gaming Ordinance noted above, which used the same list of crimes, and of legal sharing among tribal jurisdictions, especially given the prominence of Oklahoma tribes in this category. Fourteen tribal jurisdictions exclude persons with felonies or any misdemeanor convictions involving dishonesty or moral turpitude; of these, ten are in California, also suggestive of legal sharing.[30] Another 14 tribal jurisdictions exclude persons with felony convictions or convictions for any gaming offense.[31] Eight jurisdictions exclude persons with felony convictions or offenses related to gaming, dishonesty, or moral turpitude.[32] An additional eight also exclude persons with felony convictions or convictions for gaming offenses or bribery.[33] Less common are the following versions, with most of the variation involving misdemeanor exclusions:

29 For the clarity of the footnote, the full citations are omitted. The provisions are cited elsewhere in this chapter and are available on the NIGC website. Absentee-Shawnee Tribe (OK), Alabama-Coushatta Tribe (TX), Apache Tribe (OK), Caddo Nation (OK), Cherokee Nation (OK), Cheyenne River Sioux Tribe (SD), Comanche Nation (OK), Cow Creek Band of Umpqua Tribe (OR), Greenville Rancheria (CA), Ione Band of Miwok Indians (CA), Jena Band of Choctaw Indians (LA), Kaw Nation (OK), Kialegee Tribal Town (OK), Kickapoo Traditional Tribe (TX), Kiowa Indian Tribe (OK), Lac du Flambeau Band of Lake Superior Chippewa Indians (WI), Lower Elwha Tribal Community (WA), Lower Sioux Indian Community (MN), Moapa Band of Paiute Indians (NV), Nez Perce Tribe (ID), Oglala Sioux Tribe (SD), Paskenta Band of Nomlaki Indians (CA), Port Gamble S'Klallam Tribe (WA), Quartz Valley Indian Community (CA), Rosebud Sioux Tribe (SD), Round Valley Indian Tribes (CA), Santa Rosa Band of Cahuilla Indians (CA), Shinnecock Indian Nation (NY), Snoqualmie Indian Tribe (WA), Tonkawa Tribe (OK), Tonto Apache Tribe (AZ), Wichita and Affiliated Tribes (OK), Klawock Cooperative Association (AK).

30 Alturas Indian Rancheria (CA), Buena Vista Rancheria (CA), Delaware Tribe of Indians (OK), Elem Indian Colony of Pomo Indians (CA), La Posta Band of Diegueno Mission Indians (CA), Manzanita Band of Diegueno Mission Indians (CA), Mechoopda Indian Tribe (CA), Picayune Rancheria (CA), Pueblo of Jemez (NM), Pueblo of Tesuque (NM), San Pascual Band (CA), Santa Rosa Indian Community (CA), Squaxin Indian Tribe (WA), Susanville Indian Rancheria (CA).

31 Gila River Indian Community (AZ), Iowa Tribe (KS), Mescalero Apache Tribe (NM), Minnesota Chippewa Tribe (Leech Lake Band) (MN), Minnesota Chippewa Tribe (Mille Lacs Band) (MN), Mississippi Band of Choctaw Indians (MS), Pueblo of Nambe (NM), Pueblo of Pojoaque (NM), Pueblo of Santa Clara (NM), Pueblo of Taos (NM), Shoshone-Bannock Tribes (ID), Turtle Mountain Band of Chippewa Indians (ND), Winnebago Tribe (NE), Yankton Sioux Tribe (SD).

32 Citizen Potawatomi Nation (OK), Delaware Nation (OK), Grand Traverse Band of Ottawa and Chippewa Indians (MI), Little River Band of Ottawa Indians (MI), Makah Indian Tribe (WA), Prairie Band Potawatomi Nation (KS), Pueblo of San Felipe (NM), Saginaw Chippewa Indian Tribe (MI).

33 Confederated Tribes of the Grand Ronde Community (OR), Elk Valley Rancheria (CA), Fort Sill Apache Tribe (OK), Ponca Tribe (NE), Quapaw Tribe (OK), Shoshone-Paiute Tribes (NV), Wilton Rancheria (CA), Central Council of Tlingit and Haida (AK).

- Felonies alone (five jurisdictions)[34]
- Felonies plus crimes of embezzlement, theft, or moral turpitude (three jurisdictions)[35]
- Felonies plus crimes of embezzlement or dishonesty (one jurisdiction)[36]
- Felonies plus crimes of dishonesty (two jurisdictions)[37]
- Felonies plus crimes of fraud, misrepresentation, moral turpitude, or gaming (three jurisdictions)[38]
- Felonies plus crimes of fraud, misrepresentation, or gaming (three jurisdictions)[39]
- Felonies plus crimes of gaming or dishonesty (two jurisdictions)[40]
- Felonies plus crimes of moral turpitude or gaming (five jurisdictions)[41]
- Felonies plus crimes of moral turpitude (three jurisdictions, with another unclear)[42]

34 Crow Creek Sioux Tribe (SD) Gaming Ordinance (1994), Description of Procedures, §§ D (executive secretary); E (commission members); Pit River Tribe (CA) Gaming Ordinance (2004), § 4(d)(iii); Red Lake Band of Chippewa Indians (2000), §220(b)(2); Sac and Fox Nation (OK) Gaming Ordinance (2018), § 4-401(P) (note this includes only felonies with an offense involving dishonesty or violence); Yerington Paiute Tribe (NV) Gaming Ordinance (2015), art. 2, §2(G)(3)(c).

35 Ak-Chin Indian Community (AZ) Gaming Ordinance (2008), § 6.3; Colorado River Indian Tribes (AZ) Gaming Ordinance (2001), § 405(a)(Gaming Enterprise Directors); Ponca Tribe of Indians (OK) Gaming Ordinance (2017), § 35(G) (appointees of the Ponca Tribal Corporation).

36 Torres Martinez Desert Cahuilla Indians (CA) Gaming Ordinance (2020), § 6(B)(B)(b).

37 Tulalip Tribes (WA) Gaming Ordinance (2022), § 10.05.030(1)(b)(2)(C); Twenty-Nine Palms Band of Mission Indians (CA) Gaming Ordinance (2012), § 8(C)(4)(3) (removal only).

38 Augustine Band of Cahuilla Indians (CA) Gaming Ordinance (2009), § 406(e); St. Croix Chippewa Indians (WI) Gaming Ordinance (2021), 6 S.C.T.C. § 02.05(4)(d)(2); Sokaogon Chippewa Community (WI) Gaming Ordinance (2021), § 400.03(1)(e).

39 Hannahville Indian Community (MI) Gaming Ordinance (2000), § 4.11(C)(1)(d); Menominee Indian Tribe (WI) Gaming Ordinance (2008), § 2.031(3)–(4); Lac Courte Oreilles Band of Lake Superior Chippewa Indians (WI) Gaming Ordinance (1995), § 703.03(4).

40 Confederated Tribes of the Colville Reservation (WA) Gaming Ordinance (2016), § 6-5-53; Ho-Chunk Nation (WI) Gaming Ordinance (2008), § 13(b)(7).

41 Capitan Grande Band of Diegueno Mission Indians (Viejas Group) (CA) Gaming Ordinance (2018), § 3.02; La Jolla Band of Luiseno Indians (CA) Gaming Regulation 003 (2003), § C(4)(a); Pauma Band of Luiseno Mission Indians (CA) Gaming Regulation 12 (2022), § 3(C)(4)(a); Ute Mountain Ute Tribe (CO) Gaming Ordinance (2003), § 201(b); Ysleta del Sur Pueblo (TX) Gaming Ordinance (2015), § 11(2)(b).

42 The Yavapai-Prescott Indian Tribe has a gaming ordinance that excludes persons with convictions for a "felony involving theft, embezzlement or a crime involving moral turpitude." Given the placement of the commas, it is not clear whether misdemeanors involving moral turpitude are included. Yavapai-Prescott Indian Tribe (AZ) Gaming Ordinance (2011), § 24.4(C). The other three are Guidiville Rancheria (CA) Gaming Ordinance (2005), art. 2, § 5; Minnesota Chippewa Tribe (White Earth Band) (MN) Gaming Ordinance (2019), § 9(e); Seminole Nation (OK) Gaming Ordinance (2017), § 102(b)(3)–(4).

- All crimes other than misdemeanor traffic offenses (one jurisdiction)[43]
- Any offense involving gaming or moral turpitude (one jurisdiction)[44]

A smaller number of tribal jurisdictions have collateral consequences of conviction for gaming commissioner appointments that contain a sunset provision, usually for misdemeanors. The Bay Mills Indian Community excludes persons with felony or gaming offense convictions for life, or other misdemeanor convictions within the prior 5 years.[45] The Fort Independence Indian Community of Paiute Indians has a lifelong bar for felony convictions and 10 years for misdemeanors involving moral turpitude.[46] The Match-e-be-nash-she-wish Band of Pottawatomi Indians has a lifelong bar for felony convictions and a 5-year bar for misdemeanors involving theft, dishonesty, or misrepresentation, excluding felonies that were committed in defense of tribal sovereignty.[47] Finally, the Standing Rock Sioux Tribe excludes persons with felony convictions for life, petty theft for 1 year, or misdemeanors involving fraud, misrepresentation, theft, or gambling within 5 years.[48] Three tribes have sunset provisions for both felonies and misdemeanors. These include the Flandreau Santee Sioux Tribe (10 years for felonies or crimes of moral turpitude) and Shoalwater Bay Indian Tribe (10 years for felonies or misdemeanors of dishonesty).[49] Some tribes only include specific felonies in the exclusion, but with a sunset clause. The Bishop Paiute Tribe explicitly excludes persons with violent felony convictions or convictions for fraud, embezzlement, theft, or gaming offenses, but provides that a conviction will not preclude eligibility if it is more than 10 years old.[50] This provision also allows a pardon to restore eligibility.

Finally, a handful of jurisdictions have lifelong exclusions for specific offenses and sunset provisions for other felonies. These include the Forest County Potawatomi (lifelong for offenses involving gaming, fraud, or misrepresentation; 10 years for other felonies); Habematolel Pomo of Upper Lake (lifelong for crimes of dishonesty or moral turpitude; 5 years for other felonies); Omaha Tribe (lifelong for offenses of untruthfulness or dishonesty; 10 years for other felonies); Oneida Tribe (lifelong for gaming offenses, fraud,

43 Thlopthlocco Tribal Town (OK) Gaming Ordinance (2008), § 8(B)(4).

44 Note that this provision does not include felonies. Seneca-Cayuga Nation (NY) Gaming Ordinance (2013), § 9.4(d), (f).

45 Bay Mills Indian Community (MI) Gaming Ordinance (2004), § 4.11(C)(2).

46 Fort Independence Indian Community of Paiute Indians (CA) Gaming Ordinance (2016), § 109(1)–(2).

47 Match-e-be-nash-she-wish Band of Pottawatomi Indians (MI) Gaming Ordinance (2020), §§ 8.03.2(1)–(2), 8.03.5.

48 Standing Rock Sioux Tribe (SD) Gaming Ordinance (2014), §§ 23-305(d), (i), (j).

49 Flandreau Santee Sioux Tribe (SD) Tribal Code (1996), § 17-3-2(1); Shoalwater Bay Indian Tribe (WA) Gaming Ordinance (2019), § 12-3.02(c).

50 Bishop Paiute Tribe (CA) Gaming Ordinance (2012), § 405(D).

or misrepresentation; 10 years for other felonies or gaming regulatory violations); and the Sisseton-Wahpeton Oyate of the Lake Traverse Reservation (lifelong for theft, fraud, or gambling offenses; 10 years for other felonies).[51] An even more elaborate provision is that of the Yavapai-Apache Nation, which excludes persons convicted of gaming offenses, specific felonies for life (extortion, burglary, larceny, bribery, embezzlement, robbery, racketeering, money laundering, forgery, fraud, murder, manslaughter, sex offenses, rape, or kidnapping), and all other felonies within the previous 7 years.[52] Finally, the Confederated Tribes of the Chehalis Reservation has an undefined exclusion, for persons convicted of any felony or misdemeanor that suggests that one's "prior activities, criminal record, or associations" pose a threat to effective regulation of gaming or enhance the chances of unlawful practices.[53] Such an open-ended provision operates as a discretionary collateral consequence, subject to interpretation by the tribal council.

A total of ten jurisdictions do not have specified eligibility exclusions to serve as tribal gaming commissioners but have removal provisions for commissioners who are subsequently convicted while in office. Depending on the tribal jurisdiction's interpretation of these removal provisions, they may serve as a "hidden" collateral consequence if the jurisdiction is not willing to appoint a person who was previously convicted of a crime that she or he could be removed for subsequently. These include the following eight tribes: Agua Caliente Band of Cahuilla Indians (felonies only); Eastern Shawnee Tribe (felonies or crimes of dishonesty); Osage Nation (felonies or crimes of dishonesty); Pawnee Nation (felonies, crimes of untruthfulness or dishonesty); Peoria Tribe (felonies, misdemeanors involving illegal gambling or bribery); Pokagon Band of Potawatomi (felonies or crimes of dishonesty or moral turpitude); Redwood Valley Rancheria (felonies, misdemeanors of illegal gambling or bribery); and Rincon Band of Luiseno Mission Indians (felonies, misdemeanors of illegal gambling or bribery).[54] The Miami Tribe

51 Forest County Potawatomi Community (WI) Gaming Ordinance (1997), § 802(d); Habematolel Pomo of Upper Lake (CA) Gaming Ordinance (2012), § 4.10.4(3); Omaha Tribe (NE) Gaming Ordinance (2013), § 29-1-25(e)(3)–(4); Oneida Tribe (WI) Gaming Ordinance (2009), § 21.6-6(a); Sisseton-Wahpeton Oyate (SD) Gaming Ordinance (2008), § 58-03-02 (for Regulatory Authority).

52 Yavapai-Apache Nation (AZ) Gaming Ordinance (2022), § 409.

53 Confederated Tribes of the Chehalis Reservation (WA) Gaming Ordinance (2017), § 13.05.040(C).

54 Agua Caliente Band of Cahuilla Indians (CA) Gaming Ordinance (2020), § 5(G)(1); Eastern Shawnee Tribe (OK) Gaming Ordinance (2009), § 2004(1)–(3); Osage Nation (OK) Gaming Ordinance (2003), § 2.04; Pawnee Nation OK) Gaming Ordinance (2022), § 3.2(2)(i); Peoria Tribe (OK) Gaming Ordinance (2004), § 2.1(d); Pokagon Band of Potawatomi Indians (MI) Gaming Ordinance (2007), § 3.11(c); Redwood Valley Rancheria (CA) Gaming Ordinance (1995), § 2.04; Rincon Band of Luiseno Mission Indians (CA) Gaming Ordinance (2011), §7.02.

of Oklahoma has a longer list, permitting removal of a gaming commissioner for conviction of a felony or misdemeanor involving gambling, fraud, embezzlement, theft by swindle or misrepresentation, or violations of ethics or confidentiality.[55] Notably, although the Shakopee Mdewakanton Sioux Community does not have an explicit collateral exclusion for gaming commissioners other than the removal provision, it has an "indirect" exclusion since gaming commissioners must be eligible for gaming licenses.[56] In that jurisdiction, a gaming license is automatically revoked upon conviction for any felony.[57]

Tribal Gaming Directors

Some tribes have created an office equivalent to a tribal gaming director responsible for, among other things, oversight of casino operations, liaising with state and federal officials, and strategic operations. These are managerial functions rather than regulatory functions. At least 38 tribal jurisdictions impose collateral consequences for this office, often with the title of gaming director, executive director, or gaming monitor. In many of these jurisdictions, the collateral consequences of conviction for a gaming managerial office are identical to those for tribal gaming commissioners.[58] This general rule is not always true; for these exceptions, usually the restrictions for gaming commissioners or regulators are tighter than for gaming managerial offices. The Enterprise Rancheria of Maidu Indians, for instance, excludes as gaming commissioners any person convicted of a felony, gaming-related offense, fraud, embezzlement, misrepresentation, or theft.[59] However, the tribe excludes as executive director of the gaming agency persons convicted of a shorter list: any felony, fraud, theft, or embezzlement.[60] The Pawnee Nation of Oklahoma permits removal of gaming commissioners for convictions for felonies or other crimes "of any degree, an element of which pertains to untruthfulness or dishonesty."[61] For appointment to the gaming board of directors, however, the exclusion is for convictions of felonies or misdemeanors

55 Miami Tribe of Oklahoma (OK) Gaming Ordinance (2021), § 16(a).
56 Shakopee Mdewakanton Sioux Community (MN) Gaming Ordinance (2013), § 200(e).
57 Id. at § 201(c).
58 For instance, the Pueblo of Tesuque excludes persons convicted of a felony or any misdemeanor involving dishonesty or moral turpitude from serving as either gaming commissioners or as executive director of the gaming agency. Pueblo of Tesuque (NM) Gaming Ordinance (2019), §§ 5(c)(1), 6(b)(3). The Shoshone-Paiute Tribes of Duck Valley Reservation exclude any person convicted of any felony or any gambling or bribery offense from serving as either gaming commissioners or as the tribal gaming agency director. Shoshone-Paiute Tribes of Duck Valley Reservation (NV) Gaming Ordinance (2012), §§ 10(b), 11(c).
59 Enterprise Rancheria of Maidu Indians (CA) Gaming Ordinance (2013), art. 4 § 3(c)(i)–(iv).
60 Id. at art. 5 § 3(c).
61 Pawnee Nation (OK) Gaming Ordinance (2022), § 3.2(2).

involving theft, embezzlement, or moral turpitude, substantially similar but likely narrower in scope.[62] The Delaware Tribe of Indians excludes persons convicted of felonies or misdemeanors involving dishonesty or moral turpitude as gaming commissioners or as tribal gaming director; however, the bar for tribal gaming director includes a sunset provision of 10 years while the exclusion for gaming commissioner is for life.[63] A simpler version of this, perhaps reflecting different job duties, is the Campo Band of Diegueno Mission Indians ordinance, which excludes persons convicted of felonies or crimes of moral turpitude from serving as Executive Director and persons convicted of felonies or gaming offenses from serving as Gaming Monitor.[64]

Of the 38 tribal jurisdictions with collateral consequences for tribal gaming managerial positions, 12 of them exclude persons with felony convictions or with misdemeanor convictions for gaming or bribery offenses from serving, the most common variant.[65] These jurisdictions are diverse in size and geographically dispersed. Five jurisdictions, primarily in Arizona, exclude persons with convictions for felonies or crimes of moral turpitude, theft, or embezzlement.[66] Three tribes, all in California, exclude as gaming monitors any person convicted of felonies or misdemeanors involving gaming, fraud, misrepresentation, or bribery.[67] Two others, the Delaware Tribe of Indians for Gaming Director and the Pueblo of Tesuque for Executive Director, exclude persons convicted of felonies or misdemeanors involving dishonesty or moral turpitude.[68] However, the Delaware Tribe has a 10-year sunset date on the exclusion, whereas the Pueblo of Tesuque has a lifetime bar. The

62 Id. at § 4.3(2).

63 Delaware Tribe of Indians (OK) Gaming Ordinance (1999), §§6(d)(1), 16(c).

64 Campo Band of Diegueno Mission Indians (CA) Gaming Ordinance (2001), § 6(3)(c) (for Executive Director); Campo Band of Diegueno Mission Indians (CA) Gaming Ordinance (1994), § 6(C) (for Gaming Monitor).

65 Elk Valley Rancheria (CA) (gaming director); Fort Sill Apache Tribe (OK) (gaming commission director); Kaibab Band of Paiute Indians (AZ) (director); Menominee Tribe (WI) (director); Narragansett Indian Tribe (RI) (director); Peoria Tribe of Indians (OK) (director); Puyallup Tribe (WA) (director); Quapaw Tribe of Indians (OK) (director); Redwood Valley Rancheria (CA) (director); San Carlos Apache Tribe (AZ) (director), Shoshone-Paiute Tribes (NV) (director); Central Council of Tlingit and Haida (AK) (director).

66 Colorado River Indian Tribes (AZ) Gaming Ordinance (2001), § 405(a) (gaming enterprise director), § 502(a) (executive director of the tribal gaming agency); Fort McDowell Yavapai Nation (AZ) Gaming Ordinance (2020), § 504(b) (executive director); Navajo Nation (AZ) Gaming Ordinance (2019), § 2010(B)(2) (executive director); Pawnee Nation (OK) Gaming Ordinance, § 4.3(2) (board of directors); Tohono O'odham Nation (AZ) Gaming Ordinance (2021), § 402(c)(ii) (executive director).

67 Ewiiaapaayp Band of Kumeyaay Indians (CA) Gaming Ordinance (2001), § 3.01; Karuk Tribe (CA) Gaming Ordinance (2003), § 9(A); Lytton Rancheria (CA) Gaming Ordinance (1999), § 3.01.

68 Delaware Tribe of Indians (OK) Gaming Ordinance (1999), § 16(c); Pueblo of Tesuque (NM) Gaming Ordinance (2019), § 6(b)(3).

Pueblo of San Felipe excludes persons convicted of felonies or any misdemeanors involving gaming, dishonesty, or moral turpitude from serving as executive director of the gaming agency.[69] The Miami Tribe (gaming director) and the Kickapoo Tribe (general manager and executive director of the gaming commission) have the same exclusion, plus a two-year exclusion for any person convicted of any other offense except traffic violations.[70]

Several other tribes have more idiosyncratic exclusions:

- Felonies plus gaming offenses (gaming director of the Minnesota Chippewa Tribe, Mille Lacs Band)[71]
- Felonies plus gaming offenses or crimes of moral turpitude (executive director of the gaming agency, Ute Mountain Ute Tribe)[72]
- Felonies plus crimes of fraud, theft, or embezzlement (executive director of the gaming agency, Enterprise Rancheria of Maidu Indians)[73]
- Felonies plus misdemeanors of fraud, misrepresentation, moral turpitude, or gaming (chairman of the gaming commission, Nottawaseppi Huron Band of the Potawatomi)[74]
- Felonies plus misdemeanors of embezzlement, theft, gaming, or other money- or honesty-related crimes (executive director of the gaming agency, Snoqualmie Indian Tribe)[75]

Finally, four tribes do not exclude persons with criminal convictions from serving as gaming directors but have removal provisions if the incumbent is convicted of a crime. As explained above, this may serve as an eligibility criterion in disguise and therefore a "hidden" collateral consequence. The Pueblo of Acoma authorize removal of the gaming director in the event of a conviction for any misdemeanor or felony related to illegal gambling or bribery.[76] The Red Lake Band of Chippewa Indians authorizes removal of

69 Pueblo of San Felipe (NM) Gaming Ordinance (2020), § 9(B).

70 Miami Tribe (OK) Gaming Ordinance (2012), § 24(a)–(b); Kickapoo Tribe (OK) Gaming Ordinance (2014), § 110(A)–(B).

71 Minnesota Chippewa Tribe (Mille Lacs Band) (MN) Gaming Ordinance (2003), § 12(a)(3)(B).

72 Ute Mountain Ute Tribe (CO) Gaming Ordinance (2003), § 206(b)(1).

73 Enterprise Rancheria of Maidu Indians (CA) Gaming Ordinance (2013), art. 5 § 3(c).

74 Nottawaseppi Huron Band of the Potawatomi (MI) Gaming Ordinance (2000), § 306(e). Note that this tribe has a revised gaming ordinance dated 2021 that does not contain an equivalent provision.

75 Note here the similar wording to the Model NIGC Ordinance, discussed above. Snoqualmie Indian Tribe (WA) Gaming Ordinance (2015), § 8.04(C)(1).

76 The wording here suggests that *both* misdemeanors and felonies must relate to illegal gambling or bribery; other felonies are not included. Pueblo of Acoma (NM) Gaming Ordinance (2011), § 11-1-12(B).

members of the gaming board upon conviction of any felony.[77] The Squaxin Island Tribe permits removal of the gaming director for any felony or a misdemeanor involving dishonesty or moral turpitude.[78] Finally, the executive director of the gaming agency for the Sycuan Band of the Kumeyaay Nation may be removed for a conviction for a felony, gaming offense, or misdemeanor of moral turpitude.[79]

Tribal Gaming Judges

Tribal ordinances may create separate offices that serve a judicial or dispute resolution function in the tribal gaming industry, such as hearing appeals for denials of gaming licenses or contracts, patron disputes, or fines for gaming violations.[80] At least seven jurisdictions impose collateral consequences of conviction on the holders of these judicial or quasi-judicial offices. The Viejas Group of the Capitan Grande Band of Diegueno Mission Indians excludes persons with convictions for felonies or crimes of moral turpitude from serving on its Review Board.[81] The Pauma Band of Luiseno Mission Indians also excludes persons convicted of felonies or crimes of moral turpitude from serving as members of its Gaming Appellate Board.[82] The Seneca-Cayuga Nation has a collateral consequence bar for Hearing Officers, which renders ineligible persons with convictions for felonies or crimes of moral turpitude.[83] In addition, the ordinance provides for automatic removal of Hearing Officers if convicted of any felony, misdemeanors that involve dishonesty or untruthfulness, or gaming offenses.[84] The tribal council of the Colorado River Indian Tribes also appoints Hearing Officers; persons found guilty of a felony or misdemeanor involving theft, fraud, or embezzlement are ineligible.[85] Until a revised ordinance was approved in 2021, qualifications for the Mechoopda Indian Tribe of Chico Rancheria excluded as Gaming Review Board judges any person convicted of a felony or gaming offense.[86] The

77 Red Lake Band of Chippewa Indians (MN) Gaming Ordinance (2000), § 201(b). The gaming board is separate from the tribal gaming commission, which has its own collateral bar at § 220(b)(2).

78 Squaxin Island Tribe (WA) Gaming Ordinance (2021), § 6.08.170(C)(3)(a).

79 Sycuan Band of Kumeyaay Indians (CA) Gaming Ordinance (2017), § 3.04.

80 Rand & Light, supra note 26 at 121.

81 Viejas Group of Capitan Grande Band of Diegueno Mission Indians of California (CA) Gaming Ordinance (2018), § 4.03.

82 Pauma Band of Luiseno Mission Indians (CA) Gaming Ordinance (2022), Regulation 13, § 3(C)(4)(a).

83 Seneca-Cayuga Nation (OK) Gaming Ordinance (2013), § 10.4(c)–(d).

84 Id. at § 10.9(b)(i)–(ii).

85 Colorado River Indian Tribes (AZ) Gaming Ordinance (2001), § 1003.

86 Mechoopda Indian Tribe of Chico Rancheria (CA) Gaming Ordinance (2001), § 4.23.6. The 2021 Gaming Ordinance does not have this provision.

Manzanita Band of Diegueno Mission Indians has a similar exclusion.[87] The Elem Indian Colony of Pomo Indians requires its Gaming Review Board to be composed of "retired federal or state judges" who have "never been convicted of a felony or any gaming offense."[88]

Restoration of Rights for Tribal Gaming Offices

Out of the 153 tribal jurisdictions that attach collateral consequences of conviction to tribal gaming offices, at least 33 allow restoration of rights to serve in tribal gaming office, either by recognizing a pardon or providing an internal waiver process of some kind, usually conditional on evidence of rehabilitation or the passage of time. The 11 federally recognized tribes in Wisconsin are discussed separately below, because the Tribal-State Gaming Compact in Wisconsin provides legal authorization for a waiver of previous criminal offenses, though not all Wisconsin tribes have a waiver. The majority (20) of the 32 jurisdictions with a waiver process use the language provided in the NIGC Model Gaming Ordinance.[89] This provision distinguishes between non-tribal members, for whom collateral consequences act as a perpetual bar to appointment or election to a tribal gaming commission, and tribal members, whose previous convictions may be waived under certain circumstances.[90] This provision states that the appropriate authority can waive prior criminal convictions if a "significant amount of time has passed" and the candidate is "now of trustworthy character."[91] Three of these 20 tribes vary the wording slightly. The Lower Sioux Indian Community and the Rosebud Sioux Tribe use "reformed" character rather than trustworthy character.[92] The Santa Rosa Band of Cahuilla Indians requires that a significant amount of time has passed, a candidate is now of trustworthy character, *and* the candidate is now rehabilitated.[93] Restricting the waiver only to tribal

87 Manzanita Band of Diegueno Mission Indians (CA) Gaming Ordinance (2001), § 4.24.6.
88 Elem Indian Colony of Pomo Indians (CA) Gaming Ordinance (2002), § 4.23.6(1).
89 Alabama-Coushatta Tribe (TX), Apache Tribe (OK), Caddo Nation (OK), Cow Creek Band of Umpqua Tribe (OR), Ione Band of Miwok Indians (CA), Kialegee Tribal Town (OK), Kickapoo Traditional Tribe (TX), Lower Elwha Tribal Community (WA), Lower Sioux Indian Community (MN), Rosebud Sioux Tribe (SD), Paskenta Band of Nomlaki Indians (CA), Port Gamble S'Klallam Tribe (WA), Quartz Valley Indian Community (CA), Round Valley Indian Tribes (CA), Santa Rosa Band of Cahuilla Indians (CA), Shinnecock Indian Nation (NY), Tonkawa Tribe (OK), Tonto Apache Tribe (AZ), Klawock Cooperative Association (AK), Bad River Band of the Lake Superior Tribe of Chippewa Indians (WI).
90 See NIGC, Revised Model Gaming Ordinance, supra note 14 at § 8(E).
91 Id.
92 Lower Sioux Indian Community (MN) Gaming Ordinance (2006), § 7(I); Rosebud Sioux Tribe (SD) Gaming Ordinance (2007), §7(I).
93 Santa Rosa Band of Cahuilla Indians (CA) Gaming Ordinance (2023), § 8(f).

members is part of a broader policy favoring hiring of tribal members for gaming operations.

Four tribes have a similar exclusion for tribal members who wish to become gaming commissioners, but specifically provide a sunset date after which the exclusion expires. The Absentee-Shawnee Tribe allows waivers of prior criminal convictions for potential gaming commissioners if the crime is not of moral turpitude and if 10 years have passed.[94] Three other tribes, the Cheyenne River Sioux Tribe, Oglala Sioux Tribe, and Lac du Flambeau Band of Lake Superior Chippewa Indians, permit a waiver for tribal members if 10 years have passed and the person is now of trustworthy character.[95] Note that for the Cheyenne River Sioux Tribe and the Oglala Sioux Tribe gaming commissioners are elected, not appointed, so the Election Board rather than the Tribal Council issues the waiver so that the candidate may qualify for the ballot.

At least two additional tribes do not make an explicit distinction between tribal members and non-tribal members in gaming waivers but restrict membership of their tribal gaming commissions to tribal members only, so the waiver is in effect only for tribal members. The Turtle Mountain Band of Chippewa Indians authorizes the Tribal Council to consider a person with a felony conviction for appointment to the gaming commission upon a determination that the person is sufficiently rehabilitated and did not commit a gaming offense.[96] However, tribal gaming commissioners must be enrolled members of the tribe.[97] The Hannahville Indian Community limits membership on its Gaming Board of Directors only to tribal members. Directors must be elected by the whole tribal membership. Under § 4.11(C)(1)(d) of that tribe's gaming ordinance, persons with felony convictions, gaming offenses, or misdemeanors involving fraud or misrepresentation are ineligible to stand for election.[98] In addition, under § 4.11(C)(2), persons with any other criminal convictions in the preceding 5 years are also ineligible, unless pardoned or unless the tribe determines that the person "is not likely again to engage in any offensive or criminal course of conduct."[99] This waiver, however, only applies to the residual category of other offenses in § 4.11(C)(2), not to the list of more serious convictions in § 4.11(C)(1)(d). Notably, the Hannahville Indian Community's previous ordinance, dated in 1994, did

94 Absentee-Shawnee Tribe (OK) Gaming Ordinance (2023), § 7(K)(7).

95 Cheyenne River Sioux Tribe (SD) Gaming Ordinance (2018), § 13(A); Oglala Sioux Tribe (SD) Gaming Ordinance (2014), § 13(A); Lac du Flambeau Band of Lake Superior Chippewa Indians (WI) Gaming Ordinance (2012), § 43.302(9).

96 Turtle Mountain Band of Chippewa Indians (ND) Gaming Ordinance (2018), § 25.0101(3)(d).

97 Id. at § 25.0101(2)(c).

98 Hannahville Indian Community (MI) Gaming Ordinance (2000), § 4.11(C)(1)(d).

99 Id. at § 4.11(C)(2).

not contain an equivalent to § 4.11(C)(1)(d). Rather, the exclusion was for any person convicted in the last 5 years of any felony, gaming offense, or misdemeanor involving dishonesty or moral turpitude, unless pardoned by the appropriate executive or waived by the tribe.[100] By making certain convictions "unwaivable" or "unpardonable" in the 2000 ordinance, Hannahville Indian Community made its collateral exclusion stronger.

Several jurisdictions have waiver procedures for gaming commissioner candidates with previous criminal convictions, but do not limit these waivers to tribal members. One tribal jurisdiction, the Kaw Nation, uses the language of the NIGC Model Ordinance but opens the waiver to all candidates for gaming commissioner.[101] Three California tribal jurisdictions, Alturas Indian Rancheria, Habematolel Pomo of Upper Lake, and La Posta Band of Diegueno Mission Indians, have a variation that permits a waiver if "such time has passed" and an "individual has been sufficiently rehabilitated," similar to the two South Dakota tribes above but open to non-tribal members.[102] While the Alturas Indian Rancheria and the La Posta Band of Diegueno Mission Indians do not restrict membership on the gaming commission to tribal members, the Habematolel Pomo of Upper Lake requires one member of the tribal gaming commission to be a tribal member, one a non-tribal member, and the third either one.[103] One tribe has an even broader waiver, which can remove any barrier to serving as a gaming commissioner, including age, experience, or educational requirements. The Red Lake Band of Chippewa Indians authorizes the Tribal Council to "waive any requirement for persons to sit as members of the Gaming Commission," including bars to employment based on a prior conviction.[104] Though not construed as a waiver specifically, one tribe, the Match-e-be-nash-she-wish Band of Pottawatomi Indians, provides that "[s]pecial considerations may be extended to a potential Commissioner if they have a felony conviction that was to protect the sovereign rights of Indians."[105] This provision, in effect, gives the tribe discretion to find that political protests that resulted in criminal charges do not stand as a bar to serving as a gaming commissioner.

For the 11 federally recognized Indian tribes in Wisconsin, a special set of circumstances applies. The Wisconsin Tribal-State Compacts, which were negotiated between the tribes and the state government pursuant to the

100 Hannahville Indian Community (MI) Gaming Ordinance (1994), § 4.11(C)(2).
101 Kaw Nation (OK) Gaming Ordinance (2022), § 8(E).
102 Alturas Indian Rancheria (CA) Gaming Ordinance (2008), § 4.9.3(2); Habamatolel Pomo of Upper Lake (CA) Gaming Ordinance (2012), § 4.10.4(3); La Posta Band of Diegueno Mission Indians (CA) Gaming Ordinance (2007), § 4.10.3(b).
103 Habamatolel Pomo of Upper Lake (CA) Gaming Ordinance (2012), § 4.10.1.
104 Red Lake Band of Chippewa Indians (MN) Gaming Ordinance (2000), § 326(a).
105 Match-e-be-nash-she-wish Band of Pottawatomi Indians (MI) Gaming Ordinance (2020), § 8.03.5.

IGRA, contain a legal authorization for a waiver for gaming commissioners. Specifically, Section 9 of all 11 compacts states that persons with certain criminal convictions cannot serve as gaming commissioners: felonies within the previous 10 years, gambling-related offenses, fraud or misrepresentation, or violations of Wisconsin's gaming codes.[106] Section 9 contains the rider "unless the person has been pardoned," signifying that convictions that have been removed from a person's criminal record are not a bar to serving as gaming commissioner. In addition, these compacts contain an additional exception at Section 9(B), "if the Tribal Council waives such restriction by legislative resolution after the applicant or employee has demonstrated to the Council evidence of sufficient rehabilitation and present fitness."[107]

Of the 11 Wisconsin tribes, however, only 4 have a provision to waive previous criminal convictions of potential gaming commissioners. Just one ordinance—that of the Forest County Potawatomi Community—explicitly includes both the "unless pardoned" exception and the Tribal Council waiver provision that was authorized in the Tribal-State Gaming Compact.[108] As noted earlier, the Lac du Flambeau Band of Lake Superior Chippewa Indians has a waiver provision that departs from the Tribal-State Compact wording: the exclusion for gaming commissioners may be waived if the Tribe finds a "significant amount of time has passed, no less than ten (10) years from the time of conviction ... and that the person is now of trustworthy and of proper moral character."[109] The Bad River Band of the Lake Superior Tribe of Chippewa Indians is counted in the 20 tribal jurisdictions above that use the waiver provision in the NIGC Model Ordinance. This provision only applies to tribal members and only if "a significant amount of time has passed" and the person is now of "trustworthy character."[110] It does not contain the 10-year language used in the Lac du Flambeau Band ordinance.

Four more Wisconsin tribes use the "unless pardoned" language of the Tribal-State Compact, in which a conviction pardoned by the appropriate executive would not bar appointment (or election) to the tribal gaming commission. These four, the Ho-Chunk Nation, Sokaogon Chippewa Community, Lac Courte Oreilles Band of Lake Superior Chippewa Indians, and Oneida

106 For Wisconsin's Tribal-State Gaming Compacts, see State of Wisconsin Department of Administration, "Tribal Compacts and Amendments," https://doa.wi.gov/Pages/AboutDOA/TribalCompactsAndAmendments.aspx (last accessed October 27, 2023).

107 Id. See, e.g., Bad River Band of Lake Superior Chippewa Indians and State of Wisconsin Gaming Compact of 1991, § 9(A)–(B). This provision is identical to the other ten Wisconsin tribal gaming compacts.

108 Forest County Potawatomi Community (WI) Gaming Ordinance (1997), § 802(d).

109 Lac du Flambeau Band of Lake Superior Chippewa Indians (WI) Gaming Ordinance (2012), § 43.302(9).

110 Bad River Band of the Lake Superior Tribe of Chippewa Indians (WI) Gaming Ordinance (2019), § 9(F)(d)(i).

Tribe, explicitly contemplate a pardon from tribal, state, or federal authorities.[111] The Oneida Tribe adds an additional circumstance that would bar appointment or election to the tribal gaming commission beyond those listed in the Tribal-State Compact: namely, theft, fraud, or conversion where the tribe itself is the victim.[112] The remaining four Wisconsin tribes have opted not to include either the "unless pardoned" language or a waiver provision for tribal gaming commissioner appointments. The gaming ordinances of the Menominee Tribe, Red Cliff Band of Lake Superior Chippewa Indians, and the St. Croix Chippewa Indians do not have provisions for either a pardon or a waiver that would restore eligibility for a potential gaming commissioner with a prior criminal conviction.[113] The Stockbridge Munsee Community has a provision for "Tribal Gaming Waivers," including a waiver hearing process, for gaming licensees.[114] However, the provision does not restore eligibility for tribal office or employment: "A tribal gaming waiver shall not act to rehabilitate the applicant for consideration for the Commission."[115]

Gaming License Eligibility

Gaming licenses are the most complex area of collateral consequences in the entire field of tribal law. Under federal law, gaming licenses are required for persons in management positions, defined in the IGRA as PMOs or KOs; the procedure for receiving a gaming license involves an extensive background check.[116] PMOs include the chief financial officer, anyone with authority to set policy for gaming operations, and anyone with hiring authority.[117] KOs include gaming employees on the floor: bingo callers, counting room supervisors, security guards, custodians of gaming devices or cash, floor managers, pit bosses, dealers, croupiers, and others meeting a certain salary threshold.[118] Where the applicant is a business entity rather than an individual, the licensing requirement may apply to officers, directors, or shareholders or financers of 10% or more of the enterprise, as per the Tribal-State Gaming

111 Ho-Chunk Nation (WI) Gaming Ordinance (2008), § 13(b)(7); Sokaogon Chippewa Community (WI) Gaming Ordinance (2001), § 400.03(1)(e); Lac Courte Oreilles Band of Lake Superior Chippewa Indians (1995), § 703.03(4); Oneida Tribe (WI) Gaming Ordinance (2009), § 21.6-6(a).

112 Oneida Tribe (WI) Gaming Ordinance (2009), § 21.6-6(d).

113 See Menominee Tribe (WI) Gaming Ordinance (2008), § 2.031(3)–(4); Red Cliff Band of Lake Superior Chippewa Indians (WI) Gaming Ordinance (2014), § 17.10.6(a); St. Croix Chippewa Indians (WI) Tribal Code, 6 S.C.T.C. § 02.05(4)(d).

114 Stockbridge Munsee Community (WI) Gaming Ordinance (2021), §§ GMG.01.04(dd)–(ee), GMG.01.09(l)(37).

115 Id. at § GMG.01.09(h)(3)(C).

116 25 C.F.R. §§ 556.4, 558.3.

117 25 C.F.R. § 502.19.

118 25 C.F.R. § 502.14.

Compact.[119] An NIGC Bulletin dated April 20, 1994, provided guidance to tribal jurisdictions on background investigations, suitability determinations, and licensing standards. This Bulletin stated, in relevant part:

> An authorized tribal official must review a person's prior activities, criminal record, if any, and reputation, habits and associations to make a finding concerning the eligibility for employment in the gaming operation. If the authorized tribal official, in applying the standards adopted in a tribal ordinance, determines that employment poses a threat to the public interest or to the effective regulation of gaming, or enhances the dangers of unsuitable, unfair, or illegal practices and methods in the conduct of gaming, a management contractor or a tribal gaming operation shall not employ that person in a key employee or primary management official position.[120]

The wording of this provision is not strictly a collateral consequence: it merely requires a tribal gaming authority to consider a person's "criminal record" in the licensing decision. Some tribes have used the wording in the NIGC Bulletin in their exclusions. The Cloverdale Rancheria of Pomo Indians uses the language in its standards for an eligibility determination for a gaming license.[121] The Citizen Potawatomi Nation uses the phrasing in the NIGC Bulletin as a bar to employment in the gaming industry.[122]

Although federal law mandates a background check for these senior management positions, it does not specifically require persons with certain criminal convictions to be excluded from consideration entirely. However, many tribes go beyond what federal law requires in mandating exclusion for certain convictions. In total, at least 125 tribal jurisdictions (39.9%) attach collateral consequences to PMO and KO positions, bearing in mind that some provisions are difficult to classify because they may be written in a very general or highly discretionary way. Additionally, many tribes also extend these exclusions to subordinate employees or to interested third parties such as contractors, suppliers, manufacturers, or lessors. Tribes may require that persons in other roles, such as tribal gaming office holders, third-party contractors, or even non-gaming personnel, meet the eligibility standards for

119 John Maloney, "California's Tribal-State Gaming Compacts," 3 *Gaming Law Review* 311–16 (1999).

120 National Indian Gaming Commission, "Tribal Background Investigations, Suitability Determinations, and Licensing of Key Employees and Primary Management Officials," Bulletin No. 94-4 (April 20, 1994), available at: https://www.nigc.gov/images/uploads/bulletins/1994-4suitdeterminations.pdf.

121 Cloverdale Rancheria of Pomo Indians (CA) Gaming Ordinance (2005), § 10(H)(1).

122 Citizen Potawatomi Nation (OK) Gaming Ordinance (2006), § 14(c).

gaming licenses. Still other tribal jurisdictions have different licensing standards for senior management and lower-level employees or third parties.

Background Check Requirement

The IGRA requires background checks for certain officials in the Indian gaming and casino industry. Specifically, the IGRA requires that tribes have an "adequate system" that "ensures that background investigations are conducted on the primary management officials and key employees of the gaming enterprise."[123] Tribes must notify the NIGC of the results of background check investigations on applicants for these management positions and must have a "standard whereby any person whose prior activities, criminal record, if any, or reputation, habits and associations pose a threat to the public interest or to the effective regulation of gaming."[124] This background check requirement is designed to prevent infiltration by organized crime into Indian gaming, though notable links between certain Indian casinos and organized crime families have been reported in the past.[125] Under the IGRA, the tribe, not the NIGC, conducts the background check. State-regulated gaming and casino industries, however, often have a more elaborate regulatory structure than most tribal gaming authorities; in addition, the NIGC may not have the resources to scrutinize tribal background check procedures.[126]

The Code of Federal Regulations provides the minimum standards to be used in background check investigations for PMOs and KOs. Applicants for tribal gaming licenses must disclose any felony prosecution or conviction, any misdemeanor prosecution or conviction within the preceding 10 years, or any criminal charges (excluding minor traffic charges) within the previous 10 years regardless of whether the applicant was convicted.[127] The NIGC Model Gaming Ordinance provides that although the CFR requires background checks only for PMOs and KOs, a tribe "may … wish to require all employees of its gaming operation to undergo background investigations."[128] Nearly all 313 tribal gaming ordinances reviewed here have language that exactly mirrors the background check requirements of 25 C.F.R. § 556.4(a)(8)–(10).

123 27 U.S.C. § 2710(b)(2)(F).

124 Id. at § 2710(b)(2)(F)(ii). Although this provision specifically applies to Class II gaming, referring to games of chance such as bingo, it is also incorporated into the subsection regulating Class III gaming (referring to casino-style games). 27 U.S.C. § 2710(d)(1)(A)(ii) (incorporating the standards of subsection (b)).

125 Heather Saum, "Native American Gaming: Will Organized Crime Organize on the Reservation?" 3(1) *Gaming Law Review* 49, 54–55 (1999).

126 Id. at 54.

127 25 C.F.R. § 556.4(a)(8)–(10).

128 NIGC Revised Model Gaming Ordinance, supra note 14 at 20 n 19.

A small number of tribes have background check requirements that are stronger than required by federal regulations. One variation, seen in the ordinances of Pueblo of Tesuque, Shingle Springs Band of Miwok Indians, Tonto Apache Tribe, and Yavapai-Apache Nation, removes the 10-year sunset date for disclosure of prior misdemeanor convictions so that the disclosure requirement, like for felony convictions, is lifelong.[129] Other variations include specifying certain misdemeanors for which disclosure is lifelong. The Rincon Band of Luiseno Mission Indians requires disclosure of all felonies, misdemeanors within 10 years, and "any gaming-related criminal conviction, whether felony or misdemeanor."[130] The Confederated Tribes of the Umatilla Indian Reservation have a blanket provision, applying to both high and low security employees, that requires disclosure of "[a]ll criminal proceedings, except for minor traffic offenses, to which the applicant has been a party."[131] The Ewiiaapaayp Band of Kumeyaay Indians also discounts minor traffic offenses within the preceding 10 years, but includes driving while intoxicated and reckless or careless driving.[132] The Table Mountain Rancheria even requires disclosure of non-criminal lawsuits. An applicant must disclose his or her "criminal and civil record, if any, and an explanation of any crimes for which he has ever been arrested, convicted, been named or been a party to a civil suit."[133] The Fort Independence Indian Community of Paiute Indians requires disclosure of any bankruptcy proceedings filed within the previous 10 years.[134] The Cachil DeHe Band of Wintun Indians adds a requirement to disclose any conviction that has been expunged or sealed and any finding of juvenile delinquency after an applicant's 16th birthday.[135]

A handful of tribes previously had background investigation procedures that were weaker than required under 25 C.F.R. Part 556, namely by requiring disclosure of felonies only within the preceding 10 years. At least two tribes, the Comanche Nation and the Cowlitz Indian Tribe, changed their gaming ordinances to require lifelong disclosure of felony convictions.[136] However, the Shinnecock Indian Nation, Greenville Rancheria of Maidu

129 Pueblo of Tesuque (NM) Gaming Ordinance (2019), § 8(d)(3)(H)–(J); Shingle Springs Band of Miwok Indians (CA) Gaming Ordinance (2014), § 9.4(viii)–(x); Tonto Apache Tribe (AZ) Gaming Ordinance (2008), § 112(b)(8)–(10); Yavapai-Apache Nation (AZ) Gaming Ordinance (2022), § 402(b)(8)–(10).

130 Rincon Band of Luiseno Mission Indians (CA) Gaming Ordinance (2011), § 11.05(j).

131 Confederated Tribes of the Umatilla Indian Reservation (OR) Gaming Ordinance (1994), § 13(A)(2)(p).

132 Ewiiaapaayp Band of Kumeyaay Indians (CA) Gaming Ordinance (2001), § 5.03(a)(10).

133 Table Mountain Rancheria (CA) Gaming Ordinance (2006), § 5.2.3(5).

134 Fort Independence Indian Community of Paiute Indians (CA) Gaming Ordinance (2016), § 205(b)(9).

135 Cachil DeHe Band of Wintun Indians (CA) Gaming Ordinance (1994), § 8(C)(1)(h).

136 Compare Comanche Nation (OK) Gaming Ordinance (2005), § 205(15)–(16) with Comanche Nation (OK) Gaming Ordinance (2015), § 404(B)(8)–(9). Also compare Cowlitz

Indians, and White Earth Band of the Minnesota Chippewa Indians still have a provision that only requires disclosure of felonies within the preceding 10 years, which may not comply with the federal regulation.[137] Another variation is the ordinance of the Confederated Salish and Kootenai Tribes, which require disclosure of misdemeanors within the previous 5 years, rather than 10 as in the federal regulation at 25 C.F.R. § 556.4(a)(9).[138]

Eligibility for Gaming Licenses

Federal law mandates a background check for gaming licenses for PMOs and KOs, but does not specifically require any per se exclusions for prior criminal convictions. Nonetheless, because of the strictness of the federal requirement, gaming licenses for PMOs and KOs tend to be the area with the strongest exclusions in tribal gaming law. At least 125 of the 313 tribal jurisdictions explored here attach some exclusions for prior criminal convictions specifically to gaming license eligibility, bearing in mind that additional jurisdictions may have informal, discretionary, or hidden collateral consequences that are not obvious from the wording of the gaming ordinance.

The simplest construction is a categorical exclusion for felony convictions. Four tribes exclude any person with a felony conviction from receiving a gaming license and therefore, serving as a PMO or KO (Agua Caliente Band of Cahuilla Indians, Assiniboine and Sioux Tribes of Fort Peck Reservation, Augustine Band of Cahuilla Indians, and Kiowa Indian Tribe).[139] The Blackfeet Tribe excluded anyone with a felony within the past 10 years.[140] At least 11 tribes exclude any person with a felony conviction or a conviction for any gaming offense.[141] Three additional tribes exclude anyone with a

Indian Tribe (WA) Gaming Ordinance (2005), § 33(B)(8) with Cowlitz Indian Tribe (WA) Gaming Ordinance (2015), § 33(B)(8).

137 Shinnecock Indian Nation (NY) Gaming Ordinance (2020), § 10-17-1(G)(9); White Earth Band of the Minnesota Chippewa Indians (MN) Gaming Ordinance (2019), § 11(b)(8); Greenville Rancheria of Maidu Indians (CA) Gaming Ordinance (2004), § 11(E)(b)(viii).

138 Confederated Salish and Kootenai Tribes of the Flathead Reservation (MT) Gaming Ordinance (1997), § 7.03(a)(8)–(9).

139 Agua Caliente Band of Cahuilla Indians (CA) Gaming Ordinance (2020), § 8(I)(4); Assiniboine and Sioux Tribes of Fort Peck Reservation (MT) Gaming Ordinance (1998), § 413(b); Augustine Band of Cahuilla Indians (CA) Gaming Ordinance (2000), § 904(b); Kiowa Indian Tribe (OK) Gaming Ordinance (2011), § 100.19(b).

140 Blackfeet Tribe (MT) Gaming Ordinance (1997), § 3-106(A).

141 Campo Band of Diegueno Mission Indians (CA), Catawba Indian Nation (SC), Colorado River Indian Tribes (AZ), Fort McDowell Yavapai Nation (AZ), Miami Tribe (OK), Mille Lacs Band of the Minnesota Chippewa Tribe (MN), Navajo Nation (AZ), Pawnee Nation (OK), Pueblo of San Felipe (NM), Sac and Fox Tribe of the Mississippi in Iowa (IA), and the Salt River Pima-Maricopa Indian Community (AZ).

felony within the previous 10 years or a gaming offense (Alabama-Coushatta Tribe of Texas, Burns Paiute Tribe, Ysleta del Sur Pueblo).[142]

Another set of tribes add exclusions for fraud or misrepresentation. The Prairie Island Indian Community excludes anyone convicted of any felony, a gaming offense, or fraud or misrepresentation.[143] Far more common is an exclusion for any felony *within the past 10 years*, a gaming offense, or fraud or misrepresentation: 11 tribes have such an exclusion.[144] Of these 11, four tribes maintain a lifelong felony exclusion for any management entity or controlling shareholder: Eastern Band of Cherokee Indians, Ewiiaapaayp Band of Kumeyaay Indians, Hoopa Valley Tribe, and Lytton Rancheria.[145] The Omaha Tribe of Nebraska has another more elaborate variation: any felony within 10 years, any gaming offense, fraud, misrepresentation, deception, drug offense, or any felony involving dishonesty or untruthfulness.[146] The Seminole Nation flips the placement of the sunset clause: in that jurisdiction, one is excluded with a felony conviction or, within the past 10 years, any conviction involving "an element of dishonesty," to include theft or fraud.[147] Two tribes add drug crimes to this list. The Nez Perce Tribe and the Winnebago Tribe exclude any felony conviction, gaming offense, fraud, misrepresentation, deception, or drug crimes. The Nez Perce Tribe however has a 10-year sunset on all of those offenses, while the Winnebago Tribe has a 10-year sunset on felony convictions or drug offenses specifically.[148]

142 Alabama-Coushatta Tribe of Texas (TX) Gaming Ordinance (2015), § 12(11)(m)(2)(a); Burns Paiute Tribe (OR) Gaming Ordinance (2004), [page 17 on NIGC website, ordinance incomplete]; Ysleta del Sur Pueblo (TX) Gaming Ordinance (2015), § 13(1)(m).

143 Prairie Island Indian Community (MN) Gaming Ordinance (2010), § 311(B).

144 Bad River Band of the Lake Superior Tribe of Chippewa Indians (WI), Cayuga Nation (NY), Eastern Band of Cherokee Indians (NC), Enterprise Rancheria (CA), Ewiiaapaayp Band of Kumeyaay Indians (CA), Ho-Chunk Nation (WI), Hoopa Valley Tribe (CA), Lytton Rancheria (CA), Omaha Tribe (NE), Oneida Tribe (WI), St. Croix Chippewa Indians (WI).

145 Eastern Band of Cherokee Indians (NC) Gaming Ordinance (1996), § 4.03(a)(4) (note that this ordinance has subsequent amendments, but these do not appear to change this provision); Ewiiaapaayp Band of Kumeyaay Indians (CA) Gaming Ordinance (2001), § 4.03(4); Hoopa Valley Tribe (CA) Gaming Ordinance (2021), § 31.16.1(D); Lytton Rancheria (CA) Gaming Ordinance (1999), § 4.03(a)(4). Note that Lytton Rancheria has amended this portion of its ordinance in 2008 to set out new licensing standards. This new provision does not contain an exclusion for PMOs and KOs. However, the amendment does not appear to be a complete ordinance and only applies to PMOs and KOs. For that reason, the exclusion may still apply to others who need a gaming license, including management entities, controlling shareholders, gaming device suppliers, other employees, and gaming establishments. Compare Lytton Rancheria (CA) Gaming Ordinance (1999), § 4.01(a)–(b) with Lytton Rancheria (CA) Gaming Ordinance (2008), § 8.

146 Omaha Tribe (NE) Gaming Ordinance (2013), § 29-1-32(b)(2)–(3).

147 Seminole Nation (OK) Gaming Ordinance (2017), § 203(a)(7)(B).

148 Nez Perce Tribe (ID) Gaming Ordinance (2004), § 6-2-13(a)(1); Winnebago Tribe (NE) Gaming Ordinance (1994), § 9-303(6).

Another jurisdiction that combines a 10-year bar with a specific set of felony convictions is the Yavapai-Prescott Indian Tribe. In this jurisdiction, individuals are ineligible for a gaming facility operator's license, gaming manager's license, or gaming employee's license if they have been convicted, within the prior 10 years, of any gaming offense or any felony involving theft, burglary, embezzlement, assault with a deadly weapon, or murder.[149] In still another variation, the Delaware Tribe of Indians renders ineligible anyone with a conviction for any felony or "relevant misdemeanor" in the previous 10 years or anyone who was incarcerated in a state or federal penitentiary in the previous 15 years.[150]

At least eight jurisdictions, six of them in Michigan, exclude from gaming licenses any person with a criminal conviction of any kind within the preceding 5 years, though these are typically coupled with lifelong exclusions for various crimes. In addition to the 5-year bar, the Nottawaseppi Huron Band of the Potawatomi and the Saginaw Chippewa Indian Tribe add a lifelong exclusion for gaming, fraud, and misrepresentation.[151] The Hannahville Indian Community adds drug crimes in addition to gaming, fraud, and misrepresentation.[152] The Match-e-be-nash-she-wish Band of Pottawatomi Indians adds theft.[153] The Grand Traverse Band of Ottawa and Chippewa Indians has a differently worded version, excluding any conviction within 5 years as well as any gambling-related offense, "felony with an element of theft, fraud, or misrepresentation," or a misdemeanor conviction for theft, fraud, or misrepresentation that would be considered a felony in Michigan.[154] Two California tribes, Habematolel Pomo of Upper Lake and La Posta Band of Diegueno Mission Indians, follow a similar template, excluding anyone convicted of an offense within the previous 5 years, or alternatively convictions for gaming, fraud, or misrepresentation.[155] Additionally, both California tribes and the Saginaw Chippewa in Michigan also allow revocation of a license for convictions relating to embezzlement or sale of illegal drugs.[156] Another

149 Yavapai-Prescott Indian Tribe (AZ) Gaming Ordinance (2011), §§ 24.7(B)(2); 24.8(B)(1); 24.10(B)(1).
150 Delaware Tribe of Indians (OK) Gaming Ordinance (1999), § 15(e)(1)(b)–(c).
151 Nottawaseppi Huron Band of the Potawatomi (MI) Gaming Ordinance (2021), § 8.5-60(C)–(D); Saginaw Chippewa Indian Tribe (MI) Gaming Ordinance (1997), §§ 6.4.2–6.4.3.
152 Hannahville Indian Community (MI) Gaming Ordinance (2000), § 6.8(A)(10)–(11).
153 Match-e-be-nash-she-wish Band of Pottawatomi Indians (MI) Gaming Ordinance (2020), § 12.03.3(B).
154 Grand Traverse Band of Ottawa and Chippewa Indians (MI) Gaming Ordinance (2018), § 116(c)–(d).
155 Habematolel Pomo of Upper Lake (CA) Gaming Ordinance (2012), § 5.16.4(B)–(C); La Posta Band of Diegueno Mission Indians (CA) Gaming Ordinance (2007), § 5.5.4(b)–(c).
156 Habematolel Pomo of Upper Lake (CA) Gaming Ordinance (2012), § 5.12.1(9), (11), (12); La Posta Band of Diegueno Mission Indians (CA) Gaming Ordinance (2007), § 5.12.2(h); Saginaw Chippewa Indian Tribe (MI) Gaming Ordinance (1997), § 6.9.1.9.

Michigan tribe, Keweenaw Bay Indian Community, does not have a specific bar to gaming license eligibility for specific criminal convictions but provides for immediate revocation of a license for convictions involving gaming, fraud, theft, embezzlement, or the sale of illegal drugs.[157] Notably, seven of the eight jurisdictions in this category (excluding the Keweenaw Bay Indian Community) provide for pardons and/or tribal waivers to restore eligibility. Interestingly, for two of the jurisdictions, Match-e-be-nash-she-wish Band of Pottawatomi Indians and Grand Traverse Band of Ottawa and Chippewa Indians, a pardon or tribal waiver can restore eligibility for any of the listed offenses.[158] For the other five jurisdictions, a pardon or tribal waiver can only restore eligibility for the offenses that fall with in the 5-year sunset provision, not the lifelong bar for gaming, fraud, or the other offenses.

The next category of tribal jurisdictions adds crimes of moral turpitude to the exclusion for felonies and gaming offenses. This is the case with the Big Pine Paiute Tribe, Fort McDermott Paiute and Shoshone Tribes, Fort Mojave Indian Tribe, and Utu Utu Gwaitu Paiute Tribe.[159] Four tribal jurisdictions exclude persons with a felony in the previous 5 years, any gaming offense, or crimes involving fraud, misrepresentation, or moral turpitude: Confederated Salish and Kootenai Tribes; Bois Forte Band of Minnesota Chippewa Indians; Fond du Lac Band of Minnesota Chippewa Indians; and White Earth Band of Minnesota Chippewa Indians.[160] The Wampanoag Tribe of Gay Head excludes any felony in the previous 10 years, gaming offenses, fraud, misrepresentation, or crimes of moral turpitude.[161] The Tule River Indian Tribe excludes any felony within the past 10 years involving violence, theft, moral turpitude, or dishonesty, plus any offense at any time involving fraud, misrepresentation, or gambling.[162] The Stockbridge-Munsee Community excludes gaming, theft, fraud, misrepresentation, drug crimes,

157 Keweenaw Bay Indian Community (MI) Gaming Ordinance (2010), § 18B.516(B)(8).

158 Match-e-be-nash-she-wish Band of Pottawatomi Indians (MI) Gaming Ordinance (2020), § 12.03.3(B)–(C) (both provisions are pardonable); Grand Traverse Band of Ottawa and Chippewa Indians (MI) Gaming Ordinance (2018), § 116(c)–(d) (note that pardons restore eligibility for the lifelong offenses and tribal waivers restore eligibility for the 5-year offenses).

159 Big Pine Paiute Tribe (CA) Gaming Ordinance (1996), § 5(A)(b)(1); Fort McDermott Paiute and Shoshone Tribes (NV) Gaming Ordinance (1994), § 14(B)(1); Fort Mohave Indian Tribe (AZ) Gaming Ordinance (1994), § 14(B)(1); Utu Utu Gwaitu Paiute Tribe (CA) Gaming Ordinance (1996), § 5(B)(1).

160 Confederated Salish and Kootenai Tribes (MT) Gaming Ordinance (1997), § 6.03(4)(a); Minnesota Chippewa Tribe (Bois Forte Band) (MN) Gaming Ordinance (1993), § 8(F); Minnesota Chippewa Tribe (Fond du Lac Band) (MN) Gaming Ordinance (2016), § 1310(a)(5); Minnesota Chippewa Tribe (White Earth Band) (MN) Gaming Ordinance (2019), § 23(c).

161 Wampanoag Tribe of Gay Head (MA) Gaming Ordinance (2013), § 3.3(a)(3).

162 Tule River Indian Tribe (CA) Gaming Ordinance (2019), § 8(G)(2).

or any felony within the past 10 years.[163] Notably, that tribe allows a pardon to restore eligibility for gaming, theft, fraud, misrepresentation, or manufacture or sale of illegal drugs, or a waiver from the tribal council to restore eligibility for a felony within 10 years or possession of illegal drugs.[164] The Nisqually Indian Tribe excludes any person convicted of forgery, larceny, extortion, conspiracy to defraud, tax evasion, or any crime involving gaming or moral turpitude.[165] More sweeping is the Kickapoo Tribe, which excludes applicants with convictions for any felony, gaming offense, or crime of dishonesty or moral turpitude, or, within the past 2 years, any other conviction other than traffic offenses.[166]

Like several of the tribes mentioned, a handful of others have more complex hybrid provisions in which some of the listed convictions have a sunset date and some do not. The Southern Ute Indian Tribe and the Ute Mountain Ute, both in Colorado, exclude persons with any felony conviction for a gaming offense, any felony involving fraud, misrepresentation, or theft by deception, or, within the previous 10 years, any other felony, any gaming-related misdemeanor, or any misdemeanor involving fraud, misrepresentation, or theft by deception.[167] The Tulalip Tribes excludes from gaming licenses persons with criminal convictions for forgery, larceny, extortion, conspiracy to defraud, failure to make required payments or reports to government agencies; any crime involving gambling, dishonesty, or theft; or, within the past 10 years, any felony involving assault, physical harm to individuals, physical violence, or moral turpitude; or, within the past 5 years, any misdemeanor involving physical harm or non-violent felonies. Except for gaming offenses, any conviction related to defending tribal treaty rights are not grounds for denial of a license.[168]

In several cases, the tribal jurisdiction has an exclusion for gaming licenses that includes an extensive list of criminal convictions, often a combination of financial crimes and crimes against the person. The Cocopah Tribe excludes anyone with a felony conviction within the past 7 years or a conviction for any gaming offense, as well as one of 15 other offenses (extortion, burglary, larceny, bribery, embezzlement, robbery, racketeering, money laundering, forgery, fraud, murder, voluntary manslaughter, sex offenses, rape, or kidnapping).[169] The Klamath Tribes lists at least 25 offenses that result in mandatory denial of a license, including several types of sex crimes (e.g.,

163 Stockbridge-Munsee Community (WI) Gaming Ordinance (2021), § GTG.01.15(j)(2), (8).
164 Id. at § GTG.01.15(j)(2)–(3), (8).
165 Nisqually Indian Tribe (WA) Gaming Ordinance (2012), § 17.06.17(f).
166 Kickapoo Tribe (OK) Gaming Ordinance (2014), § 110(A)–(B).
167 Southern Ute Indian Tribe (CO) Gaming Ordinance (2018), § 16-5-112(4); Ute Mountain Ute (CO) Gaming Ordinance (2012), § 410(a)(4).
168 Tulalip Tribes (WA) Gaming Ordinance (2005), Regulation 7.040(b)(5)–(6).
169 Cocopah Tribe (AZ) Gaming Ordinance (2022), § 802(1)–(2).

sodomy and child pornography) and several types of crimes by deception or theft (e.g., extortion or manipulation of records, sports bribery, or unlawful credit card transactions).[170] In addition, the tribal gaming authority is also empowered to deny a license to anyone for any other type of criminal conviction, but is not required to.[171] Two Washington State tribes have a similar exclusion. The Stillaguamish Tribe lists 28 offenses, adding embezzlement, crimes of moral turpitude, and concealment of a crime.[172] Notably, the Stillaguamish exception applies to both contractors and to vendors. The Suquamish Tribe also has a substantially similar list of convictions that serve as bars to a gaming license, numbering 26 in total. Unlike the Stillaguamish ordinance, the Suquamish ordinance limits the exclusion to first- or sometimes second-degree offenses, at least for crimes against the person and sex crimes.[173] Notably, in the Suquamish ordinance, denial for high-security employees is mandatory but for low-security employees it is only mandatory for the first five offenses (aggravated murder, assault, kidnapping, rape, and sodomy), and discretionary for the other offenses.[174]

At least one jurisdiction has different eligibility exclusions depending on whether the applicant is seeking a Class II gaming license (for bingo and games of chance) or a Class III gaming license (for Vegas-style casino games). This is the Quechan Tribe of Fort Yuma Reservation in Arizona. In this jurisdiction, no employee may have a prior conviction for felonies involving theft, embezzlement, fraud, or gaming, or felony sale, possession, manufacture, or transport of illegal drugs.[175] For Class II licensees only, applicants may not have under Section 6.5.2 any misdemeanor or felony convictions for gaming offenses, fraud, or misrepresentation; or under Section 6.5.3 any conviction for sale of narcotics, fraud, misrepresentation, forgery, larceny, extortion, conspiracy to defraud, failure to make required payments or reports to government agencies, or bribery; or, within the previous 5 years, any crime involving physical harm or moral turpitude.[176] Note that the crimes under Section 6.5.2 cannot be waived or pardoned, but a pardon for all applicants or a tribal gaming waiver for tribal members can restore eligibility under Section 6.5.3. For Class III licensees, the list of excluded criminal convictions is the same but without the 5-year sunset provision, though adding sale or distribution of illegal drugs within the past 5 years.[177] Unlike Class II licenses,

170 Klamath Tribes (OR) Gaming Ordinance (1995), § 45.14(e)(1).
171 Id. at § 45.14(e)(4).
172 Stillaguamish Tribe (WA) Gaming Ordinance (2017), Chapter 4, § 4(G).
173 Suquamish Tribe (WA) Gaming Ordinance (2009), § 11.5.49(g).
174 Id. at § 11.5.50(a)–(b).
175 Quechan Tribe of the Fort Yuma Indian Reservation (AZ) Gaming Ordinance (2008), § 5.10.
176 Id. at §§ 6.5.2–6.5.3.
177 Id. at §§ 6.4.2–6.4.3, 6.14.16.

eligibility for a Class III license cannot be restored through a pardon or a tribal gaming waiver.

Another complex provision is found in the ordinance of the Pokagon Band of Potawatomi Indians in Michigan. This jurisdiction distinguishes licensees between Level 1 (PMO), Level 2 (KO), Level 3 (Non-Key Employee), and Level 4 (Non-Gaming Employee). For Level 1 licensees, applicants must not have been convicted of any felony, any gaming offense, or any other offense within the past 10 years.[178] This exclusion cannot be pardoned or waived. For Level 2 licensees, an applicant must not have been convicted of any gaming offense, fraud, misrepresentation, or any other offense within the past 5 years unless pardoned or granted a waiver.[179] For Level 3 licensees, an applicant must not have been convicted of any gaming offense, fraud or misrepresentation, or, within the previous 5 years, any other offense involving theft, fraud, dishonesty, or misrepresentation, unless pardoned or granted a waiver.[180] Finally, for all employees (including non-gaming employees), an applicant must not have been convicted of any gambling offense, fraud, or misrepresentation.[181]

Finally, the Standing Rock Sioux Tribe has different eligibility standards depending on whether the applicant is applying to gaming facilities in the portion of the reservation that is in North Dakota or in South Dakota, presumably because of different Tribal-State Gaming Compacts. For the North Dakota portion of the reservation, an applicant for a gaming license must not have had any felony conviction or, within the previous 10 years, calculated from the time of release, any misdemeanor conviction for gaming, fraud, or misrepresentation. For North Dakota applicants, a pardon restores full eligibility; in addition, a tribal gaming waiver may reduce the eligibility bar from 10 years to 5 years.[182] For the South Dakota portion of the reservation, an applicant must not have had a felony, or, within the previous 5 years, calculated from the time of release, a misdemeanor involving gaming, fraud, or misrepresentation. On the South Dakota side, these eligibility exclusions cannot be pardoned or waived.[183]

Automatic Revocation or Suspension of Gaming Licenses

At least 19 tribes do not have a specific gaming license eligibility exclusion for persons with criminal convictions but authorize revocation or suspension of a gaming license upon conviction for certain crimes. Given the broad

178 Pokagon Band of Potawatomi Indians (MI) Gaming Ordinance (2007), § 7.04(b)(1)–(2).
179 Id. at § 7.04(c).
180 Id. at § 7.04(d).
181 Id. at § 7.04(a)(3).
182 Standing Rock Sioux Tribe (SD) Gaming Ordinance (2014), § 23-504(a)(1)–(2).
183 Id. at § 23-504(a)(3).

discretion licensing officials have in determining eligibility, revocation provisions may operate as hidden or informal eligibility exclusions. The simplest are provisions authorizing revocation of gaming licenses upon a felony conviction (four jurisdictions: Fort Sill Apache Tribe, Kialegee Tribal Town, Red Lake Band of Chippewa, Shakopee Mdewakanton Sioux).[184] Two revoke for felonies or crimes of moral turpitude (Crow Creek Sioux Tribe, Central Council of Tlingit and Haida).[185] Three others revoke for felony convictions or convictions for gaming offenses: Mescalero Apache Tribe, Pueblo of Pojoaque, and Pueblo of Tesuque.[186] To this list, we can add the Reno-Sparks Indian Colony, which revokes for any felony or gross misdemeanor conviction, or any gaming conviction.[187] At least five tribal jurisdictions in California have a similar construction, with automatic revocation for any gaming offense, fraud, theft, embezzlement, or sale of illegal drugs (Alturas Indian Rancheria, San Pascual Band of Diegueno Mission Indians, Santa Rosa Indian Community, Santa Rosa Band of Cahuilla Indians, and Susanville Indian Rancheria).[188] Notably, four of those tribes have provisions with identical numbers, suggesting legal sharing among them. The Lac du Flambeau Band of Lake Superior Chippewa Indians has a slightly broader variation that authorizes revocation for gaming offenses, fraud, misrepresentation, theft, embezzlement, any drug crime, or "any other charge that threatens the integrity of tribal gaming."[189] The Delaware Nation of Oklahoma has a similar revocation provision.[190] Finally, the Sauk-Suiattle Indian Tribe has a unique provision that emphasizes financial crimes: forgery, larceny, extortion, conspiracy to defraud, tax evasion, and any crime involving gaming or moral turpitude.[191]

184 Fort Sill Apache Tribe (OK) Gaming Ordinance (2003), § 9(I)(13)(d); Kialegee Tribal Town (OK) Gaming Ordinance (2011), § 309(b)(4); Red Lake Band of Chippewa Indians (MN) Gaming Ordinance (2000), § 208(b)(4); Shakopee Mdewakanton Sioux Community (MN) Gaming Ordinance (2013), § 214(a)(5).

185 Crow Creek Sioux Tribe (SD) Gaming Ordinance (1994), § 16; Central Council of Tlingit and Haida Indian Tribes (AK) Gaming Ordinance (2016), § 24.01.016(B).

186 Mescalero Apache Tribe (NM) Gaming Ordinance (2003), § 15(A)(2); Pueblo of Pojoaque (NM) Gaming Ordinance (2012), § 10-8-11(A); Pueblo of Tesuque (NM) Gaming Ordinance (2019), § 13(a)(4).

187 Reno-Sparks Indian Colony (NV) Gaming Ordinance (1993), §13.3(b)(v), (x).

188 Alturas Indian Rancheria (CA) Gaming Ordinance (2008), § 5.12.1(9), (11); San Pascual Band of Diegueno Mission Indians (CA) Gaming Ordinance (2015), § 5.12.1(9), (11); Santa Rosa Indian Community (CA) Gaming Ordinance (2021), § 5.12.1(9), (11); Santa Rosa Band of Cahuilla Indians (CA) Gaming Ordinance (2023), § 24(b); Susanville Indian Rancheria (CA) Gaming Ordinance (2021), § 5.12.1(9), (11).

189 Lac du Flambeau Band of Lake Superior Chippewa Indians (WI) Gaming Ordinance (2012), § 43.416(2)(d)–(f).

190 Delaware Nation (OK) Gaming Ordinance (2011), § 6.8(A)(9)–(10).

191 Sauk-Suiattle Indian Tribe (WA) Gaming Ordinance (2000), § 18.1.5 (a more recent amended ordinance dated in 2019 is incomplete on the NIGC website).

Discretionary Denial or Revocation of Gaming Licenses

At least seven tribal jurisdictions give tribal gaming authorities discretion to deny or revoke a gaming license for certain criminal convictions. The wording of these provisions is quite variable. The Table Mountain Rancheria ordinance states that the tribal gaming commission "may suspend or revoke" a license for convictions involving gaming, fraud, theft, embezzlement, or moral turpitude, or any other felony.[192] The Pueblo of Isleta state that the gaming commission "may deny" an application for a felony or gross misdemeanor conviction, for convictions for gaming, theft, embezzlement, or fraud, or for "excessive DWI or DUI charges or convictions."[193] Far broader is the provision in the Pueblo of Acoma ordinance, which states that the tribal gaming commission must make a "determination of suitability." According to the provision, "the following criteria may aid in determining suitability," including whether one had any business relationship with or was employed by a person who committed a gaming offense or a felony other than a traffic offense.[194] This provision is unusual because it allows eligibility to turn on association with another person's criminal convictions.

In addition to those above, 12 additional tribal jurisdictions, mostly in California, have an identically worded provision that follows a unique template. The wording of this provision is not contained in California's Tribal-State Gaming Compacts and therefore is likely to be the product of legal sharing among these jurisdictions. The Gaming Ordinance of the Federated Indians of Graton Rancheria is illustrative: the tribal gaming commission "shall take into consideration" whether the applicant

> has ever been convicted of … forgery, larceny, extortion, conspiracy to defraud, willful failure to make required payments or reports to any [government] agency …, of bribing or otherwise unlawfully influencing a public official …, or of any felony or misdemeanor involving any gaming activity, physical harm to individuals or moral turpitude.[195]

The combination of the discretionary wording with the specific list of offenses may indicate an informal policy of excluding persons with criminal convictions from eligibility for gaming licenses, but may also provide an opportunity for rehabilitation or waiver in appropriate cases. The nine other jurisdictions with this provision are the Ak-Chin Indian Community, Capitan Grande Band of Diegueno Mission Indians (Viejas Group), Guidiville

192 Table Mountain Rancheria (CA) Gaming Ordinance (2006), § 5.13.1(9), (11), (12) (note that crimes of "moral turpitude" are listed twice).
193 Pueblo of Isleta (NM) Gaming Ordinance (2000), Chapter 5, § 11(A)(2)–(6).
194 Pueblo of Acoma (NM) Gaming Ordinance (2011), § 11-1-18(A).
195 Federated Indians of Graton Rancheria (CA) Gaming Ordinance (2008), art. 9, § 6(g).

Rancheria, La Jolla Band of Luiseno Indians, Northfork Rancheria of Mono Indians, Paskenta Band of Nomlaki Indians, Pauma Band of Luiseno Mission Indians, Pinoleville Pomo Nation, Sycuan Band of the Kumeyaay Nation, Wilton Rancheria, and Wiyot Tribe.[196]

Of these ten jurisdictions, we may notice several slight variations. First, the Wilton Rancheria and Sycuan Band ordinances use the language "may take into consideration" rather than the "shall" used in the others, which suggests greater discretion is used.[197] Second, the Sycuan Band has a slight variation in the excluded offenses, replacing failure to make payments or reports to appropriate government authorities with misappropriation of funds.[198] Third is a provision unique to the ordinance of the Pauma Band of Luiseno Mission Indians that narrows the discretion available to the tribal gaming authority. This provision states that revocation or denial of a license is mandatory if the conviction is for a felony offense, "unless the licensee is a Tribal member, in which case such a conviction is not an absolute bar to licensing" or the licensee has had the felony conviction expunged or reduced to a misdemeanor, in which it is also "not an absolute bar" to eligibility.[199] This provision in essence turns the discretionary eligibility bar into a mandatory bar with a discretionary waiver. For the Viejas Group of the Capitan Grande Band of Diegueno Mission Indians, a separate clause mandatorily denies a gaming license to any person convicted of a felony or gaming offense, so the discretionary template provision applies only to non-gaming misdemeanors.[200]

An entirely different type of discretionary denial provision is found in the ordinance of the Washoe Tribe. This provision states that the tribal gaming commission "may establish additional regulations to govern the determination of eligibility, including regulations that would permit a person convicted of certain crimes (but not crimes of moral turpitude or crimes of dishonesty)

196 Ak-Chin Indian Community (AZ) Gaming Ordinance (2008), § 9.2(d); Capitan Grande Band of Diegueno Mission Indians (Viejas Group) (CA) Gaming Ordinance (2018), § 5.09(F); Guidiville Rancheria (CA) Gaming Ordinance (1995), § 8(c)(7); La Jolla Band of Luiseno Indians (CA) Gaming Regulation 002 (2003), § 3(G); Northfork Rancheria of Mono Indians (CA) Gaming Ordinance (2017), § 8(a); Paskenta Band of Nomlaki Indians (CA) Gaming Ordinance (2022), art. 20, § 8(G); Pauma Band of Luiseno Mission Indians (CA) Gaming Regulation 1 (2022), § 9; Pinoleville Pomo Nation (CA) Gaming Ordinance (2004), § 6; Sycuan Band of the Kumeyaay Nation (2017), § 4.04(F); Wilton Rancheria (CA) Gaming Ordinance (2019), § 3-608(A)(7); Wiyot Tribe (CA) Gaming Ordinance (2004), art. 9, § 6(g).

197 Wilton Rancheria (CA) Gaming Ordinance (2019), § 3-608(A)(7); Sycuan Band of the Kumeyaay Nation (CA) Gaming Ordinance (2017), § 4.04(F).

198 Sycuan Band of the Kumeyaay Nation (CA) Gaming Ordinance (2017), § 4.04(F).

199 Pauma Band of Luiseno Mission Indians (CA) Gaming Ordinance (2022), Gaming Regulation 1, § 9.

200 Viejas Group of the Capitan Grande Band of Diegueno Mission Indians (CA) Gaming Ordinance (2018), § 5.09.

to be employed in certain gaming positions," so long as such provisions do not conflict with the background check requirements or the Tribal-State Gaming Compact.[201] This unique provision contains a clear eligibility exclusion (for convictions involving moral turpitude or dishonesty) but gives the gaming authority discretion to create other eligibility bars or a waiver process.

Combination Discretionary and Mandatory Revocation Provisions

In addition to several tribes mentioned already, at least four additional jurisdictions have a combination of discretionary and mandatory denial provisions for gaming licenses. For the Fort Belknap Indian Community, an applicant must not be guilty of "pandering or other crime or misdemeanor opposed to decency or morality," defined as either a felony that "has not been removed from the record of the individual" or a misdemeanor within the preceding 1 year that has also not been removed.[202] However, the tribal gaming authority *may* deny a license for conviction of a felony, gaming offense, embezzlement, or other crime against tribal gaming policy or to a person who is actually incarcerated in a state or federal penitentiary for a felony or gaming offense.[203]

Two Arizona tribal jurisdictions with nearly identical versions have ambiguities created by overlap between the convictions for which denial is mandatory and for which it is discretionary. The Pascua Yaqui Tribe states that the gaming authority "shall not issue" a license if the applicant has been convicted of a felony in the previous 7 years "unless that felony has been set aside" or has ever been convicted of a felony related to extortion, burglary, larceny, bribery, embezzlement, robbery, racketeering, money laundering, forgery, fraud, murder, voluntary manslaughter, sex offenses, rape, or kidnapping.[204] A second provision states that the gaming authority "may deny" a license for conviction of forgery, larceny, extortion, conspiracy to defraud, failure to make proper payments or reports to a government agency, bribing or unlawfully influencing a public official, or any felony or misdemeanor involving gaming, physical harm to individuals, or moral turpitude.[205] The Yavapai-Apache Nation has identical provisions.[206] This provision appears to be a composite from separate sources and may simply be an instance of poor drafting; the wording of the discretionary second provision mirrors the discretionary provision in the ten California jurisdictions in the previous

201 Washoe Tribe (NV) Gaming Ordinance (2015), § 20-60-60(6).
202 Fort Belknap Indian Community (MT) Gaming Ordinance (2009), § 15.2.4(B).
203 Id. at § 15.2.8(A)(2)–(6).
204 Pascua Yaqui Tribe (AZ) Gaming Ordinance (2021), § 220(A).
205 Id. at § 230(A).
206 Yavapai-Apache Nation (AZ) Gaming Ordinance (2022), §§ 409(a)–(c), 502(f).

section. The two provisions overlap and at least some of the same offenses fall within both, such as larceny, extortion, and bribery, so it is not clear whether the license denial in these cases is discretionary or mandatory. To properly give effect to both provisions, one must assume that the second discretionary provision refers only to non-felony convictions; in felony cases, the denial is mandatory.

A different variation of a hybrid provision is found in the Sac and Fox Nation of Missouri, located in Kansas. This jurisdiction provides for both mandatory denials and permissive denials. The gaming commission must deny licenses to any applicant who has been convicted of any crime involving gaming or embezzlement, but may deny for convictions involving moral turpitude, larceny, any felony, or a gross misdemeanor involving theft, embezzlement, fraud, or violence.[207] Interestingly, this provision suffers from a similar ambiguity as the Pascua Yaqui and Yavapai-Apache ordinances: namely, that embezzlement appears on both lists. In this case, one can assume that the first provision relates to felony embezzlement and the second to gross misdemeanor embezzlement.

Employment in the Gaming Industry

In some cases, tribal jurisdictions will impose collateral consequences not only on PMOs and KOs, but on non-management or non-gaming personnel, personnel working for the tribal gaming offices, or third-party contractors and suppliers. Federal law does not specifically require background checks for non-gaming employees, personnel in tribal gaming offices, or third parties involved in the gaming industry, except for management contractors.[208] However, some Tribal-State Compacts may impose more robust rules, depending on the bargain struck between tribes and state regulators.

Restrictions on Gaming Employment

Many tribes attach collateral consequences to all employees in the gaming industry, not just senior management officials. In several cases, these restrictions are less onerous than for PMOs and KOs or require a different type of license, sometimes called a "Work Permit," "Gaming Employee License," or a "Class B License." One example of a gradated collateral consequence exclusion is found in the gaming ordinance of the Pueblo of Picuris, which excludes from gaming employment any person who has, within the previous 5 years, any convictions for felony crimes, gaming offenses, theft of money

207 Sac and Fox Nation of Missouri (KS) Gaming Ordinance (1998), §§ 5(G)(1)(f), 5(G)(2)(i).
208 For a discussion of federal requirements for management contracts, see infra notes 261 et seq.

or goods, or crimes of dishonesty, but extends the exclusion to 20 years for PMOs and KOs.[209] The simplest exclusion for employees is on convictions for gaming offenses only. This is seen in the ordinance of the Pueblo of Pojoaque.[210] Seven tribes exclude employment in the gaming industry for anyone convicted of a felony or gaming offense (Arapaho Tribe of the Wind River Reservation, Colorado River Indian Tribes, Gila River Indian Community, Miami Tribe, Mississippi Band of Choctaw Indians, Pueblo of Taos, and White Mountain Apache Tribe).[211] Jamul Indian Village adds crimes of fraud or misrepresentation but allows pardons to restore eligibility.[212] The Crow Tribe excludes persons with convictions for felonies, gaming offenses, or crimes of moral turpitude, excluding juvenile misdemeanors.[213]

Two examples of jurisdictions that require gaming licenses for all employees in the gaming industry, not just PMOs and KOs, are the Poarch Band of Creeks and the Jicarilla Apache Nation. The Poarch Band of Creeks has a broader exclusion that applies to all employees: no one convicted of any felony, any gaming offense, or any misdemeanor involving theft or conversion of property.[214] For PMOs and KOs, an additional exclusion applies (although one with substantial overlap): any felony, embezzlement, theft, or any other "money-related or honesty-related crime."[215] The Jicarilla Apache Nation has an identical exclusion for all employees, but the additional exclusion for PMOs and KOs is more parsimonious. In that jurisdiction, a PMO or KO must not have been convicted of any misdemeanor involving dishonesty, violence, or moral turpitude within the previous 5 years, excluding driving under the influence of alcohol.[216]

Narrower in scope are jurisdictions that only exclude persons from employment in the gaming industry who have specific types of convictions rather than a blanket felony bar. Two tribes, the Alturas Indian Rancheria and the Santa Rosa Indian Community, both in California, exclude persons with

209 Pueblo of Picuris (NM) Gaming Ordinance (2012), § 4(E)(2)(f)(iv).

210 Pueblo of Pojoaque (NM) Gaming Ordinance (2012), § 10-8-10(K) (note that the earlier 1994 ordinance also included felonies, but this was removed in the 2012 amended ordinance).

211 Arapaho Tribe of the Wind River Reservation (WY) Gaming Ordinance (2002), § 704; Colorado River Indian Tribes (AZ) Gaming Ordinance (1994), § 602(e)(2); Gila River Indian Community (AZ) Gaming Ordinance (2016), § 22.512; Miami Tribe (OK) Gaming Ordinance (2021), § 21(d)(1); Mississippi Band of Choctaw Indians (MS) Gaming Ordinance (2021), § 15.1.14(2); Pueblo of Taos (NM) Gaming Ordinance (2009), § 11(H); and White Mountain Apache Tribe (AZ) Gaming Ordinance (2003), § 3.110(1).

212 Jamul Indian Village (CA) Gaming Ordinance (2022), § 11.6(b)(1).

213 Crow Tribe (MT) Gaming Ordinance (2013), § 13(e)(2)(A).

214 Poarch Band of Creeks (AL) Gaming Ordinance (2013), § 20-6-1(a).

215 Id. at § 20-6-1(b).

216 Jicarilla Apache Nation (NM) Gaming Ordinance (2019), § 7(b)(1)(B) (for all employees); § 7(b)(2)(E) (for PMOs and KOs).

convictions for gaming crime or for fraud, though Alturas Indian Rancheria provides for a certificate of rehabilitation to restore eligibility.[217] Also narrower in scope are jurisdictions with a sunset date for eligibility exclusions. The Ysleta del Sur Pueblo excludes persons with felony convictions in the previous 10 years or convictions for gaming offenses or crimes of moral turpitude.[218] The Seminole Tribe of Florida has an identical exclusion for both gaming licenses (for PMOs and KOs) and work permits (for other employees), excluding felonies within the past 10 years or crimes of fraud, misrepresentation, or moral turpitude.[219] The Tonkawa Tribe of Indians excludes as employees of any gaming enterprise persons with felony convictions within the past 10 years, or any gambling-related offenses, fraud, or misrepresentation.[220] A pardon restores eligibility for any of these exclusions. The Spirit Lake Tribe has an identical exclusion, except that the 10-year bar runs from the date of release from parole, probation, or incarceration rather than from the date of conviction.[221] Tribal members may seek a waiver for this exclusion if the Tribe decides that the person has been sufficiently rehabilitated.[222]

For the 12 Michigan tribes, the Tribal-State Gaming Compacts only attach collateral consequences to PMOs and KOs and separately to leases or purchase agreements for Class III gaming equipment or supplies.[223] Restrictions on gaming employees other than PMOs and KOs or third-party suppliers therefore go beyond what the Tribal-State Compact requires. The Bay Mills Indian Community excludes anyone from gaming employment with an adult felony conviction for theft, fraud, or misrepresentation, unless pardoned by the appropriate authority.[224] Hannahville Indian Community prohibits any gaming operator from employing any person convicted of theft, embezzlement, fraud, or gaming crimes, unless a certificate of rehabilitation has been issued by the tribe.[225] (Outside of Michigan, the Delaware Nation in Oklahoma has the same structure, excluding from employment anyone convicted of theft, embezzlement, fraud, or gaming crimes, and also providing

217 Alturas Indian Rancheria (CA) Gaming Ordinance (2008), § 8.3.24; Santa Rosa Indian Community of the Santa Rosa Rancheria (CA) (2021), § 8.2.24.
218 Ysleta del Sur Pueblo (TX) Gaming Ordinance (2015), § 12(5)(a)(2)(a).
219 Seminole Tribe of Florida (FL) Gaming Ordinance (2006), § 4-1.03(a)(4).
220 Tonkawa Tribe of Indians (OK) Gaming Ordinance (2014), § 11.1.
221 Spirit Lake Tribe (ND) Gaming Ordinance, § 8-14-101.
222 Id., § 8-14-101(1).
223 Michigan Gaming Control Board, "Tribal State Compacts in Michigan," https://www.michigan.gov/mgcb/tribal-casinos/tribal-state-compacts-in-michigan (last accessed October 4, 2023). Note that in all the Tribal-State Gaming Compacts, the exclusion on PMOs and KOs is at § 4(D)(2)–(3) and the exclusion for gaming equipment lessors and suppliers is at § 6(B).
224 Bay Mills Indian Community (MI) Gaming Ordinance (2014), § 10.2(BB).
225 Hannahville Indian Community (MI) Gaming Ordinance (2000), § 8.2(AH).

a certificate of rehabilitation to restore eligibility.)[226] Keweenaw Bay Indian Community prohibits a person from receiving a gaming employee license with a conviction for gaming offenses, fraud, theft, embezzlement, or the sale or possession of drugs.[227] The Little Traverse Bay Band of Odawa Indians states that the tribal gaming regulatory commission shall not issue a non-key license to anyone with a felony conviction for theft, fraud, or violence within the previous 5 years, unless pardoned.[228] The Little River Band of Ottawa Indians distinguishes between gaming employee licenses and non-gaming employee licenses. Gaming employee licenses exclude anyone with a conviction for a gaming offense, fraud, or misrepresentation committed as an adult, any other offense within the previous 5 years, or any sex crime that was committed as an adult or resulted in sex offender registration.[229] For the first two categories, a pardon by the state governor or other appropriate authority restores eligibility, but not for sex offenses.[230] Non-gaming employee licenses exclude anyone with a gambling-related conviction or a felony conviction for theft, fraud, or misrepresentation committed as an adult within the previous 3 years.[231] A pardon or, if the applicant is a tribal member, waiver by the gaming commission restores eligibility.

Unlike the Michigan Tribal-State Gaming Compacts, the Tribal-State Gaming Compacts between the State of Wisconsin and the 11 Wisconsin tribes do contain collateral consequences that attach to all employees in tribal gaming industries, including employees of gaming contractors.[232] According to this uniform provision, at Section 9(A)(1) in all the Tribal-State Compacts, employees must not have a felony conviction in the immediately preceding 10 years, any gambling-related conviction, or a conviction for fraud or misrepresentation.[233] However, the Tribal-State Compacts authorize the tribal gaming commission or tribal council to waive this restriction after the employee has demonstrated sufficient evidence of rehabilitation and present fitness.[234] Seven of the Wisconsin tribes have an exclusion that mirrors the Tribal-State Gaming Compact (Forest County Potawatomi, Ho-Chunk Nation, Lac Courte Oreilles Band of Lake Superior Chippewa Indians, Menominee Indian Tribe, Oneida Tribe of Indians, St. Croix Chippewa Indian Tribe,

226 Delaware Nation (OK) Gaming Ordinance (2011), § 8.2(AG).
227 Keweenaw Bay Indian Community (MI) Gaming Ordinance (2010), § 18(B).516(B).
228 Little Traverse Bay Band of Odawa Indians (MI) Gaming Ordinance (2005), § 5(B)(3).
229 Little River Band of Ottawa Indians (MI) Gaming Ordinance (2018), § 10.03(b)(3)–(4), (7).
230 Id.
231 Id. at § 10.02(b)(2).
232 State of Wisconsin Department of Administration, "Tribal Compacts and Amendments," https://doa.wi.gov/Pages/AboutDOA/TribalCompactsAndAmendments.aspx (last accessed October 4, 2023). Note that all Tribal-State Gaming Compacts have the same numbers.
233 Id. See § 9(A)(1) of any of the Wisconsin Tribal-State Gaming Compacts.
234 Id. See § 9(B) of any of the Wisconsin Tribal-State Gaming Compacts.

Sokaogon Chippewa Community).[235] The remaining four gaming ordinances (Bad River Band of Lake Superior Chippewa Indians, Lac du Flambeau Band of Lake Superior Chippewa Indians, Red Cliff Band of Lake Superior Chippewa Indians, Stockbridge Munsee Community) only attach collateral consequences to primary gaming licenses for PMOs and KOs, not to other employees.[236] In these jurisdictions, owing to the nature of the background check and discretionary hiring process, the exclusion for certain criminal convictions may be informal or hidden.

At least 13 tribal jurisdictions have more esoteric employment exclusions that do not specify which crimes render a person ineligible for employment, that allow but do not require a tribe to deny employment for certain crimes, or that do both. Highly discretionary provisions may disadvantage job applicants and lead to arbitrary hiring decisions. Though the wording may provide flexibility to hire a person with a criminal conviction, the lack of transparency could easily lead to hidden collateral consequences that exist in informal policy and not in written law. Nine tribes, all in California and Washington State, have nearly identical discretionary provisions that allow the gaming authority to deny in its sole discretion a Class B or Category B license based on certain criminal convictions: Confederated Tribes and Bands of the Yakama Nation, Coyote Valley Band of Pomo Indians, Hopland Band of Pomo Indians, Jamestown S'Klallam Tribe, La Jolla Band of Luiseno Indians, Scotts Valley Band of Pomo Indians, Sherwood Valley Rancheria, Stillaguamish Tribe, and Tuolumne Band of Me-Wuk Indians.[237] For instance, the Hopland Band's provision states that Class B license applicants

235 Forest County Potawatomi Community (WI) Gaming Ordinance (1995), § 7(A); Ho-Chunk Nation (WI) Gaming Ordinance (2008), § 17(c)(2); Lac Courte Oreilles Band of Lake Superior Chippewa Indians (WI) Gaming Ordinance (1995), § 704.03; Menominee Indian Tribe (WI) Gaming Ordinance (2014), § 347-20(C); Oneida Tribe of Indians (WI) Gaming Ordinance (2009), § 21.12-3(b); St. Croix Chippewa Indian Tribe (WI) Gaming Ordinance (2021), 6 S.C.T.C. § 02.10(9)(a); Sokaogon Chippewa Community (WI) Gaming Ordinance (2001), § 100.22(1).

236 See Bad River Band of Lake Superior Chippewa Indians (WI) Gaming Ordinance (2019), §§ 22–23; Lac du Flambeau Band of Lake Superior Chippewa Indians (WI) Gaming Ordinance (2012), § 43.411; Red Cliff Band of Lake Superior Chippewa Indians (WI) Gaming Ordinance (2014), § 17.14.1 (note that this provision only applies to "any gaming management position" and not to non-gaming employees); Stockbridge Munsee Community (WI) Gaming Ordinance (2021), § GMG.01.15(b).

237 Confederated Tribes and Bands of the Yakama Nation (WA) Gaming Ordinance (2020), § 11(e)(2); Coyote Valley Band of Pomo Indians (CA) Gaming Ordinance (2016), § 10(d)(2); Hopland Band of Pomo Indians (CA) Gaming Ordinance (1996), § 10(d)(2); Jamestown S'Klallam Tribe (WA) Gaming Ordinance (2019), § 7.25.01(B); La Jolla Band of Luiseno Indians (CA) Gaming Ordinance (2005), § 10.8; Scotts Valley Band of Pomo Indians (CA) Gaming Ordinance (1999), § 10(d)(2); Sherwood Valley Rancheria (CA) Gaming Ordinance (1997), § 10(d)(2); Stillaguamish Tribe (WA) Gaming Ordinance (2017), Chapter 4, § 2(B); Tuolumne Band of Me-Wuk Indians (CA) Gaming Ordinance (2012), § 9.6.2.

> must establish that they have not been convicted of a crime, or engaged in any activity, which the Gaming Commission in its sole discretion deems would render such a person a danger to the safety or integrity of the gaming activities.[238]

The Tolowa Dee-ni' Nation, also in California, has an almost identical provision but without creating a Class B license. Rather, this ordinance allows the gaming commission in its sole discretion to deny employment to "persons who are to be employed at a Gaming Facility on Tribal Lands in another capacity, such as in non-gaming related activities" upon disclosure of certain criminal convictions.[239]

Several jurisdictions allow, but do not require, a tribal gaming commission to deny a non-gaming license if convicted of certain crimes. This includes the Tulalip Tribes, which permits but does not require denial of a Category B license upon conviction for a felony or crime involving dishonesty.[240] The relevant provision in the Bishop Paiute Tribe ordinance states that the tribal gaming commission "may after a full investigation deny a license to any applicant (employee or vendor)" who has a conviction for a violent felony, forgery, larceny, extortion, conspiracy to defraud, failure to make official payments, gaming offenses, misappropriation of funds, physical harm to individuals, or crimes of moral turpitude, excluding driving under the influence.[241] This lengthy provision applies to all employees, including non-gaming employees.[242] At the extreme, the Citizen Potawatomi Nation provides an example of a provision authorizing total discretion: "No person shall be employed whose prior activity, criminal record, if any, or reputation, habits and associations pose a threat to the public interest or the effective regulation of gaming."[243] The wording of that provision appears in other tribal gaming ordinances as well because it reflects the provision in federal law at 25 C.F.R. § 556.5, except applied to all employees rather than only to PMOs and KOs.

As with gaming licenses, the Standing Rock Sioux Tribe has one of the more elaborate exclusions for non-gaming employees. In this jurisdiction, an applicant must not have had a felony conviction within the previous 5 years, or convictions for misdemeanors involving theft, gambling, misrepresentation, or fraud within 1 year, with both times calculated from release.[244] However, the tribal gaming commission may waive the felony bar for tribal members only if they have not committed a felony in the preceding 1 year,

238 Hopland Band of Pomo Indians (CA) Gaming Ordinance (1996), § 10(d)(2).
239 Tolowa Dee-ni' Nation (CA) Gaming Ordinance (2015), Art. 3, § 6.0.
240 Tulalip Tribes (WA) Gaming Ordinance (2005), § 4(b)(1)(vii)(C).
241 Bishop Paiute Tribe (CA) Gaming Ordinance (2012), § 304(F).
242 Id. at § 301.
243 Citizen Potawatomi Nation (OK) Gaming Ordinance (2006), § 14(c).
244 Standing Rock Sioux Tribe (SD) Gaming Ordinance (2014), § 23-504(b)(1).

calculated from release, and have none of the excluded misdemeanor convictions. The waiver process includes provision for a hearing and a determination that the job applicant has been rehabilitated. However, even with the waiver, a person with a felony conviction may not assume the duties of a PMO or KO at any time unless she or he has a gaming license.[245]

Restrictions on Gaming Commission Employment

At least 13 jurisdictions attach collateral consequences of conviction to employment in the tribal gaming commission office or regulatory agency, including for investigators. Notably, 6 of the 13 jurisdictions are in Arizona and reflect wording in that state's Tribal-State Gaming Compact (2021), which includes "Tribal Gaming Office employee" in its restrictions on gaming licenses for employees in tribal gaming industries. Arizona's Tribal-State Gaming Compact specifically excludes from tribal gaming employment, including employment in a tribal gaming office, anyone with a conviction for a gaming offense, anyone convicted of a felony in the past 7 years unless it has been "set aside," or anyone convicted of any "felony relating to extortion, burglary, larceny, bribery, embezzlement, robbery, racketeering, money laundering, forgery, fraud, murder, voluntary manslaughter, sex offenses, rape or kidnapping."[246] One Arizona tribe, the Tohono O'odham Nation, has adopted the provision in the Tribal-Gaming Compact in identical form for gaming regulatory licenses.[247] Notably, that jurisdiction also uses the identical exclusion for gaming manager's licenses, gaming employee's licenses, and gaming facility operator's licenses.[248] However, the other Arizona tribes included in this category have exclusions for gaming office employees broader than that required by the Compact.

These restrictions are typically separate from collateral consequences that attach to gaming commissioners or directors of gaming agencies, which this study classifies as restrictions on appointment to tribal office rather than restrictions on employment. The simplest exclusions for gaming regulatory employees are for felony convictions and for gaming offenses. This exclusion is found in the gaming ordinances of the Gila River Indian Community and the Salt River Pima-Maricopa Indian Community, both in Arizona, and the Quapaw Tribe in Oklahoma.[249] The Shoshone Paiute Tribes of the Duck Valley Reservation add bribery to this list for staff of the Tribal Gaming

245 Id. at § 23-504(b)(2)–(3).
246 Arizona Tribal-State Gaming Compact (2021), § 5(d)(1)–(3).
247 Tohono O'odham Nation (AZ) Gaming Ordinance (2021), § 402(f).
248 Id. at §§ 502(b), 602(a), 802.
249 Gila River Indian Community (AZ) Gaming Ordinance (2003), § 320; Salt River Pima-Maricopa Indian Community (AZ) Gaming Ordinance (AZ) Gaming Ordinance (2016), § 15.5-13; Quapaw Tribe of Indians (OK) Gaming Ordinance (2012), §§ 10(C), 11(D).

Agency, while the Ute Mountain Ute add crimes of moral turpitude to their exclusion for gaming investigators.[250] Some tribes have a sunset provision. The Delaware Tribe of Indians excludes convictions for all felonies and crimes of dishonesty or moral turpitude within the past 10 years for investigator positions.[251] The Tonkawa Tribe excludes gaming offenses, any felony in the previous 10 years, or any offense of fraud or misrepresentation.[252] In its 2003 gaming ordinance, the Navajo Nation excluded from employment in the Gaming Regulatory Office any felony within the past 10 years and any gaming offense, though this provision was not included in the revised 2019 amended ordinance.[253] The Yavapai-Prescott Indian Tribe excluded any gaming offense within the past 10 years and only specific felonies within the previous 10 years, namely for theft, burglary, embezzlement, assault with a deadly weapon, or murder.[254]

Several tribes use a different template. Two tribal jurisdictions use the framing of "money- or honesty-related" crime, which was originally used in the NIGC Model Gaming Ordinance. These are the Fort McDowell Yavapai Nation, which excludes anyone with a felony conviction or convictions for embezzlement, theft, or money- or honesty-related crimes, and the Snoqualmie Indian Tribe, which excludes persons convicted of any felony, gaming offense, misdemeanor embezzlement or theft, or any money- or honesty-related crime.[255] Finally, one jurisdiction, the Stockbridge Munsee Community in Wisconsin, excludes as staff in its Compliance Department anyone with a conviction for any felony, gaming offense, or misdemeanor involving dishonesty, fraud, misrepresentation, or moral turpitude.[256] This jurisdiction has waivers for gaming license eligibility exclusions, including previous criminal convictions; however, staff of the Compliance Department are ineligible for these waivers.[257]

Restrictions on Third Party Licenses or Agreements

Exclusions from involvement in tribal gaming based on previous criminal convictions extend to third-party licenses and contracts, to include management

250 Shoshone Paiute Tribes of the Duck Valley Reservation (NV) Gaming Ordinance (2012), §§ 10(c), 11(d). These provisions are otherwise identical to the Quapaw Tribe's ordinance. Ute Mountain Ute Tribe (CO) Gaming Ordinance (2003), § 206(c).
251 Delaware Tribe of Indians (OK) Gaming Ordinance (1999), § 15(b).
252 Tonkawa Tribe of Indians (OK) Gaming Ordinance (2014), § 11.1 (provision extends to all employees in the gaming industry as well).
253 Navajo Nation (AZ) Gaming Ordinance (2003), § 402(c).
254 Yavapai-Prescott Indian Tribe (AZ) Gaming Ordinance (2011), § 24.4(L).
255 Fort McDowell Yavapai Nation (AZ) Gaming Ordinance (2020), § 503; Snoqualmie Indian Tribe (WA) Gaming Ordinance (2015), § 8.04(C).
256 Stockbridge Munsee Community (WI) Gaming Ordinance (2021), § GMG.01.11(d)(2).
257 Id. at § GMG.01.11(d)(3).

contractors, suppliers, vendors, manufacturers, lessees, operators, stockholders, and financiers. These exclusions can come in the form of eligibility for a special license (such as a supplier's license or vendor's license) or as a condition to tribal approval of the outside contract. As one federal prosecutor wrote, unscrupulous individuals may avoid mandatory NIGC background checks by contracting themselves out as vendors or suppliers instead of through employment in casino management.[258] She describes one case in which a known supplier of unlawful casino video games contracted with the Seminole Tribe for 40% of the profits (the tribe retained the other 60%) to provide video games in four casinos. By holding himself out as a machine vendor rather than a gaming manager, the contractor avoided detection in an NIGC background check, which would have revealed a previous federal felony conviction, alleged ties to organized crime, and an unpaid tax debt.[259]

The strictest third-party restrictions are on management contracts, that is, contracts with professional casino operating firms, because Congress had the explicit aim to ensure that tribal gaming revenue remained with the tribe rather than negotiated away to an outside party. In one infamous case, a federal judge temporarily closed a blackjack facility on the Lummi Reservation when two individuals working for the management contractor were found to have felony convictions.[260] For this reason, the IGRA requires the NIGC to approve all management contracts.[261] "Congress intended to insure through this process, first, that Indian tribes (rather than outside parties) are the primary beneficiaries of Indian gaming and, second, that Indian gaming is shielded from organized crime and other corrupting influences."[262] However, because of the strict rules on management contracts, third-party contractors may try to portray their role as a lease, financing agreement, consulting contract, or the like, since non-management contracts need not comply with the NIGC background check rules.[263] This helps explain many tribes' efforts to extend background checks, eligibility exclusions, and revocation and suspension provisions based on prior criminal convictions to other types of contractors besides management contractors.

258 Linda A. Epperley, "Indian Gaming Offices and Tribal White Collar Crime," 58(4) *United States Attorneys' Bulletin* 64–73, 66 (2010).

259 Id. at 66–67.

260 Angela Firkus & David L. Parman, "Indian Reservation Gaming: Much at Stake," 9(4) *OAH Magazine of History* 22–27, 23 (1995); "$1 Million Bid to Start Casino on Lummi Land," *Seattle Times* (June 18, 1990), available at: https://archive.seattletimes.com/archive/?date=19900618&slug=1077809.

261 25 U.S.C. § 2711.

262 Kevin K. Washburn, "The Mechanics of Indian Gaming Management Contract Approval," 8(6) *Gaming Law Review* 333–46, 333 (2004).

263 Washburn, supra note 6 at 432.

At least eight tribal jurisdictions attach collateral consequences to contractors. Of these, five exclude persons with felony convictions or convictions for gaming offenses (Kaibab Band of Paiute Indians, Kalispel Indian Community, Menominee Tribe, Shoalwater Bay Indian Tribe, and Spokane Tribe).[264] The Forest County Potawatomi Community excludes persons with a felony in the prior 10 years, gaming offense convictions, or convictions for fraud or misrepresentation.[265] The Squaxin Island Indian Tribe has a discretionary revocation provision for contractor's licenses for crimes of moral turpitude or dishonesty.[266] The Klamath Tribes in Oregon authorize denial of a gaming contract if the applicant, or any owner or key employee of the applicant, has been convicted of any one of 25 offenses, mostly violent, sexual, financial, or honesty-related crimes.[267]

Another eight jurisdictions attach collateral consequences specifically to management contracts, five of them in Oklahoma. Likely, many other jurisdictions subsume management contracts into broader gaming license eligibility restrictions, contractor restrictions, or restrictions on employment. For tribes that rely on management contractors to operate tribal casinos or gaming establishments, these exclusions apply at a minimum to principals, shareholders, officers, or partners of the contracting firm. Under federal law, management contracts must be approved by the Chair of the NIGC.[268] Of these eight jurisdictions, seven of them exclude as management contractors any person with a conviction for any felony or any gaming offense (Capitan Grande Band of Diegueno Mission Indians (Viejas Group), Coquille Indian Tribe, Ottawa Tribe of Oklahoma, Otoe-Missouria Tribe, Sault Ste. Marie Tribe of Chippewa Indians, Shawnee Tribe, and Tonkawa Tribe).[269] The

264 Kaibab Band of Paiute Indians (AZ) Gaming Ordinance (1994), § 5.04; Kalispel Indian Community (WA) Gaming Ordinance (2022), § 11-15.04(1); Menominee Tribe (WI) Gaming Ordinance (2014), § 347-21(D)(1)(b); Shoalwater Bay Indian Tribe (WA) Gaming Ordinance (2019), § 12-16.04(a); Spokane Tribe (WA) Gaming Ordinance (1996), § 4.04(a).

265 Forest County Potawatomi Community (WI) Gaming Ordinance (1995), § 7A (applies to contractors, employees of contractors, shareholders, or officers of contractors).

266 Squaxin Island Tribe (WA) Gaming Ordinance (2021), § 6.08.380(F).

267 Klamath Tribes (OR) Gaming Ordinance (1995), § 45.15(f).

268 25 U.S.C. § 2711; 25 C.F.R. Part 531.

269 Capitan Grande Band of Diegueno Mission Indians (Viejas Group) (CA) Gaming Ordinance (2018), § 6.04(A); Coquille Indian Tribe (OR) Gaming Ordinance (2020), § 198.300(5)(a); Ottawa Tribe of Oklahoma (OK) Gaming Ordinance (1998), § 3-8; Otoe-Missouria Tribe (OK) Gaming Ordinance (2018), § 5; Sault Ste. Marie Tribe of Chippewa Indians (MI) Gaming Ordinance (2017), § 42.603(1); Shawnee Tribe (OK) Gaming Ordinance (2003), § 38; Tonkawa Tribe (OK) Gaming Ordinance (2014), § 6.2(C)(1).

sixth tribe, Redwood Valley or Little River Band of Pomo Indians, excludes felony convictions only.[270]

At least 16 jurisdictions attach collateral consequences for gaming licenses for other third-party involvement in the gaming or casino industry.[271] These include gaming manufacturers, suppliers, equipment lessors, stockholders, partners of manufacturers, operators, retailers, or vendors. This number is likely an undercount, since jurisdictions may include third-party licenses or agreements in broader categorical exclusions. In perhaps the simplest expression of this, the Colorado River Indian Tribes excludes persons with felony convictions or gaming offense convictions from manufacturer or supplier licenses.[272] The Spirit Lake Tribe prohibits leases or purchase agreements with any lessor or seller (principal thereof) who has been convicted of a felony or gambling-related crime within the previous 5 years.[273] Notably, the Tribal-State Gaming Compact between the Standing Rock Sioux Tribe and the state of North Dakota has an identical provision.[274] However, no such provision exists in the Standing Rock Sioux Tribe's gaming compact with the state of South Dakota. The Lower Sioux Indian Community (in its original 1993 ordinance) and the Bois Forte Band of the Minnesota Chippewa Tribe prohibit lease agreements for video games of chance if any principal was convicted of a felony within the previous 5 years, or any felony or gross misdemeanor involving fraud, misrepresentation, or gambling.[275] One tribe, the Tohono O'odham Nation, extends the sunset period to 7 years for licenses for gaming facility operators, manufacturers, distributors, financers, and vendors of gaming services or equipment.[276] This exclusion is identical to the one the tribe has on gaming commission employment, above, which reflects the Arizona Tribal-State Gaming Compact language. The Standing Rock Sioux

270 Redwood Valley or Little River Band of Pomo Indians (CA) Gaming Code (1995), § 4.04(a).

271 This also does not include special disclosure requirements that apply to vendors or other third-party participants, even if these can serve as hidden collateral consequences. An example of this is the Iowa Tribe of Oklahoma, which requires disclosure for vendors of any convictions for felonies, gaming offenses, or fraud or misrepresentation. Iowa Tribe of Oklahoma (OK) Gaming Ordinance (2005), § 14(a)(3)(F).

272 Colorado River Indian Tribes (AZ) Gaming Ordinance (1994), § 602(d).

273 Spirit Lake Tribe (ND) Gaming Ordinance (1994), § 8-17-103(1).

274 Amended Gaming Compact Between the Standing Rock Sioux Tribe and the State of North Dakota (2022), § 19.3, available at: https://www.bia.gov/sites/default/files/dup/assets/as-ia/oig/pdf/508_compliant_2022.12.19_standing_rock_sioux_tribe_tribal_state_gaming_compact.pdf (last accessed October 30, 2023).

275 Lower Sioux Indian Community (MN) Gaming Ordinance (1993), § 11(D)(4) (this provision does not appear in the 2010 amended ordinance); Bois Forte Band of the Minnesota Chippewa Tribe (MN) Gaming Ordinance (1993), § 9(B).

276 Tohono O'odham Nation (AZ) Gaming Ordinance (2021), § 502(b) (gaming facility operators), § 702(a) (for gaming device manufacturers, vendors, distributors, and financers).

Tribe also has a vendor exclusion that mirrors its complex gaming license exclusion for PMOs and KOs, detailed above.[277]

As with the Arizona tribes mentioned above, the Tribal-State Gaming Compacts in Michigan attach identical restrictions to purchase agreements or leases, excluding anyone with a conviction for any gambling-related offense, fraud, or misrepresentation, or who has been convicted within the past 5 years of any other felony unless it has been pardoned.[278] The gaming ordinances of Michigan tribes, however, may be more restrictive than required by the Tribal-State Compact. The Little River Band of Ottawa Indians adheres to the baseline, denying a supplier's license to any person convicted of a felony in the previous 5 years or to gambling offenses, fraud, or misrepresentation, but does not include the pardon language.[279] The Sault Ste. Marie Tribe of Chippewa Indians has the same exclusion as the others for gaming device supplier's licenses and for management contractors, including allowing a pardon to restore eligibility, but adds an additional 5-year bar on felony convictions for vendors and lessors that is not required by the Compact.[280] Two other Michigan tribes even extend the bar to 10 years. For a gaming supplier's license, the Pokagon Band of Potawatomi Indians excludes persons with felonies in the past 10 years, plus anyone convicted of a gaming offense or felony fraud or misrepresentation.[281] The Nottawaseppi Huron Band of the Potawatomi has a slightly broader exclusion for a gaming vendor's license, excluding felonies within 10 years, gaming offenses, theft-related offenses, or felony fraud or misrepresentation.[282]

Other tribal jurisdictions also set a 10-year sunset date for criminal convictions for third-party licenses. In the simplest expression, two South Dakota jurisdictions, the Crow Creek Sioux Tribe and the Flandreau Santee Sioux Tribe, exclude persons convicted of a felony within the past 10 years as manufacturers, operators, or retailers of gaming products or services.[283] The Eastern Band of Cherokee Indians requires suppliers of gaming goods or services to be eligible for a gaming license, therefore excluding anyone with a felony conviction in the previous 10 years, or any conviction for

277 Standing Rock Sioux Tribe (SD) Gaming Ordinance (2014), § 23-607(a)(3)–(4).

278 All 12 Michigan Tribal-State Gaming Compacts have the same Section 6(B) which provides for this. See Michigan Gaming Control Board, "Tribal-State Compacts in Michigan," https://www.michigan.gov/mgcb/tribal-casinos/tribal-state-compacts-in-michigan (last accessed October 27, 2023).

279 Little River Band of Ottawa Indians (MI) Gaming Commission Rules (1999), Rule 2(E).

280 Sault Ste. Marie Tribe of Chippewa Indians (MI) Gaming Ordinance (2017), §§ 42.506(3)(b)–(c), 42.716(2).

281 Pokagon Band of Potawatomi Indians (MI) Gaming Ordinance (2007), § 8.05(a)–(b).

282 Nottawaseppi Huron Band of the Potawatomi (MI) Gaming Ordinance (2021), § 8.5-75(A)–(B).

283 Crow Creek Sioux Tribe (SD) Gaming Ordinance (1994), § 26(3); Flandreau Santee Sioux Tribe (SD) Gaming Ordinance (1996), § 17-6-3.

gaming offenses, fraud, misrepresentation, or crimes of moral turpitude.[284] The Seminole Nation of Oklahoma uses a similar construction, requiring any gaming vendor or gaming financer to meet the standards for receiving a gaming license. This excludes any person convicted of a felony or, within 10 years, an offense involving dishonesty.[285] Two other tribes have a 10-year sunset provision, though these are more complex. The Ute Mountain Ute denies manufacturer or distributor licenses to persons convicted of a gaming felony, a felony of fraud, misrepresentation, or theft by deception, or, within the past 10 years, any other felony or any misdemeanor involving fraud, misrepresentation, or theft by deception.[286] The Yavapai-Prescott Indian Tribe excludes as gaming device manufacturers, distributors, suppliers, or financiers any person, or principal of any business, convicted within the past 10 years of a gaming offense or a felony for theft, burglary, embezzlement, assault with a deadly weapon, or murder.[287]

Restoration of Eligibility for Gaming Licenses

In total, at least 45 tribal jurisdictions provide for a restoration of the right to a gaming license, either by allowing a pardon or expungement to restore eligibility for a gaming license or by creating a tribal waiver process. The former requires an external statutory or constitutional clemency authority to clear the underlying conviction; the latter is purely a creation of tribal law. Tribal jurisdictions in Michigan and Wisconsin are overrepresented in this category, comprising 21 of the 45 jurisdictions, owing to the wording of the Tribal-State Gaming Compacts in those states.[288] One jurisdiction, the Salt River Pima-Maricopa Indian Community, has an altogether different legal structure: its tribal gaming commission can issue a waiver of the requirement to have a vendor's license rather than waive the restriction of eligibility due to a prior criminal conviction "if licensing the vendor is not

284 Eastern Band of Cherokee Indians (NC) Gaming Ordinance (1996), § 16-4.03(a)(4) (applies to suppliers of gaming goods or services).

285 Seminole Nation of Oklahoma (OK) Gaming Ordinance (2017), § 203(a)(7)(B).

286 Ute Mountain Ute Tribe (CO) Gaming Ordinance (2012), § 410(a).

287 Yavapai-Prescott Indian Tribe (AZ) Gaming Ordinance (2011), § 24.9(B).

288 In the Michigan gaming compacts, the uniform provision at § 4(D)(3) contemplates a pardon or tribal waiver to restore eligibility. See Michigan Gaming Control Board, "Tribal-State Compacts in Michigan," https://www.michigan.gov/mgcb/tribal-casinos/tribal-state-compacts-in-michigan (last accessed October 28, 2023). The provision is numbered the same in all the compacts. In the Wisconsin gaming compacts, the uniform provision at § 9(A)(1)–(2) also contemplates a pardon or tribal waiver to restore eligibility. See State of Wisconsin Department of Administration, "Tribal Compacts and Amendments," https://doa.wi.gov/Pages/AboutDOA/TribalCompactsAndAmendments.aspx (last accessed October 28, 2023). The provision is numbered the same in all the compacts.

necessary in order to protect the public interest."[289] Another jurisdiction, the Burns Paiute Tribe, renders persons with certain convictions ineligible for a gaming license even if those offenses are expunged from their record, but the tribal gaming commission creates a process for waiving the eligibility criteria.[290] In two additional jurisdictions, not included in the total, the gaming ordinance is unclear whether a pardon restores eligibility. Fort Belknap Indian Community restores eligibility for gaming licenses if a conviction was "removed from the record" and the Yavapai-Apache Nation restores eligibility if a conviction is "set aside," but these may refer to expungements or record sealing rather than pardons.[291]

In at least eight jurisdictions, a pardon of an offense from an appropriate authority restores eligibility for gaming license without exception. Seven of these jurisdictions are in Wisconsin (Forest County Potawatomi Community, Ho-Chunk Nation, Lac Courte Oreilles Band of Lake Superior Chippewa Indians, Menominee Indian Tribe, Red Cliff Band of Lake Superior Chippewa Indians, St. Croix Chippewa Indians, and Sokaogon Chippewa Community).[292] The remaining jurisdiction is the Tonkawa Tribe in Oklahoma.[293] The Ho-Chunk Nation also has a separate waiver process. The tribal council may waive the criminal conviction exclusion upon a showing of rehabilitation and fitness, with an exclusion for casino owners and management contractors for whom ineligibility cannot be waived.[294]

A handful of jurisdictions allow pardons to restore eligibility for a gaming license but make exceptions for certain crimes. Bay Mills Indian Community provides that a pardon of any crime except gaming offenses restores eligibility.[295] The Sault Ste. Marie Tribe of Chippewa Indians excludes gaming offenses, fraud, and misrepresentation in contemplating pardons to restore

289 Salt River Pima-Maricopa Indian Community (AZ) Gaming Ordinance (2016), § 15.5-10.

290 Burns Paiute Tribe (OR) Gaming Ordinance (2004), pages 17–19 (note the missing pages and provision numbering in the gaming ordinance on the NIGC website).

291 Fort Belknap Indian Community (MT) Gaming Ordinance (2009), § 15.2.4(B); Yavapai-Apache Nation (AZ) Gaming Ordinance (2022), § 409(b).

292 Forest County Potawatomi Community (WI) Gaming Ordinance (1995), § 7(A)(1); Ho-Chunk Nation (WI) Gaming Ordinance (2008), § 17(c)(2); Lac Courte Oreilles Band of Lake Superior Chippewa Indians (WI) Gaming Ordinance (1995), § 704.03(1)(b); Menominee Indian Tribe (WI) Gaming Ordinance (2014), § 347-20(C); Red Cliff Band of Lake Superior Chippewa Indians (WI) Gaming Ordinance (2014), § 17.14.1; St. Croix Chippewa Indians (WI) Gaming Ordinance (2021), 6 S.C.T.C. § 02.10(9)(a); Sokaogon Chippewa Community (WI) Gaming Ordinance (2001), § 100.22(1)(a). The Bad River Band of the Lake Superior Tribe of Chippewa Indians also had this provision in its original 1993 ordinance, but this was not retained in the 2019 amended ordinance. Bad River Band of the Lake Superior Tribe of Chippewa Indians (WI) Gaming Ordinance (2003), § 550.7(d)(2)(A)(2).

293 Tonkawa Tribe (OK) Gaming Ordinance (2014), § 11.1.

294 Ho-Chunk Nation (WI) Gaming Ordinance (2008), §§ 17(c)(2) (pardon), 17(c)(4) (waiver).

295 Bay Mills Indian Community (MI) Gaming Ordinance (1997), § 10.2(BB).

eligibility for gaming device supplier licenses.[296] The Habematolel Pomo of Upper Lake also excludes gaming offenses, fraud, or misrepresentation from restoration of eligibility through a pardon.[297] Five other tribal jurisdictions have the same pardon exclusion for gaming offenses, fraud, or misrepresentation, but separately provide a waiver process for tribal members who are not likely to engage in criminal activity in the future. These are the La Posta Band of Diegueno Mission Indians, Match-e-be-nash-she-wish Band of Pottawatomi Indians, Nottawaseppi Huron Band of the Potawatomi, Quechan Tribe of the Fort Yuma Indian Reservation (for Class II licenses only, not Class III), and the Saginaw Chippewa Indian Tribe.[298]

In addition to the tribal jurisdictions mentioned above, several others allow a pardon to restore eligibility and separately provide a waiver process for offenses that are not pardoned. The Spirit Lake Tribe allows either a pardon or a waiver for tribal members to restore eligibility.[299] Three other jurisdictions, the Jamul Indian Village, Oneida Tribe of Wisconsin, and the Prairie Island Indian Community, allow pardons to restore eligibility but also allow the tribe to grant "pardons" restoring eligibility, which effectively operate as tribal waivers.[300] In the Hannahville Indian Community, a pardon can restore eligibility for all crimes except drug crimes, but the tribe can waive the restriction for tribal members if they are not likely to engage in future criminal conduct.[301] The Grand Traverse Band of Ottawa and Chippewa Indians uses the same language for its certificate of rehabilitation to tribal members; in addition, it also provides for a pardon to restore eligibility but without the exclusion for drug crimes.[302] Little Traverse Bay Band of Odawa Indians and Little River Band of Ottawa Indians allow pardons for any underlying crime to restore eligibility for employee licenses and provide

296 Sault Ste. Marie Tribe of Chippewa Indians (MI) Gaming Ordinance (2017), § 42.506(3)(b)–(c).

297 Habematolel Pomo of Upper Lake (CA) Gaming Ordinance (2012), § 5.16.4(B)–(C).

298 La Posta Band of Diegueno Mission Indians (CA) Gaming Ordinance (2007), § 5.5.4(b)–(c); Match-e-be-nash-she-wish Band of Pottawatomi Indians (MI) Gaming Ordinance (2020), § 12.03.3(C) (note that the waiver does not apply for felony convictions for gaming offenses, fraud, or misrepresentation, but these may be pardoned); Nottawaseppi Huron Band of the Potawatomi (MI) Gaming Ordinance (2021), § 8.5-60(D) (note that the waiver does not apply for felony convictions for gaming offenses, fraud, or misrepresentation, but these may be pardoned); Quechan Tribe of the Fort Yuma Indian Reservation (AZ) Gaming Ordinance (2008), § 6.5.3; Saginaw Chippewa Tribe (MI) Gaming Ordinance (1997), § 6.4.3.

299 Spirit Lake Tribe (SD) Gaming Ordinance (1994), § 8-14-101(b).

300 Jamul Indian Village (CA) Gaming Ordinance (2022), § 11.6(1); Oneida Tribe of Indians (WI) Gaming Ordinance (2009), § 21.12-3(b); Prairie Island Indian Community (MN) Gaming Ordinance (2010), § 311(B).

301 Hannahville Indian Community (MI) Gaming Ordinance (2000), § 6.8(A)(11), (14).

302 Grand Traverse Band of Ottawa and Chippewa Indians (MI) Gaming Ordinance (2018), § 116(c)–(d).

for a waiver for tribal members if they are rehabilitated or unlikely to engage in future criminal conduct.[303]

Besides providing for restoration of eligibility through a pardon, the Stockbridge Munsee Community has a "tribal gaming waiver policy" for gaming license ineligibility due to prior criminal convictions. This does not restore eligibility for employment with the gaming compliance department. The gaming compliance department makes a report to the gaming commission, which will hold a hearing on the waiver application and provide a recommendation to the tribal council, which will make the ultimate decision.[304] The tribal gaming waiver appears to be open to all applicants, not only tribal members. As noted above, the Standing Rock Sioux Tribe allows pardons and waivers to restore eligibility for gaming licenses in some instances, but only for the North Dakota portion of the reservation and not for the South Dakota portion, owing to the different standards in the Tribal-State Gaming Compacts for each state.[305] Specifically, the Tribal-State Compact between North Dakota and the Standing Rock Sioux Tribe contains collateral consequences that prohibit employment by a person with a conviction in the previous 10 years for any felony, gaming offense, or fraud or misrepresentation, unless pardoned or waived by the tribe if the applicant has been "sufficiently rehabilitated."[306] The Tribal-State Compact between South Dakota and the Standing Rock Sioux does not contain an equivalent provision. For eligibility for non-gaming employment, a different process applies that is uniform for both the North Dakota and South Dakota portions of the reservation. For non-gaming employees, the tribal gaming commission may waive the felony bar for tribal members only, provided the applicant has not had a felony conviction or certain misdemeanor convictions, or was released from custody, within the previous year. The applicant must apply for a waiver from the gaming commission and request a hearing. The commission will determine whether the applicant "has been properly rehabilitated" and is not otherwise ineligible.[307]

Tribes that solely have waiver procedures to restore eligibility for a gaming license have different variations in who can apply for the waiver, whether the waiver applies to all offenses or only to specific ones, and the standard

303 Little Traverse Bay Band of Odawa Indians (MI) Gaming Ordinance (2005), § 5(B)(3); Little River Band of Ottawa Indians (MI) Gaming Ordinance (2018), § 10.02(b)(4).

304 Stockbridge Munsee Community (WI) Gaming Ordinance (2021), §§ GMG.01.04(dd)–(ee), GMG.01.09(l)(37).

305 Standing Rock Sioux Tribe (SD) Gaming Ordinance (2014), § 23-504(a).

306 Amended Gaming Compact Between the Standing Rock Sioux Tribe and the State of North Dakota (2022), § 10.1(B), available at: https://www.bia.gov/sites/default/files/dup/assets/as-ia/oig/pdf/508_compliant_2022.12.19_standing_rock_sioux_tribe_tribal_state_gaming_compact.pdf (last accessed October 30, 2023).

307 Standing Rock Sioux Tribe (SD) Gaming Ordinance (2014), § 23-504(b)(2).

that the applicant for a waiver must meet. These jurisdictions also vary as to whether the waiver must be made by the tribal legislature or the tribal gaming commission, or whether it must involve state gaming officials. The Alabama-Coushatta Tribe permits waivers for tribal members only if a "significant amount of time" has passed and the applicant is now of "trustworthy character."[308] The Alturas Indian Rancheria broadens the waiver to all applicants, not just tribal members, and uses a less demanding waiver standard, namely, if "such time has passed" and the applicant is "sufficiently rehabilitated."[309] Using a slightly different standard, the Minnesota Chippewa Tribe (Bois Forte Band) and Minnesota Chippewa Tribe (Fond du Lac Band) both open tribal waivers to everyone, not just tribal members, with evidence of "sufficient rehabilitation" and "present fitness" for employment.[310]

The Suquamish Indian Tribe has a more complex provision with a waiver clause and an exclusion for certain political offenses concerning tribal treaty rights. The waiver clause, for enrolled tribal members, allows the tribal gaming commission in agreement with the state gaming agency to waive criteria for a gaming license if the applicant "does not pose a material risk of engaging in unlawful activity."[311] A second provision, pertaining not just to tribal members but to anyone enrolled in any federally recognized Indian tribe, states that a gaming license may not be denied if the conviction occurred before the U.S. Supreme Court upheld state criminal jurisdiction over hunting or fishing offenses or cigarette or alcohol sales. In addition, non-gaming offenses committed as part of a protest over tribal sovereignty rights do not render an applicant ineligible.[312] Another example of a jurisdiction that requires input from state gaming regulators is the Klamath Tribes of Oregon. To request a waiver, the Klamath Tribes require both the tribe and state gaming regulators to meet and agree on a possible waiver, considering the passage of time, age at conviction, severity of the offense, overall criminal record, reputation of the applicant, and nature of the position.[313]

Some tribes attach numerous conditions to gaming license waivers. For the Cayuga Nation, the tribe may waive an ineligible conviction based on "extenuating circumstances" that show a conviction "will not have a meaningful effect on the applicant's fitness or ability to perform" the job and the

308 Alabama-Coushatta Tribe (TX) Gaming Ordinance (2015), § 11(6)(a)(3)(a).

309 Alturas Indian Rancheria (CA) Gaming Ordinance (2008), § 8.3.24.

310 Minnesota Chippewa Tribe (Bois Forte Band) (MN) Gaming Ordinance (1993), § 8(F); Minnesota Chippewa Tribe (Fond du Lac Band) (MN) Gaming Ordinance (2016), § 1310(a)(5)(i).

311 Suquamish Indian Tribe (WA) Gaming Ordinance (2009), § 11.5.52(a).

312 Id. at § 11.5.52(b)–(c).

313 Klamath Tribes (OR) Gaming Ordinance (1995), § 45.14.

applicant is "of good moral character."[314] However, the conviction must be of a single low-level felony or an aggravated sentence based on multiple low-level convictions of a traffic offense; 5 years must have passed since the expiration of sentence without any additional convictions; and the felony must be non-violent, and if alcohol- or drug-related, must accompany completion of a treatment program.[315] In Minnesota, the Red Lake Band of Chippewa Indians and the Shakopee Mdewakanton Sioux Community allow the gaming commission to waive the felony bar if the felony is not gaming related or a crime in which a tribal government was the victim. In addition, "a period of time" must have elapsed and the applicant must be found to be "a reasonable member of society."[316]

Another jurisdiction that places conditions on its waiver is the Delaware Nation of Oklahoma. This jurisdiction can grant a certificate of rehabilitation to a tribal member who was found ineligible for a gaming license if the excluded conviction is more than 10 years old. The en banc tribal commission must weigh the "particular circumstances and behavior" of the applicant with the "public welfare" to find the applicant fit to serve.[317] The Sac and Fox Nation of Kansas provides waivers for enrolled tribal members or other Native American applicants with established connections to the tribe. To waive ineligibility, an applicant must provide all relevant court records with proof of good character, to cover any felonies within the previous 2 years or any felonies of violence, dishonesty, theft, or moral turpitude within 5 years. The provision requires a hearing in person before the tribal gaming commission.[318]

Enforcement in Action: Oneida Gaming Commission Cases

Several illustrative cases from the Oneida Tribe of Wisconsin show how collateral consequences of conviction are applied in gaming-related cases and provide some justifications. In *House v. Oneida Gaming Commission*, the appellants were convicted of drunk driving and were denied gaming licenses under the felony exclusion of the Oneida Gaming Ordinance.[319] The appellants argued that the denial was arbitrary and capricious since the

314 Cayuga Nation (NY) Gaming Ordinance (2003), § 8(D)(2)(a). Note, however, that this provision may be superseded by the 2018 ordinance, which does not contain a waiver provision.
315 Id. at § 8(D)(2)(a)(i)–(vi).
316 Red Lake Band of Chippewa Indians (MN) Gaming Ordinance (2000), § 326(b)–(c); Shakopee Mdewakanton Sioux Community (MN) Gaming Ordinance (2013), § 326.
317 Delaware Nation (OK) Gaming Ordinance (1995), § 12.4.
318 Sac & Fox Nation (KS) Gaming Ordinance (1998), § 5(P).
319 House v. Oneida Gaming Commission, No. 02-AC-038 (Oneida App. Comm., May 30, 2003).

convictions were not related to gaming or fraud. The Ordinance, they asserted, was overbroad since a drunk driving conviction did not threaten gaming operations.[320] The Appellate Commission rejected their contention since the Oneida Gaming Ordinance excluded persons convicted of felonies of fraud or misrepresentation, gaming-related offenses, or, within the previous 10 years, any other felonies.[321] "It has been deemed against the public interest to license and employ recent felons in gaming operations under the law," the Appellate Commission wrote, adding that the word "felony" might be broad but was not ambiguous or subjective.[322] The appellants were properly terminated because maintaining a gaming license was one of the criteria of their employment.

Two other cases proved more complex because the gaming license denial and the personnel decision were made independently of one another. In *Oneida Bingo & Casino v. Lopez*, the respondent was a slot technician who participated in a party after hours at the slot warehouse, where he was seen taking coins from the bases of machines.[323] He was terminated both for holding the party, which included alcohol, and for theft of coins. The Personnel Commission disagreed, finding that none of the allegations were proven, and additionally determined that the respondent was wrongly terminated because the gaming establishment should have used progressive discipline or provided a warning. The Personnel Commission based its decision in part on the respondent's acquittal in state circuit court where he was found not guilty of stealing money. However, he was found guilty of stealing washers worth approximately five cents apiece. The Personnel Committee found that stealing washers did not reach the level of an egregious act warranting termination and instead required a warning with progressive discipline.[324]

The Appellate Commission reversed. Although the Personnel Commission correctly found that the respondent's termination was a personnel matter and therefore progressive discipline should have been used, the Personnel Commission failed to apply the Oneida Gaming Ordinance. The Gaming Ordinance stated that a person convicted of "theft of any kind" cannot be employed in the conduct of any game, without exception.[325] In this case, the

320 Id. at ¶ 27.

321 The Oneida Tribe ordinances on the NIGC website have different numbering than the numbers used in the decision, likely because the NIGC website is missing an amendment to the original 1994 ordinance. However, the most recent ordinance, approved in 2015, has substantially similar wording. Oneida Tribe of Indians (WI) Gaming Ordinance (2015), § 21.12-3(b)(2)–(4).

322 *House*, supra note 319 at ¶¶ 30–32.

323 Oneida Bingo & Casino v. Lopez, No. 99-EP-0039 (Oneida App. Comm., Jan. 28, 2000).

324 Id. at ¶¶ 14–18.

325 This provision was repealed beginning with the 2009 amended ordinance, so it has no equivalent in the current gaming ordinance. For the original provision, see Oneida Tribe of Indians (WI) Gaming Ordinance (1994), art. 7, § F(2).

respondent was convicted of stealing washers which, though of negligible value, was still the crime of theft. The Appellate Commission found that the Gaming Ordinance prohibition on employment by persons convicted of theft preempted the Oneida Personnel Policies and Procedures. The respondent, therefore, was not entitled to reinstatement to his position.[326]

A subsequent case did not involve a criminal conviction but resulted in a similar conflict between personnel policies and the discretionary denial provision in the Oneida Gaming Ordinance. In *Kapla v. Oneida Gaming Commission*, the appellant, a poker dealer, was terminated from Oneida Bingo & Casino after a surveillance officer witnessed another vehicle pull alongside the appellant's car and place a $100.00 bill inside the gas tank.[327] The appellant had dealt cards to the driver of the other vehicle earlier in the evening, and surveillance footage revealed that she retrieved the money from the gas tank later. She subsequently admitted the money was a tip and she was terminated for violations of the Oneida Personnel Policies and Procedures. Subsequently, she appealed her termination, which was reduced to a 3-week suspension. However, the Oneida Gaming Commission suspended her gaming license 4 weeks later based on her dishonesty to the surveillance officer and the acceptance of an unlawful gift.[328]

Under the Oneida Gaming Ordinance, the Gaming Commission "shall not license any person … whose prior activities, criminal record, if any, or reputation, habits, and associations pose a threat to the public interest" or contribute to unfair or unlawful gaming operations.[329] The appellant appealed the suspension of her gaming license and the Oneida Gaming Commission held an administrative review hearing that found adequate basis for the license suspension. She was subsequently terminated from her position. The Oneida Personnel Commission denied a grievance hearing since her license had been suspended. She appealed both the Gaming Commission's suspension of her license and the Personnel Commission's refusal to hold a grievance hearing to the Oneida Appellate Commission.[330]

The Oneida Appellate Commission first ruled in favor of the Oneida Gaming Commission, finding that Kapla had admitted she received a $100.00 tip from a customer and failed to notify gaming management. She also lied to an investigator. These activities supported a finding that her activities "pose a threat to the effective operation of gaming and enhance the danger of illegal

326 *Lopez*, supra note 323 at ¶¶ 23–27.
327 Kapla v. Oneida Gaming Commission, No. 07-AC-007/008 (Onedia App. Comm., Aug. 14, 2007).
328 Id. at ¶¶ 10–20.
329 In the current ordinance, this provision is at Oneida Tribe of Indians (WI) Gaming Ordinance (2015), § 21.12-3(c).
330 *Kapla*, supra note 327 at ¶¶ 25–32.

practices."[331] The Appellate Commission found, however, that the Personnel Commission had erred in not providing her with a grievance hearing. The Personnel Commission had wrongly assumed that the revocation of her gaming license was the grounds for her termination rather than the underlying conduct. Termination may only occur for disciplinary violations of Oneida personnel policies and in this case the Personnel Commission had not investigated. As a corollary, the Oneida Gaming Commission had no authority over employment matters.[332] The Appellate Commission upheld the denial of the gaming license and dismissed the appeal regarding termination of employment as untimely.

These cases, when read together, show how the collateral consequences in gaming ordinances interact with employment law. In both cases, the employee's termination for wrongdoing was found to be irregular under the tribe's personnel policies, yet reinstatement was denied because the Oneida Gaming Ordinance had specific exclusions for wrongdoing. In all instances, the proscriptions in the Gaming Ordinance were found to be superior to the personnel provisions, reflecting the importance of gaming operations and the seriousness with which this industry polices potential violations.

331 Id. at ¶¶ 61–62.
332 Id. at ¶¶ 75–76.

Chapter 7

Restrictions on Civil Rights and Tribal Social Services

Restrictions on civil rights or social services are among the most problematic forms of collateral consequences of conviction. Unlike restrictions on tribal office, employment in the casino industry, or eligibility for licenses and permits, the exclusions covered in this chapter do not focus on occupational privileges but rather on core individual rights or entitlements that affect all members of the community, including the most vulnerable. Restrictions on voting or serving on a jury reduce civic participation and may cumulatively affect political or legal legitimacy if criminal convictions result in systematic exclusion.[1] In addition, restrictions on core rights or social services can also burden the innocent. Children or household members may be disadvantaged if a parent or family member is excluded from tribal housing, driving, or inheritance, not to mention loss of parental rights or employment.[2] However, the most notable finding of this chapter is a positive one: collateral consequences related to civil rights and social services in tribal law are considerably less common than restrictions on tribal office, occupational licenses, or gaming employment.

Recognizing that blanket collateral consequences are problematic, some tribes have qualified their exclusions on core civil rights for persons with criminal convictions. The Cherokee Nation provides that a sentence of imprisonment suspends all civil rights except the right to enter into employment contracts, subject to approval of the tribal court, when this benefits the vocational training or post-incarceration employment of the person in confinement.[3] The system used by the Pueblo of Acoma could serve as a model for other jurisdictions. The Pueblo of Acoma Tribal Code specifically

1 Alec C. Ewald, "'Because I Feel Like I Want to Be Heard, You Know?' Carceral Citizenship and Collateral Consequences," *Law and Policy* [OnlineFirst] (2023), https://doi.org/10.1111/lapo.12225.

2 See, e.g., Barbara Mulé & Michael Yavinsky, "Saving One's Home: Collateral Consequences for Innocent Family Members," 30(4) *New York University Review of Law and Social Change* 689–700 (2006).

3 Cherokee Nation (OK) Tribal Code, Title 21, § 65.

DOI: 10.4324/9781003432548-7

spells out what civil rights are lost because of a criminal conviction and provides for how to restore them. The code excludes persons with criminal convictions from offices of trust or from jury service, but specifically does not exclude them from tribal employment unless a "reasonable relationship" exists between the conviction and the duties of the office. A convicted person may also seek a restoration of rights.[4] Another positive example are jurisdictions that specifically protect the rights of juveniles by providing that juvenile delinquency proceedings are not criminal proceedings and a finding of guilt in juvenile court is not a conviction. This is the case with the Spirit Lake Tribe, which has an explicit provision protecting persons with juvenile delinquency convictions from collateral consequences.[5] The next chapter makes the normative case for pardons, expungements, and other restoration of rights mechanisms, which can help reduce the harms of collateral consequences.

Jury Service

The most common collateral consequence of conviction that relates to civil rights under tribal law is exclusion from serving on a tribal court jury. Interestingly, a survey conducted more than three decades ago of the 50 U.S. states revealed that lifelong exclusion from jury service for a felony conviction was among the most common collateral consequences in U.S. law, more common than lifelong restrictions on voting or public employment.[6] This survey of tribal law found something similar. Restrictions on jury service are comparatively common in Indian Country. Serving on a jury is "a signifier of full citizenship," one long denied in American history to women and minority groups; in addition, empirical evidence has shown that jurors who have been convicted of a crime are not more sympathetic to a defendant, neutralizing another objection.[7] Arguably, exclusion from jury service for prior convictions fails to distinguish between the offender and their previous criminal act, preferring to shame former offenders without regard to underlying criminological considerations.[8]

In total, at least 22 tribal jurisdictions exclude persons with felony or other convictions from serving on a jury. The following tribes have an exclusion for felony convictions only: Assiniboine and Sioux Tribes of the Fort

4 Pueblo of Acoma (NM) Tribal Code, § 5-5-3(A)–(F).

5 Spirit Lake Tribe (ND) Tribal Code, § 23-6-119(C).

6 Velmer S. Burton, Francis T. Cullen & Lawrence F. Travis, "The Collateral Consequences of a Felony Conviction: A National Survey of State Statutes," 51(3) *Federal Probation* 52–60, 58–59 (1987).

7 Briana L. McGinnis, "Beyond Disenfranchisement: Collateral Consequences and Equal Citizenship," 6(1) *Politics, Groups, and Identities* 59–76, 67–68 (2018).

8 Id. at 70.

Peck Indian Reservation, Comanche Nation, Coushatta Tribe of Louisiana, Pueblo of Acoma, Pueblo of Isleta, Red Lake Band of Chippewa Indians, Sault Ste. Marie Tribe of Chippewa Indians, Shawnee Tribe, Shoshone Tribe of the Wind River Reservation, Standing Rock Sioux Tribe, Te-Moak Tribe of Western Shoshone Indians, Yomba Shoshone Tribe, and Yurok Tribe.[9] Several tribes have variations from the majority rule. The Mashantucket Pequot Indian Tribe and Las Vegas Tribe of Paiute Indians only exclude persons from serving on a jury for felony convictions within the previous 5 years.[10] The Little Traverse Bay Band of Odawa Indians extends the felony exclusion to 10 years, except crimes involving domestic violence for which the bar is lifelong.[11] The Omaha Tribe of Nebraska has an exclusion for felony convictions and Class A misdemeanors, defined in that tribe to mean an offense that can be punishable by 6 months or more in prison.[12] The Ute Indian Tribe of the Uintah and Ouray Reservation and the Yankton Sioux Tribe also include Class A misdemeanors.[13] The Poarch Band of Creeks states that eligible jurors must not have lost the right to vote in federal or state elections "because of a conviction for any offense involving moral turpitude."[14] The Winnebago Tribe allows this right to be restored with a pardon: "Any person convicted of a felony within the preceding five years for which he/she did not receive a pardon is not eligible for jury duty."[15] Another provision of the Winnebago Tribe's code broadens the felony exclusion to crimes involving moral turpitude.[16]

Uniquely, at least one tribal jurisdiction with an exclusion for jury service allows for a waiver of this exclusion. The Spirit Lake Tribe in North Dakota excludes from jury service any person with a state or federal felony conviction

9 Assiniboine and Sioux Tribes of the Fort Peck Indian Reservation (MT) Tribal Code, Title 6, § 507(b); Comanche Nation (OK) Tribal Code, Title 3, § 1-15B(1); Coushatta Tribe of Louisiana (LA) Tribal Code, Title 2, Chapter 5, § 7(b); Pueblo of Acoma (NM) Tribal Code, § 3-2-6(C)(3)(d); Pueblo of Isleta (NM) Resolution No. 2001-134, § 2A; Red Lake Band of Chippewa Indians (MN) Tribal Code, Title 4, § 407.02; Sault Ste. Marie Tribe of Chippewa Indians (MI) Tribal Code, § 70.126(3); Shawnee Tribe (OK) Tribal Code, § 16.04.150(G)(2); Shoshone Tribe of the Wind River Reservation (WY) Tribal Code, § 1-6-1(1); Standing Rock Sioux Tribe (SD) Tribal Code, § 3-507(c)(4); Te-Moak Tribe of Western Shoshone Indians (NV) Tribal Code, § 1-3-34(A); Yomba Shoshone Tribe (NV) Law and Order Code, Title 2, § H(3); Yurok Tribe of the Yurok Reservation (CA) Tribal Code, § 2.10.1000(g)(2).

10 Mashantucket Pequot Indian Tribe (MA) Tribal Code, Title 2, Chapter 1, § 21(b); Las Vegas Tribe of Paiute Indians (NV) Tribal Code, § 4-60-020(d).

11 Little Traverse Bay Band of Odawa Indians (MI) Tribal Code, § 9.706(B)(1)(c).

12 Omaha Tribe of Nebraska (NE) Tribal Code, §§ 1-6-1 (jury qualifications), 5-3-6(a)(definition of Class A offense).

13 Ute Indian Tribe of the Uintah and Ouray Reservation (UT) Tribal Code, § 1-6-1(1)–(2); Yankton Sioux Tribe (SD) Tribal Code, § 1-6-1(1).

14 Poarch Band of Creeks (AL) Tribal Code, § 6-2-1(d).

15 Winnebago Tribe (NE) Tribal Code, Title 1B, Rule 1B-402.

16 Id., Title 2, § 2-713(2)(G).

or a tribal court conviction resulting in 60 days of imprisonment. However, a person with such a conviction may apply to the Tribal Council for a waiver. The Tribal Council will pass a resolution waiving the jury service exclusion, though this only applies to the conviction(s) listed in the resolution and not subsequent convictions.[17]

Firearm or Weapon Possession

After restrictions on jury selection, the next most common collateral consequence related to civil rights is a limitation on possession of a gun or other firearm. As a threshold matter, the Second Amendment of the U.S. Constitution protecting the "right to bear arms" does not apply in Indian Country.[18] Similarly, the right to bear arms does not appear in the federal Indian Civil Rights Act of 1968, which laid out minimum individual rights protections with input from tribal leaders.[19] Several tribes, such as the Navajo Nation, Little River Band of Ottawa Indians, and Nottawaseppi Huron Band of the Potawatomi, have a qualified constitutional right to bear arms in their tribal constitutions.[20] More common are tribes that have modest gun control measures to include permit requirements, background checks, prohibitions on certain types of guns, or prohibitions on possessing guns in sensitive areas.[21] This analysis focuses on restrictions on ownership or possession of guns by persons with certain criminal convictions. The simplest expression is a prohibition on firearm possession by any person with a felony conviction for firearms-related offenses. This is the formulation used by the Hannahville Indian Community, which prohibits possession of a pistol by any person previously convicted of a felony involving threats, force, violence, or use of a firearm.[22] The Saginaw Chippewa Indian Tribe has substantially the same provision.[23] The Menominee Indian Tribe has a blanket ban on possession and use of firearms or ammunition for any person with a felony conviction or any person found not guilty by reason of insanity or mental disease.[24]

17 Spirit Lake Tribe (ND) Tribal Code, § 2-8-103(2)–(3).
18 Ann Tweedy, "Indian Tribes and Gun Regulation: Should Tribes Exercise Their Sovereign Rights to Enact Gun Bans or Stand-Your-Ground Laws?" 78(2) *Albany Law Review* 885–907 (2014).
19 Angela R. Reilly, "Indians and Guns," 100(5) *Georgetown Law Journal* 1675–746, 1712 (2012).
20 Tweedy, supra note 18 at 889–90, citing Navajo Nation (AZ) Bill of Rights, 1 N.N.C. § 6; Little River Band of Ottawa Indians (MI) Constitution, Art. 3, § 1(k); Nottawaseppi Huron Band of the Potawatomi (MI) Constitution, Art. 7, § 1(a)(11).
21 Tweedy, supra note 18 at 890–91.
22 Hannahville Indian Community (MI) Legal Code, §1.2103(1).
23 Saginaw Chippewa Indian Tribe (MI) Tribal Code, § 1.2103(a)–(b).
24 Menominee Indian Tribe (WI) Tribal Code, § 321-10.

Some tribes make provision for restoration of the right to possess a firearm. The Cherokee Nation prohibits any person with a felony conviction from possessing a pistol, machine gun, homemade or modified guns, or other firearms that could be concealed, unless that person has been fully pardoned and has been certified as an officer of the peace.[25] The Ho-Chunk Nation has an exclusion for firearm possession by any person with a felony conviction or any person found not guilty of a felony by reason of mental disease or defect, but also allows restoration of rights through a pardon.[26] The Ho-Chunk Nation also prohibits persons with violent felony convictions from possessing body armor, unless they have been pardoned.[27] The Choctaw Nation specifically provides that individuals whose non-violent felonies are pardoned by the proper authorities have their right to possess a firearm restored, including the right to perform the duties of a peace officer, gunsmith, or firearms repairman.[28] The Jamestown S'Klallam Tribe also provides that a pardon or annulment of conviction restores the right to carry a firearm.[29] Not all tribes allow restoration of the right to possess a firearm. The Cayuga Nation of New York has an elaborate expungement process for criminal convictions but makes clear that "the expungement of a felony conviction does not relieve an individual of complying with law relating to the use or possession of firearms by persons convicted of a felony."[30] The Oneida Nation has a similar provision.[31] For the Yurok Tribe, expungement of a criminal conviction does not restore the right to possess a firearm if the person is under a court order prohibiting firearms possession.[32] In a variation, the Ely Shoshone Tribe prohibits possession of an electronic stun device if that person has a felony conviction unless she or he has received a pardon, so long as the pardon does not include a restriction on the right to bear arms. This code also prevents sale or transfer of an electronic stun gun to a person with a felony conviction, unless pardoned, subject to the same proviso.[33]

In some tribes, restrictions on firearms possession are specific to crimes involving domestic violence. The Confederated Tribes of the Chehalis Reservation prohibit persons from possessing firearms if they have been convicted of any crime of domestic violence that involved the use or threat of physical force or a deadly weapon.[34] The firearms prohibition for the Lower

25 Cherokee Nation (OK) Tribal Code, Title 21, Chapter 53, § 1283.
26 Ho-Chunk Nation (WI) Tribal Code, § 941.29.
27 Id. at § 941.291.
28 Choctaw Nation (OK) Tribal Code, § 1283(B).
29 Jamestown S'Klallam Tribe (WA) Law and Order Code, Title 21, § 3.2.41.040(3).
30 Cayuga Nation (NY) Tribal Code, Chapter 10, § 1001(6).
31 Oneida Nation (NY) Tribal Code, Chapter 10, § 1001(f).
32 Yurok Tribe of the Yurok Reservation (CA) Tribal Code, § 2.10.1110(c).
33 Ely Shoshone Tribe (NV) Tribal Code, §§ 202.357(2)(a), 202.357(4)(b).
34 Confederated Tribes of the Chehalis Reservation (OR) Tribal Code, § 4.85.020.

Elwha Indian Community, Winnebago Tribe, and the Nottawaseppi Huron Band of the Potawatomi is on persons convicted of domestic violence or family violence, to include threat or use of physical harm to an intimate partner or family member.[35] Similar exclusions can be found in the laws of the Pueblo of Laguna (domestic violence/abuse) and Stillaguamish Tribe (domestic violence, dating violence, or family violence).[36] The Mescalero Apache Tribe has a narrower exclusion, stating that a person convicted of a domestic violence offense cannot possess a firearm for a period of 3 years after conviction.[37] The Ponca Tribe disallows firearms possession for any person convicted of a felony or a misdemeanor crime of domestic violence.[38] The Reno-Sparks Indian Colony makes possession of a weapon a criminal offense if a person has been convicted of a felony or is subject to a domestic violence order.[39]

Still other tribes base the exclusion on the type of weapon involved, usually to exempt hunting rifles. For instance, the Confederated Tribes of Siletz Indians prohibits persons with any type of criminal conviction from possessing a firearm with a barrel less than 18 inches in length or smaller than 26 inches in total, to exclude guns that are fired from the shoulder like rifles.[40] The tribe has a second prohibition for persons with criminal convictions on possession of switchblade knives or other knives that are spring-loaded.[41] The Dry Creek Rancheria Band of Pomo Indians has an identically worded statute.[42] The Squaxin Island Tribe prohibits a person convicted of a crime of violence or a firearm-related felony from possessing a "pistol or short firearm."[43] The Nez Perce Tribe has a felony bar for all dangerous weapons, not limited to firearms, except for possession of "a hunting bow ... solely for the purpose of exercising her or his treaty hunting right."[44] The Yurok Tribe has a felony bar for possession of automatic or semi-automatic firearms or explosive weapons.[45]

Some tribes have automatic restoration of the right to own a firearm after a period of time has passed. The Rosebud Sioux Tribe prohibits any person with a felony conviction from possessing a firearm. However, this section

35 Lower Elwha Indian Community (WA) Tribal Code, § 16.05.11; Notawaseppi Huron Band of the Potawatomi (MI) Tribal Code, § 7.4-65; Winnebago Tribe (NE) Tribal Code, § 12-204(1).

36 Pueblo of Laguna (NM) Tribal Code, § 7-4-11(2); Stillaguamish Tribe (WA) Domestic Violence Code, § 10(A).

37 Mescalero Apache Tribe (NM) Tribal Code, § 9-6-3.

38 Ponca Tribe of Nebraska (NE) Tribal Code, § 1-8-4(1).

39 Reno-Sparks Indian Colony (NV) Tribal Code, § 4-12-205(a).

40 Confederated Tribes of Siletz Indians (OR) Tribal Code, § 12.120.

41 Id. at § 12.121(a).

42 Dry Creek Rancheria Band of Pomo Indians (CA) Tribal Code, Title 4, § 4(35)–(36).

43 Squaxin Island Tribe (WA) Law and Order Code, § 9.12.825.

44 Nez Perce Tribe (ID) Tribal Code, § 4-1-126.

45 Yurok Tribe of the Yurok Reservation (CA) Tribal Code, §15.10.110(a).

does not apply if a person has been discharged from imprisonment, probation, or parole more than 5 years earlier.[46] In other jurisdictions, restoration of the right to own a gun requires a petition or waiver process. The Tulalip Tribes of Washington have a specific statute for restoration of the right to possess a firearm. According to that law, a person convicted of a felony offense except murder, manslaughter, robbery, assault, terrorism, and other violent offenses may petition for restoration of firearm rights if more than 5 years has passed since conviction and the petitioner has no weapons-related offenses in the previous 10 years.[47] For persons prohibited from possessing a firearm due to a misdemeanor conviction for domestic violence, dating violence, stalking, or sexual assault, a petitioner may seek restoration of rights 3 years after conviction if the petitioner had no weapons-related offenses in the previous 10 years.[48] To restore firearm rights, the tribal court may hold a public hearing and the petitioner must prove with clear and convincing evidence that he or she is not a danger to the public and that the circumstances of the original offense are unlikely to occur again.[49]

Voting Rights

Disenfranchisement of persons with criminal convictions is among the most serious constraints on civil rights and among the most controversial. Stripping voting rights of persons with criminal records may affect election outcomes, hamper reintegration of returning offenders, and disproportionately constrain the voice of minority or urban communities.[50] The Indian Civil Rights Act may have implications for voting rights under tribal law. In the 1970s, several federal courts confronted the question as to whether tribes were required to lower the voting age in tribal elections from 21 to 18 concomitant with the Twenty-Sixth Amendment of the U.S. Constitution. Although these challenges were generally rejected, this does not mean that disenfranchisement in tribal elections could not violate the equal protection requirements of the Indian Civil Rights Act, as for example with a jurisdiction that disenfranchises women.[51] Possibly, disenfranchisement in tribal elections due to prior criminal convictions may also be vulnerable on these grounds.

46 Rosebud Sioux Tribe (SD) Tribal Code, § 5-11-6.
47 Tulalip Tribes of Washington (WA) Tribal Code, § 11.40.010(2).
48 Id. at § 11.40.010(3).
49 Id. at § 11.40.020.
50 Bryan Lee Miller & Joseph F. Spillane, "Civil Death: An Examination of Ex-Felon Disenfranchisement and Reintegration," 14(4) *Punishment & Society* 402–28 (2012).
51 Gary D. Kennedy, "Tribal Elections: An Appraisal after the Indian Civil Rights Act," 3(2) *American Indian Law Review* 497, 502–03 (1975).

In tribal law, explicit restrictions on voting by persons with past criminal convictions are uncommon. These may also manifest as limitations on absentee voting in tribal elections for persons who are presently incarcerated off the reservation. In this survey, only one tribal jurisdiction was found to explicitly disenfranchise persons with felony convictions. The constitution of the Seneca Nation in New York provides that all persons 21 and older who have not been convicted of a felony can vote in tribal elections and hold tribal office.[52] The Winnemucca Indian Colony of Nevada has an election ordinance authorizing absentee voting for voters "incarcerated for minor offenses," defined as less than 30 days' imprisonment or a $50 fine.[53] This ordinance implies that persons serving lengthier sentences for more serious crimes may not vote absentee. Likely, other tribal jurisdictions have limitations on absentee voting for persons who are presently incarcerated.

Exclusion, Disenrollment, and Banishment

Exclusion (of either tribal or non-tribal members), banishment from a reservation, or disenrollment from tribal membership are among the harshest punishments available under tribal law. These are also among the most ancient sanctions for addressing social deviance or crime in tribal society. To put it another way,

> [h]indered by their limited civil and criminal jurisdiction, frustrated with their inability to impose meaningful sanctions, and fearful of further disruption, harm, and violence to their communities, tribal governments recognize that the old customs of banishment and exclusion are powerful and effective means of reestablishing order and safety.[54]

Although in traditional practice decisions to exclude or banish would not be subject to legal challenge, today these punishments create concerns surrounding due process and treatment of political dissidents.[55] Tribes have the sovereign right to control their own membership; however, whether the federal Indian Civil Rights Act allows a banished or disenrolled tribal member to sue the tribe in federal court for a due process violation is still an open question.[56] On the other hand, banishment may be justified as culturally appropriate or even transformative or rehabilitative for offenders, especially

52 Constitution of the Seneca Nation of Indians (NY), art. 10.
53 Winnemucca Indian Colony (NV), Election Ordinance No. 301, § 1(d)(2).
54 Patrice H. Kunesh, "Banishment as Cultural Justice in Contemporary Tribal Legal Systems," 37(1) *New Mexico Law Review* 85–146, 88 (2007).
55 Id. at 89.
56 Mary Swift, "Banishing *Habeas* Jurisdiction: Why Federal Courts Lack Jurisdiction to Hear Tribal Banishment Actions," 86(4) *Washington Law Review* 941–80 (2011).

if complemented by a reintegration ritual following return to the reservation after the banishment period.[57] Notably, tribal exclusion ordinances vary in whether they apply to tribal members or only to non-tribal members. In one analysis, 32 tribal codes authorized exclusion of non-tribal members who threatened a tribe's well-being.[58] Commonly, tribes allow exclusion from the reservation for persons who have been convicted of state or federal criminal law to prevent the reservation from becoming a refuge for a fugitive.[59]

Provisions that exclude persons with criminal convictions from tribal membership are not common. The Enterprise Rancheria of Maidu Indians authorizes disenrollment from the tribe for a tribal member convicted of a violent felony.[60] The Lummi Tribe authorizes disenrollment from the tribe for a person convicted of a crime "which threatens the well-being, economic or social welfare, or culture of the Lummi Nation and its members."[61] This tribe has a process for reenrollment if the tribal member had no conviction for similar crimes within 5 years.[62] In another variation, the Lower Sioux Indian Community deny tribal residency for enrollment purposes to persons who are incarcerated, regardless of the location of the prison facility. Tribal residency is required for parents to pass on tribal membership to their children, so a child of an incarcerated parent may lose membership in the tribe.[63] However, the tribe has a process for reestablishing residency after living on the reservation continuously for 5 years.[64] The Sac and Fox Tribe of the Mississippi in Iowa authorizes disenrollment from the tribe for convictions of murder, rape, treason, or incest, or multiple convictions for drug trafficking, manufacturing, or distribution.[65] The Mohegan Tribe of Indians in Connecticut stops short of total disenrollment. Rather, conviction of a felony results in the loss of "good standing," and as a result the Council of Elders may suspend that person's tribal "rights, benefits, and privileges," which appears to include essential rights like voting.[66]

Unlike disenrollment from the tribe, exclusion from the reservation is a sanction that may be applied to both tribal members and non-tribal members.

57 Colin Miller, "Banishment from within and without: Analyzing Indigenous Sentencing under International Human Rights Standards," 80(2) *North Dakota Law Review* 253–88, 253, 260 (2004).
58 David E. Wilkins & Shelly Hulse Wilkins, *Dismembered: Native Disenrollment and the Battle for Human Rights* 53 (University of Washington Press, 2017).
59 Jeremy Wood, "Tribal Exclusion Authority: Its Sovereign Basis with Recommendations for Federal Support," 6(2) *American Indian Law Journal* 197–269, 209 (2018).
60 Constitution of the Enterprise Rancheria of Maidu Indians (CA), art. 3, § 7(C).
61 Lummi Nation (WI) Tribal Code, § 34.07.010(d).
62 Id. at § 34.07.040(a).
63 Lower Sioux Indian Community (MN) Enrollment Ordinance §§ 1.4(H), 2.1(E).
64 Id. at § 6.1.
65 Sac and Fox Tribe of the Mississippi in Iowa (IA) Tribal Code, § 10-6101(a).
66 Mohegan Tribe of Indians (CT) Tribal Code, Article 2, § 31-24(a)(1).

The Omaha Tribe has a vaguely worded provision that authorizes exclusion from the reservation for "repeated commission of criminal offenses."[67] The Nottawaseppi Huron Band of the Potawatomi authorizes both exclusion and disenrollment for different reasons. Disenrollment may occur when a tribal member is convicted of criminal treason in the tribal court.[68] Exclusion may occur when a person is convicted of a crime of domestic violence, serious offenses such as murder, arson, rape, assault with a deadly weapon, or sexual offense involving a murder or vulnerable adult, or crimes related to cultural heritage of the tribe such as unlawful excavation.[69] Reenrollment is possible if the tribal member was exonerated of the crime.[70] The Makah Indian Tribe authorizes a 1-year period of banishment from the reservation for two or more domestic violence convictions involving the same victim if the victim is a tribal member.[71] The Pauma Band of Luiseño Mission Indians permits exclusion for "conviction of a crime by tribal, state, or federal court."[72] The Wiyot Tribe also has a broad provision excluding from tribal lands persons convicted of any felony or misdemeanor that is violent or that injures, damages, or threatens the peace of the tribe and its membership.[73] The Tulalip Tribes allow exclusion for any act that violates criminal or civil laws, even if the tribe does not have jurisdiction over them, including criminal traffic offenses. Additionally, the tribe can also exclude any registered sex offender.[74]

Several tribes have more complex provisions. The Penobscot Nation has two exclusion ordinances. The first is for tribal members: this provision authorizes a 6-month banishment for minor sex offenses and lifelong banishment for sexually violent sex offenses.[75] The other is for non-tribal members: a person will be automatically denied visitation or residency within the Penobscot Nation for drug convictions, sexual abuse, violent felonies within the previous 15 years, sex offenses, or domestic violence, among other crimes.[76] More troublingly, the law states that such automatic denials are not subject to review or appeal.[77] The Shoalwater Bay Indian Tribe has a complex exclusion ordinance for tribal members who commit sexual abuse of minors, violations of sex offender registration requirements, or, more problematically, commission of any crime under tribal, federal, state, or foreign

67 Omaha Tribe (NE) Tribal Code, § 16-1-3.
68 Constitution of the Nottawaseppi Huron Band of the Potawatomi (MI), art. 3, § 6(a)(1).
69 Nottawaseppi Huron Band of the Potawatomi (MI) Tribal Code, § 8.16-5.
70 Id.
71 Makah Indian Tribe of the Makah Reservation (WA) Tribal Code, § 11.4.09(h).
72 Pauma Band of Luiseño Mission Indians (CA) Exclusion Ordinance, § 3(2).
73 Wiyot Tribe (CA) Tribal Code, § 3.10.050(B).
74 Tulalip Tribes (WA) Tribal Code, § 2.40.050(3), (13).
75 Penobscot Nation (ME) Tribal Code, Chapter 13, § 6-A-1.
76 Penobscot Nation (ME) Adrian's Law, § 3.
77 Id.

laws.[78] The Utu Utu Gwaitu Paiute Tribe authorizes exclusion from the reservation for persons required to register as sex offenders or habitual offenders who have three or more convictions within the previous 3 years. If the person excluded is a minor, his or her parents must also be excluded.[79] The Spokane Tribe has a strong ordinance requiring mandatory exclusion for non-tribal members convicted of drug crimes, felony convictions for domestic or sexual violence, neglect or violent crimes against minors and vulnerable adults, or any other violent felonies.[80]

Criminal convictions may also bar enrollment or reenrollment in the tribe. The Sauk-Suiattle Indian Tribe does not permit enrollment into the tribe by way of adoption for a person convicted of a felony or major crime.[81] The Cherokee Nation states that persons who voluntarily relinquish their tribal citizenship must wait 5 years before reenrolling in the tribe; however, if a person were convicted of a felony or misdemeanor of moral turpitude, they would not be eligible to reenroll as a tribal citizen.[82]

Guardianship and Conservatorship Rights

Criminal convictions may bar a person's appointment as a guardian ad litem or conservator for a juvenile or vulnerable adult. Due to a high rate of elder abuse on Indian reservations, some tribes have adopted policies on elder abuse, to include criminal code provisions and guardianship frameworks.[83] Tribes that exclude persons with felony convictions from serving as a guardian or conservator include the Burns Paiute Tribe, Quechan Tribe of the Fort Yuma Indian Reservation, and Winnebago Tribe.[84] The Northern Cheyenne Tribe, Oglala Sioux Tribe, Poarch Band of Creeks, and Salt River Pima-Maricopa Indian Community terminate juvenile guardianship automatically upon conviction of a felony.[85] The Eastern Band of Cherokee Indians excludes persons convicted of "a felony or other crime," which would presumably include at least some misdemeanors.[86] The Nooksack Indian Tribe excludes as guardians ad litem persons convicted of felonies, crimes of moral

78 Shoalwater Bay Indian Tribe (WA) Tribal Code, § 4A.2.010(1).
79 Utu Utu Gwaitu Paiute Tribe (CA) Tribal Code, § 7-10-010(a), (c).
80 Spokane Tribe of the Spokane Reservation (WA) Tribal Code, § 21-3.02.
81 Sauk-Suiattle Indian Tribe (WA) Enrollment Ordinance, § 15.
82 Cherokee Nation (OK) Tribal Code, Chapter 4, § 34(K)(2).
83 Justin Siegler, "Injustice in Indian Country: The Need for a Serious Response for Native American Elder Abuse," 19(2) *Elder Law Journal* 415–48, 428 (2012).
84 Burns Paiute Tribe (OR) Tribal Code, § 5.2.342(c); Quechan Tribe of the Fort Yuma Indian Reservation (AZ) Tribal Code, § 6.3.23(B)(3); Winnebago Tribe (NE) Tribal Code, § 18-215.
85 Northern Cheyenne Tribe (MT) Tribal Code, § 3-6-7(D)(2); Oglala Sioux Tribe (SD) Law and Order Code, Chapter 3, § 54.7; Poarch Band of Creeks (AL) Tribal Code, § 10-7-8(a); Salt River Pima-Maricopa Indian Community (AZ) Tribal Code, § 10-124(a)(3)(p).
86 Eastern Band of Cherokee Indians (NC) Tribal Code, § 35A-1105(b).

turpitude, drug crimes, domestic violence, or sex offenses.[87] The Sycuan Band of the Kumeyaay Nation denies as proposed conservators any person with convictions for felonies and serious misdemeanors.[88]

Several jurisdictions have more complex provisions that either provide a more elaborate list of exclusions or that contemplate restoration of rights. The Oneida Indian Tribe does not permit guardians ad litem who have been convicted of a felony "unless the person received a pardon or forgiveness," or any other crime involving a child.[89] The Spirit Lake Tribe has a longer list of exclusions for guardians for vulnerable adults. These include convictions for violent sex crimes, violent felonies, or arson, as well as convictions within the previous 5 years for maltreatment, neglect, assault, drug offenses (including misdemeanors), theft, robbery, or domestic violence.[90] The Morongo Band of Mission Indians does not permit as conservators for vulnerable adults anyone with criminal convictions for felony child abuse or neglect, spousal abuse, child pornography, crimes involving violence, to include murder, rape, and sexual assault.[91] In addition, the tribe has a 5-year bar for criminal convictions involving physical assault, battery, or drug- or alcohol-related crimes, and a 20-year bar for crimes of moral turpitude.[92]

Inheritance Rights

Several tribes exclude persons with previous criminal convictions from serving as personal representative of an estate, either as an executor (if decedent died with a will) or as administrator (if decedent died without a will). The Nez Perce Tribal Code states that persons convicted of a felony, a misdemeanor involving moral turpitude, or their equivalents under tribal law may not act as personal representative of an estate.[93] The Spokane Tribe and Kalispel Indian Community have similar exclusions for crimes of moral turpitude but do not exclude other felonies.[94] By contrast, the Washoe Tribe of Nevada and California excludes persons convicted of all felonies from serving as an executor or administrator of an estate, but does not exclude misdemeanors involving moral turpitude.[95] The Mescalero Apache Tribe also excludes

87 Nooksack Indian Tribes (WA) Tribal Code, § 18.08.080(A).
88 Sycuan Band of the Kumeyaay Nation (CA) Conservatorship Code, § 7(b)(2).
89 Oneida Indian Tribe (WI) Tribal Code, § 708.8-2(a).
90 Spirit Lake Tribe (ND) Tribal Code, § 24-3-600(D).
91 Morongo Band of Mission Indians (CA) Vulnerable Adult Protection Ordinance, #42, § 11(A)(8).
92 Id.
93 Nez Perce Tribe (ID) Tribal Code, Chapter 10-4, § 10-4-3.
94 Spokane Tribe of the Spokane Reservation (WA) Tribal Code, Chapter 5, § 5-8.01; Kalispel Indian Community (WA) Tribal Code, § 6-13.01.
95 Washoe Tribe of Nevada and California (NV) Tribal Code, Title 25, §§ 25-138-020(1)(b), 25-139-010(2).

persons with felony convictions from serving as administrator or administratrix of an estate.[96] The Morongo Band of Mission Indians does not permit as conservators of an estate persons who have a felony conviction for abuse or neglect or violent crimes; in addition, the tribe has a 5-year bar on convictions involving physical assault, battery, or drug and alcohol crimes, and a 20-year bar for convictions involving moral turpitude, embezzlement, or bribery.[97]

Whether a will is properly executed on an Indian reservation is a matter for federal law, not state or tribal law.[98] The Board of Indian Appeals in the U.S. Department of the Interior has confirmed that under federal Indian law, a witness attesting to a will is not disqualified by having a felony conviction.[99] However, in a case where a decedent attempted to devise a firearm in a will to a person with a previous felony conviction, the Board dismissed the claim as untimely and therefore did not reach the merits.[100] The question remains open then whether the devise fails when the tribe prohibits possession of a firearm by a person with a previous criminal conviction.

Rights of Parents and Foster Parents

Some tribes restrict the rights of parents or foster parents with a criminal conviction. For parental rights, the Keweenaw Bay Indian Community has a straightforward authorization to terminate parental rights where a parent has been convicted of murder, manslaughter, sexual assault, or felony assault of a child.[101] The Ponca Tribe of Nebraska authorizes termination of parental rights where the parent was convicted of rape or sexual assault against the other parent.[102] The Pokagon Band of Potawatomi Indians and the Quechan Tribe of the Fort Yuma Indian Reservation have a broader exclusion: in those tribes, parental rights may be terminated if a parent has been convicted of a violent or sexual offense against any person or "any other crime that proves the unfitness of the parent."[103] The Muscogee (Creek) Nation has a similarly narrow exclusion for parents who were convicted of

96 Mescalero Apache Tribe of the Mescalero Reservation (NM) Tribal Code, Chapter 7, § 7-2-1.

97 Morongo Band of Mission Indians (CA) Vulnerable Adult Protection Ordinance, #42, § 11(B)(7).

98 25 U.S.C. 373; 43 C.F.R. 4.260-262; Estate of Carrie Standing Haddon Miller, 10 I.B.I.A. 128 (1982).

99 Estate of Sally Fawbush, 34 I.B.I.A. 254 (2000).

100 Estate of Lorraine M. Miller, 64 I.B.I.A. 333 (2017), 66 I.B.I.A. (2018).

101 Keweenaw Bay Indian Community (MI) Tribal Code, § 4.707(C), citing 42 U.S.C. § 675(5)(E).

102 Ponca Tribe of Nebraska (NE) Tribal Code, § 3-8-4(1)(h).

103 Pokagon Band of Potawatomi Indians (MI) Child Protection Code, § 24(B)(5); Quechan Tribe of the Fort Yuma Indian Reservation (AZ) Tribal Code, § 6-3-20(H)(e).

physical or sexual abuse of a child or failing to protect the child from such abuse, or for causing the death of the child's sibling as a result of abuse or neglect.[104] The tribe also authorizes termination of parental rights where a parent is incarcerated for more than 10 years, taken in conjunction with other factors such as the relationship between the parent and the child, any history of abuse, child's age, and previous criminal record.[105] The Shoshone Tribe of the Wind River Reservation also authorizes termination of parental rights due to incarceration, but the exclusion is much broader than with the Muscogee (Creek) Nation. For the Wind River Shoshone, a parent may have his or her parental rights terminated for incarceration for any felony conviction regardless of length of incarceration, where a showing has been made that the parent is unfit to have custody.[106]

Some tribes have collateral consequences that relate to foster parenting. The Confederated Tribes of Siletz Indians does not allow as foster parents persons with criminal convictions for child abuse or neglect, spousal abuse, crimes against children, or violent crimes excluding simple assault or battery, or, within the last 5 years, a conviction for felony assault or battery or a drug-related offense.[107] The Nez Perce Tribe, Omaha Tribe, and Eastern Band of Cherokee Indians have substantively identical exclusions for foster parents or family foster home licenses.[108] However, the Eastern Band of Cherokee Indians has a discretionary provision to restore eligibility to receive a license for a foster home considering the nature of the crime, time since the crime took place, age of the offender when the crime was committed, and other criteria including a letter of support from the foster care agency's executive director.[109] The Mescalero Apache Tribe excludes as foster parents anyone convicted in the last 7 years of a felony, serious offense involving child abuse, neglect, or violence, or any sex offense.[110]

Several tribes restrict adoption rights. For the Oglala Sioux Tribe, consent to adoption is not necessary from a parent who has been convicted of adultery, any felony, or a crime of moral turpitude.[111] For the Oneida Tribe of Wisconsin, a prospective adoptive parent with a criminal record that has not been pardoned or forgiven may still be eligible to adopt if he or she shows

104 Muscogee (Creek) Nation (OK) Tribal Code, Title 6, § 1-901(5)-(6).
105 Id. at § 1-901(7).
106 Shoshone Tribe of the Wind River Reservation (WY) Tribal Code, § 9-2-1(1)(d).
107 Confederated Tribes of Siletz Indians (OR) Tribal Code, § 8.034(f)(4)(K).
108 Nez Perce Tribe (ID) Tribal Code, § 5-1-25(d)(2)–(3); Omaha Tribe (NE) Tribal Code, § 24-1-3(c)(1)–(4); Eastern Band of Cherokee Indians (NC) Tribal Code, § 10A CAR 70E .1114(a)–(c).
109 Eastern Band of Cherokee Indians (NC) Tribal Code, § 10A CAR 70E .1114(d).
110 Mescalero Apache Tribe (NM) Tribal Code, § 11-13-2(A)(5).
111 Oglala Sioux Tribe (SD) Law and Order Code, Chapter 3, § 53.3(1).

with clear and convincing evidence that adoption is in the best interests of the child.[112]

Other Civil Rights Restrictions

Some tribes have other types of civil rights restrictions for previous criminal convictions in their tribal codes:

- **Driver's licenses**: some jurisdictions attach restrictions to an individual's ability to have a tribal driver's license, to drive on a reservation, or to be employed in positions that require driving. The Pueblo of San Ildefonso Tribal Code denies a chauffeur license to anyone with three convictions for driving under the influence of drugs or alcohol, and the right to drive on the reservation entirely with a subsequent conviction.[113] The Tulalip Tribes of Washington require applicants for a commercial driver's license to have no convictions for driving under the influence within the previous 7 years and exclude persons with felony convictions from tribal employment requiring a commercial driver's license.[114] The Lac Courte Oreilles Band of Lake Superior Chippewa Indians restricts driving of tribal vehicles to persons who have not had a conviction in the past 1 year of reckless driving, driving without a license, negligent homicide, or other driving-related offenses.[115] At least one tribe, the Spirit Lake Tribe, provides a process to restore driving privileges if a conviction is later reversed or overturned; in this instance, the registrar of the tribal court is responsible for restoring driving privileges.[116]
- **Ownership of an animal**: a prior criminal conviction could affect a person's legal possession of an animal. The Hannahville Indian Community prevents persons with a previous criminal conviction within the previous 5 years from receiving a permit for a "restricted animal," defined as a wolf, wolf hybrid, pit bull terrier, or rottweiler. The provision does not distinguish between previous felony or misdemeanor convictions.
- **Registration as a violent offender**: violent offender registries, especially when made public and not solely for use by police, appear to have little criminological benefit beyond the shame and exclusion that they produce.[117] The Reno-Sparks Indian Colony has a mandatory registration process for violent offenders who visit, work, or live on the reservation.

112 Oneida Tribe (WI) Tribal Code, § 708.42-3.
113 Pueblo of San Ildefonso (NM) Tribal Code, Part 25.1.3, § 25.1.3.040(c).
114 Tulalip Tribes of Washington (WA) Tribal Code, Title 1, Chapter 1.30, § 1.30.360(3).
115 Lac Courte Oreilles Band of Lake Superior Chippewa Indians (WI) Tribal Code, Title 14, § 4.1005(1)(e).
116 Spirit Lake Tribe (ND) Tribal Code, § 6-7-112.
117 McGinnis, supra note 7 at 64–65.

These persons must register with the police department and be fingerprinted. Convictions for the following offenses result in a registration requirement: homicide, aggravated battery, aggravated stalking, terrorist threats, criminal endangerment, robbery, false imprisonment, kidnapping, criminal child abuse, arson, aggravated burglary, and "any equivalent offense" under tribal, state, or federal law.[118]

Tribal Housing

Exclusions for persons with criminal convictions from tribal housing or tribal-owned homesteads are often broader than other forms of collateral consequences, and in some cases not even contingent on conviction of a crime. In the Pinoleville Pomo Nation, an arrest or conviction for any drug-related offense results in immediate termination of a tenant's lease and ineligibility for tribal housing, although use of any drugs without an arrest or conviction also results in eviction.[119] The Rincon Band of Luiseño Mission Indians allows eviction of persons or their possessions from their houses for conviction of a felony.[120] This tribe appears to have communal land ownership for houses, so this eviction ordinance is distinct from the exclusion or banishment ordinances summarized above.

Collateral restrictions on tribal housing may have a sunset date. The Washoe Tribe of Nevada and California renders ineligible for housing assistance for 7 years any person who is convicted of crimes such as assault, intimidation, burglary, arson, trespass, and others. For misdemeanor domestic violence, a single conviction within 7 years does not disqualify a tribal member from on-reservation services. However, two convictions for misdemeanor domestic violence in 7 years may result in disqualification if clear and convincing evidence shows that the tenant threatens the right to peaceful enjoyment of one's residence.[121] The Pueblo of Santa Ana have a homeownership program for low-income families. Applicants for admission to this program must not have been convicted within the previous 3 years of felony drug offenses, sexual abuse of children, offenses involving bodily harm, or theft or destruction of property. This provision does not apply "if the person has completed a rehabilitation program and has completed all probationary terms imposed by the jurisdiction that convicted the offender."[122] This

118 Reno-Sparks Indian Colony (NV) Tribal Code, § 4-1-301(a)–(b).
119 Pinoleville Pomo Nation (CA) Housing Department, Eligibility and Occupancy Policy, § 11(K).
120 Rincon Band of Luiseño Mission Indians (CA) Tribal Code, § 15.504(a)(4).
121 Washoe Tribe of Nevada and California (NV) WHA Board of Commissioners, Criminal and Drug Related Activity Policy, *see* http://washoehousingauthority.com/policies.
122 Pueblo of Santa Ana (NM) Tamaya Housing Inc. Homeownership Program Policies and Procedures, § 3(A)(13).

program also provides for termination of a lease for any criminal activity that threatens the health and safety of others, including vandalism, arson, and assault, with expedited eviction for drug-related crimes.[123]

Some tribes have a provision for waiver or restoration of rights. The Lac Courte Oreilles Band of Lake Superior Chippewa Indians excludes from tribal housing anyone convicted of a crime or violation of a local ordinance concerning public safety. Notably, though, this may be waived pursuant to the tribe's Pardon and Forgiveness Code, restoring this right.[124] However, the tribe has additional exclusions from tribal housing for other types of offenses. No person convicted of a sex offense for which 10-year or lifetime sex offender registration is required may receive or live in tribal housing; this provision does not provide for a restoration of rights under the Pardon and Forgiveness Code.[125] In addition, the tribe has two additional exclusions: a 5-year bar for persons with convictions for use or possession of controlled substances with intent to deliver and a 3-year bar for persons with convictions for simple use or possession of controlled substances or drug paraphernalia. Notably, unlike sex offenses, both drug-related exclusions may be waived under the Pardon and Forgiveness Code.[126] Other tribes have housing restrictions specific to sex offenders. The Winnebago Tribe states that sex offenders are not permitted to lease, rent, or reside in tribal housing units or reside on any tribally owned land.[127] This is in addition to a restriction stating that sex offenders may not live within 1,000 feet of a school, childcare facility, youth program facility, or playground.[128] Turtle Mountain Band of Chippewa Indians has multiple exclusions from its tribal housing rental program. An applicant is ineligible if any member of the household has a drug conviction unless she or he has completed a rehabilitation program; has been convicted of violent criminal activity or gang activity within the previous 3 years; or is currently subject to a sex offender registration requirement, which is retroactive to 2003.[129]

Tribal Employment

Many tribes have background check requirements and exclusions from general tribal employment for persons with certain criminal convictions. This can be a major limitation, because tribal governments may be the largest

123 Id. at §§ 3(B)(2)(f), 3(B)(7)(a).
124 Lac Courte Oreilles Band of Lake Superior Chippewa Indians (WI) Tribal Code, Title 11, § 7.506(2).
125 Id. at § 7.506(4).
126 Id. at § 7.506(6), (7).
127 Winnebago Tribe (NE) Tribal Code, § 7-1705(1)–(3).
128 Id. at § 7-1703(1).
129 Turtle Mountain Band of Chippewa Indians (ND) Tribal Code, § 42.1401(1).

employer on the reservation. The Oglala Sioux Tribe has a personnel requirement that may disqualify applicants for tribal employment if they were convicted of a criminal offense or other crime involving moral turpitude.[130] By contrast, other tribes stop short of a blanket exclusion on criminal convictions for tribal employees. The Standing Rock Sioux Tribe has a condition of employment for anyone in "a position dealing with sensitive or confidential information, a position involving financial dealings or a position of public trust" that he or she does not have a conviction for theft, embezzlement, or other finance-related felony. However, a conviction for unpaid child or dependent support is not an automatic bar, so long as the employee pays child or dependent support as a payroll deduction while employed.[131] Some employment-related restrictions pertain specifically to alcohol-related convictions. The Fort Belknap Indian Community authorizes mandatory termination on final conviction for any conviction related to driving under the influence of alcohol. An employee may reapply when he or she completes all requirements of the sentence.[132]

Several jurisdictions have more limited exclusions, either restricted to specific responsibilities or individual tribal agencies. For the Little Traverse Bay Band of Odawa Indians, persons convicted of domestic violence may not be hired or promoted to the position of manager or supervisor, or that has managerial or supervisory responsibilities over another person in tribal government or tribal enterprises. This provision sunsets 7 years after conviction.[133] The Salt River Pima-Maricopa Indian Community has an exclusion specifically for employees of the tribal financial division or the tribal health and human services division for persons convicted of any felony or crime involving violence, or found liable in any civil judgment involving fraud, misrepresentation, material omission, misappropriation, theft, or conversion.[134]

Collateral consequences may also attach to a Tribal Employment Rights Ordinance (TERO), which authorizes a Native American hiring preference for employers on or near Indian reservations. Title VII of the Civil Rights Act of 1964 excludes Indian tribes and private employers operating on reservations from its definition of employment discrimination to protect tribal hiring preferences.[135] Some tribes exclude persons with criminal convictions from a tribal hiring preference. The Quinault Indian Nation has an exception in its TERO, stating that the hiring preference for tribal members does not apply if the applicant has been convicted of "violent or financial crimes" or has "a

130 Oglala Sioux Tribe (SD) Tribal Code, Chapter 17, § E(1)(6)(C).
131 Standing Rock Sioux Tribe (SD) Tribal Code, § 18.201(8).
132 Fort Belknap Indian Community (MT) Resolution 106-04, § 120.8.
133 Little Traverse Bay Band of Odawa Indians (MI) Tribal Code, § 9.1503(A).
134 Salt River Pima-Maricopa Indian Community (AZ) Tribal Code, art. 9, § 10-304(c)(5).
135 42 U.S.C. § 2000e-2(i).

history of sexual or other harassment."[136] The Mohegan Tribe of Indians has a TERO that requires employers on the reservation to exercise an employment preference for tribal members. These employers are certified as Native American Entities or Mohegan Entities, a designation that they may lose if they hire an employee who has a criminal conviction for "an offense that indicates a lack of business integrity or honesty," including fraud in performance of a contract.[137]

At least one jurisdiction has a "Ban the Box" type policy that prohibits employment discrimination based on prior arrests or that prevents disclosure of arrests in an initial employment application. The code of the Poarch Band of Creeks prohibits discrimination based on prior arrest record. This prohibits employers from requiring disclosure of prior arrests except when the arrest prevents an employee from being bondable under a fidelity bond, that is, from receiving insurance coverage for employee theft or other employee-related crimes.[138] This provision does not apply if the applicant is facing pending charges that "substantially relate to the circumstances of the particular job or licensed activity."[139] The provision also does not apply if the applicant is actually convicted of a felony, unless pardoned; denied a gaming license or liquor sales license because of gaming offenses or offenses involving controlled substances; or unemployable under the federal Indian Child Protection Act, as described in the next section.[140]

The exclusion mentioned above that a prospective employee may not be bondable because of theft against the tribe has come up in another jurisdiction as well. After it opened a casino, the Oneida Tribe of Indians in Wisconsin purchased a tribal insurance policy to protect tribal assets. This policy prohibited hiring employees who committed theft against the tribe. In one instance, an employee was denied a job with the Oneida Farm, a tribal agricultural enterprise, because he had been found civilly liable for theft of tires that belonged to the tribe. However, he was not convicted of criminal charges and rather received a deferred prosecution agreement. He sought a declaratory judgment from the Oneida Appeals Commission that he was eligible for employment. In *Ellis v. Barton*, the Appeals Commission rejected his contention that he was eligible because he did not have a criminal conviction.[141] While the Commission conceded that he could not use the tribal pardon process since he had not been convicted, it maintained that the Oneida Tribe had to adhere to its contractual agreements in its insurance

136 Quinault Indian Nation (WA) Tribal Code, § 97.03.010(i)(1)(B).
137 Mohegan Tribe of Indians (CT) Tribal Code, art. 5 § 4-109.
138 Poarch Band of Creeks (AL) Tribal Code, § 33-4-6(a).
139 Id. at § 33-4-6(b).
140 Id. at § 33-4-6(c)–(g).
141 Ellis v. Barton, No. 03-TC-342 (Oneida App. Comm., Jan. 19, 2004).

policy. The Commission instead suggested that either the insurance company consent to an extension of coverage or the Oneida Business Committee alter the insurance policy.[142] This is an example of a hidden collateral consequence because it is not specifically included in the Oneida Code or another publicly available law.

Tribal Employment Involving Children

For employment involving children, the federal Indian Child Protection and Family Violence Prevention Act requires tribes to perform background checks for potential employees and requires tribal employers to deny employment to or dismiss an employee for any felony conviction or two or more misdemeanors "involving crimes of violence; sexual assault, sexual molestation, sexual exploitation, sexual contact or prostitution; crimes against persons; or offenses committed against children."[143] An employer has discretion to deny employment to or terminate an employee with a conviction for an offense involving a child victim, a sex crime, or a drug felony.[144] This provision allows employers to consider a pardon, expungement, set aside, or other court order.[145] Some tribes have integrated this requirement into tribal law, and a few have a harsher exclusion. As required by federal law, the Eastern Band of Cherokee Indians has a mandatory background check for positions related to children, which requires employees to disclose any previous criminal convictions. This extends to volunteers as well. Persons who are hired must "meet the standards of character required for an individual's fitness to have responsibility for the safety and well-being of children."[146] The Eastern Band does not exclude any specific criminal convictions automatically.

Some tribes include a list of excluded criminal convictions that are more extensive or more specific than the federal law. The Quileute Tribe has a mandatory background check for tribal employees, contractors, and volunteers in jobs involving children. No employees or volunteers may have a previous conviction for any felony or two or more misdemeanors involving violence, sexual assault, molestation, exploitation, indecent liberties, prostitution, crimes against persons, or offenses against children.[147] The Oglala Sioux Tribe excludes employees with drug convictions or child abuse convictions from tribal employment that involves working with children.[148] The Standing Rock Sioux Tribe has a more complex restriction on tribal

142 Id. at ¶¶ 19–20.
143 25 CFR § 63.19(a).
144 25 CFR § 63.19(b).
145 25 CFR § 63.19(c).
146 Eastern Band of Cherokee Indians (NC) Tribal Code, §§ 95-69, 95-70.
147 Quileute Tribe of the Quileute Reservation (WA) Tribal Code, Chapter 5, § 5.1(A)(2).
148 Oglala Sioux Tribe (SD) Personnel Policies and Procedures, Amendments, §§ 2, 14.

employees who work with children and vulnerable adults. Excluded from these positions are persons with convictions "involving a crime of violence, sexual assault, molestation, exploitation, contact or prostitution or other crimes against persons." As with other tribal employment, unpaid child or dependent support convictions do not render an applicant ineligible so long as the employee continues payroll deduction for this support pursuant to a tribal court order.[149] The Fond du Lac Band of the Minnesota Chippewa Tribe has a blanket exclusion for any tribal enterprise or program with duties and responsibilities involving children, which are designated "CA," "CB," or "CC" depending on the extent of involvement with children. For tribal businesses designated as "CA," involving the most extensive involvement with children, employees or volunteers must not have a criminal conviction for, *inter alia*, family violence, child abuse or neglect, sexual assault, prostitution, violent crimes, or, within the preceding 5 years, gross misdemeanor crimes of theft, fraud, or misrepresentation, including refusing to submit to a drug test.[150]

These criminal conviction exclusions may be included in the statutes of tribal day care centers. The Samish Indian Nation requires a background check for employees or volunteers at its Longhorse Early Learning Center and in its Head Start programs. Persons with convictions for crimes involving children, violent crimes, sexual crimes, or other crimes against persons are ineligible for employment or volunteer positions and subject to termination, reassignment, administrative leave, or exclusion from tribal events.[151] Similar to its restriction on day care licensees, the Swinomish Indian Tribal Community excludes as staff members or volunteers at its day care center any person who has been convicted of a crime involving child abuse or physical harm to another person.[152]

Other Social Services

Some tribal jurisdictions exclude persons with criminal convictions from certain types of monetary benefits or other services. These include:

- **Gaming and casino dividends**: at least one tribe suspends distribution of tribal gaming dividends based on a criminal conviction. The United Auburn Indian Community in California authorizes suspension of a tribal member's per capita payments upon a felony arrest warrant or conviction

149 Standing Rock Sioux Tribe (SD) Tribal Code, § 18.201(8).
150 Fond du Lac Band of the Minnesota Chippewa Tribe (MN) Ordinance 13/94, § 104.
151 Samish Indian Nation (WA) Tribal Code, § 5-16-009(6).
152 Swinomish Indian Tribal Community (WA) Tribal Code, § 15-01.220(A)(4).

resulting in incarceration.[153] These lucrative quarterly distributions are paid to tribal members from the tribe's gaming revenues.[154]

- **Weatherization checks**: criminal convictions may affect a person's ability to receive a payment from the tribe to prepare a personal home for winter. The Pueblo of Pojoaque Tribal Code states that checks made to incarcerated tribal members to weatherize their homes must be placed in a trust fund until the tribal member is released from incarceration.[155]
- **School expulsion**: the Eastern Band of Cherokee Indians authorizes the tribal school board, on the recommendation of the school principal and superintendent, to expel any juvenile aged 14 or older who has been convicted of a felony and who poses a "clear threat to the safety and health of other students or employees." If expelled, the code makes clear that the tribe has no duty to provide special educational services to students with special needs.[156]

153 Constitution of the United Auburn Indian Community (CA), art. 8 § 3 (Amendment 1).
154 Tavares v. Whitehouse, 851 F.3d 863, 870 (2017).
155 Pueblo of Pojoaque (NM) Tribal Code, § I-14(a).
156 Eastern Band of Cherokee (SC) Tribal Code, § 115-5(d).

Chapter 8

Pardons, Expungements, and Restoration of Rights in Tribal Law

Protecting individual rights in tribal law may conflict with cultural revitalization or the protection of traditional decision making in Indian Country. The tendency to privilege the individual right at the expense of the communitarian interest, including through adversarial criminal proceedings with formal legal representation within a hierarchical court system, no doubt reflects Anglo-American cultural influence.[1] However, restoration of individual rights after a crime or a wrong might be reconciled with traditional notions of forgiveness and peacemaking. Peacemaking rituals are designed to benefit the community and protect tribal social norms, to include one's relationship to others as part of one's identity, through the presence of a third-party mediator who seeks to find a mutually agreeable solution.[2] Restoration of rights procedures fundamentally involve reintegration of a person in his or her community, sometimes with an apology or acknowledgment of guilt.

This chapter explores the basic restoration of rights procedures in tribal law. The broadest structure is a pardon or expungement procedure which is open to all persons with convictions. Earlier chapters of this book have also catalogued waivers for specific rights such as running for tribal office or receiving a gaming license. If we conceive of a pardon or expungement as a bundle of sticks, entirely erasing a criminal conviction from one's record, other devices such as commutations of sentence or waivers for specific rights comprise something less than the whole bundle. Another example of this, explored below, is reduction of registration periods for persons on tribal sex offender registries, a peculiar device that is specifically created by federal law and available to tribes that choose to adopt it. Owing to its discretionary nature, it is akin to a commutation of sentence, notwithstanding efforts to

1 Carole E. Goldberg, "Individual Rights and Tribal Revitalization," 35(3) *Arizona State Law Journal* 889, 937 (2003).

2 Robert B. Porter, "Strengthening Tribal Sovereignty Through Peacemaking: How the Anglo-American Legal Tradition Destroys Indigenous Societies," 28(2) *Columbia Human Rights Law Review* 235, 251–54 (1997).

DOI: 10.4324/9781003432548-8

characterize sex offender registries as "non-punitive."[3] Finally, this chapter addresses several tribal court decisions that have addressed whether a pardon device may be implied in tribal law even when not specifically provided for. These challenges consider whether an implied pardon power can exist as part and parcel of an executive or legislature's general constitutional powers.

Pardon and Expungement Powers in Tribal Law

The pardon power is an ancient, primitive power that appeared in many legal systems where a sovereign had power of life over death. Its existence has been reported not only in medieval Europe but also in centralized polities throughout the precolonial world in Asia and Africa; in Islamic legal theory the Qur'an provides support for a victim's pardon.[4] For Native American tribal authorities, which tended not to have the unitary conception of executive power that the pardon requires, the existence of pardons is overwhelmingly the product of Anglo-American influence, just as culturally foreign as criminal jurisdiction in modern tribal courts.[5] However, one could overgeneralize too far. Many indigenous value structures recognized compromise, conciliation, redemption, and restoration of harmony that could be compatible with modern forms of legal forgiveness. For instance, the Coast Salish people of the Pacific Northwest have specific rituals for apology and reparation that require a wrongdoer to admit fault. The longhouse gathering is one example: under pressure from family members, the offender must face elders and other community members in a longhouse to receive "strong words" and agree to a settlement resolving the dispute.[6]

With that said, pardons in some tribal jurisdictions have at this point developed a long history. Not surprisingly, the Five Civilized Tribes in the American Southeast (Cherokee, Chickasaw, Choctaw, Muscogee, and Seminole) have the longest documented history of tribal pardons because these are precisely the jurisdictions that had the earliest and most profound Anglo-American cultural influence.[7] In 1839, the Cherokee Tribe passed an Act for the Punishment of Criminal Offenses, which authorized a pardon for

3 Wayne A. Logan, "Populism and Punishment: Sex Offender Registration and Community Notification in the Courts," 26(1) *Criminal Justice* 37, 38 (2011).

4 Andrew Novak, *Comparative Executive Clemency: The Constitutional Pardon Power and the Prerogative of Mercy in Global Perspective* 6–15 (Routledge, 2016).

5 See, e.g., Gloria Valencia-Weber, "Tribal Courts: Custom and Innovative Law," 24(2) *New Mexico Law Review* 225 (1994).

6 Bruce Granville Miller, "Bringing Culture in: Community Responses to Apology, Reconciliation, and Reparations," 30(4) *American Indian Culture and Research Journal* 1–17, 9–10 (2006).

7 See, e.g., Andrew Denson, *Demanding the Cherokee Nation: Indian Autonomy and American Culture, 1830–1900* 16–20 (University of Nebraska Press, 2015).

death sentences. After a conviction for murder, the trial court had 5 days to petition the Principal Chief for a pardon before the execution was carried out. The Principal Chief exercised this power in concert with the Assistant Chief and Executive Council.[8] In 1900, the Choctaw Nation granted a pardon for a tribal member wrongfully convicted of murder. The General Council passed a pardon resolution and the Principal Chief signed it.[9]

The Muscogee (Creek) Nation had a particularly active pardon history. The Principal Chief served as the final appeal for criminal cases since the Muscogee Supreme Court only heard appeals in non-criminal cases. The Principal Chief granted pardons freely, especially when the law conflicted with traditional notions of Muscogee justice. By the 1890s, pardons were especially common for the capital crime of theft with two prior convictions, as the Muscogee considered the death penalty too harsh. The tribal archives hold more than 130 pardon applications dated between 1870 and 1896, many of which contain petitions or letters vouching for the convicted person.[10] Pardons were also used for political crimes during the Muscogee civil wars. Harring writes that the Principal Chief's unrestricted pardon power was a means of "mediating between the formal requirements of the new legal system and traditional Creek notions of law and justice."[11] The Muscogee had uncovered the enduring benefit of the pardon power in most of the world's legal systems and across time: the flexibility to temper formal law.

After the civil wars ended, the 1893 Constitution of the Muscogee (Creek) Nation reinforced the formal pardon power. The constitution stated that any citizen who was convicted of a felony and received punishment was to live an exemplary life for five years. Following this, he or she could make an application for a pardon to the Principal Chief signed by at least ten respectable citizens and approved by a tribal court judge. Such a pardon would restore the right to hold tribal office. In addition, the Constitution authorized a "full, free and unconditional pardon" for "all political offenses growing out of the late trouble in our Nation." This provision is equivalent to a general amnesty. One who was charged with a political offense had to take an oath to support the constitution.[12] In 1896, the Muscogee National Council added an additional provision, which stated that any person convicted of larceny three times and subsequently pardoned by the Principal Chief was considered

8 Cherokee Tribe, An Act for the Punishment of Criminal Offenses (1839) [HeinOnline].

9 Choctaw Nation, Bill No. 6, An Act for the Pardon of Johnson Jacob (1900) [HeinOnline].

10 Sidney L. Harring, *Crow Dog's Case: American Indian Sovereignty, Tribal Law, and United States Law in the Nineteenth Century* 87–88 (Cambridge University Press, 1994).

11 Sidney L. Harring, "Crazy Snake and the Creek Struggle for Sovereignty: The Native American Legal Culture and American Law," 34(4) *American Journal of Legal History* 365, 370 (1990).

12 Constitution and Laws of the Muskogee Nation, Under Act of October 15, 1892 (1893), Chapter XXIX, §§ 404–10 [HeinOnline].

to have been pardoned for the earlier offenses as well. However, if a person were again convicted of larceny after the pardon, the offender would receive the penalty of 50 lashes.[13]

During the term of U.S. President Franklin Roosevelt, the federal government more profoundly influenced the development of tribal law systems. The 1934 Indian Reorganization Act advocated a tribal constitutional structure analogous to that of the U.S. federal system, with three branches of government and a written constitution approved by the U.S. Secretary of the Interior.[14] One of the main architects of President Roosevelt's "Indian New Deal," Felix S. Cohen in the Department of the Interior, prepared an influential memorandum on drafting tribal constitutions in 1934. This memorandum included a pardon power in the chapter on drafting a judicial code:

> Consideration should be given to the question of whether the power to grant parole, reprieve, or absolute pardon should lie with the sentencing court, the tribal council, or some official of the tribe, such as the governor or the president of the council.[15]

Another example of federal influence on tribal pardon and expungement mechanisms is the Model Indian Juvenile Code. In 1986, Congress required the U.S. Secretary of the Interior to develop a Model Indian Juvenile Code to make tribal law consistent with U.S. federal law concerning juvenile delinquency, especially for alcohol- and drug-related cases.[16] The Model Indian Juvenile Code provides that all records in juvenile criminal proceedings shall be confidential and not open to inspection except after a hearing in which the juvenile and her or his guardians are fully represented.[17] In addition, when the juvenile turns 25, all records and files shall be expunged and no further use or inspection of those files is permitted.[18]

As the following sections show, tribal jurisdictions chose an array of legal structures for pardons, expungements, and restoration of rights. As the following typology shows, legal forgiveness could come from the executive,

13 Creek Nation, Acts and Resolutions of the National Council of the Muskogee Nation of 1893 and 1899, Inclusive (1900), Acts and Resolutions of 1893, § 203 (October 29, 1896) [HeinOnline].

14 Angelique Wambdi Eaglewoman & Stacy L. Leeds, *Mastering American Indian Law* 19 (2d ed., Carolina Academic Press, 2019).

15 Felix S. Cohen, *On the Drafting of Tribal Constitutions* 126 (David E. Wilkins, ed., University of Oklahoma Press, 2020).

16 25 U.S.C. § 2454.

17 Model Indian Juvenile Code, § 1.04.210 (rev. 2016), available at: https://www.bia.gov/sites/default/files/dup/assets/bia/ojs/ojs/pdf/idc2-047015.pdf.

18 Id. at § 1.04.230.

legislature, judiciary, some combination of the above, or a specially appointed pardons board or committee.

Executive Acting Alone

An executive with the unrestrained power to grant free or conditional pardons is paradigmatic of the Anglo-American common law conception of pardons. In the Anglophone world, this power descended from the king's prerogative of mercy in medieval England, which was delegated to colonial governors and ultimately codified in many constitutions around the world, including the United States.[19] This type of pardon structure would likely be completely unfamiliar to precontact conceptions of political power, though over the past two centuries some tribal authorities have developed a more centralized, personal idea of political power that is compatible with a free pardon. Before the Major Crimes Act of 1885 which gave federal courts jurisdiction over serious offenses in Indian Country, the Principal Chief of the Muscogee (Creek) Nation granted pardons, even in cases that were eligible for the death penalty.[20] The flexibility of the pardon power allowed mediation between conflicting legal norms.

In several tribal jurisdictions, the pardon power is clearly established in the tribal executive acting alone. The constitutions of Big Lagoon Rancheria and Death Valley Timbi-sha Shoshone Tribe provide the pardon power to their tribal chairpersons.[21] The Minnesota Chippewa Tribe (Mille Lacs Band) provides the pardon power to the chief executive.[22] The Chickasaw Nation authorizes the tribal governor to grant commutations or conditional pardons for any conviction except impeachment, an exclusion clearly reflecting Anglo-American influence. This provision allows the Chickasaw governor unlimited discretion to release a convicted person from prison for health reasons or revoke a pardon if lawful conditions are violated.[23] The Pascua Yaqui Tribe allows the Chairman of the Tribal Council to grant a reprieve, commutation, or pardon in her or his discretion, unless the person was convicted twice of the same offense. The Chairman must report any clemency grant to the full Tribal Council.[24] The Mescalero Apache and Jicarilla Apache constitutions

19 Harold J. Krent, "Conditioning the President's Conditional Pardon Power," 89 *California Law Review* 1665, 1672 (2001), Jeffrey Crouch, *The Presidential Pardon Power* 10–15 (University of Kansas Press, 2009).

20 Sidney L. Harring, *Crow Dog's Case: American Indian Sovereignty, Tribal Law, and United States Law in the Nineteenth Century* 87–88 (Cambridge University Press, 1994).

21 Big Lagoon Rancheria (CA) Constitution, art. 10, § 1(e); Death Valley Timbi-sha Shoshone Tribe (CA), art. 7, § 1(a)(6).

22 Minnesota Chippewa Tribe (Mille Lacs Band) (MN) Tribal Code, Title 4, § 6(k).

23 Chickasaw Tribal Code, §§ 5-701.9, 5-701.10, 5-701.11.

24 Pascua Yaqui Tribe (AZ) Tribal Code, 3 PYTC § 2-2-450(E).

grant the pardon power to their tribal presidents specifically to restore the right to run for elected tribal office.[25] Revised in 2021, the Mescalero Apache Tribal Code clarifies that the president's pardon power is restricted to restoring the right to run for tribal office and is not a general pardon power; it also adds the proviso that the president cannot pardon her or himself.[26]

The Cherokee Nation and Shawnee Tribe, both in Oklahoma, have identical provisions that delegate to the Cherokee Principal Chief or Shawnee Chairman, respectively, the ability to grant pardons or commutations of sentence to any person convicted and sentenced to at least 1 year imprisonment. Applications must include additional materials such as recommendations from "credible persons," a statement of facts, and a rationale for the pardon, and provide notice to the victims. The decision nonetheless is for the executive alone.[27]

Executive Alone with Legislative or Membership Veto

In at least 11 jurisdictions, all in Oklahoma or Kansas, the executive is empowered to grant pardons or commutations but provide a window of time, typically 60 days, for the tribal council or tribal supreme court justices to object to the pardon and trigger a vote of the tribal membership to veto the proposed clemency grant. In tribal law, this device is called "Executive Order for Relief from Judgment." For instance, the Absentee-Shawnee Tribe allows the Chief Executive Officer of the tribe to grant pardons or commutations, a copy of which must be filed with the court clerk and sent to all members of the tribal supreme court and legislature. Within 60 days, any of them may object to the proposed pardon or commutation and provide written reasons; if so, the pardon is placed on the ballot for the full tribal membership at the next scheduled election.[28] An identical provision exists in nine other tribal codes: Cheyenne and Arapaho Tribes, Kaw Nation, Kickapoo Tribe of Indians (Kansas), Kickapoo Tribe (Oklahoma), Miami Tribe, Quapaw Tribe, Sac & Fox Nation of Missouri (Kansas), Sac & Fox Nation (Oklahoma), and Seminole Nation.[29] A tenth jurisdiction, the Prairie Band of Potawatomi, had

25 Mescalero Apache Tribe (NM) Constitution, art. 22, § 1(f); Jicarilla Apache Tribe (AZ) Constitution, art. 16(f).

26 Mescalero Apache Tribe (NM) Tribal Code (2021), § 9-8-1.

27 Cherokee Nation (OK) Tribal Code, Title 51, Chapter 2, §§ 56–57; Shawnee Nation (OK) Tribal Code, §§ 3.04.060, 3.04.070.

28 Absentee-Shawnee Tribe (OK) Tribal Code of Criminal Procedure, § 606.

29 Cheyenne and Arapaho Tribe (OK) Law and Order Code, Title 2(C), § 606; Kaw Nation (OK) Tribal Code, Title 8, § 606; Kickapoo Tribe of Indians (KS) Tribal Code, Title 11, § 606; Kickapoo Tribe (OK) Criminal Procedure Code, § 606; Miami Tribe (OK) Criminal Procedure Code, § 606; Quapaw Tribe (OK) Criminal Procedure Act, § 106; Sac & Fox Nation of Missouri (KS) Tribal Code, Title 11, § 606; Sac & Fox Nation (OK) Tribal Code, Title 11, § 606; Seminole Nation (OK) Tribal Code, Title 7, § 606.

the same provision until it was repealed in 1999.[30] In all cases, the pardon or commutation becomes effective if no one objects.

In 2001, the Muscogee (Creek) Nation passed a similar version with several notable exceptions. In the Muscogee provision, the Principal Chief can "recommend" to the National Council to pardon or commute any sentence when doing so "promotes the ends of justice." This is then transmitted to the court clerk and distributed to each justice of the tribal supreme court and the National Council. Any justice or a *majority* of the National Council may object to the proposed pardon and provide a statement of reasons. The pardon or commutation then dies.[31] This provision has two material differences from the template above. First, a single objecting legislator is not sufficient; rather, a majority of the legislature must disapprove. Second, the Muscogee version does not allow a vote of the full tribal membership to override the objectors. In essence, this provision makes objecting to the pardon more difficult, but once made the objection defeats the pardon.

Executive Considers Recommendation from Pardon Board

Another clemency model is where an executive makes the ultimate pardon decision, but must receive a favorable recommendation of a pardons board. Among the Turtle Mountain Band of Chippewa Indians of North Dakota, the tribal chairman can issue a pardon on recommendation of the Pardon Board. The Board includes five members, one from each district plus a chairman appointed by the tribal chairman and tribal council. In this jurisdiction, an applicant must submit three references and a small fee to the pardon clerk, who prepares it for the Pardon Board's quarterly meetings. An applicant is eligible for a pardon 5 years after the conviction. The Pardon Board will make a recommendation to the tribal chairman; if the pardon is denied, an applicant may apply again 6 months later.[32] The Pardon Board has significant restrictions on its authority. It cannot hear applications from persons with three or more tribal misdemeanor convictions or applications involving infractions less than 5 years old. In addition, the Pardon Board is also not competent to hear applications for convictions under the Indian Major Crimes Act (even if also a crime under tribal law) or misdemeanor drug dealing or distribution convictions. Before application is made, drug use-related infractions require an intensive drug treatment program lasting at least 90 days.[33]

30 See Prairie Band of Potawatomi (KS) Tribal Code, § 16-6-6 (deleted 1999).
31 Muscogee (Creek) Nation (OK) Tribal Code, Title 14, § 1-703(A).
32 Turtle Mountain Band of Chippewa Indians Tribal Code, Chapters 26.0706–26.0708.
33 Id., Chapter 16.0707.

Legislature Acting Alone

Yet another variation is where a tribal legislature makes the ultimate clemency decision. In the Menominee Tribe of Wisconsin, the tribal legislature has the pardon power in misdemeanor cases 5 years after conviction in the tribal court. Pardons may not be given for felony convictions or violent offenses. An applicant pays a filing fee and the legislature reviews the pardon petition at the next regular meeting. Decisions are final, but an applicant is not limited in the number of times she or he may apply.[34] The Kickapoo Traditional Tribe of Texas has a more limited legislative pardon provision that is specifically for one of two purposes. First, the council may restore the right to run for tribal office or serve on tribal boards or commissions. In this jurisdiction, any person convicted of a crime resulting in banishment or exclusion from tribal lands becomes ineligible to serve in elected or appointed tribal office for not less than 5 years, extending to the length of the term of the banishment or exclusion. This may be overturned by the tribal council, which is authorized to reduce a sentence of banishment or exclusion to 10 years after 10 years have passed since the conviction.[35] The tribal council may also grant a free pardon to any person 7 years after conviction upon receiving new evidence "which proves beyond a reasonable doubt that the offender was never guilty of the crime."[36] This provision may be criticized because it imposes a burdensome waiting period for an offender who is factually innocent of the underlying offense.

Legislature Considers Recommendation of Pardon Board

In some jurisdictions, the legislature may appoint a pardons board or commission to hear petitions and make recommendations, but ultimately the decision is one for the legislature itself. The Oneida Tribe of Wisconsin has such a procedure, enacted in 2016 to replace an ad hoc process that the Oneida Business Committee had created.[37] This new process allows the Oneida Business Committee to grant pardons, but requires a recommendation from the Pardon and Forgiveness Screening Committee. The Screening Committee reviews the background of the case, presides over a hearing, and makes a formal recommendation to the Business Committee. An applicant may apply for either pardon or forgiveness. Pardons are for tribal members and can restore housing rights or other tribal benefits. Forgiveness is for any individual, not just tribal members, and intended to restore eligibility for employment or occupational licenses or permits. An applicant may seek

34 Menominee Indian Tribe of Wisconsin Tribal Code, Chapter 81, §§ 81-3 to 81-5.
35 Kickapoo Traditional Tribe (TX) Tribal Code, Chapter 18 (Penal Code), § 3.
36 Id.
37 Oneida Pardon Ordinance, Resolution No. 2-19-93-I (February 19, 1993) (repealed).

pardon or forgiveness 1 year after the conviction. The Screening Committee holds a public hearing with testimony from the applicant, victims, witnesses, or other interested parties. When the Oneida Business Committee considers the Screening Committee's recommendation, the applicant may testify to the full Business Committee. The recommendation and ultimate decision may impose conditions on the pardon, such as that the applicant not serve in specific jobs or have caregiving responsibilities.[38]

In 2019, the Lac Courte Oreilles Band of Lake Superior Chippewa Indians, also in Wisconsin, enacted a similar ordinance creating a Pardon and Forgiveness Screening Committee. The Committee is composed of five tribal members, none of whom may be a member of the Tribal Governing Board. Like in the Oneida Nation, applicants may apply to the Pardon and Forgiveness Screening Committee seeking either pardon for a tribal court conviction (tribal members only) or forgiveness (all individuals) to restore eligibility for tribal housing, employment, occupational housing, or foster care license. The Steering Committee will review the applicant's background, evidence, and testimony, preside over a hearing, and make a formal, written recommendation to the Tribal Governing Board. The Steering Committee may consider, for instance, letters of reference or support, drug test results, a statement expressing remorse, proof of payment of fines or fees, and other supporting materials.[39] A negative drug test is required for drug-related convictions.[40] The Tribal Governing Board may approve a pardon or forgiveness with conditions, either on the recommendation of the Steering Committee or on its own initiative. Neither pardon nor forgiveness absolves the requirement for sex offender registration, certain employment restrictions that are "substantially related" to the care of other people or animals, or tribal housing rights for certain periods of time in the event of drug-related convictions.[41]

Legislative Committee Sits as Pardon Board

Unlike the Wisconsin jurisdictions above, which exclude members of the tribal council from serving as members of the advisory pardons body, the Blackfeet Tribe in Montana requires members of the Board of Pardons and Parole to be members of the Tribal Business Council. In this way, the Board of Pardons operates as a legislative committee. The Board is made up of three members of the Business Council who vote by majority to grant pardons or parole. The Board must hold a hearing before approving pardons or parole.[42]

38 Oneida Nation (WI) Code of Laws, Title 1, §§ 126.1-126.10.

39 Lac Courte Oreilles Band of Lake Superior Chippewa Indians (WI) Tribal Code of Law, § MCC.6.3.030.

40 Id. at § MCC.6.3.040.

41 Id. at §§ MCC.6.3.060, MCC.6.3.070(f).

42 Blackfeet Tribe (MT) Law and Order Code, Chapter 4, § 4.

Pardon Board Acting Alone

In at least three jurisdictions, the pardon board alone makes the decision to grant clemency. The Assiniboine and Sioux Tribes of the Fort Peck Indian Reservation in Montana authorizes the Tribal Pardon Commission to grant pardons. The Commission has five members who are chosen by the chairman with recommendations from the tribal executive board. Applicants are eligible to apply 5 years after a misdemeanor conviction or 10 years after a felony conviction. Applications are publicly posted and the Commission holds a public hearing. Members of the Commission serve 2-year terms and may be removed from their position by a two-thirds vote of the other members.[43] Application is made to the Pardons Clerk, at least 10 years after a final felony conviction or 5 years after a final misdemeanor conviction. The Pardons Clerk provides public notice to members of the tribe and arranges a public hearing before the Commission; applicants may have counsel present and the tribal prosecutor is permitted to testify under oath. A recommendation from the Chief Judge of the Fort Peck Tribal Court may also be obtained. The Commission's decisions are made by majority and not subject to appeal.[44]

The Standing Rock Sioux Tribe has a similar structure, in which an appointed board, the Tribal Pardon Commission, makes the ultimate pardon decision. The Commission is composed of four members serving 2-year terms, appointed by the tribal chairman, ratified by a majority vote of the tribal council members. This jurisdiction has a shorter waiting period: applicants may apply for a pardon 2 years after a misdemeanor conviction or 5 years after a felony conviction. The Commission holds a public hearing on the application and receives recommendations from the chief judge of the tribal court and the prosecutor in the case. Hearings are held quarterly, and the applicant may have counsel present. The tribal prosecutor may also testify under oath in opposition to the pardon. Three of the four members of the Commission must approve the pardon for it to be granted. A decision may not be appealed. The Commission may only grant pardons, not commutations of sentence or remissions of fines or forfeitures. Finally, each enrolled member of the Standing Rock Sioux Tribe may only use the pardon procedure one time in their lives, regardless of whether the conviction is for a misdemeanor or a felony.[45] The Shoshone-Bannock Tribes of Idaho also have a board structure. There, the Board of Pardons and Parole consists of the chief judge of the tribal court, a member of the Fort Hall business council,

43 Assiniboine and Sioux Tribes (MT), Fort Peck Tribes Comprehensive Code of Justice, Title 6, Subchapter 2, § 906.

44 Id., §§ 907–09.

45 Standing Rock Sioux Tribal Code of Justice, Title IV, Chapter 4, §§ 4-401 to 4-406. See also, Standing Rock Sioux Tribal Commission Policies and Procedures, Resolution 002-14 (approved Jan. 8, 2014).

and an additional member of the tribe who is unrelated to the applicant. The Board can pardon or parole with a majority vote. The parole requirement for a hearing and the numerous exclusions from parole, especially for violent or sex offenses, do not apply to pardons.[46]

Tribal Court Makes Decision

This typology uses "pardon" or "commutation of sentence" to refer to discretionary decisions to reduce or cancel punishment for convicted persons and restore rights. It is legally distinct from court-ordered revision or modification of sentences, although in practice these terms may be used interchangeably since judicial and executive functions in tribal law may not be totally separate, especially in small jurisdictions. Several jurisdictions use the term "commutation" to refer to a court-ordered sentence reduction, which often accompanies an application process similar to executive clemency and relies on similar considerations. For the purposes of this typology, a revision or modification of sentence will be used for sentences that are still in progress, while the term expungement will be used for court-ordered cancellation of punishment after the sentence has been completely served.

Many jurisdictions have a procedure in which the tribal court may modify or revise a sentence. Although these are sometimes referred to as "commutations," they are more akin to a parole mechanism than a pardon. For instance, the Hopi Tribe, Pascua-Yaqui Tribe, and Saginaw-Chippewa Indian Tribe have "commutation" procedures that allow the tribal court to reduce a sentence after the applicant has served half the sentence with good behavior.[47] Among the Northern Cheyenne Tribe, Chippewa-Cree Indians of the Rocky Boy's Reservation, Sisseton-Wahpeton Oyate, and Shoshone-Bannock, a presiding judge is authorized to grant a commutation at any time to a person who has served a sentence without misconduct.[48] A slightly different framework is used by the Crow Creek Sioux Tribe, Omaha Tribe of Nebraska, Seminole Nation of Oklahoma, and Ute Indian Tribe of the Uintah and Ouray Reservation. These jurisdictions have an "Order Removing Disqualification or Disability Based on Conviction," which removes any legal disabilities

46 Shoshone-Bannock Tribes Law and Order Code, Title 5, Chapter 1, § 5-1-51(h)(2)-(4).

47 Hopi Indian Tribe Law and Order Code, § 2.12.6; Saginaw Chippewa Indian Tribal Code, § 1.1607; Pascua Yaqui Tribe (AZ) Tribal Code, 4 PYTC § 4-80.

48 Chippewa-Cree Indians of the Rocky Boy's Reservation (MT) Tribal Code, § 8.4; Northern Cheyenne Tribe (MT) Rules of Criminal Procedure Code, Title V, Rule 42; Sisseton-Wahpeton Oyate (SD) Codes of Law, § 24-01-42; Shoshone-Bannock Tribes (ID) Law and Order Code, § 5-1-51(i).

arising from conviction after a defendant serves her or his sentence of probation and has not been convicted of another offense.[49]

Hannahville Indian Community in Michigan has a court-driven procedure that is best likened to an expungement process. This jurisdiction allows the tribal court to suspend or commute a sentence based on good conduct or interests of justice.[50] For an "order setting aside conviction," which removes or cancels the conviction, an applicant must wait 3 years after serving his or her sentence, assuming no other convictions in that time. No individual may use this process more than twice in his or her lifetime. For crimes against persons, notification must be given to the victim; if any fines or fees are owed, these must be paid. The court then appoints an ad hoc review committee composed of the tribal prosecutor, defense counsel, chief of police, and probation officer, who hold a hearing with the applicant and make a recommendation to the tribal court.[51] The tribal court then makes the ultimate decision as to expunging the conviction. If the applicant succeeds, the conviction is deemed never to have occurred, and cannot be used to bar the applicant from employment or for sentencing enhancements for subsequent convictions. The applicant is entitled to appeal if the tribal court denies the order.[52] Notably, Hannahville's expungement process has several exclusions: crimes under the Major Crimes Act (felonies), aggravated assault or assault with a weapon, sex offenses including registration as a sex offender, and traffic offenses.[53]

The Sault Ste. Marie Tribe of Chippewa Indians has a similar process for setting aside a conviction. The main difference from the Hannahville ordinance is that the applicant must wait 5 years rather than 3 after serving her or his sentence. This jurisdiction also has different exclusions: homicide, abuse of office, sex offenses including registration as a sex offender, conspiracy to commit any of the above, or traffic offenses. The procedure may only be used one time.[54] In this jurisdiction, the applicant files with the police department first, which reviews its records and forwards the application to the tribal court and tribal prosecutor. The tribal prosecutor notifies the victims in the case. The tribal court holds a hearing and the prosecutor may contest the application. The trial judge makes the final decision. If the applicant is successful, the conviction is sealed and may not be used against the applicant unless she or he applies for employment with the law enforcement department.[55]

49 Crow Creek Sioux Tribe (SD) Tribal Code, § 10-2-15; Omaha Tribe (NE) Tribal Code, §5-3-17; Seminole Nation (OK) Tribal Court, Title 7, § 807; Ute Indian Tribe of the Uintah and Ouray Reservation (UT) Tribal Code, § 13-3-18(1).
50 Hannahville Indian Community (MI) Tribal Code, §§ 1.1606, 1.1607.
51 Id. at § 1.1608(1)–(7).
52 Id. at § 1.1608(8)–(11).
53 Id. at § 1.1608(2).
54 Sault Ste. Marie Tribe of Chippewa Indians (MI) Tribal Code, § 77.101(1)–(2).
55 Id. at §§ 77.102, 77.104.

The Hopi Tribe has a simpler expungement process. In that jurisdiction, a convicted person is informed when the sentence is completed of the right to have the judgment of guilt set aside. This process requires an application to the tribal court in writing. If a judge grants the expungement, the person is "released from all penalties and disabilities resulting from the conviction."[56] Similarly, for the Three Affiliated Tribes of the Fort Berthold Indian Reservation in North Dakota, the chief judge of the tribal district court may expunge a criminal record. A petition must be sworn under oath and provide the reasons for requesting expungement; the procedure may only be performed once for each individual and only after 7 years have passed since the conviction. Expungements are limited to misdemeanor offenses and exclude felonies, domestic violence convictions, or some serious misdemeanors. In making the expungement decision, the judge will consider the nature of the offense, prior criminal history, evidence of rehabilitation, and reasons for the request.[57]

The Southern Ute Indian Tribe has an expungement process that requires filing an application with the tribal court and serving the tribal prosecutor's office. The tribal court holds a hearing with the prosecutor and, if relevant, the victim. An applicant may seek to expunge an arrest that did not result in conviction, including if the applicant was acquitted or if the statute of limitations had passed. For offenses resulting in conviction, the petition must provide reasons to expunge, evidence of rehabilitation, and other criminal history.[58] The exclusions, however, are broad. Expungements may not be granted for offenders with three or more convictions and the offender may only apply once every 2 years (or within 5 years of a conviction in another court). A petitioner must wait 10 years after release from probation, parole, or incarceration and must have paid in full restitution, fines, and fees. The process also has many exclusions: convictions for homicide, abduction, sexual offenses, fraud, crimes of dishonesty (including theft, robbery, and burglary), assault of a peace officer, offenses using deadly weapons, domestic violence with a weapon, and all alcohol- and drug-related driving offenses.[59] If the tribal court grants the expungement, all disabilities resulting from the conviction are removed. If denied, the applicant may appeal.

The Yurok Tribe has two court-ordered expungement processes, one for misdemeanors and one for felonies. In the misdemeanor process, a convicted person may request, after 1 year, to remove the guilty verdict provided she or he has no other convictions and has completed the entire sentence. The

56 Hopi Tribe (AZ) Tribal Code, § 2.12.6.

57 Resolution of the Governing Body of the Three Affiliated Tribes of the Fort Berthold Indian Reservation, No. 08-170 (16 October 2008).

58 Southern Ute Indian Tribe (CO) Tribal Code, §§ 28-1-103, 28-1-104, 28-1-105.

59 Id. at § 28-1-105(1)–(2).

tribal court may release the convicted person from all disabilities or penalties resulting from the conviction.[60] For felonies, the convicted person may use the same process, but the effects of the expungement are more limited. First, the convicted person must wait for a period equivalent to the time served on the sentence. Unlike for misdemeanors, felony expungement does not absolve the applicant from obligations to disclose the conviction for employment or licensing purposes or running for office and it may be considered for enhanced sentencing as a prior conviction. It also does not restore the right to possess a firearm.[61]

One of the most forgiving clemency structures is found in the law of the Pueblo of Acoma. In that jurisdiction, the tribal code clearly spells out which civil rights are lost due to a criminal conviction, to include holding public office of trust or profit and serving on a jury. However, persons with criminal convictions are not disqualified from tribal employment or from any occupation or license unless a "reasonable relationship" exists between the conviction and the functions of the office, with an exception for employment in law enforcement.[62] The Pueblo of Acoma has several different methods for restoring rights lost by a criminal conviction. If a person has been convicted of two or more felonies, she or he may have civil rights restored by the judge who processes the discharge from probation. For other persons with criminal convictions, the chief tribal court judge is empowered to restore civil rights upon an application to the clerk of the court.[63] To expunge a record, 5 years must pass without any further convictions. The applicant must show by clear and convincing evidence his or her good conduct, service to the Pueblo, and need. This record will be reinstated and the convicted person charged with contempt if she or he commits an additional felony after the expungement occurred.[64] For a person who has served a full jail sentence, the chief tribal court judge may restore civil rights after 2 years have passed.[65] A person convicted of any offense may also apply to set aside the conviction. This requires an application to the trial court judge, who may then lift any penalty or disability resulting from conviction.[66] The tribal code also contains a provision allowing restoration of rights under tribal law due to conviction in U.S. federal court. This requires an application to the clerk of the tribal court. If a person was convicted of two or more felonies in federal court, she or he must wait 2 years and may apply for restoration of rights with the presiding

60 Yurok Tribe (CA) Tribal Code, § 2.10.1090.
61 Id. at § 2.10.1100.
62 Pueblo of Acoma (NM) Tribal Code, § 5-5-3(A), (E)–(F).
63 Id. at § 5-5-4(A)–(B).
64 Id. at § 5-5-4(C).
65 Id. at § 5-5-5(A).
66 Id. at § 5-5-6

judge of the tribal court.[67] Additionally, the Pueblo of Acoma tribal court has automatic restoration of rights for a first offense under the tribal code, so long as the first-time offender has served the entire sentence or completed probation.[68]

The Quapaw Tribe provides for an expungement by application to the tribal court. A person is eligible for expungement if charges were dropped, the conviction overturned on appeal, or if she or he was acquitted, pardoned by the chair of the tribal council, exonerated due to DNA evidence, a victim of identity theft, or a juvenile under age 16.[69] Upon an application, the tribal court will hold a hearing with notice to the tribal prosecutor, marshals service, and any other relevant party. The tribal court may decide to seal the person's criminal record, limit access to the record, or maintain the record. A decision may be appealed by the applicant, the tribal prosecutor, or the marshals service. Once a record is expunged, the conviction is deemed to have never occurred and the successful applicant does not need to report the conviction to any educational institution, employer, or government agency.[70] The Quapaw Tribal Code also provides for automatic expungement for victims of identity theft whose name or likeness was appropriated by another person in the course of committing a crime.[71]

Marijuana or Drug Court Expungements

Several tribal jurisdictions have legislative enactments that expunge convictions for simple marijuana use or possession. For the Arapaho Tribe of the Wind River Reservation, the tribal code states that the tribe has no jurisdiction to prosecute any person for possessing, consuming, or cultivating marijuana for personal use. The law expunges all previous convictions and directs the tribal court to destroy all records.[72] The Mashantucket Pequot Indian Tribe uses a petition process rather than an automatic expungement. In that jurisdiction, a person convicted in the tribal court of possession of small amounts of cannabis may request erasure of the conviction.[73] As of 2022, an amendment to the Nez Perce Tribal Code was pending that, if passed, would vacate convictions for possessing less than 40 grams of marijuana or other paraphernalia.[74] This follows the U.S. Department of Agriculture's approval

67 Id. at §§ 5-5-8 to 5-5-9.
68 Id. at § 5-5-10.
69 Quapaw Tribe (OK) Criminal Procedure Act, § 135(a).
70 Id. at § 136(b)–(c).
71 Id. at § 137.
72 Arapaho Tribe of the Wind River Reservation (WY) Tribal Code, § 24-205.
73 Mashantucket Pequot Indian Tribe (CT) Tribal Code, § 2-2(d)(v).
74 Nez Perce Tribe (ID) Tribal Code Proposed Amendments (2022), § 2.10.57, available at: https://nezperce.org/wp-content/uploads/2022/01/Proposed-amendments-to-Ch.-2-1-Criminal-Procedure.pdf (last accessed November 5, 2023).

of the Nez Perce Tribe's industrial hemp cultivation ordinance in 2021.[75] At least one tribe has a drug court expungement process. The Poarch Band of Creeks allows a drug court judge to recommend to the trial judge that a drug conviction be expunged upon completion of a drug treatment program.[76]

Expungements for Human Trafficking Victims

Like marijuana expungements, restorations of rights for human trafficking victims constitutes a novel form of tribal legal forgiveness, which operates in part to protect sex workers or persons convicted of prostitution. The Fort Belknap Indian Community in Montana has a provision for victim access to expungement in its law against human trafficking. This law states that a person convicted of "a non-violent offense, including prostitution," while a victim of human trafficking or as the result of being a victim of human trafficking may apply to the tribal court for an expungement of the conviction. Documentation from another government agency that the person was a victim at the time of the offense creates a legal presumption that the offense was a result of being a victim of human trafficking.[77] On the other side of the country, the Nottawaseppi Huron Band of the Potawatomi in Michigan has an identical provision.[78]

Traditional Forgiveness Process

The Lummi Nation of Washington State uses a kind of traditional council of elders to make decisions on legal forgiveness. Here, four elders are randomly drawn from the 12-member *Ch'qi'n'txw* Pool, which comprises three elders from the Cultural Committee, three from the Law and Justice Commission, three from the Health and Family Services Commission, and three from the community at large and appointed by the Business Council. The *Ch'qi'n'txw* Panel must comprise one elder from each of these four groups. An applicant applies with a statement of facts, grounds for petition, a copy of the criminal judgment, an affidavit from the probation department, and a background check. One applies to the tribal court, which makes the petition public. If the applicant is eligible (that is, has met the waiting period requirements and submitted all required documents), the *Ch'qi'n'txw* Panel holds a public hearing and makes a unanimous decision. If the Panel cannot make a unanimous decision, the petition must be denied. The Panel's decision is final and cannot be appealed.[79]

75 Nez Perce Tribe (ID) Tribal Code, Title 6, Chapter 13 (Hemp Regulatory Code) (2021).
76 Poarch Band of Creeks (AL) Tribal Code, § 3-3-4(b)(5).
77 Fort Belknap Indian Community (MT) Tribal Code, Title 6, Part 7, § 18(A)–(B).
78 Nottawaseppi Huron Band of the Potawatomi (MI) Tribal Code, § 8.23-9(A)–(B).
79 Lummi Tribe of the Lummi Reservation Tribal Code, Chapter 5.12, § 5.12.010 et seq.

Restoration of Rights for Registered Sex Offenders

This section considers the issue of sex offender registration in Indian Country. The introduction of sex offender registration in Title I of the Adam Walsh Child Protection and Safety Act, better known as the Sex Offender Registration and Notification Act (SORNA), provides a discretionary process for reducing periods of sex offender registration. However, tribes can opt to refuse this reduction process. In addition, as noted below, some jurisdictions contain an expungement or pardon process unique to juvenile sex offenders or create exceptions for sex offenses that render them unpardonable. Sex offender registration is itself a collateral consequence of conviction. Notably, though, registration may trigger other collateral consequences, such as restrictions on housing, internet use, travel, or employment.[80] These secondary collateral consequences are not included in this section and are not required by SORNA. As noted throughout this book, specific collateral consequences attach to sex-related convictions in many areas of tribal law.

Some tribes have passed special exclusions for registered sex offenders in their SORNA ordinances. One example is the Confederated Tribes of the Warm Springs Reservation of Oregon, which has a child safety zone exclusion. Under this ordinance, a sex offender whose victim was under 14 years old cannot park or loiter in an area specifically designed or frequented by children; attend events for children or contact a childcare facility unless she or he has custody of a child; or establish or maintain a residence within 500 feet of a school or other area designated for children.[81] The Turtle Mountain Band of Chippewa Indians has an elaborate SORNA ordinance that excludes registered sex offenders from being present or residing within 500 feet of a school, park, playground, recreation facility, or gymnasium.[82] This jurisdiction also excludes registered sex offenders and their immediate families from tribal rental housing.[83] The Winnebago Tribe excludes registered sex offenders from tribal rental housing but increases the exclusion zone to 1000 feet outside of schools and playgrounds, though the statute permits a judge to grant exceptions in certain cases such as if the sex offender is a juvenile.[84]

80 Lori McPherson, "The Sex Offender Registration and Notification Act (SORNA) at 10 Years: History, Implementation, and the Future," 64(3) *Drake Law Review* 741–96, 785 et seq. (2016).

81 Confederated Tribes of the Warm Springs Reservation of Oregon, "Sex Offender Registry: FAQs," https://warmsprings.nsopw.gov/FAQs.aspx (last accessed November 2, 2023).

82 Turtle Mountain Band of Chippewa Indians (ND) Tribal Code, § 42.1305.

83 Id. at § 42.1401(1).

84 Winnebago Tribe (NE) Tribal Code, §§ 7-1703, 7-1705.

Reduction of Sex Offender Registration Periods

Unlike with the Indian Gaming Regulatory Act, which was passed with significant tribal input and creates a process whereby the federal government can mediate disputes between tribes and states over Indian gaming, Congress's extension of sex offender registries to Indian Country created a host of complications involving tribal sovereignty and criminal jurisdiction. In 2006, Congress passed SORNA, as Title I of the Adam Walsh Child Protection and Safety Act. SORNA incorporated tribal jurisdictions into the reciprocal state and federal sex offender registries, in part to ensure continuous coverage and prevent reservations from becoming safe havens for sex offenders.[85] Because of the speedy passage of SORNA through Congress, tribal input in the legislation was minimal. For tribal governments, adopting SORNA delegates some oversight to the government of the state in which the tribe is located, which some tribes see as a loss of sovereignty.[86] At the time SORNA was passed, tribal governments did not have access to the federal or state criminal justice databases that would allow them to monitor registrants or implement a procedure for registering, creating an opening for the state government to take over this role. In addition to loss of funds, tribes that refuse to enact a SORNA law will involuntarily have their registration and enforcement responsibilities over sex offenders delegated to the state government.[87]

In addition, SORNA had several unintended consequences for tribes. First, it required states and the federal government to recognize sex-related criminal convictions in tribal court even though these courts' recognition of other tribal convictions is far from settled.[88] Second, it complicated matters when tribes had more *restrictive* sex offender registries than the surrounding state. For instance, the Confederated Tribes of the Umatilla Reservation had a compliant SORNA statute even when Oregon did not, creating an enforcement gap in the other direction.[89] Finally, SORNA did not fully resolve whether states can impose sex offender registration on tribes, including by requiring sex offenders living on reservations to register twice. Several state and federal cases from Arizona and New Mexico resolved the question differently.[90]

SORNA divided sex offenders into three tiers. Tier 1 is for first-time offenders who do not fall in Tiers 2 or 3. Tier 2 offenders committed a repeated Tier 1 offense or an offense against a minor. Tier 3 offenders committed a repeated Tier 2 offense or aggravated sexual abuse or kidnapping.

85 Virginia Davis & Kevin K. Washburn, "Sex Offender Registration in Indian Country," 6(1) *Ohio State Journal of Criminal Law* 3–24, 12–13 (2008)
86 McPherson, supra note 80 at 759.
87 Id. at 769.
88 Davis & Washburn, supra note 85 at 12–13.
89 McPherson, supra note 80 at 770.
90 Id. at 771.

For Tier 2 and Tier 3, the offense must be punishable by at least 1 year imprisonment.[91] Tier 1 offenders must register in person once per year for 15 years; Tier 2 offenders must register every 6 months for 25 years; and Tier 3 offenders every 3 months for life.[92] However, for Tier 1 and Tier 3 offenders, SORNA allows reduction of these registration periods if certain criteria are met. Specifically, a Tier 1 registrant may seek a reduction of the period of sex offender registration from 15 years to 10 years by maintaining a clean record and completing a sex offender treatment program. A Tier 3 registrant who committed her or his crime as a juvenile may seek reduction to 25 years with a clean record.[93] Notably, tribal jurisdictions that adopt SORNA may also include a reduction period for Tier 1 and Tier 3 registrants.[94] Because reduction of sex offender registration is a discretionary restoration of rights and may absolve a registrant of onerous collateral consequences, it is included in this chapter.

Just as the National Indian Gaming Commission provides a Model Gaming Ordinance to tribal jurisdictions, so too does the Office of Sex Offender Sentencing, Monitoring, Apprehending, Registering, and Tracking (SMART) in the Office of Justice Programs, U.S. Department of Justice, provide a model tribal SORNA ordinance. Section 4.02(C) of the model SORNA ordinance covers reduction of sex offender registration periods. This provision states that for first-time or low-level sex offenses, a Tier 1 sex offender registrant may have a period of registration reduced to 10 years with a clean record. For Tier 3 lifelong registrants who committed a repeated or aggravated offense, the period of registration may be reduced to 25 years if the individual was convicted as a juvenile and maintained a clean record.[95] However, the Model SORNA ordinance is careful to point out in an annotation that "reduction of registration periods is optional," and, if tribes opt to include a reduction provision, they should spell out the procedural mechanism for doing so specifically in the tribal code.[96]

91 34 U.S.C. § 20911(2)–(4).
92 34 U.S.C. § 20918.
93 34 U.S.C. § 20915(b).
94 Lori McPherson, "Sex Offender Registration in Indian Country: SORNA Implementation and 18 U.S.C. Sec. 2250," 69(2) *Department of Justice Journal of Federal Law and Practice* 209–50, 223 (2021).
95 Office of Sex Offender Sentencing, Monitoring, Apprehending, Registering, and Tracking, Office of Justice Programs, U.S. Department of Justice, "Model Tribal Sex Offender Registration Code" (2017), § 4.02(C), available at: https://smart.ojp.gov/model-tribal-code (last accessed November 1, 2023).
96 Id. at 15 (see annotation corresponding to § 4.02(C).

As of 2023, 137 tribal jurisdictions are compliant with SORNA.[97] Twelve tribes are not.[98] The remaining tribes are incorporated into their state SORNA systems, either because state criminal law presumptively applies to the reservations under Public Law 280 or because the tribes elected (or are deemed to have elected) to join their state SORNA systems.[99] Notably, only 18 of the 50 states and four of the five U.S. territories are compliant with SORNA. This has led to the anomalous situation that some tribes that are within state jurisdiction under Public Law 280 may have their own compliant SORNA statute when the surrounding state does not. For instance, the Menominee Tribe in Wisconsin is compliant with SORNA while the State of Wisconsin, which has mandatory Public Law 280 criminal jurisdiction over Wisconsin's Indian Country, is not compliant.[100]

Although only slightly more than half of the 137 substantially implemented tribal SORNA ordinances could be found in a publicly accessible format, the clear majority rule in Indian Country is to adopt a reduction provision for sex offender registration. Among published tribal codes, this survey found at least 54 tribal jurisdictions that have sex offender reduction provisions that mirror the Model SORNA Ordinance published by SMART in the Office of Justice Programs. Of these 54 jurisdictions, the full sex offender registration ordinance was available in 46 of them.[101] In seven

97 Office of Sex Offender Sentencing, Monitoring, Apprehending, Registering, and Tracking, Office of Justice Programs, U.S. Department of Justice, "Jurisdictions That Have Substantially Implemented SORNA," https://smart.ojp.gov/sorna/substantially-implemented (last accessed November 1, 2023).

98 Office of Sex Offender Sentencing, Monitoring, Apprehending, Registering, and Tracking, Office of Justice Programs, U.S. Department of Justice, "SORNA Implementation Status," https://smart.ojp.gov/sorna/sorna-implementation-status (search for Tribes under Jurisdiction Type in the search filters) (last accessed November 1, 2023). The 12 jurisdictions are the Confederated Tribes of the Chehalis Reservation (WA), Muckleshoot Indian Tribe (WA), Nez Perce Tribe (ID), Onondaga Nation (NY), Pueblo of Cochiti (NM), Pueblo of San Felipe (NM), Pueblo of Santa Clara (NM), Pueblo of Tesuque (NM), Swinomish Indian Tribal Community (WA), and Taos Pueblo (NM).

99 Davis & Washburn, supra note 85 at 13–14.

100 See "Jurisdictions That Have Substantially Implemented SORNA," supra note 97.

101 Absentee-Shawnee Tribe of Indians (OK), Alabama-Coushatta Tribe (TX), Arapaho Tribe of the Wind River Reservation (WY), Cheyenne River Sioux Tribe (SD), Colorado River Indian Tribes (AZ), Confederated Tribes and Bands of the Yakama Nation (WA), Confederated Tribes of the Warm Springs Reservation (OR), Flandreau Santee Sioux Tribe (SD), Fort McDowell Yavapai Nation (AZ), Hannahville Indian Community (MI), Hualapai Indian Tribe (AZ), Kalispel Indian Community (WA), Little River Band of Ottawa Indians (MI), Little Traverse Bay Band of Odawa Indians (MI), Makah Indian Tribe (WA), Menominee Indian Tribe (WI), Mescalero Apache Tribe (NM), Mississippi Band of Choctaw Indians (MS), Muscogee (Creek) Nation (OK), Nisqually Indian Tribe (WA), Nooksack Indian Tribe (WA), Nottawaseppi Huron Band of the Potawatomi (MI), Omaha Tribe (NE), Oneida Nation (NY), Pokagon Band of Potawatomi Indians (MI), Port Gamble S'Klallam Tribe (WA), Prairie Band Potawatomi Nation (KS), Pueblo of Laguna

other jurisdictions, SMART noted the reduction provision in the SORNA Substantial Implementation Review decision.[102] Finally, the Keweenaw Bay Indian Community includes information about its sex offender reduction on its SORNA website.[103] Specifically, these provisions allow reduction of a 15-year registration period to 10 years for Tier 1 offenders and reduction of a lifetime registration period to 25 years for Tier 3 juvenile offenders. The Model SORNA Ordinance does not contain a reduction provision for Tier 2 offenders.

An additional handful of jurisdictions have reduction provisions that depart from the Model SORNA Ordinance. The Nez Perce Tribe and the Seminole Nation of Oklahoma allow reduction for Tier 1 offenders from a 15-year registration period to a 10-year registration period with a clean record but do not allow reduction for Tier 3 juvenile offenders as per the Model SORNA Ordinance.[104] On the other hand, three jurisdictions add a feature that neither the original Adam Walsh Act nor the Model SORNA Ordinance have: reduction for Tier 2 sex offenders. The Pueblo of Santa Ana and Standing Rock Sioux Tribe provide that with a clean record, a Tier 1 offender may reduce a 15-year registration period to 10 years, a Tier 2

(NM), Pueblo of San Ildefonso (NM), Quinault Indian Nation (WA), Reno-Sparks Indian Colony (NV), Sac & Fox Tribe of the Mississippi (IA), Saginaw Chippewa Indian Tribe (MI), Saint Regis Mohawk Tribe (NY), Salt River Pima-Maricopa Indian Community (AZ), Shoalwater Bay Indian Tribe (WA), Shoshone-Paiute Tribes of the Duck Valley Reservation (NV), Southern Ute Indian Tribe (CO), Spokane Tribe (WA), Squaxin Island Tribe (WA), Suquamish Tribe (WA), Swinomish Indian Tribal Community (WA), Turtle Mountain Band of Chippewa Indians (ND), Washoe Tribe (NV), Winnebago Tribe (NE), Wyandotte Nation (OK).

102 Office of Sex Offender Sentencing, Monitoring, Apprehending, Registering, and Tracking, Office of Justice Programs, U.S. Department of Justice, "SORNA Substantial Implementation Review: Ely Shoshone Tribe" (November 2014), https://smart.ojp.gov/sites/g/files/xyckuh231/files/media/document/ely-shoshone-tribe.pdf; "SORNA Substantial Implementation Review: Fort Mojave Indian Tribe" (May 2023), https://smart.ojp.gov/fort-mojave; "SORNA Substantial Implementation Review: Metlakatla Indian Community, Annette Islands Reserve," (December 2020), https://smart.ojp.gov/sites/g/files/xyckuh231/files/media/document/Metlakatla_SI_Review_2020.pdf; "SORNA Substantial Implementation Review: Eastern Band of Cherokee Indians" (March 2015), https://smart.ojp.gov/sites/g/files/xyckuh231/files/media/document/easternbandofcherokee.pdf; SORNA Substantial Implementation Review: Oglala Sioux Tribe" (March 2023), https://smart.ojp.gov/implementation-review-oglala-sioux-tribe.pdf; "SORNA Substantial Implementation Review: Rosebud Sioux Tribe" (March 2017), https://smart.ojp.gov/sites/g/files/xyckuh231/files/media/document/rosebud-sioux-tribe.pdf; SORNA Substantial Implementation Review: Tonto Apache Tribe" (October 2015), https://smart.ojp.gov/sites/g/files/xyckuh231/files/media/document/tontoapachetribe.pdf.

103 Keweenaw Bay Indian Community (MI), "Sex Offender Registry: FAQs," https://kbic.nsopw.gov/FAQs.aspx (last accessed November 2, 2023).

104 Nez Perce Tribe (ID) Tribal Code, § 4-6-30(b); Seminole Nation of Oklahoma (OK) Tribal Code, Title 6C, § 420(b)(1)–(2).

offender may reduce a 25-year registration period to 15 years, and a Tier 3 offender may reduce a lifetime period of registration to 25 years, which is more lenient than provided for in the Adam Walsh Act or Model SORNA Ordinance.[105] The Pueblo of Acoma Tribal Code has a more limited version that states:

> A Tier 2 offender may have his or her period of registration reduced to 15 years if he or she was adjudicated delinquent of an offense as a juvenile that required Tier 3 registration and he or she has maintained a clean record for 15 years.[106]

At least 12 tribal jurisdictions have explicitly rejected a provision that would allow for a reduction in sex offender registration periods, including the largest tribal jurisdiction, the Navajo Nation.[107] Of these, the full ordinance was reviewed in 11 jurisdictions and the information about the remaining one, the Havasupai Tribe of Arizona, comes from the SORNA Substantial Implementation Review decision.[108] Most of these ordinances adopted the "frequency" and "duration" provisions of the Model SORNA Ordinance but without the "reduction" portion.[109] Several, however, departed from this template.[110] Although it does not include a reduction provision, the Osage Nation's SORNA ordinance incorporates some of the leniency that the

105 Pueblo of Santa Ana (NM) Tribal Code, § 8-21-14(B); Standing Rock Sioux Tribe (SD) Tribal Code, § 4-1629(B).

106 Pueblo of Acoma (NM) Tribal Code, § 18-4-25(B)(2).

107 These jurisdictions are the Grand Traverse Band of Ottawa and Chippewa Indians (MI), Havasupai Tribe (AZ), Mashantucket Pequot Indian Tribe (CT), Navajo Nation (AZ), Osage Nation (OK), Poarch Band of Creeks (AL), Puyallup Tribe (WA), Sault Ste. Marie Tribe of Chippewa Indians (MI), Shoshone-Bannock Tribes of the Fort Hall Reservation (ID), Skokomish Indian Tribe (WA), Spirit Lake Tribe (ND), and Yavapai-Prescott Indian Tribe (AZ).

108 Office of Sex Offender Sentencing, Monitoring, Apprehending, Registering, and Tracking, Office of Justice Programs, U.S. Department of Justice, "SORNA Substantial Implementation Review: Havasupai Tribe" (November 2016), available at: https://smart.ojp.gov/sites/g/files/xyckuh231/files/media/document/havasupai-tribe.pdf (last accessed November 2, 2023).

109 Grand Traverse Band of Ottawa and Chippewa Indians (MI) Tribal Code, § 4.04(g)(1); Mashantucket Pequot Indian Tribe (CT) Tribal Code, 38 M.P.T.L. ch.3 § 1(i); Navajo Nation (AZ) Tribal Code, Title 17, Chapter 5, Subchapter 10, § 2107(A)–(B); Osage Nation (OK) Tribal Code, § 5-314(E); Poarch Band of Creeks (AL) Tribal Code, § 38-4-20; Puyallup Tribe (WA) Tribal Code, § 5.16.390; Sault Ste. Marie Tribe of Chippewa Indians (MI) Tribal Code, § 72.407; Shoshone-Bannock Tribes of the Fort Hall Reservation (ID) Tribal Code, § 13-1-30; Skokomish Indian Tribe (WA) Criminal Code, § 9.02B.420; Spirit Lake Tribe (ND), § 20-3-102; Yavapai-Prescott Indian Tribe (AZ) Tribal Code, § 36.32.

110 E.g., the Yavapai-Prescott Indian Tribe (AZ) Tribal Code, Chapter 36 (Sex Offender Registration Code) includes the frequency and duration requirements of registration in a different section, Verification and Appearance Requirements, § 36.32.

reduction provision would provide. This jurisdiction incorporates shorter registration periods for juvenile offenders (10 years for Tier 1, 20 years for Tier 2, and life for Tier 3) than for adult offenders (15 years for Tier 1, 25 years for Tier 2, and life for Tier 3).[111]

Expungement or Pardon of Sex Offender Registration

Several jurisdictions allow a pardon or expungement to end the registration requirement for sex offenders, either by pardoning the underlying offense or by commuting or waiving the registration requirement. The SORNA ordinance of the Sisseton-Wahpeton Oyate of the Lake Traverse Reservation specifically excludes sex offenders who have been pardoned and are no longer required to register as a sex offender.[112] The Southern Ute Indian Tribe has an elaborate petition process to allow juvenile Tier 1 or Tier 2 sex offenders to discontinue the requirement for registration or internet posting if the juvenile completed his or her sentence and has not been subsequently convicted of unlawful sexual behavior. The tribal court must consider recommendations from the parole or probation officer, treatment provider, and prosecuting attorney. The court may also consider the views of the victim. Following notice and a hearing, the tribal court may order the registration discontinued and the internet posting to end. If the juvenile was convicted of a sex offense in another jurisdiction and reprieved, the Southern Ute Tribe may reciprocally remove the juvenile offender's name from the registry.[113]

Sex Offender Registration as Ineligible for Pardon or Commutation

In several jurisdictions, sex offenses may be excluded from pardons, expungements, or commutations of sentence. The Tohono O'odham Nation renders ineligible from pardon, parole, or commutation of sentence several specific sex-related crimes, including sexual assault, sexual abuse, causing a minor to engage in prostitution, failing to register as a sex offender, or abusing, neglecting, or exploiting a vulnerable or incapacitated adult.[114] Also in Arizona, the Pascua Yaqui Tribe and White Mountain Apache Tribe have similar provisions for sexual assault and sexual assault of a spouse. These are ineligible for pardon, parole, or commutation of sentence under the tribal codes. However, the Pascua Yacqui Tribe allows a judge discretion to order counseling instead, so the offense of sexual assault of a spouse does not

111 Osage Nation (OK) Tribal Code, § 5-314(E).
112 Sisseton-Wahpeton Oyate of the Lake Traverse Reservation (SD), § 75-03-04(A)(3).
113 Southern Ute Indian Tribe (CO) Tribal Code, § 23-1-108(3)(a)–(e).
114 Tohono O'odham Nation (AZ) Tribal Code, Title 7, §§ 9.1(C), 9.2(D), 9.11(C), 9-3901(B)(2); Title 17, § 1.12(A)(1) (code is not consecutively numbered).

become unpardonable until the second conviction. For the White Mountain Apache Tribe, it is always unpardonable.[115] The Colorado River Indian Tribes specifically provide that juvenile records for tribal sex offenses cannot be expunged under tribal law, creating an exception to the general rule in the tribal children's code that juvenile delinquency records are expunged and sealed on an offender's eighteenth birthday.[116] The Gila River Indian Community excludes from its expungement process anyone convicted of a crime for which she or he must register as a sex offender or any crime with a sexual motivation.[117] Other jurisdictions specifically provide that a pardon cannot remove the registration obligation of a sex offender. This is the case with the Oneida Tribe of Wisconsin.[118]

An Implied Pardon or Expungement Power in Tribal Law?

Many tribal jurisdictions do not possess a pardon power in their constitutions, codes, bylaws, or ordinances. Several tribal courts have addressed whether the tribes could have a pardon power that is implied in the executive's or legislature's other powers. These often messy challenges have arisen when either the tribal executive or the legislative council has attempted to issue a pardon that is then challenged by one of the other branches of government in tribal court. Generally, these courts have not found an implied pardon power. In the final case, involving the Hopi Tribe, the question at issue was not specifically whether an implied pardon power existed in tribal law, but whether traditional concepts of forgiveness and mercy would allow a tribal court to expunge a prior conviction and allow a dismissed employee to be reinstated. In that case, the court set aside the previous conviction upon a showing that the individual was sufficiently rehabilitated.

Salish and Kootenai Tribes (Montana)

The procedural background for the executive clemency challenge originated in a criminal appeal, in which defendant Anthony Crossguns was convicted of three counts of domestic violence. Chief Judge of the Tribal Court William Joseph Moran sentenced Crossguns to tribal jail for 3 years. This decision was upheld on appeal by a three-judge appellate panel of the tribal court on February 3, 1995.[119] Crossguns then petitioned the Tribal Council for an

115 Pascua Yaqui Tribe (AZ) Tribal Code, 4 PYTC §§ 2-60, 2-70; White Mountain Apache Tribe (AZ) Criminal Code, §§ 4.6(C), 4.7.
116 Colorado River Indian Tribes (AZ) Tribal Code, § 1-902.
117 Gila River Indian Community (AZ) Tribal Code, § 5.409(D)(2)–(3).
118 Oneida Tribe (WI) Tribal Code, § 126.9-1(c).
119 Crossguns v. Confederated Salish and Kootenai Tribes, Cause No. AP-CR-239-92 and AP-CR-284-92 (Feb. 3, 1995) (CSKT App. Ct.).

executive clemency order, arguing that the length and conditions of punishment were cruel and unusual.[120] On March 10, 1995, the Tribal Council voted 5-3 to issue a conditional pardon to Crossguns, which was issued by Tribal Chairman Michael Pablo the next day. Crossguns, a member of the Blackfeet Tribe, was pardoned on the condition that he not return to the Flathead Reservation for 2.5 years.[121] Thereafter, Crossguns was released from tribal jail. The tribal prosecutor who objected to the clemency order for Crossguns was fired. On May 19, 1995, Judge Leslie Kallowat, one of the judges on the appellate panel in Crossguns, issued a dissent to the February 3, 1995, decision, arguing that the Tribal Council had acted irregularly when it tried to pardon Crossguns, when it pressured the tribal judges to acquit him, and when it released him from jail. Judge Kallowat wrote that the Tribal Council's decision to release the defendant even though the Court upheld the sentence violated the separation of powers. Judge Kallowat explained that the Tribal Council could adopt a pardon procedure by a constitutional amendment or bylaw, but it had not done so and therefore could not issue pardons.[122]

Two weeks before Judge Kallowat issued her dissent to the Crossguns decision, Chief Judge Moran sued the Tribal Council and Chairman at the Salish and Kootenai Court of Appeals, seeking declaratory relief in tribal court that the executive clemency order for Crossguns was unlawful.[123] Moran wanted a declaratory judgment that the executive clemency order was unlawful and a temporary restraining order to prevent the Tribal Council from removing him from his position for bringing the case. The Tribal Council argued that the Court of Appeals was not competent to hear the case, believing the temporary restraining order was baseless and that the question of executive clemency was a non-justiciable political question.[124] In *Moran v. Confederated Salish and Kootenai Tribes*, dated October 23, 1995, the Court of Appeals remanded the executive clemency question to the tribal court. After affirming its jurisdiction to hear the dispute over the temporary restraining order, the Court explained that whether the Salish and Kootenai tribes had an executive clemency power was an internal matter to be decided by tribal law. The relevant inquiry was whether the membership of the tribe had delegated the sovereign power to pardon to the Tribal Council, and, if so, whether the Council lawfully exercised that power.[125] The Court remanded the question

120 Moran v. Confederated Salish and Kootenai Tribes, Cause No. AP-95-282-CV (June 9, 1995) (CSKT Civil Ct. App.) at 2–3.

121 "Judge Sues Tribal Leaders over Jurisdiction," *The Billings Gazette*, May 12, 1995, 14C.

122 Crossguns v. Confederated Salish and Kootenai Tribes, Cause No. AP-CR-239-92 and AP-CR-284-92 (May 19, 1995) (CSKT App. Ct.) (Kallowat, J., dissenting).

123 *Moran*, supra note 120 at 4–6.

124 Id. at 7–9.

125 Id. at 39–42.

to the Tribal Court to look to the tribal constitution, by-laws, and applicable ordinances and resolutions to determine whether an executive clemency power existed and was properly delegated to the Tribal Council. This validated the point made in Judge Kallowat's dissent in the Crossguns case.

The Moran lawsuit settled before the trial court could hear the remanded question about whether an executive clemency power existed. After the Tribal Council removed Moran as Chief Judge of the Tribal Court, he sued for breach of employment contract. In December 1995, he ran for and was elected to the Tribal Council, at which the lawsuit seemed like an embarrassment, according to an article in the *Missoulian*. As part of the settlement, a constitutional review commission was appointed to consider the tribe's separation of powers.[126] However, the Chief Justice of the Court of Appeals, Robert Peregoy, was also forced to resign after the decision in *Moran* and brought an additional lawsuit against the Tribal Council for breach of contract, which was subsequently dismissed.[127] Currently, the revised tribal code of the Salish and Kootenai Tribe does not include a pardon power or executive clemency, but it contains an expungement process for deferred sentences and a parole and probation system.[128]

Rosebud Sioux Tribe (North Dakota)

In 2006, the Rosebud Sioux Tribal Court found that the President of the Tribe had no authority under the constitution or tribal codes to exercise the pardon power. In this case, *Rosebud Sioux Tribe v. Keith Horse Looking*, the Tribal Court denied the defendant's request to recognize the President's pardon in court.[129] The defendant, a tribal spiritual leader, was ordered to serve a 60-day jail sentence for aggravated assault and other crimes. However, before the warrant was issued, the President sent a letter to the chief judge of the tribal court issuing a pardon. Although the President claimed that he had consulted with the Sicangu Lakota Treaty Council, the legislative body of the Rosebud Sioux reservation, this consultation apparently never took place. The Prosecutor objected to the pardon, arguing that it would "undermine the integrity" of the tribal court as the President had "no authority in law" to pardon any convicted defendant.[130]

126 John Stromnes, "Suit against Tribes Called a 'Draw'," *The Missoulian*, Feb. 15, 1996, B3.

127 John Stromnes, "Lawsuit against Tribe Dismissed," *The Missoulian*, Dec. 12, 1999, https://missoulian.com/lawsuit-against-tribe-dismissed/article_828407de-e2e3-59c7-b5f8-2a38d55e01fc.html.

128 Confederated Salish and Kootenai Tribal Laws Codified, Title II, Chapter 2 (Criminal Procedure), § 2-2-1208.

129 Rosebud Sioux Tribe v. Keith Horse Looking, 33 I.L.R. 6092, 6092 (Aug 21, 2006).

130 Id. at 6092–93.

As a threshold matter, the Rosebud Sioux Tribal Court explained that the pardon power was not necessarily an inherent power of the executive branch on the model of the British prerogative of mercy, but rather belonged to the people as sovereign. To that end, only the people could enact or authorize a pardon power, through either their elected representatives or the constitution drafting process. Although the U.S. federal constitution and the state constitution of South Dakota had created a pardon power, the "controlling authority, if any be found, must rest in the Constitution and Laws of the Rosebud Sioux Tribe."[131] If the constitution or laws of the Tribe are silent, the Court is to look at customs and traditions of the Tribe, then to the customs and laws of other tribes, and only then to federal and state law. In this case, the parties agree that the Tribe's constitution and laws do not create a pardon power, so the remaining question is whether such a power is implied. According to the tribal court, the U.S Supreme Court has ruled that the failure of a tribal constitution to specifically articulate a specific power does not preclude existence of an implied power.[132] The tribal court also cited *Moran v. Salish and Kootenai Tribes* (1995), described above, which recognized that a tribal pardon power could be implied in the constitution.[133]

> Yet in the instant case, there is no evidence that the Rosebud Sioux Tribe, either in its Constitution or through the official acts of the Tribal Council, has ever set into place a process by which the power of the pardon could be exercised by any Tribal Officer.[134]

The Court explained that although the Tribe had authority to create a pardon power, it apparently had not done so.

The Court also rejected the Tribal President's view that a pardon power could be implied in the constitutional powers to "manage" or "administer" the Tribe's affairs. Looking to the U.S. and South Dakota constitutions, the Court reasoned that these also authorize the executives to "manage" or "administer" but also create a separate pardon power, suggesting that pardons "fall outside the scope of general management or administration." In addition, the Court noted that the customs and traditions of the Rosebud Sioux did not support an implied pardon either, citing a letter from the Sicangu Lakota Treaty Council that argued that the pardon power did not exist in traditional law.[135] Perhaps the most notable aspect of the Court's

131 Id. at 6094.
132 See Merrion v. Jicarilla Apache Tribe, 455 U.S. 130 (1982).
133 See Moran v. Confederated Salish and Kootenai Tribes, Cause No. AP-95-282-CV (June 9, 1995) (CSKT Civil Ct. App.).
134 *Keith Horse Looking*, 33 I.L.R. at 6094.
135 Id.

reasoning from the perspective of comparative law is the Court's analysis of other tribes' pardon powers. The Court described different pardon models, including where the tribal council made the ultimate decision, as with the Standing Rock Sioux Tribe; where a tribal chairman made the decision, as with the White Mountain Apache; where a tribal executive can pardon but the legislature had a period to overturn the pardon, as with the Pawnee Tribe of Oklahoma; or where a special pardon commission or board made the decision, such as the Sault Ste. Marie Tribe of Chippewa Indians or the Blackfeet Tribe.[136] This notable use of comparative law is an example of how ideas and legal structures in tribal law can influence other jurisdictions. The increasing availability of tribal law on the internet may make this type of judicial sharing more pronounced in the future.

According to the Rosebud Sioux Tribal Court, the existence of pardon mechanisms in other tribal jurisdictions did not suggest that such a pardon power existed in Rosebud Sioux law. "What becomes exceedingly clear is that those Indian tribes that have determined to provide for a pardon authority have created it," rather than rely on an implied power.[137] The Court commented on the diversity of these pardon mechanisms, which relied variously on a tribal executive, council, special board, or multi-tiered process that involved executive, legislative, and judicial actors. However, "many tribes have not granted their executive branch the pardon power, and thus they have not established procedures for the application, consideration and grant/denial process."[138] The Rosebud Sioux were one of these "non-pardon" tribes, as the tribal constitution and legislature had never set up such a process. For this reason, the defendant's pardon was invalid and his request for modification of sentence denied.

Navajo Nation (Arizona)

In 2014, the Supreme Court of the Navajo Nation ruled that the Navajo constitution did not include a pardon power, rejecting arguments that such a power was implied in Navajo law even if it was not explicitly stated. The dispute arose over the contested 2014 election for President of the Navajo Nation, in which the Supreme Court found the Navajo Board of Election Supervisors in contempt for failing to fulfill responsibilities under the Navajo Election Code.[139] A candidate for Navajo President in the Democratic primary election was disqualified and the runner-up, Russell Begaye, was to be

136 Id. at 6094–95.
137 Id. at 6095.
138 Id.
139 Tsosie & Whitethorne v. Navajo Board of Election Supervisors, No. SC-CV-68-14 (Navajo Nation, Feb. 20, 2015).

automatically placed on the general election ballot. However, the Board of Election Supervisors voted not to remove the disqualified candidate's name from the ballot and refused to postpone the election. The Supreme Court found the members of the Board of Elections Supervisors in indirect civil contempt for their open defiance of the Court order, and removed them as Election Supervisors.[140] Subsequently, on December 30, 2014, the Navajo Nation Council passed two resolutions, the first nullifying the 2014 primary election for office of Navajo President and scheduling a special election, and the second pardoning and reinstating the Election Supervisors after their removal by the Supreme Court.[141] As to the first resolution nullifying the 2014 primary election, the Supreme Court reiterated that Navajo election law was explicit that the Election Supervisors must place the runner-up in the primary election on the general election ballot if the winner of the election was ineligible.[142] As to the second resolution, the Supreme Court determined that the Navajo Nation had no pardon process in its legal system, and therefore the Navajo Council's attempt to pardon and reinstate the ousted Election Supervisors was unlawful.[143]

In the pardon holding, the Court reasoned that the Navajo Nation Code did not bestow the power to pardon on any branch of government, rejecting the Council's claim that the power to pardon was an implied power implicitly reserved to the Council under Title II of the Navajo Nation Code. This provision states, "all powers not delegated are reserved to the Navajo Nation Council."[144] According to the Court, non-delegated powers are reserved to the Navajo people, not the Council; the Council could not alter the separation of powers without a referendum. In a footnote, the Council explained that the Navajo people must give "careful thought" to the idea that the Council should be able to pardon government officials, owing to a 2011 corruption scandal that implicated several Council members. The Court wrote: "The people must seriously consider whether it will permit our politicians to police themselves to the ultimate extent of wiping the slate clean for each other."[145] The Court also rejected the Council's argument that an earlier Council pardon, passed in 1995, created a precedent for future pardons. According to the Court, this 1995 pardon was never challenged at the Supreme Court and in any event was controversial at the time it was issued. Contemporaneous statements by the Chief Legislative Counsel and the Navajo Attorney General both expressed reservations about the existence of a pardon power.[146] The

140 Id. at 2.
141 Id. at 2–3.
142 Id. at 9–10.
143 Id. at 10–17.
144 Id. at 12–13, citing 2 N.N.C. § 102(B).
145 Id. at 13 n. 7.
146 Id. at 11–12.

Court's comment that a pardon power would exonerate the crimes of the powerful may be an unfair characterization and should be challenged as such. As this analysis has laid out, tribal law contains thousands of collateral consequences of conviction, and a restoration of rights mechanism such as a pardon can help reintegrate or rehabilitate many formerly convicted people, including vulnerable ones. The faulty assumption that the main purpose of the pardon power is to exonerate corruption by self-serving politicians may feed penal populism and contribute to overcriminalization in tribal law.

The Supreme Court also refused to find an analogue for the pardon power in traditional *Diné* law. Although the Council argued that forgiveness is a "core Navajo value," the Court explained that forgiveness was "not equivalent or even interchangeable with the *bilagáana* [Anglo-American] word 'pardon'." The Court rejected "the use of semantics to elucidate Navajo concepts that can only be truly understood through *diné bizaad* [Navajo language]." The Court believed that the concept of a pardon came from English law, in which the king had the royal prerogative to shield his subjects from punishment.[147] The Navajo did have a concept known as *k'é* (kinship or community) that can restore *hózhó* (harmony) or *nalyeeh* (distributive justice or peacemaking), which allows "individuals who caused harm and discord to apologize, seek compassion and return to society."[148] This concept, however, requires the individuals who caused harm to acknowledge wrongdoing and seek forgiveness. According to the Court, in the traditional process, the offender must be "more self-critical than anyone else" and must

> own up to his/her actions in a manner more complete than expected, offer an apology as an extension of utmost respect to the people harmed, and slowly rebuild relationships to restore harmony so as not to lower social standards.[149]

The Court explained that the Council's pardon ordinance did not properly comport with the traditional requirements, and the separation of powers in the Navajo constitution did not permit the Council to usurp the Court's inherent power to punish.

Hopi Tribe (Arizona)

A different result came from Hopi tribal courts, which essentially found an implied expungement power based on a traditional forgiveness concept. On June 3, 1990, the plaintiff Cameron Timms was arrested for possession of

147 Id. at 13–14.
148 Id. at 14.
149 Id. at 14–15.

alcohol, resisting arrest, assault, and aiding and abetting, to which he pled guilty.[150] On December 28, 1990, he was sentenced to a fine of $125 and 90 days in jail, later reduced to 1 year of probation. Eight years later, when he was an employee of a high school, he was terminated for having a previous "crime of violence" (assault conviction) while working in a position that involved regular contact with Indian children, as prohibited under U.S. federal law.[151] In 1999, he filed a motion to dismiss his prior convictions because he was not an enrolled member of the tribe at the time, but the tribal trial court dismissed his motion as untimely. He subsequently filed another motion to set aside the prior convictions. The tribal trial court found that Hopi law did not contain a provision for setting aside convictions.[152]

The Hopi Appellate Court reversed. The Court found that the "deeply rooted" Hopi concept of *ookwalni* (forgiveness and mercy) required consideration of whether Timms could set aside the previous conviction. Hopi law required the tribal courts to consider the "customs, traditions and culture of the Hopi Tribe."[153] The Appellate Court found that Timms was "clearly deserving of *ookwalni*." The plaintiff was 11 years older, attended college, and became "a respected member of the community." He had no further criminal convictions since. The Court received letters praising him, including from his supervisor at the high school. The plaintiff also had support from a prior supervisor and the high school principal, who called him "an exemplary employee and very caring individual."[154] The tribal prosecutor did not object. The Court therefore found that Timms had "served his punishment and shown sufficient rehabilitation" to find the "tradition of *ookwalni* … properly involved and controlling."[155]

Conclusion on the Implied Pardon Power

When read together, the first three decisions, from the Confederated Salish and Kootenai Tribes, Rosebud Sioux Tribe, and Navajo Nation, generally deny the existence of an implied pardon power in a tribal council's or tribal executive's general constitutional power to manage or administer the tribe. However, the decision from the Hopi Tribe nonetheless suggests that an implied pardon or expungement power can exist when it is grounded in a traditional forgiveness or mercy tradition. Even where a pardon power is provided for in a tribal constitution, the great diversity of pardon and restoration of rights mechanisms in tribal law is good reason for tribal jurisdictions

150 Timms v. Hopi Tribe, Case No. 00AC000011 (Hopi App. Ct., March 23, 2001).
151 See 25 U.S.C. § 3207(b).
152 As relayed in the procedural history, *Timms v. Hopi Tribe*, supra note 150 at ¶ 15.
153 Id. at ¶ 17, citing Hopi Resolution H-12-76.
154 Id. at ¶¶ 23–25.
155 Id. at ¶¶ 26–29.

to lay out a specific statutory procedure for previously convicted persons to apply for relief. As a normative matter, this would have the benefit of allowing persons with prior convictions to know their rights under tribal law and produce a more transparent, regular decision-making process. This would have the added benefit of preventing the kind of arbitrariness that the Navajo Supreme Court warned against, such as self-serving politicians pardoning themselves. Although self-dealing or corruption is a risk with a broad pardon power, it does not have to be the paradigm, and, as this analysis shows, many options exist for creating safeguards to prevent this type of harm. The facts in *Timms v. Hopi Tribe* serve as a counterexample to the Navajo Supreme Court's negative characterization of the pardon power.

Appendix

Tribal name	State	Executive and Legislative	Administrators and Personnel	Licenses and Permits	Rights and Services	Gaming Ordinances	Restoration of Rights
Absentee-Shawnee Tribe of Indians	OK	Tribal council	None found	None found	Jury service	Commissioners	Tribal pardon; sex offender reduction; juvenile expungement; gaming waivers
Agua Caliente Band of Cahuilla Indians	CA	None found	Judges	None found	None found	Commissioners; licenses	None found
Ak-Chin Indian Community	AZ	Tribal council	None found	None found	None found	Commissioners; licenses	None found
Alabama-Coushatta Tribe	TX	None found	Judges; peacemakers; court administrators	None found	Jury service	Board of regulators; licenses; employment	Sex offender reduction
Alabama-Quassarte Tribal Town	OK	None found	None found	None found	None found	None found	None found
Alturas Indian Rancheria	CA	None found	None found	None found	None found	Commissioners; licenses; employment	Gaming waiver
Apache Tribe	OK	Tribal council	None found	Liquor license; solid waste permit	None found	Commissioners	Gaming waiver
Arapaho Tribe of the Wind River Reservation	WY	Tribal council	Magistrates	None found	None found	Licenses; work permits	Sex offender reduction; marijuana expungements
Aroostook Band of Micmacs	ME	None found	None found	None found	None found	None found	None found

Assiniboine and Sioux Tribes of the Fort Peck Indian Reservation	MT	Executive board	Judges; court administrators; election officials; tribal rights review board; water administrators	Lay counselors	None found	Licenses	Tribal pardon
Augustine Band of Cahuilla Indians	CA	None found	None found	None found	None found	Commissioners; licenses	None found
Bad River Band of the Lake Superior Tribe of Chippewa Indians	WI	Tribal council	Membership enrollment committee	None found	None found	Commissioners; licenses	None found
Bay Mills Indian Community	MI	Executive council	Judges	Liquor license	None found	Commissioners; employment	None found
Bear River Band of the Rohnerville Rancheria	CA	None found	Judges	Liquor license	None found	None found	None found
Berry Creek Rancheria of Maidu Indians	CA	None found	None found	None found	None found	None found	None found
Big Lagoon Rancheria	CA	Business council	None found	None found	None found	None found	Election waiver
Big Pine Paiute Tribe of the Owens Valley	CA	None found	None found	None found	None found	Licenses	None found
Big Sandy Rancheria of Western Mono Indians	CA	None found	None found	None found	None found	None found	None found
Big Valley Band of Pomo Indians	CA	None found	None found	None found	None found	None found	None found
Bishop Paiute Tribe	CA	Tribal council	None found	None found	None found	Commissioners; licenses; employment	None found
Blackfeet Tribe	MT	Business council	Judges	None found	None found	Licenses	Tribal pardons

Tribal name	State	Executive and Legislative	Administrators and Personnel	Licenses and Permits	Rights and Services	Gaming Ordinances	Restoration of Rights
Blue Lake Rancheria	CA	Business council	Judges	None found	None found	Commissioners; directors; licenses; contracts	None found
Bridgeport Indian Colony	CA	Tribal council	Judges	None found	None found	None found	None found
Buena Vista Rancheria of Me-Wuk Indians	CA	None found	None found	Liquor license	None found	Commissioners	None found
Burns Paiute Tribe	OR	None found	Judges; election board members	None found	Guardianship for juveniles	Licenses	Gaming waiver
Cabazon Band of Mission Indians	CA	Business committee	None found	None found	None found	None found	None found
Cachil DeHe Band of Wintun Indians	CA	Community council	None found	None found	None found	None found	None found
Caddo Nation	OK	Tribal council	Election board members	None found	None found	Commissioners	None found
Cahuilla Band of Indians	CA	None found	None found	None found	None found	None found	None found
Cahto Tribe of the Laytonville Rancheria	CA	None found	None found	None found	None found	None found	None found
California Valley Miwok Tribe	CA	None found	None found	None found	None found	None found	None found
Campo Band of Diegueno Mission Indians	CA	None found	None found	None found	None found	Executive director; gaming monitor; employment	None found

Capitan Grande Band of Diegueno Mission Indians: *Barona Group*	CA	None found	None found	None found	None found	None found	None found
Capitan Grande Band of Diegueno Mission Indians: *Viejas Group*	CA	None found	None found	None found	None found	Commissioners; licenses; management contracts	None found
Catawba Indian Nation	SC	None found	None found	None found	None found	Licenses	None found
Cayuga Nation	NY	None found	Judges	None found	None found	Licenses	Expungement; gaming waiver; pardons for judicial candidates
Cedarville Rancheria	CA	Executive Committee	None found	Liquor license	None found	None found	None found
Chemehuevi Indian Tribe	CA	Tribal council	None found	None found	None found	None found	None found
Cher-Ae Heights Indian Community of the Trinidad Rancheria	CA	None found	None found	None found	None found	None found	None found
Cherokee Nation	OK	Tribal council	Blanket exclusion	None found	Firearm possession	Commissioners	Tribal pardon; juvenile expungement
Cheyenne and Arapaho Tribes, Oklahoma	OK	District legislator; governor; lieutenant governor	Police officers; judges	None found	Jury service	None found	Tribal pardon
Cheyenne River Sioux Tribe	SD	Tribal council	None found	None found	None found	Commissioners	Sex offender reduction; gaming waiver

Tribal name	State	Executive and Legislative	Administrators and Personnel	Licenses and Permits	Rights and Services	Gaming Ordinances	Restoration of Rights
Chickahominy Indian Tribe	VA	None found	None found	None found	None found	None found	None found
Chickahominy Indian Tribe - Eastern Division	VA	None found	None found	None found	None found	None found	None found
Chickasaw Nation	OK	Tribal legislature; executive offices	Judges	Liquor license	Jury service	None found	Tribal pardon
Chicken Ranch Rancheria of Me-Wuk Indians	CA	None found	None found	Liquor license	None found	None found	None found
Chippewa Cree Indians of the Rocky Boy's Reservation	MT	Business committee	Police officers	None found	None found	None found	Judicial commutation
Chitimacha Tribe	LA	Tribal council	None found	Liquor license	None found	None found	Expungement
Choctaw Nation	OK	Tribal council	Blanket exclusion; peacemakers	Attorneys	Jury service	Licenses; employment	Expungement
Citizen Potawatomi Nation	OK	Executive officers; legislators	Judges	None found	Jury service	Commissioners; gaming director; general manager; employment	Tribal pardon; juvenile expungement
Cloverdale Rancheria of Pomo Indians	CA	None found	None found	None found	None found	Licenses	None found
Cocopah Tribe	AZ	Tribal council	None found	None found	None found	General manager; licenses; employment in gaming commission	None found

Coeur D'Alene Tribe	ID	None found	None found	None found	None found	None found	None found
Cold Springs Rancheria of Mono Indians	CA	Tribal council	None found	None found	None found	None found	None found
Colorado River Indian Tribes	AZ	Chairman; vice-chairman	None found	Liquor license; hemp license	None found	None found	Suspension of sentence; sex offender reduction
Comanche Nation	OK	Tribal council	Tribal administrator; tribal prosecutor	None found	Jury service	Commissioners	None found
Confederated Salish and Kootenai Tribes of the Flathead Reservation	MT	None found	Judges	Lay representative	None found	Licenses	Expungement; deferred sentence
Confederated Tribes of the Chehalis Reservation	WA	Business committee	Judges; fish and wildlife committee	Commercial marijuana license; motor vehicle parts recycling license; business agent license	Firearm possession	Commissioners	Deferred prosecution
Confederated Tribes of the Colville Reservation	WA	Business council	Judges; police officers	Marijuana sales	None found	Commissioners; employment in gaming commission	None found
Confederated Tribes of the Coos, Lower Umpqua and Siuslaw Indians	OR	Tribal council	Judges; police officers; election board members	None found	None found	None found	None found

Tribal name	State	Executive and Legislative	Administrators and Personnel	Licenses and Permits	Rights and Services	Gaming Ordinances	Restoration of Rights
Confederated Tribes of the Goshute Reservation	NV	None found	Goshute Federal Corporation Board of Directors	None found	None found	None found	None found
Confederated Tribes of the Grand Ronde Community	OR	None found	Judges; fish and wildlife committee members	None found	None found	Commissioners; director of gaming commission	None found
Confederated Tribes of Siletz Indians	OR	None found	Judges; athletic commission members	Liquor license	Foster parents; firearm possession	None found	None found
Confederated Tribes of the Umatilla Indian Reservation	OR	None found	Judges; fish and wildlife commissioners	None found	None found	Commissioners	Expungement; juvenile expungement; gaming waiver
Confederated Tribes of the Warm Springs Reservation	OR	Tribal council	Judges	Marijuana permit	None found	None found	Sex offender reduction
Confederated Tribes and Bands of the Yakama Nation	WA	None found	None found	None found	Hunting if firearm conviction	Class B licenses	Sex offender reduction
Coquille Indian Tribe	OR	Tribal council	Judges; court clerk	None found	None found	Management contracts	Expungement
Cortina Indian Rancheria (Kletsel Dehe Band of Wintun Indians)	CA	Tribal council	None found	None found	None found	None found	None found
Coushatta Tribe	LA	None found	Judges	Attorneys; lay representatives	Jury service	None found	Juvenile expungement

Cow Creek Band of Umpqua Tribe of Indians	OR	None found	None found	None found	None found	Gaming monitor; licenses; employment	None found
Cowlitz Indian Tribe	WA	Tribal council	None found	None found	None found	None found	None found
Coyote Valley Band of Pomo Indians	CA	None found	None found	Liquor license	None found	None found	None found
Crow Tribe	MT	Executive and legislative positions	Judges; court clerk	None found	None found	Commissioners; blanket exclusion for all employees	Deferred and suspended sentence; sex offender expungement
Crow Creek Sioux Tribe	SD	Tribal council; chairman	None found	None found	None found	Commissioners; licenses; stockholders or partners of manufacturers, operators, or retailers	Order removing disability based on conviction
Death Valley Timbi-sha Shoshone Tribe	CA	Tribal council	Judges	None found	None found	None found	Tribal pardon; election waiver
Delaware Nation	OK	Executive committee	Election committee members	None found	None found	Commissioners; licenses	Gaming waiver
Delaware Tribe of Indians	OK	Tribal council	Judges	Lay representatives	None found	Commissioners; gaming director; investigators	None found
Dry Creek Rancheria Band of Pomo Indians	CA	None found	Judges	None found	Firearm or weapon possession	None found	None found
Duckwater Shoshone Tribe	NV	Tribal council	None found	None found	None found	None found	None found

Tribal name	State	Executive and Legislative	Administrators and Personnel	Licenses and Permits	Rights and Services	Gaming Ordinances	Restoration of Rights
Eastern Band of Cherokee Indians	NC	Tribal council; chief or vice-chief; school board	Judges; hospital governing board; housing committee members; public health advisory board members	Pawnbrokers license; family foster home license; handgun sales license; trader's permit (for check cashing services); business agents; bondsman license	Employment with children; guardianship; school expulsion; firearm possession	Licenses; employment; suppliers of gaming goods	Expungement; restoration of rights; juvenile expunction; sex offender reduction
Eastern Shawnee Tribe	OK	Tribal council	None found	None found	None found	Commissioners	None found
Elem Indian Colony of Pomo Indians of the Sulphur Bank Rancheria	CA	Tribal council	None found	None found	None found	Commissioners; gaming review board judges	None found
Elk Valley Rancheria	CA	Tribal council	None found	Liquor license	None found	Commissioners; gaming director; management contractors	None found
Ely Shoshone Tribe	NV	Tribal council	None found	None found	Possession of an electronic stun device	None found	None found
Enterprise Rancheria of Maidu Indians	CA	Tribal council	Judges; election board members	None found	Disenrollment from tribe	Commissioners; executive director; licenses; management contractors; employment	Gaming waiver

Ewiiaapaayp Band of Kumeyaay Indians	CA	None found	None found	None found	None found	Gaming monitor; licenses	None found
Federated Indians of Graton Rancheria	CA	Tribal council	None found	None found	None found	Licenses	None found
Flandreau Santee Sioux Tribe	SD	Tribal council	Tobacco control board members; coroner	Marijuana licenses	None found	Commissioners; temporary licenses; permissions for manufacturers, operators, or retailers	Suspension of sentence; sex offender reduction
Forest County Potawatomi Community	WI	Executive council	None found	None found	None found	Commissioners; employment; contractors	Gaming waiver
Fort Belknap Indian Community	MT	Tribal council	None found	None found	Tribal employment for alcohol-related convictions	Licenses	Expungement for trafficking victim
Fort Bidwell Indian Community	CA	Tribal council	None found	None found	None found	None found	None found
Fort Independence Indian Community of Paiute Indians	CA	Tribal council	None found	None found	None found	Commissioners; board of directors	None found
Fort McDermitt Paiute and Shoshone Tribes of the Fort McDermitt Indian Reservation	NV	Tribal council; executive officers	Judges	None found	None found	Licenses	None found

Tribal name	State	Executive and Legislative	Administrators and Personnel	Licenses and Permits	Rights and Services	Gaming Ordinances	Restoration of Rights
Fort McDowell Yavapai Nation	AZ	Tribal council; president; vice-president; treasurer; secretary	Judges	None found	None found	Executive director of gaming regulatory agency; employees of gaming regulatory agency; licenses	Stay of execution of sentence; sex offender reduction
Fort Mojave Indian Tribe	AZ	Tribal council	None found	None found	None found	Licenses	None found
Fort Sill Apache Tribe	OK	Business committee	None found	None found	None found	Commissioners; gaming director; licenses	None found
Gila River Indian Community	AZ	Tribal council	None found	None found	None found	Commissioners; licenses; employees of gaming facilities or gaming commission	Expungement; commutation of sentence by court
Grand Traverse Band of Ottawa and Chippewa Indians	MI	Tribal council	Judges; tribal prosecutors	None found	None found	Commissioners; licenses; employees; contractors	Gaming waiver
Greenville Rancheria	CA	Tribal council	None found	None found	None found	Commissioners	Tribal pardon; waiver for gaming commissioners
Grindstone Indian Rancheria of Wintun-Wailaki Indians	CA	None found	None found	None found	None found	None found	None found

Guidiville Rancheria	CA	Tribal council	None found	None found	None found	Commissioners; licenses	None found
Habematolel Pomo of Upper Lake	CA	Executive council	Blanket exclusion on appointees; judges	None found	None found	Commissioners; licenses	None found
Hannahville Indian Community	MI	None found	Judges; court clerks; magistrates	None found	Firearm possession; ownership of restricted animal	Gaming board of directors; licenses; employment	Suspension or commutation of sentence by court; order setting aside conviction; gaming waiver
Havasupai Tribe of the Havasupai Reservation	AZ	None found	None found	None found	None found	None found	None found
Ho-Chunk Nation	WI	Legislators; president	Judges; insurance review commission	None found	Firearm or body armor possession	Commissioners; licenses; employment	Gaming waiver; election waiver
Hoh Indian Tribe	WA	Business committee	Judges; court clerk	None found	None found	None found	None found
Hoopa Valley Tribe	CA	Tribal council	Judges	None found	None found	Licenses; employment	None found
Hopi Tribe	AZ	Tribal council; chairman; vice-chairman	Judges; judicial commission members	None found	Jury service	None found	Suspension or commutation of sentence; expungement
Hopland Band of Pomo Indians	CA	Tribal council	Judges; peacemakers	Liquor license	None found	Class A licenses; Class B licenses	Election waiver; deferral of fines
Houlton Band of Maliseet Indians	ME	None found	None found	None found	None found	None found	None found
Hualapai Indian Tribe	AZ	Tribal council	Judges	None found	None found	None found	Early release; sex offender reduction
Iipay Nation of Santa Ysabel	CA	None found	None found	None found	None found	None found	None found

Tribal name	State	Executive and Legislative	Administrators and Personnel	Licenses and Permits	Rights and Services	Gaming Ordinances	Restoration of Rights
Inaja Band of Diegueno Mission Indians of the Inaja and Cosmit Reservation	CA	None found	None found	None found	None found	None found	None found
Ione Band of Miwok Indians	CA	Tribal council	None found	None found	None found	Commissioners	Waiver for gaming commissioners
Iowa Tribe of Kansas and Nebraska	KS	Executive Committee	None found	Hemp license	None found	Commissioners	None found
Iowa Tribe of Oklahoma	OK	Tribal council	Judges	None found	None found	Commissioners; executive director; licenses; vendors	Tribal pardon; juvenile expungement
Jackson Band of Miwuk Indians	CA	None found	None found	None found	None found	None found	None found
Jamestown S'Klallam Tribe	WA	Tribal council	Judges; natural resource committee membership; blanket for all tribal board and commissions	Attorneys	Employment with natural resources department	Class A licenses; Class B licenses	Restoration of right to possess firearm
Jamul Indian Village	CA	Executive Committee	None found	Liquor license	None found	Commissioners; licenses	None found
Jena Band of Choctaw Indians	LA	None found	None found	None found	None found	Commissioners	None found
Jicarilla Apache Nation	NM	Tribal council	Judges	Liquor license	None found	Commissioners; tribal gaming board members; licenses; employment;	Tribal pardon

Kaibab Band of Paiute Indians	AZ	Tribal council	Judges	None found	None found	Gaming director; contractors	Reduction of sentence
Kalispel Indian Community	WA	Business committee	Judges	None found	Personal representative of estate	Contractors	Sex offender reduction
Karuk Tribe	CA	Tribal council	None found	None found	None found	Gaming monitor	None found
Kashia Band of Pomo Indians of the Stewarts Point Rancheria	CA	Tribal council	Economic development committee member; blanket for tribal employees and appointees	None found	None found	None found	None found
Kaw Nation	OK	Tribal council	Judges; magistrates	None found	None found	Commissioners	Tribal pardon; Waiver for gaming commissioners
Kewa Pueblo	NM	None found	None found	None found	None found	None found	None found
Keweenaw Bay Indian Community	MI	None found	Judges; court clerks	None found	Parental rights	Licenses; employment	Sex offender reduction
Kialegee Tribal Town	OK	None found	None found	None found	None found	Commissioners	Waiver for gaming commissioners
Kickapoo Tribe of Indians	KS	Tribal council	Judges	Attorneys	Jury service	None found	Tribal pardon
Kickapoo Tribe of Oklahoma	OK	None found	Judges; members of utility management board	None found	None found	General manager; executive director of gaming commission; key employees	Tribal pardon; juvenile expungement
Kickapoo Traditional Tribe of Texas	TX	Traditional council	Blanket exclusion for tribal boards; judges; housing authority board of commissioners; police officers; police reservists	None found	None found	Commissioners	Reduction for ineligibility period for tribal office; waiver for gaming commissioners

Tribal name	State	Executive and Legislative	Administrators and Personnel	Licenses and Permits	Rights and Services	Gaming Ordinances	Restoration of Rights
Kiowa Indian Tribe	OK	Tribal council; president; vice-president	Judge; judicial commission members; election commission members	None found	None found	Commissioners; licenses	None found
Klamath Tribes	OR	None found	Judges; judicial commission members; peacemakers	None found	Jury service	Licenses; low-security employees	Gaming waiver
Koi Nation of Northern California	CA	Tribal council	None found	None found	None found	None found	None found
Kootenai Tribe	ID	None found	None found	None found	None found	None found	None found
La Jolla Band of Luiseno Indians	CA	None found	None found	None found	None found	Commissioners; executive director; Class A licenses; Class B licenses; contractors	None found
La Posta Band of Diegueno Mission Indians	CA	None found	None found	None found	None found	Commissioners; licenses	None found
Lac Courte Oreilles Band of Lake Superior Chippewa Indians	WI	Governing board	Pardon screening committee; public safety board members; police officers	None found	Tribal housing	Commissioners; employment; contracts	Tribal pardon; election waiver
Lac du Flambeau Band of Lake Superior Chippewa Indians	WI	None found	Judges	None found	None found	Commissioners; licenses	None found

Lac Vieux Desert Band of Lake Superior Chippewa Indians	MI	Tribal council	Judges	None found	None found	None found	Election waiver
Las Vegas Tribe of Paiute Indians	NV	None found	Judges	None found	Jury service	None found	None found
Little Shell Band of Chippewa Indians	MT	Tribal council	None found	None found	None found	None found	None found
Little River Band of Ottawa Indians	MI	Tribal council	Judges; tribal prosecutor; housing commissioners; Muschigon construction company board of directors	None found	None found	Commissioners; licenses; non-gaming employee license; supplier license	Gaming waiver; sex offender reduction
Little Traverse Bay Bands of Odawa Indians	MI	Tribal council; chairperson; vice-chairperson	Judges; conservation enforcement officers; economic development board of directors	Hemp license	Jury selection; tribal employment	Commissioners; licenses; non-key licenses	Gaming waiver for non-key employees; sex offender reduction
Lone Pine Paiute-Shoshone Tribe	CA	None found	None found	None found	None found	None found	None found
Los Coyotes Band of Cahuilla and Cupeno Indians	CA	None found	None found	None found	None found	None found	None found
Lovelock Paiute Tribe	NV	None found	None found	Marijuana licenses	None found	None found	None found
Lower Brule Sioux Tribe	SD	Tribal council	Election board members	None found	None found	None found	None found
Lower Elwha Tribal Community	WA	Community council	Game committee member	Designated hunter	Firearm possession	Commissioners	Waiver for gaming commissioners

Tribal name	State	Executive and Legislative	Administrators and Personnel	Licenses and Permits	Rights and Services	Gaming Ordinances	Restoration of Rights
Lower Sioux Indian Community	MN	Community council	Judges	None found	Disenrollment	Commissioners; leases for video games of chance	Waiver for gaming commissioners; reinstatement for disenrollment
Lummi Tribe	WA	Business council	Police officers; water resources manager	None found	Disenrollment	None found	Ch'qi'n'txw (expungement); reinstatement for disenrollment; suspension of sentence
Lytton Rancheria of California	CA	None found	None found	None found	None found	Gaming monitor; licenses	None found
Makah Indian Tribe	WA	None found	Police officers	None found	Banishment for domestic violence	Commissioners	Sex offender reduction
Manchester Band of Pomo Indians	CA	None found	None found	None found	None found	None found	None found
Manzanita Band of Diegueno Mission Indians	CA	None found	None found	None found	None found	Commissioners; judges of gaming review board	None found
Mashantucket Pequot Indian Tribe	CT	Tribal council	None found	Attorneys; liquor license	Foster parents; jury service	None found	Marijuana expungements
Mashpee Wampanoag Tribe	MA	Tribal council	Judges	Attorneys	None found	None found	Waiver for attorneys

Match-e-be-nash-she-wish Band of Pottawatomi Indians	MI	None found	Judges	Liquor license	None found	Commissioners; licenses; employment; gaming service suppliers	None found
Mechoopda Indian Tribe of Chico Rancheria	CA	Tribal council	None found	None found	None found	Commissioners; judges of gaming review board	None found
Menominee Indian Tribe	WI	Legislators	Judges; economic development board of directors; tribal enterprises board of directors; police chief; police commission members	None found	Firearm possession	Commissioners; director; employment; contracts	Tribal pardon; expungement; sex offender reduction
Mesa Grande Band of Diegueno Mission Indians	CA	Business committee	None found	None found	None found	None found	None found
Mescalero Apache Tribe of the Mescalero Reservation	NM	Tribal council; president; vice-president	Judges; school board members	None found	Administrator of an estate; firearm possession; foster parents	Commissioners	Election waiver; sex offender reduction; deferred sentence
Miami Tribe	OK	Tribal council	Judges	None found	None found	Commissioners; gaming director; licenses; licenses for non-gaming employees	Tribal pardon
Miccosukee Tribe of Indians	FL	Tribal council	Hemp control officer	Hemp license	None found	None found	None found
Middletown Rancheria of Pomo Indians	CA	None found	None found	Liquor license	None found	None found	None found

Tribal name	State	Executive and Legislative	Administrators and Personnel	Licenses and Permits	Rights and Services	Gaming Ordinances	Restoration of Rights
Minnesota Chippewa Tribe: *Bois Forte Band (Nett Lake)*	MN	Business committee	None found	None found	None found	Licenses; leases of video games of chance	Gaming waiver
Minnesota Chippewa Tribe: *Fond du Lac Band*	MN	Business committee	None found	None found	Employment involving children	Licenses	Gaming waiver; restoration of right to employment involving children
Minnesota Chippewa Tribe: *Grand Portage Band*	MN	Business committee	Judges	None found	Jury service	None found	None found
Minnesota Chippewa Tribe: *Leech Lake Band*	MN	Business committee	None found	None found	None found	Board of directors	None found
Minnesota Chippewa Tribe: *Mille Lacs Band*	MN	Business committee	Judges	None found	Exclusion from reservation for drug crimes	Commissioners; gaming director; licenses; contractors	Tribal pardon; lift exclusion for drug crimes
Minnesota Chippewa Tribe: *White Earth Band*	MN	Business committee	None found	None found	None found	Commissioners; licenses	None found
Mississippi Band of Choctaw Indians	MS	Tribal council; chief	Judges	Attorneys; lay advocates; boxing commission licenses; business agents	None found	Commissioners; licenses; work permits	Suspension of sentence; sex offender reduction

Moapa Band of Paiute Indians	NV	None found	None found	None found	None found	Commissioners	None found
Modoc Tribe	OK	Elected council	Judges	None found	None found	None found	None found
Mohegan Tribe of Indians	CT	Tribal council; Council of elders	Judges; magistrates; election committee members; utility management board members; ethics commission members; freedom of information commission members	Liquor license; attorneys; business agents; child day care center license	Tribal membership; tribal employment preference	None found	Election waiver
Monacan Indian Nation	VA	Tribal council; chief; assistant chief; treasurer	Judges	None found	None found	None found	None found
Mooretown Rancheria of Maidu Indians	CA	Tribal council	None found	Liquor license	None found	None found	None found
Morongo Band of Mission Indians	CA	None found	Judges; court clerks	None found	Conservatorship for adults	None found	None found
Muckleshoot Indian Tribe	WA	Tribal council	None found	None found	None found	None found	None found
Muscogee (Creek) Nation	OK	Principal chief; second chief	Judges; judicial officers; attorney general; lighthorse officers; tribal secretary; Eufaula boarding school board members; election board members; controller	Liquor license; tobacco license; labor organization agent	Firearm possession; jury service; parental rights; guardianship	None found	Tribal pardon; sex offender reduction
Nansemond Indian Nation	VA	None found	None found	None found	None found	None found	None found
Narragansett Indian Tribe	RI	None found	None found	None found	None found	Gaming director	None found

Tribal name	State	Executive and Legislative	Administrators and Personnel	Licenses and Permits	Rights and Services	Gaming Ordinances	Restoration of Rights
Navajo Nation	AZ	Tribal council; president; vice-president	Board of education members; land board members; farm board members; grazing committee members; school board members; election board members; nursing home administrator; labor commission members; utility authority board of commissioners	Pawnbroker permit; manufactured housing license; blanket exclusion for business and procurement contracts; veterinary licenses; fuel distributor license	None found	Executive director; licenses; employment in gaming regulatory office	Business and procurement waiver
Nez Perce Tribe	ID	Executive committee	Judges; court clerks; utility department board members	Attorneys	Weapon possession; foster parents; adoption; representative of an estate	Commissioners; licenses	Sex offender reduction; marijuana expungement; deferred prosecution; juvenile expungement
Nisqually Indian Tribe	WA	Tribal council	None found	Liquor license; marijuana license; business agents	None found	None found	Sex offender reduction; juvenile expungement; deferred prosecution; tribal council review of court decisions

Nooksack Indian Tribe	WA	Tribal council	Election board members; ballot clerk	Shellfish license; fishing license; business agents	Guardian ad litem	None found	Sex offender reduction; shellfish ordinance expungement
Northern Cheyenne Tribe	MT	Tribal council	Judges	Solid waste permit; attorneys	Guardianship of a juvenile	None found	Judicial commutation
Northfork Rancheria of Mono Indians	CA	Tribal council	Election board member	None found	None found	Licenses	None found
Northwestern Band of Shoshone Nation	UT	Tribal council	None found	None found	None found	None found	None found
Nottawaseppi Huron Band of the Potawatomi	MI	Tribal council	None found	Liquor license; solicitor license	Disenrollment; exclusion; parental rights; jury service; firearm possession	Commissioners; licenses; employment; gaming vendor license	Delayed sentencing; expungement for trafficking victims; sex offender reduction
Oglala Sioux Tribe	SD	Tribal council	Coroner; election board members; judges of court of election appeals	Grazing permit	Adoption; guardianship; blanket employment exclusion; employment involving children	Commissioners; licenses	Waiver for gaming commissioners; sex offender reduction; suspension of sentence
Ohkay Owingeh (formerly Pueblo of San Juan)	NM	Tribal council	None found	None found	None found	None found	None found

Tribal name	State	Executive and Legislative	Administrators and Personnel	Licenses and Permits	Rights and Services	Gaming Ordinances	Restoration of Rights
Omaha Tribe	NE	Tribal council	Judges; court clerks; police officers	None found	Jury service; exclusion; foster parents	Commissioners; licenses	Order removing disability based on conviction; suspended sentence; sex offender reduction
Oneida Nation	NY	None found	None found	None found	None found	None found	Expungement; juvenile expungement; sex offender reduction
Oneida Tribe of Indians	WI	Tribal council	Judges; police commission members	Attorneys; hemp license	Guardian ad litem; child custody; adoption	Commissioners; licenses	Tribal pardon
Onondaga Nation	NY	None found	None found	None found	None found	None found	None found
Osage Nation	OK	Congress; principal chief; assistant principal chief	Secretary of the nation; treasurer	None found	None found	Commissioners; licenses	Juvenile expungement
Ottawa Tribe	OK	Business committee	None found	Liquor license	None found	Management contracts	None found
Otoe-Missouria Tribe of Indians	OK	Tribal council	Judges; election board members	Hemp license	None found	Licenses; employment; management contracts	None found
Paiute Indian Tribe of Utah	UT	Tribal council	Election board members	None found	None found	None found	None found
Paiute-Shoshone Tribe of the Fallon Reservation and Colony	NV	Business council	Judges	None found	None found	None found	None found

Pala Band of Mission Indians	CA	None found	None found	None found	None found	None found	Record sealing
Pamunkey Tribe	VA	None found	None found	None found	None found	None found	None found
Pascua Yaqui Tribe	AZ	Tribal council	Judges; athletic commission members	None found	None found	Licenses	Judicial commutation
Paskenta Band of Nomlaki Indians	CA	Tribal council; chairperson; vice-chairperson; treasurer	None found	None found	None found	Commissioners; licenses	None found
Passamaquoddy Tribe	ME	Tribal council; governors	None found	None found	None found	None found	None found
Pauma Band of Luiseno Mission Indians	CA	None found	None found	None found	Exclusion	Commissioners; executive director; members of gaming appellate board; licenses	None found
Pawnee Nation	OK	Business council	Judges	Attorneys	Jury service	Commissioners; board of directors; licenses	Tribal pardon; juvenile expungement
Pechanga Band of Luiseno Mission Indians	CA	None found	None found	None found	None found	None found	None found
Penobscot Nation	ME	Tribal council; chief; vice-chief	Judges	None found	Exclusion; banishment for sex offenders	None found	None found
Peoria Tribe of Indians	OK	Business committee	None found	Liquor license	None found	Commissioners; gaming director	None found
Picayune Rancheria of Chukchansi Indians	CA	Tribal council	Judges; judicial council members	Cannabis license; liquor license; lay advocate	None found	Commissioners	None found

Tribal name	State	Executive and Legislative	Administrators and Personnel	Licenses and Permits	Rights and Services	Gaming Ordinances	Restoration of Rights
Pinoleville Pomo Nation	CA	None found	None found	None found	Tribal housing	Licenses	None found
Pit River Tribe	CA	None found	Housing commissioners	None found	Foster parents	Commissioners	None found
Poarch Band of Creeks	AL	Tribal council	Ethics board members; election board members		Jury service; guardianship; foster parents	Commissioners; licenses	Judicial commutation; prohibition of employment discrimination for previous conviction
Pokagon Band of Potawatomi Indians	MI	Tribal council	Judges; election board members; cannabis regulatory commissioners	Cannabis licenses; hunting and gathering license; liquor license	Cannabis-related employment; parental rights	Commissioners; licenses; supplier licenses	Deferred sentence; sex offender reduction
Ponca Tribe of Indians	OK	Business Committee	Election board members	Liquor license	None found	Commissioners	None found
Ponca Tribe	NE	Tribal council	Judges; tribal corporation board of directors; election board members; housing authority commissioners	None found	Weapon possession; disenrollment; parental rights	Commissioners	None found
Port Gamble S'Klallam Tribe	WA	None found	Judges; police officers; fisheries committee member	Designated hunter	Banishment	Commissioners	Waiver for gaming commissioners; appeal of banishment
Potter Valley Tribe	CA	Tribal council	None found	None found	None found	None found	None found
Prairie Band Potawatomi Nation	KS	Tribal council	Tribal prosecutor	Hemp license	Jury service	Commissioners	Sex offender reduction
Prairie Island Indian Community	MN	Community council	Judges	None found	None found	Commissioners; licenses	None found

Pueblo of Acoma	NM	Blanket exclusion from tribal office	Judges	Lay counsel; liquor license; cigarette license	Jury service	Commissioners; licenses	Restoration of civil rights; juvenile record sealing; sex offender reduction
Pueblo of Cochiti	NM	None found	None found	None found	None found	None found	None found
Pueblo of Jemez	NM	None found	None found	None found	None found	Commissioners	None found
Pueblo of Isleta	NM	Tribal council; governor	Judges	Liquor license	Jury service	Licenses; temporary work permits; temporary vendor permits	None found
Pueblo of Laguna	NM	Staff officers; village representatives	Judges	Liquor license; vendor's permit; lay advocates	Firearm possession	None found	Modification of banishment order; deferred sentence; sex offender reduction
Pueblo of Nambe	NM	None found	None found	None found	None found	Commissioners	None found
Pueblo of Picuris	NM	None found	None found	Liquor license; hemp license	None found	Licenses	None found
Pueblo of Pojoaque	NM	Tribal council	Judges; utility board members; police officers	Consumer financial services license	Weatherization checks; foster parents	Commissioners; licenses; employment	Judicial commutation
Pueblo of San Felipe	NM	None found	None found	None found	None found	Commissioners; executive director; licenses	None found
Pueblo of San Ildefonso	NM	None found	Judges; court clerks	Driver or chauffer license	None found	None found	Juvenile expungement; sex offender reduction
Pueblo of Sandia	NM	None found	None found	Liquor license	None found	None found	None found

Tribal name	State	Executive and Legislative	Administrators and Personnel	Licenses and Permits	Rights and Services	Gaming Ordinances	Restoration of Rights
Pueblo of Santa Ana	NM	None found	None found	Liquor license; grazing permit; hunting and fishing permit	Tribal housing	None found	Juvenile expungement; sex offender reduction; reduction of tribal housing exclusion period
Pueblo of Santa Clara	NM	None found	None found	None found	None found	Commissioners	None found
Pueblo of Taos	NM	None found	None found	Liquor license	None found	Commissioners; licenses	None found
Pueblo of Tesuque	NM	None found	None found	Liquor license	None found	Commissioners; executive director; licenses	None found
Pueblo of Zia	NM	None found	None found	None found	None found	None found	None found
Puyallup Tribe	WA	Tribal council	Cannabis committee members; fisheries management commission members; shellfish commission members	Designated hunters; shellfish license	Blanket exclusion for tribal employment	Gaming director	None found
Pyramid Lake Paiute Tribe	NV	None found	None found	Marijuana license	None found	None found	None found

Quapaw Tribe of Indians	OK	Business committee	None found	None found	Jury service	Commissioners; director of gaming agency; staff of gaming commission; staff of tribal gaming agency	Tribal pardon; expungement; juvenile record sealing; sex offender reduction; automatic expungement for identity theft; suspension of sentence
Quartz Valley Indian Community	CA	None found	None found	None found	None found	Commissioners	Waiver for gaming commissioners
Quechan Tribe of the Fort Yuma Indian Reservation	AZ	Tribal council	Judges; police officers	None found	Jury service; parental rights; guardianship	Licenses	Class II gaming waiver; juvenile expungement; suspended sentence
Quileute Tribe	WA	Tribal council	Election board members; elders panel	None found	Employment involving children	None found	Suspended sentence
Quinault Indian Nation	WA	None found	None found	None found	Tribal employment preference	None found	None found
Ramona Band of Cahuilla	CA	None found	None found	None found	None found	None found	None found
Rappahannock Tribe	VA	None found	None found	None found	None found	None found	None found
Red Cliff Band of Lake Superior Chippewa Indians	WI	None found	Law enforcement commission members	None found	None found	Commissioners; licenses	None found

Tribal name	State	Executive and Legislative	Administrators and Personnel	Licenses and Permits	Rights and Services	Gaming Ordinances	Restoration of Rights
Red Lake Band of Chippewa Indians	MN	Tribal council; chairman; secretary; treasurer	None found	Game and fish license	Handgun permit; jury service	Commissioners; gaming board members; licenses	Waiver for gaming commissioners
Redding Rancheria	CA	None found	None found	Liquor license	None found	None found	None found
Redwood Valley or Little River Band of Pomo Indians	CA	Tribal council	None found	None found	None found	Commissioners; gaming director; management contracts	None found
Reno-Sparks Indian Colony	NV	Tribal council	Judges	Marijuana license; attorneys; lay representatives; liquor license	Violent offender registration; weapon possession	Licenses	Deferred sentence; sex offender reduction
Resighini Rancheria	CA	None found	None found	Liquor license	None found	None found	None found
Rincon Band of Luiseno Mission Indians	CA	Business committee	None found	None found	Tribal housing	Commissioners	None found
Robinson Rancheria	CA	Business council; chairperson; vice-chairperson; secretary; treasurer	None found	None found	None found	None found	None found
Rosebud Sioux Tribe	SD	Tribal council	None found	None found	None found	Commissioners	Waiver for gaming commissioners; sex offender reduction
Round Valley Indian Tribes	CA	Tribal council	Housing authority board of commissioners	None found	None found	Commissioners	Waiver for gaming commissioners
Sac & Fox Tribe of the Mississippi	IA	None found	Probation-parole officers; election committee members	Liquor license	Disenrollment	Management contracts	Sex offender reduction; juvenile expungement

Sac & Fox Nation of Missouri	KS	Tribal council	None found	Liquor license	None found	Licenses	Tribal pardon; gaming waiver
Sac & Fox Nation	OK	None found	Judges	None found	Jury service	Commissioners	Tribal pardon; juvenile expungement
Saginaw Chippewa Indian Tribe	MI	Tribal council	Judges; court clerks	None found	Possession of a pistol	Commissioners; licenses; employees	Judicial commutation; juvenile expungement; gaming waiver; sex offender reduction
St. Croix Chippewa Indians	WI	Tribal council	Judges	Liquor license	None found	Commissioners; licenses	None found
Saint Regis Mohawk Tribe	NY	Tribal council; chief; sub-chief; clerk	Judges; cannabis advisory board members; police commission members; traffic court judges	Cannabis license	None found	None found	Sex offender reduction
Salt River Pima-Maricopa Indian Community	AZ	Community council	Judges; financial services institution board member; judicial conduct and discipline commission member	Blanket for all licenses; amusement licenses; cigarette licenses	Guardianship; employment with financial and health and human services agencies	Licenses; employment with gaming regulatory agency; gaming services license	Gaming license waiver; sex offender reduction
Samish Indian Nation	WA	Tribal council	None found	Liquor license	Employment with early childhood learning center and head start	None found	None found
San Carlos Apache Tribe	AZ	Tribal council; chairman; vice-chairman	None found	None found	None found	Gaming director	None found
San Juan Southern Paiute Tribe	AZ	Tribal council	None found	None found	None found	None found	None found

Tribal name	State	Executive and Legislative	Administrators and Personnel	Licenses and Permits	Rights and Services	Gaming Ordinances	Restoration of Rights
San Manuel Band of Mission Indians	CA	None found	Judges	Attorneys	None found	None found	None found
San Pasqual Band of Diegueno Mission Indians	CA	Business committee	Election board member	None found	None found	Commissioners; licenses	None found
Santa Rosa Indian Community	CA	Tribal council	None found	None found	None found	Commissioners; licenses; employment	None found
Santa Rosa Band of Cahuilla Indians	CA	None found	None found	None found	None found	Commissioners; licenses	Waiver for gaming commissioners
Santa Ynez Band of Chumash Mission Indians	CA	None found	None found	None found	None found	None found	None found
Santee Sioux Nation	NE	None found	None found	None found	None found	None found	None found
Sauk-Suiattle Indian Tribe	WA	Tribal council	Judges; utility authority commissioners	None found	Enrollment of adopted members	None found	None found
Sault Ste. Marie Tribe of Chippewa Indians	MI	Board of directors; chairperson	Conservation committee members	Private security guard license; liquor license	Jury selection	Management contracts; device supplier contracts; vendors; lessors	Conviction set-aside
Scotts Valley Band of Pomo Indians	CA	Tribal council	Judges	None found	None found	Class B licenses	None found

Seminole Nation	OK	General council; chief; assistant chief	Judges; court clerks; foster home licensing commission members; police officers (cross-deputization); hemp commission members	Attorneys; liquor license	Jury selection; employment with head start	Licenses; vendors; financiers	Tribal pardon; juvenile expungement; order removing disability based on conviction
Seminole Tribe	FL	Tribal council	None found	Liquor license	None found	Licenses; work permits	None found
Seneca Nation of Indians	NY	None found	Hemp compliance administrator	Hemp license	Voting rights	None found	None found
Seneca-Cayuga Nation	OK	None found	None found	None found	None found	Commissioners; hearing officers	None found
Shakopee Mdewakanton Sioux Community	MN	None found	None found	None found	None found	Commissioners; licenses	Gaming waiver
Shawnee Tribe	OK	Business council; chief	Tax commissioner	None found	None found	Management contracts	Tribal pardon; juvenile record sealing
Sherwood Valley Rancheria of Pomo Indians	CA	Tribal council	None found	None found	None found	Class B licenses	None found
Shingle Springs Band of Miwok Indians	CA	None found	None found	None found	None found	None found	None found
Shinnecock Indian Nation	NY	None found	None found	None found	None found	Commissioners	Waiver for gaming commissioners
Shoalwater Bay Indian Tribe	WA	Tribal council	Utility authority commissioners	Liquor license	Exclusion	Commissioners; contracts	Sex offender reduction
Shoshone Tribe of the Wind River Reservation	WY	None found	Judges	Lay advocates	Jury service; parental rights	None found	Juvenile record sealing

Tribal name	State	Executive and Legislative	Administrators and Personnel	Licenses and Permits	Rights and Services	Gaming Ordinances	Restoration of Rights
Shoshone-Bannock Tribes of the Fort Hall Reservation	ID	Business council	None found	Liquor license	None found	Commissioners	Judicial commutation; suspension of sentence
Shoshone-Paiute Tribes of the Duck Valley Reservation	NV	Tribal council	None found	None found	None found	Commissioners; gaming agency director; staff of commission and gaming agency	Sex offender reduction
Sisseton-Wahpeton Oyate of the Lake Traverse Reservation	SD	None found	Judges	Attorneys	None found	Regulatory authority members and employees	Judicial commutation
Skokomish Indian Tribe	WA	None found	None found	Designated hunter	None found	None found	None found
Skull Valley Band of Goshute Indians	UT	None found	None found	None found	None found	None found	None found
Snoqualmie Indian Tribe	WA	Tribal council	Judges	Designated hunter; solid waste permit	None found	Commissioners; executive director; commission staff	None found
Soboba Band of Luiseno Indians	CA	None found	None found	None found	None found	None found	None found
Sokaogon Chippewa Community	WI	None found	Judges	None found	None found	Commissioners; employment	None found
Southern Ute Indian Tribe	CO	Tribal council	None found	None found	None found	Licenses	Sex offender reduction

Spirit Lake Tribe	ND	None found	Judges; peacemakers; environmental quality commission members	None found	Jury service; guardianship	Employment; leases; purchase agreements	Gaming waiver for employees; jury waiver; juvenile expungement; sentence suspension; restoration of driving privileges
Spokane Tribe	WA	Business council	Judges; wildlife committee members	None found	Representative of an estate; exclusion	Contracts	Sex offender reduction
Squaxin Island Tribe	WA	Tribal council	Judges	Business agents	Firearm possession	Commissioners; gaming director; contractor license	Sex offender reduction
Standing Rock Sioux Tribe	SD	Tribal council	Judges; chief clerk; court administrator; housing board of commissioners; tax commissioners; game, fish, and wildlife conservation commissioners; water administrator; employment and contracting rights commissioners; election commissioners; election judges; election clerks; school board members; tribal prosecutor; public defender	Business license; liquor license; hemp license	Tribal employment; employment with children; jury service	Commissioners; licenses; non-gaming staff	Tribal pardon; sex offender reduction; gaming waiver for employment

Tribal name	State	Executive and Legislative	Administrators and Personnel	Licenses and Permits	Rights and Services	Gaming Ordinances	Restoration of Rights
Stockbridge Munsee Community	WI	None found	Judges; court clerks; members of judiciary commission	None found	None found	Commissioners; licenses; employment with compliance department	Gaming waiver (licenses only)
Stillaguamish Tribe of Indians	WA	Board of directors	Judges	None found	Firearm possession	Commissioners; Class A licenses; Class B licenses	None found
Summit Lake Paiute Tribe	NV	None found	None found	None found	None found	None found	None found
Suquamish Indian Tribe of the Port Madison Reservation	WA	Tribal council	Judges; court clerks; manager of Suquamish Evergreen Corporation (marijuana); administrative law judges; resources, fish, wildlife, and shellfish committee members	Designated hunters		Licenses; contracts	Gaming waiver
Susanville Indian Rancheria	CA	Tribal council	Election board members	Liquor license	None found	Commissioners; conditional licenses	None found
Swinomish Indian Tribal Community	WA	Tribal senate	Judges; police officers; natural resource commission members; utility authority commissioners	Fish and game licenses; day care center license	Jury service; firearm possession; day care center employment	None found	Sex offender reduction

Sycuan Band of the Kumeyaay Nation	CA	None found	None found	None found	Conservatorship	Executive director; licenses; vendor licenses	None found
Table Mountain Rancheria	CA	Tribal council	None found	None found	None found	Licenses	None found
Tejon Indian Tribe	CA	Executive committee	None found	None found	None found	None found	None found
Te-Moak Tribe of Western Shoshone Indians of Nevada	NV	Tribal council	Judges; band election committee members; election board members; poll officials	None found	Jury service	None found	None found
Thlopthlocco Tribal Town	OK	None found	None found	None found	None found	Commissioners	None found
Three Affiliated Tribes of the Fort Berthold Reservation	ND	Tribal council	None found	None found	None found	None found	Expungement
Tohono O'odham Nation	AZ	Tribal council	Judges	None found	None found	Executive director; gaming manager license; employee license; regulatory license; gaming facility operator license	Juvenile record sealing
Tolowa Dee-ni' Nation	CA	Tribal council	None found	None found	None found	Licenses	None found
Tonawanda Band of Seneca	NY	None found	None found	None found	None found	None found	None found
Tonkawa Tribe of Indians	OK	Tribal council	None found	Liquor license	None found	Commissioners; licenses; management contracts	Waiver for gaming commissioners

Tribal name	State	Executive and Legislative	Administrators and Personnel	Licenses and Permits	Rights and Services	Gaming Ordinances	Restoration of Rights
Tonto Apache Tribe	AZ	Tribal council	None found	None found	None found	Commissioners	Waiver for gaming commissioners; sex offender reduction
Torres Martinez Desert Cahuilla Indians	CA	Tribal council	None found	None found	None found	Commissioners	None found
Tule River Indian Tribe	CA	Tribal council	Judges	None found	None found	Licenses	None found
Tulalip Tribes	WA	Tribal council	Judges; hunting commission members; tribal employment rights commissioners; police officers	Commercial driver's license; peddler's license	None found	Commissioners; Category A licenses; Category B licenses	Deferred prosecution; restoration of firearm rights
Tunica-Biloxi Indian Tribe	LA	Tribal council	Judges	None found	None found	None found	Reduction or modification of sentence
Tuolumne Band of Me-Wuk Indians	CA	Community council	None found	Liquor license	None found	Class B licenses	None found
Turtle Mountain Band of Chippewa Indians	ND	Tribal council	None found	None found	None found	Commissioners	Tribal pardon; waiver for gaming commissioners
Tuscarora Nation	NY	None found	None found	None found	None found	None found	None found
Twenty-Nine Palms Band of Mission Indians	CA	None found	None found	Liquor license	None found	Commissioners	None found
United Auburn Indian Community of the Auburn Rancheria	CA	Tribal council	None found	None found	Per capita payments of gaming revenues	None found	None found

United Keetoowah Band of Cherokee Indians	OK	Tribal council	Election board members	None found	None found	None found	None found
Upper Mattaponi Tribe	VA	Tribal council	None found	None found	None found	None found	None found
Upper Sioux Community	MN	Board of Trustees	Judges	Lay advocate	Jury service	None found	None found
Upper Skagit Indian Tribe	WA	None found	None found	None found	None found	None found	None found
Ute Indian Tribe of the Uintah & Ouray Reservation	UT	Business committee	Police officers	None found	Jury service	None found	Order removing disability based on conviction
Ute Mountain Ute Tribe	CO	Tribal council	None found	None found	None found	Commissioners; executive director; licenses; investigators; manufacturer or distributor license	None found
Utu Utu Gwaitu Paiute Tribe of the Benton Paiute Reservation	CA	None found	None found	None found	Exclusion	Licenses	None found
Walker River Paiute Tribe of the Walker River Reservation	NV	None found	None found	None found	None found	None found	None found
Wampanoag Tribe of Gay Head (Aquinnah)	MA	None found	None found	None found	None found	Licenses; work permits	None found
Washoe Tribe	NV	None found	Judges	Attorneys; lay advocates	Tribal housing; executor of an estate; administrator of an estate	Licenses	Sex offender reduction

Tribal name	State	Executive and Legislative	Administrators and Personnel	Licenses and Permits	Rights and Services	Gaming Ordinances	Restoration of Rights
White Mountain Apache Tribe of the Fort Apache Reservation	AZ	Tribal council	Judges	None found	None found	Licenses; employment	Expungement
Wichita and Affiliated Tribes	OK	None found	None found	Liquor license	None found	Commissioners	None found
Wilton Rancheria	CA	Tribal council	None found	None found	None found	Commissioners; licenses	None found
Winnebago Tribe	NE	Tribal council	Judges; hemp oversight licensing commission members; economic development authority board of trustees	None found	Jury service; sex offender residency; firearm possession; guardianship or conservatorship	Commissioners; licenses	Sex offender reduction; juvenile expungement
Winnemucca Indian Colony	NV	None found	None found	None found	None found	None found	None found
Wiyot Tribe	CA	Tribal council	None found	None found	Exclusion	Licenses	None found
Wyandotte Nation	OK	Board of directors	Judges	Attorneys	None found	None found	Sex offender reduction
Yankton Sioux Tribe	SD	Business committee	None found	Hunting and fishing license	Jury service	Commissioners	None found
Yavapai-Apache Nation of the Camp Verde Indian Reservation	AZ	Tribal council	Judges; community development and financial institution board of directors; construction board of directors; enrollment board members; event committee members	None found	None found	Commissioners; licenses; gaming commission staff	Waiver for event committee members

Yavapai-Prescott Indian Tribe	AZ	Board of directors	None found	None found	None found	Commissioners; operator license; manager license; employee license; regulatory license; manufacturer, distributor, supplier, financier license	None found
Yerington Paiute Tribe of the Yerington Colony & Campbell Ranch	NV	Tribal council	None found	None found	None found	Commissioners	None found
Yocha Dehe Wintun Nation	CA	Tribal council	None found	None found	None found	None found	None found
Yomba Shoshone Tribe	NV	Tribal council	Judges	None found	Jury service	None found	Judicial cancellation of fines
Ysleta del Sur Pueblo	TX	None found	Judges	None found	None found	Commissioners; licenses; employment	None found
Yurok Tribe	CA	Tribal council	Housing authority board of commissioners	Hemp license	Jury service; firearm possession	None found	Expungement
Zuni Tribe	NM	Tribal council	Judges	None found	None found	None found	None found

Note: in the “Administrators Personnel” column, “judges” refers to all trial judges, appellate judges, and supreme court justices, even if different collateral consequences attach to each. However, judges of courts of special jurisdiction are listed separately. In the “Gaming Ordinance” column, “licenses” refers to gaming licenses for Primary Management Officials (PMOs) and Key Officers or Employees (KOs) after they complete the required background checks, as required by the Indian Gaming Regulatory Act, 29 U.S.C. § 2710(b)(2)(F). Other types of gaming licenses, for instance, to non-gaming employees, vendors, or contractors, are at the discretion of the tribe and listed separately.

Index